The Glorious Qur'an

TRANSLATION

Translated by
Mohammed Marmaduke Pickthall

Published by
Tahrike Tarsile Qur'an, Inc.
Publishers and Distributors of The Holy Qur'an
80-08 51st Avenue
Elmhurst, New York 11373-4141
www.koranusa.org

Published by
Tahrike Tarsile Qur'an, Inc.
Publishers and Distributors of Holy Qur'an
80-08 51st Avenue
Elmhurst, New York 11373-4141
E-mail: read@koranusa.org
www.koranusa.org

Fifth US Edition 2009

Library of Congress Catalog Number: 99 075684
British Library Cataloguing in Publication Data

ISBN: 978-1-879402-51-5

INTRODUCTION

The Qur'an is a divine message revealed by God to Prophet Muhammad (Peace be upon him—PBUH) over a period of 23 years. In 610 AD while Prophet Muhammad (PBUH) was meditating in the cave of Hira, outside the city of Makkah, Angel Gabriel visited Muhammad commanding him to "read" (Chapter 96: Verse 1). This was the first verse revealed to Muhammad from God (Glorified is He). Over the next several years, Prophet Muhammad (PBUH) continued to receive revelations from God, which were ultimately compiled into 114 chapters (*Suwaar*).

The revelation of the Qur'an came during different times, some verses were revealed after specific events while the seven verses that make The Opening (*Surat al-Fateha*) was revealed twice. The chapters of the Qur'an tend to be arranged with the place of revelation, generally chapters revealed in Madinah are longer and placed in the first half of the Qur'an and chapters revealed in Makkah tend to be shorter and are placed in the later end. Although some verses can be read on their own, many verses need to be understood through background knowledge of the time's culture, the Arabic language, and the history of revelation of the verse. To gain a better understanding of certain verses, one should refer to translations which include commentaries. The best reading is to take the Qur'an as a complete guidance rather than attempting to interpret verses on their own.

Arabic is the language that was used for the revelation of divine message. It was also the language of the people that the Qur'an was initially revealed to. The Arabic language is known for its poetic and linguistic excellence. This puts limitations on the translation and interpretation of the Qur'an. Translation, such as the one presented in the following pages, should be looked at as simple interpretations of the Qur'an. For a thorough and complete understanding, the Qur'an should be understood in its original Arabic language.

Finally, the Qur'an is a continuation of the revelation that came to Moses in the form of the Torah (*Taurat*), Jesus with the Bible (*Injeel*) and David in the Psalms (*Zabur*): "*The same religion He has established for you as that which He enjoined on Noah—that which We have sent by inspiration to you—and that which We enjoined on Abraham, Moses, and Jesus; namely, that you should remain steadfast in religion, and make no divisions therein ...*" (42:13). Mary, mother of Prophet Jesus, has a chapter dedicated in her name and is one of few women to be mentioned by name. The Qur'an was revealed not to distinguish Islam as a separate religion, but the revelation of God came as the final message that embodies a universal message for people of all times.

Tahrike Tarsile Qur'an, Inc., April 2009

LIST OF CHAPTERS / SÛRAHS

SÛRAH 1

Al-Fâtihah, "The Opening", or *Fâtihatu'l-Kitâb*, "The Opening of the Scripture" or *Ummu'l-Qur'ân*, "The Essence of the Koran," as it is variously named, has been called the Lord's Prayer of the Muslims . It is an essential part of all Muslim worship, public and private, and no solemn contract or transaction is complete unless it is recited. The date of revelation is uncertain, but the fact that it has always, from the very earliest times, formed a part of Muslim worship, there being no record or remembrance of its introduction, or of public prayer without it, makes it clear that it was revealed before the fourth year of the Prophet's Mission (the tenth year before the Hijrah); because we know for certain that by that time regular congregational prayers were offered by the little group of Muslims in Mecca. In that year, as the result of insult and attack by the idolaters, the Prophet arranged for the services, which had till then been held out of doors, to take place in a private house.

This sûrah is also often called *Saba'an min al-Mathâni*, "Seven of the Oft-repeated" ("verses" being understood), S. 15:87, words which are taken as referring to this sûrah .

THE OPENING

Revealed at Mecca

In the name of Allah, the Beneficent, the Merciful .
1. Praise be to Allah, Lord of the Worlds,
2. The Beneficent, the Merciful.
3. Owner of the Day of Judgment.
4. Thee (alone) we worship; Thee (alone) we ask for help.
5. Show us the straight path,
6. The path of those whom Thou hast favoured;
7. Not (the path) of those who earn Thine anger nor of those who go astray.

SÛRAH 2

Al-Baqarah "The Cow", is so named from the story of the yellow heifer (vv. 67-71). As is the case with many other sûrahs, the title is taken from some word or incident which surprised the listeners . All suggestions to the contrary notwithstanding, it seems probable that the whole of this sûrah was revealed during the first four years after the Hijrah, and that by far the greater portion of it was revealed in the first eighteen months of the Prophet's reign at Al-Madînah—that is to say, before the battle of Badr.

The Jewish tribes, once paramount in Yathrib had, not very long before the coming of Al-Islâm, been reduced by the pagan Arab tribes of Aûs and Khazraj, each Jewish tribe becoming an adherent of one or the other. But they had preserved a sort of intellectual ascendancy owing to their possession of the Scripture and their fame for occult science, the pagan Arabs consulting their rabbis on occasions and paying heed to what they said. Before the coming of Al-Islâm, these Jewish rabbis had often told their neighbours that a Prophet was about to come, and had often threatened them that, when he came, they (the Jews) would destroy the pagan Arabs as the tribes of A'âd and Thamûd had been destroyed of old. So plainly did they describe the coming prophet, that pilgrims from Yathrib recognised the Prophet, when he addressed them in Mecca, as the same whom the Jewish doctors had described to them. But the Jewish idea of a Prophet was one who would give them dominion, not one who would make them brethren of every pagan Arab who chose to accept Al-Islâm. When they found that they could not make use of the newcomer, they opposed him and tried to bewilder him with questions from their theology, speaking to him as men who possessed superior wisdom; failing to perceive that, from a prophet's standpoint, theology is childish nonsense, the very opposite of religion, and its enemy; religion, for the Prophet, being not a matter of conjecture and speech, but of fact and conduct.

Ibn Ishâq states definitely that vv. 1-141 were revealed concerning these Jewish rabbis and such of the new converts to Al-Islâm as were half-hearted and inclined to them. There follows the order to change the *Qiblah* (The place toward which the Muslims turn their face in Prayer) from Jerusalem to the Ka'bah at Mecca, which was built by Abraham, the choice of Jerusalem having led to a misunderstanding on the part of the Jews that the Prophet was groping his way toward their religion and stood in need of their guidance and instruction.

All through the sûrah runs the note of warning, which sounds indeed throughout the whole Koran, that it is not the mere profession of a creed, but righteous conduct which is true religion. There is the repeated announcement that the religion of Abraham, to which Judaism and Christianity (which springs from Judaism) trace their origin, is the only true religion, and that religion consists in the surrender of man's will and purpose to the Will and Purpose of the Lord of Creation as manifested in His creation and revealed by way of guidance through successive Prophets. Of sincerity in that religion the one test is conduct, and the standard of that religion is for all alike.

At the time when this sûrah was revealed at Al-Madînah, the Prophet's own tribe, the pagan Qureysh at Mecca, were preparing to attack the Muslims in their place of refuge. Cruel persecution was the lot of Muslims who had stayed in Meccan territory or who journeyed thither, and Muslims were being prevented from performing the pilgrimage. The possible necessity of fighting had been foreseen in the terms of the oath, taken at Al-'Aqabah by the Muslims of Yathrib before the Flight, to defend the Prophet as they would their own wives and children, and the first commandment to flight was revealed to the Prophet before his flight from Mecca; but there was no actual fighting by the Muslims until the battle of Badr. Many of them were reluctant, having before been subject to a rule of strict non-violence. It was with difficulty that they could accept the idea of fighting even in self-defence, as can be seen from several verses in this sûrah; which contains also rules for fasting and the pilgrimage, bequest, almsgiving, divorce and contracts, and verses which discountenance usury, strong drink and gambling. It concludes with a statement of the universal character of Al-Islâm, the religion of Allah's sovereignty, and a prayer for the forgiveness of shortcomings.

This sûrah might be described as the Koran in little. It contains mention of all the essential points of the Revelation, which are elaborated elsewhere. This accounts for the precedence given to it in the arrangement of the Book.

The period of revelation is the years 1 and 2. A.H. for the most part, certain verses of legislation being considered as of later date.

THE COW

Revealed at Al-Madînah

In the name of Allah, the Beneficent, the Merciful.

1. Alif. Lâm. Mîm.

2. This is the Scripture whereof there is no doubt, a guidance unto those who ward off (evil).

3. Who believe in the Unseen, and establish worship, and spend of that We have bestowed upon them;

4. And who believe in that which is revealed unto thee (Muhammad) and that which was revealed before thee, and are certain of the Hereafter.

5. These depend on guidance from their Lord. These are

the successful.

6. As for the disbelievers, whether thou warn them or thou warn them not it is all one for them; they believe not.

7. Allah hath sealed their hearing and their hearts, and on their eyes there is a covering. Theirs will be an awful doom.

8. And of mankind are some who say: We believe in Allah and the Last Day, when they believe not.

9. They think to beguile Allah and those who believe, and they beguile none save themselves; but they perceive not.

10. In their hearts is a disease, and Allah increaseth their disease. A painful doom is theirs because they lie.

11. And when it is said unto them: Make not mischief in the earth, they say: We are peacemakers only.

12. Are not they indeed the mischief-makers? But they perceive not.

13. And when it is said unto them: Believe as the people believe, they say: Shall we believe as the foolish believe? Are not they indeed the foolish? But they know not.

14. And when they fall in with those who believe, they say: We believe; but when they go apart to their devils they declare: Lo! we are with you; verily we did but mock.

15. Allah (Himself) doth mock them, leaving them to wander blindly on in their contumacy.

16. These are they who purchase error at the price of guidance, so their commerce doth not prosper, neither are they guided.

17. Their likeness is as the likeness of one who kindleth fire, and when it sheddeth its light around him Allah taketh away their light and leaveth them in darkness, where they cannot see.

18. Deaf, dumb and blind; and they return not.

19. Or like a rainstorm from the sky, wherein is darkness, thunder and the flash of lightning. They thrust their fingers in their ears by reason of the thunder-claps, for fear of death. Allah encompasseth the disbelievers (in His guidance).

20. The lightning almost snatcheth away their sight from them. As often as it flasheth forth for them they walk therein, and when it darkeneth against them they stand still. If Allah willed, He could destroy their hearing and their sight. Lo! Allah is Able to do all things.

21. O mankind! Worship your Lord, who hath created you and those before you, so that ye may ward off (evil).

22. Who hath appointed the earth a resting-place for you, and the sky a canopy; and causeth water to pour down from the sky, thereby producing fruits as food for you. And do not

set up rivals to Allah when ye know (better).

23. And if ye are in doubt concerning that which We reveal unto Our slave (Muhammad), then produce a sûrah of the like thereof, and call your witnesses beside Allah if ye are truthful.

24. And if ye do it not—and ye can never do it—then guard yourselves against the fire prepared for disbelievers, whose fuel is of men and stones.

25. And give glad tidings (O Muhammad) unto those who believe and do good works; that theirs are Gardens underneath which rivers flow; as often as they are regaled with food of the fruit thereof, they say: This is what was given us aforetime, and it is given to them in resemblance. There for them are pure companions; there for ever they abide.

26. Lo! Allah disdaineth not to coin the similitude even of a gnat. Those who believe know that it is the truth from their Lord; but those who disbelieve say: What doth Allah wish (to teach) by such a similitude? He misleadeth many thereby, and He guideth many thereby; and He misleadeth thereby only miscreants.

27. Those who break the covenant of Allah after ratifying it, and sever that which Allah ordered to be joined, and (who) make mischief in the earth: Those are they who are the losers.

28. How disbelieve ye in Allah when ye were dead and He gave life to you! Then he will give you death, then life again, and then unto Him ye will return.

29. He it is Who created for you all that is in the earth. Then turned He to the heaven, and fashioned it as seven heavens. And He is Knower of all things.

30. And when thy Lord said unto the angels: Lo! I am about to place a viceroy in the earth, they said: Wilt Thou place therein one who will do harm therein and will shed blood, while we, we hymn Thy praise and sanctify Thee? He said: Surely I know that which ye know not.

31. And He taught Adam all the names, then showed them to the angels, saying: Inform me of the names of these, if ye are truthful.

32. They said: Be glorified! We have no knowledge saving that which Thou hast taught us. Lo! Thou, only Thou, art the Knower, the Wise.

33. He said: O Adam! Inform them of their names, and when he had informed them of their names, He said: Did I not tell you that I know the secret of the heavens and the earth? And I know that which ye disclose and which ye hide.

34. And when We said unto the angels: Prostrate yourselves

before Adam, they fell prostrate, all save Iblîs. He demurred through pride, and so became a disbeliever.

35. And We said: O Adam! Dwell thou and thy wife in the Garden, and eat ye freely (of the fruits) thereof where ye will; but come not nigh this tree lest ye become wrongdoers.

36. But Satan caused them to deflect therefrom and expelled them from the (happy) state in which they were; and We said: Fall down, one of you a foe unto the other! There shall be for you on earth a habitation and provision for a time.

37. Then Adam received from his Lord words (of revelation), and He relented toward him. Lo! He is the Relenting, the Merciful.

38. We said: Go down, all of you, from hence; but verily there cometh unto you from Me a guidance; and whoso followeth My guidance, there shall no fear come upon them neither shall they grieve.

39. But they who disbelieve, and deny Our revelations, such are rightful owners of the Fire. They will abide therein.

40. O Children of Israel! Remember favour wherewith I favoured you, and fulfil your (part of the) covenant, I shall fulfil My (part of the) covenant, and fear Me.

41. And believe in that which I reveal, confirming that which ye possess already (of the Scripture), and be not first to disbelieve therein, and part not with my revelations for a trifling price, and keep your duty unto Me.

42. Confound not truth with falsehood, nor knowingly conceal the truth.

43. Establish worship, pay the poor-due, and bow your heads with those who bow (in worship).

44. Enjoin ye righteousness upon mankind while ye yourselves forget (to practise it)? And ye are readers of the Scripture! Have ye then no sense?

45. Seek help in patience and prayer; and truly it is hard save for the humble-minded.

46. Who know that they will have to meet their Lord, and that unto Him they are returning.

47. O Children of Israel! Remember My favour wherewith I favoured you and how I preferred you to (all) creatures.

48. And guard yourselves against a day when no soul will in aught avail another, nor will intercession be accepted from it, nor will compensation be received from it, nor will they be helped.

49. And (remember) when We did deliver you from Pharaoh's folk, who were afflicting you with dreadful torment,

slaying your sons and sparing your women: That was a tremendous trial from your Lord.

50. And when We brought you through the sea and rescued you, and drowned the folk of Pharaoh in your sight.

51. And when We did appoint for Moses forty nights (of solitude), and then ye chose the calf, when he had gone from you, and were wrongdoers.

52. Then, even after that, We pardoned you in order that ye might give thanks.

53. And when We gave unto Moses the Scripture and the Criterion (of right and wrong), that ye might be led aright.

54. And when Moses said unto his people: O my people! Ye have wronged yourselves by your choosing of the calf (for worship) so turn in penitence to your Creator, and kill (the guilty) yourselves . That will be best for you with your Creator and He will relent toward you. Lo! He is the Relenting, the Merciful.

55. And when ye said: O Moses! We will not believe in thee till we see Allah plainly; and even while ye gazed the lightning seized you.

56. Then We revived you after your extinction, that ye might give thanks.

57. And we caused the white cloud to overshadow you and sent down on you the manna and the quails, (saying):
Eat of the good things wherewith We have provided you — We wronged them not, but they did wrong themselves.

58. And when We said: Go into this township and eat freely of that which is therein, and enter the gate prostrate, and say: "Repentance." We will forgive you your sins and will increase (reward) for the right-doers.

59. But those who did wrong changed the word which had been told them for another, and We sent down upon the evildoers wrath from Heaven for their evil-doing.

60. And when Moses asked for water for his people, We said: Smite with thy staff the rock. And there gushed out therefrom twelve springs (so that) each tribe knew their drinking-place. Eat and drink of that which Allah hath provided, and do not act corruptly, making mischief in the earth.

61. And when ye said: O Moses! We are weary of one kind of food; so call upon thy Lord for us that He bring forth for us of that which the earth groweth — of its herbs and its cucumbers and its corn and its lentils and its onions. He said: Would ye exchange that which is higher for that which is lower? Go down to settled country, thus ye shall get that which

ye demand. And humiliation and wretchedness were stamped
upon them and they were visited with wrath from Allah . That
was because they disbelieved in Allah's revelations and slew
the prophets wrongfully. That was for their disobedience and
transgression.

62. Lo ! those who believe (in that which is revealed unto
thee, Muhammad), and those who are Jews, and Christians, and
Sabaeans—whoever believeth in Allah and the Last Day and
doeth right—surely their reward is with their Lord, and there
shall no fear come upon them neither shall they grieve.

63. And (remember, O Children of Israel) when We made a
covenant with you and caused the Mount to tower above you,
(saying): Hold fast that which We have given you, and
remember that which is therein, that ye may ward off (evil).

64. Then, even after that, ye turned away, and if it had not
been for the grace of Allah and His mercy ye had been among
the losers.

65. And ye know of those of you who broke the Sabbath,
how We said unto them: Be ye apes, despised and hated!

66. And We made it an example to their own and to
succeeding generations, and an admonition to the Godfearing.

67. And when Moses said unto his people: Lo ! Allah
commandeth you that ye sacrifice a cow, they said: Dost thou
make game of us ? He answered: Allah forbid that I should
be among the foolish !

68. They said: Pray for us unto thy Lord that He make clear
to us what (cow) she is . (Moses) answered: Lo ! He saith Verily
she is a cow neither with calf nor immature; (she is) between
the two conditions; so do that which ye are commanded.

69. They said: Pray for us unto thy Lord that He make clear
to us of what colour she is. (Moses) answered: Lo ! He saith
Verily she is a yellow cow. Bright is her colour, gladdening
beholders.

70. They said: Pray for us unto thy Lord that make clear to
us what (cow) she is. Lo ! cows are much alike to us; and lo !
if Allah wills, we may be led aright.

71. (Moses) answered: Lo ! He saith: Verily she is a cow
unyoked; she plougheth not the soil nor watereth the tilth;
whole and without mark. They said: Now thou bringest the
truth. So they sacrificed her, though almost they did not.

72. And (remember) when ye slew a man and disagree
concerning it and Allah brought forth that which ye were
hiding.

73. And We said: Smite him with some of it. Thus Allah
bringeth the dead to life and showeth you His portents so that

ye may understand.

74. Then, even after that, your hearts were hardened and became as rocks, or worse than rocks, for hardness. For indeed there are rocks from out which rivers gush, and indeed there are rocks which split asunder so that water floweth from them. And indeed there are rocks which fall down for the fear of Allah. Allah is not unaware of what ye do.

75. Have ye any hope that they will be true to you when a party of them used to listen to the Word of Allah, then used to change it, after they had understood it, knowingly?

76. And when they fall in with those who believe, they say: We believe. But when they go apart one with another they say: Prate ye to them of that which Allah hath disclosed to you that they may contend with you before your Lord concerning it? Have ye then no sense?

77. Are they then unaware that Allah knoweth that which they keep hidden and that which they proclaim?

78. Among them are unlettered folk who know the Scripture not except from hearsay. They but guess.

79. Therefore woe be unto those who write the Scripture with their hands and then say, "This is from Allah," that they may purchase a small gain therewith. Woe unto them for that their hands have written, and woe unto them for that they earn thereby.

80. And they say: The fire (of punishment) will not touch us save for a certain number of days. Say: Have ye received a covenant from Allah — truly Allah will not break His covenant — or tell ye concerning Allah that which ye know not?

81. Nay, but whosoever hath done evil and his sin surroundeth him; such are rightful owners of the Fire; they will abide therein.

82. And those who believe and do good works: such are rightful owners of the Garden. They will abide therein.

83. And (remember) when We made a covenant with the Children of Israel, (saying): Worship none save Allah (only), and be good to parents and to kindred and to orphans and the needy, and speak kindly to mankind; and establish worship and pay the poor-due. Then, after that, ye slid back, save a few of you, being averse.

84. And when We made with you a covenant (saying): Shed not the blood of your people nor turn (a party of) your people out of your dwellings. Then ye ratified (Our covenant) and ye were witnesses (thereto).

85. Yet ye it is who slay each other and drive out a party of your people from their homes, supporting one another

against them by sin and transgression—and if they came to you as captives ye would ransom them, whereas their expulsion was itself unlawful for you—Believe ye in part of the Scripture and disbelieve ye in part thereof? And what is the reward of those who do so save ignominy in the life of the world, and on the Day of Resurrection they will be consigned to the most grievous doom. For Allah is not unaware of what ye do.

86. Such are those who buy the life of the world at the price of the Hereafter. Their punishment will not be lightened, neither will they have support.

87. And verily We gave unto Moses the Scripture and We caused a train of messengers to follow after him, and We gave unto Jesus, son of Mary, clear proofs (of Allah's sovereignty), and We supported him with the holy Spirit. Is it ever so, that when there cometh unto you a messenger (from Allah) and with that which ye yourselves desire not, ye grow arrogant, and some ye disbelieve and some ye slay?

88. And they say: Our hearts are hardened. Nay, but Allah hath cursed them for their unbelief. Little is that which they believe.

89. And when there cometh unto them a scripture from Allah, confirming that in their possession—though before that they were asking for a signal triumph over those who disbelieved—and when there cometh unto them that which they know (to be the Truth) they disbelieve therein. The curse of Allah is on disbelievers.

90. Evil is that for which they sell their souls: that they should disbelieve in that which Allah hath revealed, grudging that Allah should reveal of His bounty unto whom He will of His bondmen. They have incurred anger upon anger. For disbelievers is a shameful doom.

91. And when it is said unto them: Believe in that which Allah hath revealed, they say: We believe in that which was revealed unto us. And they disbelieve in that which cometh after it, though it is the truth confirming that which they possess. Say (unto them, O Muhammad): Why then slew the Prophets of Allah aforetime, if ye are (indeed) believers?

92. And Moses came unto you with clear proofs (of Allah's sovereignty), yet, while he was away, ye chose the calf (for worship) and ye were wrongdoers.

93. And when We made with you a covenant and caused the Mount to tower above you, (saying): Hold fast by that which We have given you, and hear (Our Word), they said: We hear and we rebel. And (worship of) the calf was made to sink into

their hearts because of their rejection (of the Covenant). Say (unto them): Evil is that which your belief enjoineth on you, if ye are believers.

94. Say (unto them): If the abode of the Hereafter in the providence of Allah is indeed for you alone and not for others of mankind (as ye pretend), then long for death (for ye must long for death) if ye are truthful.

95. But they will never long for it, because of that which their own hands have sent before them. Allah is Aware of evildoers.

96. And thou wilt find them greediest of mankind for life and (greedier) than the idolaters. (Each) one of them would like to be allowed to live a thousand years. And to live (a thousand years) would by no means remove him from the doom. Allah is Seer of what they do.

97. Say (O Muhammad, to mankind): Who is an enemy to Gabriel ! For he it is who hath revealed (this Scripture) to thy heart by Allah's leave, confirming that which was (revealed) before it, and a guidance and glad tidings to believers.

98. Who is an enemy to Allah, and His angels and His messengers, and Gabriel and Michael! Then, lo! Allah (Himself) is an enemy to the disbelievers.

99. Verily We have revealed unto thee clear tokens, and only miscreants will disbelieve in them.

100. Is it ever so that when ye make a covenant a party of you set it aside ? The truth is, most of them believe not.

101. And when there cometh unto them a messenger from Allah, confirming that which they possess, a party of those who have received the Scripture fling the Scripture of Allah behind their backs as if they knew not.

102. And follow that which the devils falsely related against the kingdom of Solomon. Solomon disbelieved not; but the devils disbelieved, teaching mankind magic and that which was revealed to the two angels in Babel, Hârût and Mârût. Nor did they (the two angels) teach it to anyone till they had said: We are only a temptation, therefore disbelieve not (in the guidance of Allah). And from these two (angels) people learn that by which they cause division between man and wife; but they injure thereby no-one save by Allah's leave. And they learn that which harmeth them and profiteth them not. And surely they do know that he who trafficketh therein will have no (portion) in the Hereafter; and surely evil is the price for which they sell their souls, if they but knew.

103. And if they had believed and kept from evil, a recompense from Allah would be better, if they only knew.

104. O ye who believe, say not (unto the Prophet): "Listen to us" but say "Look upon us," and be ye listeners. For disbelievers is a painful doom.

105. Neither those who disbelieve among the People of the Scripture nor the idolaters love that there should be sent down unto you any good thing from your Lord. But Allah chooseth for His mercy whom He will, and Allah is of infinite bounty.

106. Such of Our revelations as We abrogate or cause to be forgotten, we bring (in place) one better or the like thereof. Knowest thou not that Allah is Able to do all things?

107. Knowest thou not that it is Allah unto Whom belongeth the sovereignty of the heavens and earth; and ye have not, beside Allah, any friend or helper?

108. Or would ye question your messenger as Moses was questioned aforetime? He who chooseth disbelief instead of faith, verily he hath gone astray from a plain road.

109. Many of the People of the Scripture long to make you disbelievers after your belief, through envy on their own account, after the truth hath become manifest unto them. Forgive and be indulgent (toward them) until Allah give command. Lo! Allah is Able to do all things.

110. Establish worship, and pay the poor-due; and whatever of good ye send before (you) for your souls, ye will find it with Allah. Lo! Allah is Seer of what you do.

111. And they say: None entereth Paradise unless he be a Jew or a Christian. These are their own desires. Say: Bring your proof (of what ye state) if ye are truthful.

112. Nay, but whosoever surrendereth his purpose to Allah while doing good, his reward is with his Lord; and there shall no fear come upon them neither shall they grieve.

113. And the Jews say the Christians follow nothing (true), and the Christians say the Jews follow nothing (true); yet both are readers of the Scripture. Even thus speak those who know not. Allah will judge between them on the Day of Resurrection concerning that wherein they differ.

114. And who doth greater wrong than he who forbiddeth the approach to the sanctuaries of Allah lest His name should be mentioned therein, and striveth for their ruin ? As for such, was never meant that they should enter them except in fear. Theirs in the world is ignominy and theirs in the Hereafter is an awful doom.

115. Unto Allah belong the East and West, and whithersoever ye turn, there is Allah's countenance. Lo! Allah is All Embracing All-Knowing.

116. And they say: Allah hath taken unto Himself a Son. Be

He glorified! Nay, but whatsoever is in the heavens and the earth is His. All are subservient unto Him.

117. The Originator of the heavens and the earth! When He decreeth a thing, He saith unto it only: Be! and it is.

118. And those who have no knowledge say: Why doth not Allah speak unto us, or some sign come unto us? Even thus, as they now speak; spake those (who were) before them. Their hearts are all alike. We have made clear the revelations for people who are sure.

119. Lo! We have sent thee (O Muhammad) with the truth, a bringer of glad tidings and a warner. And thou wilt not be asked about the owners of hell-fire.

120. And the Jews will not be pleased with thee, nor will the Christians, till thou follow their creed. Say: Lo! the guidance of Allah (Himself) is Guidance. And if thou shouldst follow their desires after the knowledge which hath come unto thee, then wouldst thou have from Allah no protecting friend nor help.

121. Those unto whom We have given the Scripture, who read it with the right reading, those believe in it. And whoso disbelieveth in it, those are they who are the losers.

122. O Children of Israel! Remember My favour wherewith I favoured you and how I preferred you to (all) creatures.

123. And guard (yourselves) against a day when no soul will in aught avail another, nor will compensation be accepted from it, nor will intercession be of use to it; nor will they be helped.

124. And (remember) when his Lord tried Abraham with (His) commands, and he fulfilled them, He said: Lo! I have appointed thee a leader for mankind. (Abraham) said: And of my offspring (will there be leaders)? He said: My covenant includeth not wrongdoers.

125. And when We made the House (at Mecca) a resort for mankind and a sanctuary, (saying): Take as your place of worship the place where Abraham stood (to pray). And We imposed a duty upon Abraham and Ishmael, (saying): Purify My house for those who go around and those who meditate therein and those who bow down and prostrate themselves (in worship).

126. And when Abraham prayed: My Lord! Make this a region of security and bestow upon its people fruits, such of them as believe in Allah and the Last Day, He answered: As for him who disbelieveth, I shall leave him in contentment for a while, then I shall compel him to the doom of fire—a hapless journey's end!

127. And when Abraham and Ishmael were raising the

foundations of the House, (Abraham prayed): Our Lord!
Accept from us (this duty). Lo! Thou, only Thou, art the
Hearer, the Knower.

128. Our Lord! And make us submissive unto Thee and of
our seed a nation submissive unto Thee, and show us our ways
of worship, and relent toward us. Lo! Thou, only Thou, art
the Relenting, the Merciful.

129. Our Lord! And raise up in their midst a messenger
from among them who shall recite unto them Thy revelations,
and shall instruct them in the Scripture and in wisdom and
shall make them grow. Lo! Thou, only Thou, art the Mighty,
Wise.

130. And who forsaketh the religion of Abraham save him
who befooleth himself? Verily We chose him in the world, and
lo! in the Hereafter he is among the righteous.

131. When his Lord said unto him: Surrender! he said: I
have surrendered to the Lord of the Worlds.

132. The same did Abraham enjoin upon his sons, and also
Jacob, (saying): O my sons! Lo! Allah hath chosen for you the
(true) religion; therefore die not save as men who have
surrendered (unto Him).

133. Or were ye present when death came to Jacob, when he
said unto his sons: What will ye worship after me? They said:
We shall worship thy God, the God of thy fathers, Abraham
and Ishmael and Isaac, One God, and unto Him we have
surrendered.

134. Those are a people who have passed away. Theirs is that
which they earned, and yours is that which ye earn. And ye
will not be asked of what they used to do.

135. And they say: Be Jews or Christians, then ye will be
rightly guided. Say (unto them, O Muhammad): Nay, but (we
follow) the religion of Abraham, the upright, and he was not
of the idolaters.

136. Say (O Muslims): We believe in Allah and that which
is revealed unto us and that which was revealed unto Abraham,
and Ishmael, and Isaac, and Jacob, and the tribes, and that
which Moses and Jesus received, and that which the Prophets
received from their Lord. We make no distinction between any
of them, and unto Him we have surrendered.

137. And if they believe in the like of that which ye believe,
then are they rightly guided. But if they turn away, then are
they in schism, and Allah will suffice thee (for defence) against
them. He is the Hearer, the Knower.

138. (We take our) colour from Allah, and who is better than
Allah at colouring. We are His worshippers.

21

139. Say (unto the People of the Scripture): Dispute ye with us concerning Allah when He is our Lord and your Lord? Ours are our works and yours your works. We look to Him Alone.

140. Or say ye that Abraham, and Ishmael, and Isaac, and Jacob, and the tribes were Jews or Christians? Say: Do ye know best, or doth Allah? And who is more unjust than he who hideth a testimony which he hath received from Allah? Allah is not unaware of what ye do.

141. Those are a people who have passed away; theirs is that which they earned and yours that which ye earn. And ye will not be asked of what they used to do.

142. The foolish of the People will say: What hath turned them from the qiblah which they formerly observed? Say: Unto Allah belong the East and the West. He guideth whom He will unto a straight path.

143. Thus We have appointed you a middle nation, that ye may be witnesses against mankind, and that the Messenger may be a witness against you. And We appointed the qiblah which ye formerly observed only that We might know him who followeth the Messenger, from him who turneth on his heels. In truth it was a hard (test) save for those whom Allah guided. But it was not Allah's purpose that your faith should be in vain, for Allah is full of pity, Merciful toward mankind.

144. We have seen the turning of thy face to heaven (for guidance, O Muhammad). And now verily We shall make thee turn (in prayer) toward a qiblah which is dear to thee. So turn thy face toward the Inviolable Place of Worship, and ye (O Muslims), wheresoever ye may be, turn your faces (when ye pray) toward it. Lo! those who have received the Scripture know that (this Revelation) is the Truth from their Lord. And Allah is not unaware of what they do.

145. And even if thou broughtest unto those who have received the Scripture all kinds of portents, they would not follow thy qiblah, nor canst thou be a follower of their qiblah; nor are some of them followers of the qiblah of others. And if thou shouldst follow their desires after the knowledge which hath come unto thee, then surely wert thou of the evildoers.

146. Those unto whom We gave the Scripture recognise (this revelation) as they recognise their sons. But lo! a party of them knowingly conceal the truth.

147. It is Truth from thy Lord (O Muhammad), so be not thou of those who waver.

148. And each one hath a goal toward which he turneth; so vie with one another in good works. Wheresoever ye may be,

Allah will bring you all together. Lo! Allah is Able to do all things.

149. And whencesoever thou comest forth (for prayer, O Muhammad) turn thy face toward the Inviolable Place of Worship. Lo! it is the Truth from thy Lord. Allah is not unaware of what ye do.

150. Whencesoever thou comest forth turn thy face toward the Inviolable Place of Worship; and wheresoever ye may be (O Muslims) turn your faces toward it (when ye pray) so that men may have no argument against you, save such of them as do injustice—Fear them not, but fear Me!—and so that I may complete My grace upon you, and that ye may be guided.

151. Even as We have sent you a messenger from among you, who reciteth unto you Our revelations and causeth you to grow, and teacheth you the Scripture and wisdom, and teacheth you that which ye knew not.

152. Therefore remember Me, I will remember you. Give thanks to Me, and reject not Me.

153. O ye who believe! Seek help in steadfastness and prayer. Lo! Allah is with the steadfast.

154. And call not those who are slain in the way of Allah "dead ." Nay, they are living, only ye perceive not.

155. And surely We shall try you with something of fear and hunger, and loss of wealth and lives and crops; but give glad tidings to the steadfast.

156. Who say, when a misfortune striketh them: Lo! we are Allah's and lo! unto Him we are returning.

157. Such are they on whom are blessings from their Lord, and mercy. Such are the rightly guided.

158. Lo! (the mountains) As-Safâ and Al-Marwah are among the indications of Allah. It is therefore no sin for him who is on pilgrimage to the House (of God) or visiteth it, to go around them (as the pagan custom is). And he who doeth good of his own accord (for him), lo! Allah is Responsive, Aware.

159. Those who hide the proofs and the guidance which We revealed, after We had made it clear in the Scripture: such are accursed of Allah and accursed of those who have the power to curse.

160. Except such of them as repent and amend and make manifest (the truth). These it is toward whom I relent. I am the relenting, the Merciful.

161. Lo! those who disbelieve, and die while they are disbelievers; on them is the curse of Allah and of angels and of men combined.

162. They ever dwell therein. The doom will not be lightened

for them, neither will they be reprieved.

163. Your God is One God; there is no God save Him, the Beneficent, the Merciful.

164. Lo! in the creation of the heavens and the earth, and the difference of night and day, and the ships which run upon the sea with that which is of use to men, and the water which Allah sendeth down from the sky, thereby reviving the earth after its death, and dispersing all kinds of beasts therein, and (in) the ordinance of the winds, and the clouds obedient between heaven and earth: are signs (of Allah's sovereignty) for people who have sense.

165. Yet of mankind are some who take unto themselves (objects of worship which they set as) rivals to Allah, loving them with a love like (that which is the due) of Allah (only) — Those who believe are stauncher in their love for Allah — Oh, that those who do evil had but known, (on the day) when they behold the doom, that power belongeth wholly to Allah, and that Allah is severe in punishment.

166. (On the day) when those who were followed disown those who followed (them), and they behold the doom, and all their aims collapse with them.

167. And those who were but followers will say: If a return were possible for us, we would disown them even as they have disowned us. Thus will Allah show them their own deeds as anguish for them, and they will not emerge from the Fire.

168. O mankind! Eat of that which is lawful and wholesome in the earth, and follow not the footsteps of the devil. Lo ! he is an open enemy for you.

169. He enjoineth upon you only the evil and the foul, and that ye should tell concerning Allah that which ye know not.

170. And when it is said unto them: Follow that which Allah hath revealed, they say: We follow that wherein we found our fathers . What ! Even though their fathers were wholly unintelligent and had no guidance?

171. The likeness of those who disbelieve (in relation to the messenger) is as the likeness of one who calleth unto that which heareth naught except a shout and cry. Deaf, dumb, blind, therefore they have no sense.

172. O ye who believe! Eat of the good things wherewith We have provided you, and render thanks to Allah if it is (indeed) He whom ye worship.

173. He hath forbidden you only carrion, and blood, and swineflesh, and that which hath been immolated to (the name of) any other than Allah. But he who is driven by necessity, neither craving nor transgressing, it is no sin for him . Lo ! Allah

is forgiving, Merciful.

174. Lo! those who hide aught of the Scripture which Allah hath revealed, and purchase a small gain therewith, they eat into their bellies nothing else than fire. Allah will not speak to them on the Day of Resurrection, nor will He make them grow. Theirs will be a painful doom.

175. Those are they who purchase error at the price of guidance, and torment at the price of pardon. How constant are they in their strife to reach the Fire!

176. That is because Allah hath revealed the Scripture with the truth. Lo! those who find (a cause of) disagreement in the Scripture are in open schism.

177. It is not righteousness that ye turn your faces to the East and the West; but righteous is he who believeth in Allah and the Last Day and the angels and the Scripture and the Prophets; and giveth his wealth, for love of Him, to kinsfolk and to orphans and the needy and the wayfarer and to those who ask, and to set slaves free; and observeth proper worship and payeth the poor-due. And those who keep their treaty when they make one, and the patient in tribulation and adversity and time of stress. Such are they who are sincere. Such are the God-fearing.

178. O ye who believe! Retaliation is prescribed for you in the matter of the murdered; the freeman for the freeman, and the slave for the slave, and the female for the female. And for him who is forgiven somewhat by his (injured) brother, prosecution according to usage and payment unto him in kindness. This is an alleviation and a mercy from your Lord. He who transgresseth after this will have a painful doom.

179. And there is life for you in retaliation, O men of understanding, that ye may ward off (evil).

180. It is prescribed for you, when one of you approacheth death, if he leave wealth, that he bequeath unto parents and near relatives in kindness. (This is) a duty for all those who ward off (evil).

181. And whoso changeth (the will) after he hath heard it — the sin thereof is only upon those who change it. Lo! Allah is Hearer, Knower.

182. But he who feareth from a testator some unjust or sinful clause, and maketh peace between the parties, (it shall be) no sin for him. Lo! Allah is Forgiving, Merciful.

183. O ye who believe! Fasting is prescribed for you, even as it was prescribed for those before you, that ye may ward off (evil).

184. (Fast) a certain number of days; and (for) him who is sick among you, or on a journey, (the same) number of other

days; and for those who can afford it there is a ransom: the feeding of a man in need — But whoso doeth good of his own accord, it is better for him: and that ye fast is better for you if ye did but know —

185. The month of Ramadân in which was revealed the Qur'ân, a guidance for mankind, and clear proofs of the guidance, and the Criterion (of right and wrong). And whosoever of you is present, let him fast the month, and whosoever of you is sick or on a journey, (let him fast the same) number of other days. Allah desireth for you ease; He desireth not hardship for you; and (He desireth) that ye should complete the period, and that ye should magnify Allah for having guided you, and that peradventure ye may be thankful.

186. And when My servants question thee concerning Me, then surely I am nigh. I answer the prayer of the suppliant when he crieth unto Me, so let them hear My call and let them trust in Me, in order that they may be led aright.

187. It is made lawful for you to go unto your wives on the night of the fast. They are raiment for you and ye are raiment for them. Allah is aware that ye were deceiving yourselves in this respect and He hath turned in mercy toward you and relieved you. So hold intercourse with them and seek that which Allah hath ordained for you, and eat and drink until the white thread becometh distinct to you from the black thread of the dawn. Then strictly observe the fast till nightfall and touch them not, but be at your devotions in the mosques. These are the limits imposed by Allah, so approach them not. Thus Allah expoundeth His revelations to mankind that they may ward off (evil).

188. And eat not up your property among yourselves in vanity, nor seek by it to gain the hearing of the judges that ye may knowingly devour a portion of the property of others wrongfully.

189. They ask thee, (O Muhammad), of new moons. Say: They are fixed seasons for mankind and for the pilgrimage. It is not righteousness that ye go to houses by the backs thereof (as do the idolaters at certain seasons), but the righteous man is he who wardeth off (evil). So go to houses by the gates thereof, and observe your duty to Allah, that ye may be successful.

190. Fight in the way of Allah against those who fight against you, but begin not hostilities. Lo! Allah loveth not aggressors.

191. And slay them wherever ye find them, and drive them out of the places whence they drove you out, for persecution

is worse than slaughter. And fight not with them at the Inviolable Place of Worship until they first attack you there, but if they attack you (there) then slay them. Such is the reward of disbelievers.

192. But if they desist, then lo! Allah is Forgiving, Merciful.

193. And fight them until persecution is no more, and religion is for Allah. But if they desist, then let there be no hostility except against wrongdoers.

194. The forbidden month for the forbidden month, and forbidden things in retaliation. And one who attacketh you, attack him in the manner as he attacked you. Observe your duty to Allah, and know that Allah is with those who ward off (evil).

195. Spend your wealth for the cause of Allah, and be not cast by your own hands to ruin; and do good. Lo! Allah loveth the beneficent.

196. Perform the pilgrimage and visit (to Mecca) for Allah. And if ye are prevented, then send such gifts as can be obtained with ease, and shave not your heads until the gifts have reached their destination. And whoever among you is sick or hath an ailment of the head must pay a ransom of fasting or almsgiving or offering. And if ye are in safety, then whosoever contenteth himself with the visit for the Pilgrimage (shall give) such gifts as can be had with ease. And whosoever cannot find (such gifts), then a fast of three days while on the pilgrimage, and of seven when ye have returned; that is, ten in all. That is for him whose folk are not present at the Inviolable Place of Worship. Observe your duty to Allah, and know that Allah is severe in punishment.

197. The pilgrimage is (in) the well-known months, and whoever is minded to perform the pilgrimage therein (let him remember that) there is (to be) no lewdness nor abuse nor angry conversation on the pilgrimage. And whatsoever good ye do Allah knoweth it. So make provision for yourselves (hereafter); for the best provision is to ward off evil. Therefore keep your duty unto Me, O men of understanding.

198. It is no sin for you that ye seek the bounty of your Lord (by trading). But, when ye press on in the multitude from 'Arafât, remember Allah by the sacred monument. Remember Him as He hath guided you, although before ye were of those astray.

199. Then hasten onward from the place whence the multitude hasteneth onward, and ask forgiveness of Allah. Lo! Allah is Forgiving, Merciful.

200. And when ye have completed your devotions, then

remember Allah as ye remember your fathers or with a more lively remembrance. But of mankind is he who saith: "Our Lord! Give unto us in the world,' and he hath no portion in the Hereafter.

201. And of them (also) is he who saith: "Our Lord! Give unto us in the world that which is good and in the Hereafter that which is good, and guard us from the doom of Fire."

202. For them, there is in store a goodly portion out of that which they have earned. Allah is swift at reckoning.

203. Remember Allah through the appointed days. Then whoso hasteneth (his departure) by two days, it is no sin for him, and whoso delayeth, it is no sin for him; that is for him who wardeth off (evil). Be careful of your duty to Allah, and know that unto Him ye will be gathered.

204. And of mankind there is he whose conversation on the life of this world pleaseth thee (Muhammad), and he calleth Allah to witness as to that which is in his heart; yet he is the most rigid of opponents.

205. And when he turneth away (from thee) his effort in the land is to make a mischief therein and to destroy the crops and the cattle; and Allah loveth not mischief.

206. And when it is said unto him: Be careful of thy duty to Allah, pride taketh him to sin. Hell will settle his account, an evil resting-place.

207. And of mankind is he who would sell himself, seeking the pleasure of Allah; and Allah hath compassion on (His) bondmen.

208. O ye who believe! Come, all of you, into submission (unto Him); and follow not the footsteps of the devil. Lo! he is an open enemy for you.

209. And if ye slide back after the clear proofs have come unto you, then know that Allah is Mighty, Wise.

210. Wait they for naught else than that Allah should come unto them in the shadows of the clouds with the angels? Then the case would be already judged. All cases go back to Allah (for judgement).

211. Ask of the Children of Israel how many a clear revelation We gave them! He who altereth the grace of Allah after it hath come unto him (for him), lo! Allah is severe in punishment.

212. Beautified is the life of the world for those who disbelieve; they make a jest of the believers. But those who keep their duty to Allah will be above them on the Day of Resurrection. Allah giveth without stint to whom He will.

213. Mankind were one community, and Allah sent (unto

them) Prophets as bearers of good tidings and as warners, and
revealed therewith the Scripture with the truth that it might
judge between mankind concerning that wherein they differed. And only those unto whom (the Scripture) was given
differed concerning it, after clear proofs had come unto them,
through hatred one of another. And Allah by His Will guided
those who believe unto the truth of that concerning which
they differed. Allah guideth whom He will unto a straight
path.

214. Or think ye that ye will enter Paradise while yet there
hath not come unto you the like of (that which came to) those
who passed away before you? Affliction and adversity befell
them, they were shaken as with earthquake, till the messenger
(of Allah) and those who believed along with him said: When
cometh Allah's help? Now surely Allah's help is nigh.

215. They ask thee, (O Muhammad), what they shall spend.
Say: That which ye spend for good (must go) to parents and
near kindred and orphans and the needy and the wayfarer. And
whatsoever good ye do, lo! Allah is Aware of it.

216. Warfare is ordained for you, though it is hateful unto
you; but it may happen that ye hate a thing which is good for
you, and it may happen that ye love a thing which is bad for
you. Allah knoweth, ye know not.

217. They question thee (O Muhammad) with regard to
warfare in the sacred month. Say: Warfare therein is a great
(transgression), but to turn (men) from the way of Allah, and
to disbelieve in Him and in the Inviolable Place of Worship, and
to expel his people thence, is a greater with Allah; for
persecution is worse than killing. And they will not cease from
fighting against you till they have made you renegades from
your religion, if they can. And whoso becometh a renegade and
dieth in his disbelief such are they whose works have fallen
both in the world and the Hereafter. Such are rightful owners
of the Fire: they will abide therein.

218. Lo! those who believe, and those who emigrate (to
escape the persecution) and strive in the way of Allah, these
have hope of Allah's mercy. Allah is Forgiving, Merciful.

219. They question thee about strong drink and games of
chance. Say: In both is great sin, and (some) utility for men; but
the sin of them is greater than their usefulness. And they ask
thee what they ought to spend. Say: That which is superfluous.
Thus Allah maketh plain to you (His) revelations, that haply
ye may reflect.

220. Upon the world and the Hereafter. And they question
thee concerning orphans. Say: to improve their lot is best. And

if ye mingle your affairs with theirs, then (they are) your brothers. Allah knoweth him who spoileth from him who improveth. Had Allah willed He could have overburdened you. Allah is Mighty, Wise.

221. Wed not idolatresses till they believe; for lo! a believing bondwoman is better than an idolatress though she please you; and give not your daughters in marriage to idolaters till they believe, for lo! a believing slave is better than an idolater though he please you. These invite unto the Fire, and Allah inviteth unto the Garden, and unto forgiveness by His grace, and expoundeth thus His revelations to mankind that haply they may remember.

222. They question thee (O Muhammad) concerning menstruation. Say: It is an illness, so let women alone at such times and go not in unto them till they are cleansed. And when they have purified themselves, then go in unto them as Allah hath enjoined upon you. Truly Allah loveth those who turn unto Him, and loveth those who have a care for cleanness.

223. Your women are a tilth for you (to cultivate) so go to your tilth as ye will, and send (good deeds) before you for your souls, and fear Allah, and know that ye will (one day) meet Him. Give glad tidings to believers, (O Muhammad).

224. And make not Allah, by your oaths, a hindrance to your being righteous and observing your duty unto Him and making peace among mankind. Allah is Hearer, Knower.

225. Allah will not take you to task for that which is unintentional in your oaths. But He will take you to task for that which your hearts have garnered. Allah is Forgiving, Clement.

226. Those who forswear their wives must wait four months; then, if they change their mind, lo! Allah is Forgiving, Merciful.

227. And if they decide upon divorce (let them remember that) Allah is Hearer, Knower.

228. Women who are divorced shall wait, keeping themselves apart, three (monthly) courses. And it is not lawful for them that they should conceal that which Allah hath created in their wombs if they are believers in Allah and the Last Day. And their husbands would do better to take them back in that case if they desire a reconciliation. And they (women) have rights similar to those (of men) over them in kindness, and men are a degree above them. Allah is Mighty, Wise.

229. Divorce must be pronounced twice and then (a woman) must be retained in honour or released in kindness. And it is not lawful for you that ye take from women aught of that which ye have given them; except (in the case) when both fear that

they may not be able to keep the limits (imposed by) Allah.
And if ye fear that they may not be able to keep the limits
of Allah, in that case it is no sin for either of them if the
woman ransom herself. These are the limits (imposed by)
Allah. Transgress them not. For whoso transgresseth Allah's
limits: such are wrong-doers.

230. And if he hath divorced her (the third time), then she
is not lawful unto him thereafter until she hath wedded
another husband. Then if he (the other husband) divorce her
it is no sin for both of them that they come together again if
they consider that they are able to observe the limits of Allah.
These are the limits of Allah. He manifesteth them for people
who have knowledge.

231. When ye have divorced women, and they have
reached their term, then retain them in kindness or release
them in kindness. Retain them not to their hurt so that ye
transgress (the limits). He who doeth that hath wronged his
soul. Make not the revelations of Allah a laughing-stock (by
your behaviour), but remember Allah's grace upon you and
that which He hath revealed unto you of the Scripture and of
wisdom, whereby He doth exhort you. Observe your duty to
Allah and know that Allah is Aware of All things.

232. And when ye have divorced women and they reach
their term, place not difficulties in the way of their marrying
their husbands if it is agreed between them in kindness. This
is an admonition for him among you who believeth in Allah
and the Last Day. That is more virtuous for you, and cleaner.
Allah knoweth: ye know not.

233. Mothers shall suckle their children for two whole years;
(that is) for those who wish to complete the suckling. The duty
of feeding and clothing nursing mothers in a seemly manner
is upon the father of the child. No one should be charged
beyond his capacity. A mother should not be made to suffer
because of her child, nor should he to whom the child is born
(be made to suffer) because of his child. And on the (father's)
heir is incumbent the like of that (which was incumbent on the
father). If they desire to wean the child by mutual consent and
(after) consultation, it is no sin for them; and if ye wish to give
your children out to nurse, it is no sin for you, provided that
ye pay what is due from you in kindness. Observe your duty
to Allah, and know that Allah is Seer of what ye do.

234. Such of you as die and leave behind them wives, they
(the wives) shall wait, keeping themselves apart, four months
and ten days. And when they reach the term (prescribed for
them) then there is no sin for you in aught that they may do

with themselves in decency. Allah is Informed of what ye do.

235. There is no sin for you in that which ye proclaim or hide in your minds concerning your troth with women. Allah knoweth that ye will remember them. But plight not your troth with women except by uttering a recognised form or words. And do not consummate the marriage until (the term) prescribed is run. Know that Allah knoweth what is in your minds, so beware of Him; and know that Allah is Forgiving, Clement.

236. It is no sin for you if ye divorce women while yet ye have not touched them, nor appointed unto them a portion. Provide for them, the rich according to his means, and the straitened according to his means, a fair provision. (This is) a bounden duty for those who do good.

237. If ye divorce them before ye have appointed unto them a portion, then (pay the) half of that which ye appointed, unless they (the women) agree to forgo it in whose hand is the marriage tie. To forgo is nearer to piety. And forget not kindness among yourselves. Allah is Seer of what ye do.

238. Be guardians of your prayers, and of the midmost prayer, and stand up with devotion to Allah.

239. And if ye go in fear, then (pray) standing or on horseback. And when ye are again in safety, remember Allah, as He hath taught you that which (heretofore) ye knew not.

240. (In the case of) those of you who are about to die and leave behind your wives, they should bequeath unto their wives a provision for the year without turning them out, but if they go out (of their own accord) there is no sin for you in that which they do of themselves within their rights. Allah is Mighty, Wise.

241. For divorced women a provision in kindness: a duty for those who ward off (evil).

242. Thus Allah expoundeth unto you His revelations so that ye may understand.

243. Bethink thee (O Muhammad) of those of old, who went forth from their habitations in their thousands, fearing death, and Allah said unto them: Die, and then He brought them back to life. Lo! Allah is Lord of Kindness to mankind, but most of mankind give not thanks.

244. Fight in the way of Allah, and know that Allah is Hearer, Knower.

245. Who is it that will lend unto Allah a goodly loan, so that He may give it increase manifold? Allah straiteneth and enlargeth. Unto Him ye will return.

246. Bethink thee of the Leaders of the Children of Israel

after Moses, how they said unto a Prophet whom they had:
Set up for us a King and we will fight in Allah's way. He said:
Would ye then refrain from fighting if fighting were
prescribed for you? They said: Why should we not fight in
Allah's way when we have been driven from our dwellings
with our children? Yet, when fighting was prescribed for
them, they turned away, all save a few of them. Allah is
Aware of evildoers.

247. Their Prophet said unto them: Lo! Allah hath raised up
Saul to be a king for you. They said: How can he have
kingdom over us when we are more deserving of the
kingdom than he is, since he hath not been given wealth
enough? He said: Lo! Allah hath chosen him above you, and
hath increased him abundantly in wisdom and stature. Allah
bestoweth His sovereignty on whom He will. Allah is All-
Embracing, All-Knowing.

248. And their Prophet said unto them: Lo! the token of his
kingdom is that there shall come unto you the ark wherein is
peace of reassurance from your Lord, and a remnant of that
which the house of Moses and the house of Aaron left behind,
the angels bearing it. Lo! herein shall be a token for you if (in
truth) ye are believers.

249. And when Saul set out with the army, he said: Lo! Allah
will try you by (the ordeal of) a river. Whosoever therefore
drinketh thereof he is not of me, and whosoever tasteth it not
he is of me, save him who taketh (thereof) in the hollow of his
hand. But they drank thereof, all save a few of them. And after
he had crossed (the river), he and those who believed with
them, they said: We have no power this day against Goliath
and his hosts. But those who knew that they would meet their
Lord exclaimed: How many a little company hath overcome a
mighty host by Allah's leave! Allah is with the steadfast.

250. And when they went into the field against Goliath and
his hosts they said: Our Lord! Bestow on us endurance, make
our foothold sure, and give us help against the disbelieving
folk.

251. So they routed them by Allah's leave and David slew
Goliath; and Allah gave him the kingdom and wisdom, and
taught him of that which He willeth. And if Allah had not
repelled some men by others the earth would have been
corrupted. But Allah is a Lord of Kindness to (His) creatures.

252. These are the portents of Allah which we recite unto
thee (Muhammad) with truth, and lo! thou art of the number
of (Our) messengers.

253. Of these messengers, some of whom We have caused

to excel others, and of whom there are some unto whom Allah spake, while some of them He exalted (above others) in degree; and We gave Jesus, son of Mary, clear proofs (of Allah's sovereignty) and We supported him with the Holy Spirit. And if Allah had so willed it, those who followed after them would not have fought one with another after the clear proofs had come unto them. But they differed, some of them believing and some disbelieving. And if Allah had so willed it, they would not have fought one with another; but Allah doeth what He will.

254. O ye who believe! Spend of that wherewith We have provided you ere a day come when there will be no trafficking nor friendship, nor intercession. The disbelievers, they are the wrongdoers.

255. Allah! There is no God save Him, the Alive, the Eternal. Neither slumber nor sleep overtaketh Him. Unto Him belongeth whatsoever is in the heavens and whatsoever is in the earth. Who is he that intercedeth with Him save by His leave? He knoweth that which is in front of them and that which is behind them, while they encompass nothing of His knowledge save that He will. His throne includeth the heavens and the earth, and He is never weary of preserving them. He is the Sublime, the Tremendous.

256. There is no compulsion in religion. The right direction is henceforth distinct from error. And he who rejecteth false deities and believeth in Allah hath grasped a firm handhold which will never break. Allah is Hearer, Knower.

257. Allah is the Protecting Friend of those who believe. He bringeth them out of darkness into light. As for those who disbelieve, their patrons are false deities. They bring them out of light into darkness. Such are rightful owners of the Fire. They will abide therein.

258. Bethink thee of him who had an argument with Abraham about his Lord, because Allah had given him the kingdom; how, when Abraham said: My Lord is He who giveth life and causeth death, he answered: I give life and cause death. Abraham said, Lo! Allah causeth the sun to rise in the East, so do thou cause it to come up from the West. Thus was the disbeliever abashed. And Allah guideth not wrong-doing folk.

259. Or (behink thee of) the like of him who, passing by a township which had fallen into utter ruin, exclaimed: How shall Allah give this township life after its death? And Allah made him die a hundred years, then brought him back to life. He said: How long hast thou tarried? (The man) said: I have tarried a day or part of a day. (He) said: Nay, but thou hast tarried for

a hundred years. Just look at thy food and drink which have rotted! Look at thine ass! And, that We may make thee a token unto mankind, look at the bones, how We adjust them and then cover them with flesh! And when (the matter) became clear unto him, he said: I know now that Allah is Able to do all things.

260. And when Abraham said (unto his Lord): My Lord! Show me how Thou givest life to the dead, He said: Dost thou not believe? Abraham said: Yea, but (I ask) in order that my heart may be at ease. (His Lord) said: Take four of the birds and cause them to incline unto thee, then place a part of them on each hill, then call them, they will come to thee in haste. And know that Allah is Mighty, Wise.

261. The likeness of those who spend their wealth in Allah's way is as the likeness of a grain which groweth seven ears, in every ear a hundred grains. Allah giveth increase manifold to whom He will. Allah is All-Embracing, All-Knowing.

262. Those who spend their wealth for the cause of Allah and afterwards make not reproach and injury to follow that which they have spent; their reward is with their Lord, and there shall no fear come upon them, neither shall they grieve.

263. A kind word with forgiveness is better than almsgiving followed by injury. Allah is Absolute, Clement.

264. O ye who believe! Render not vain your almsgiving by reproach and injury, like him who spendeth his wealth only to be seen of men and believeth not in Allah and the Last Day. His likeness is as the likeness of a rock whereon is dust of earth; a rainstorm smiteth it, leaving it smooth and bare. They have no control of aught of that which they have gained. Allah guideth not the disbelieving folk.

265. And the likeness of those who spend their wealth in search of Allah's pleasure, and for the strengthening of their souls, is as the likeness of a garden on a height. The rainstorm smiteth it and it bringeth forth its fruit twofold. And if the rainstorm smite it not, then the shower. Allah is Seer of what ye do.

266. Would any of you like to have a garden of palm-trees and vines, with rivers flowing underneath it, with all kinds of fruit for him therein; and old age hath stricken him and he hath feeble off-spring; and a fiery whirlwind striketh it and it is (all) consumed by fire. Thus Allah maketh plain His revelations unto you, in order that ye may give thought.

267. O ye who believe! Spend of the good things which ye have earned, and of that which we bring forth from the earth for you, and seek not the bad (with intent) to spend thereof (in

charity) when ye would not take it for yourselves save with disdain; and know that Allah is Absolute, Owner of Praise.

268. The devil promiseth you destitution and enjoineth on you lewdness. But Allah promiseth you forgiveness from Himself with bounty. Allah is All-Embracing, All-Knowing.

269. He giveth wisdom unto whom He will, and he unto whom wisdom is given, he truly hath received abundant good. But none remember except men of understanding.

270. Whatever alms ye spend or vow ye vow, lo! Allah knoweth it. Wrong-doers have no helpers.

271. If ye publish your almsgiving, it is well, but if ye hide it and give it to the poor, it will be better for you, and will atone for some of your ill-deeds. Allah is Informed of what ye do.

272. The guiding of them is not thy duty (O Muhammad) but Allah guideth whom He will. And whatsoever good thing ye spend, it is for yourselves, when ye spend not save in search of Allah's countenance; and whatsoever good thing ye spend, it will be repaid to you in full, and ye will not be wronged.

273. (Alms are) for the poor who are straitened for the cause of Allah, who cannot travel in the land (for trade). The unthinking man accounteth them wealthy because of their restraint. Thou shalt know them by their mark: They do not beg of men with importunity. And whatsoever good thing ye spend, lo! Allah knoweth it.

274. Those who spend their wealth by night and day, by stealth and openly, verily their reward is with their Lord, and there shall no fear come upon them neither shall they grieve.

275. Those who swallow usury cannot rise up save as he ariseth whom the devil hath prostrated by (his) touch. That is because they say: Trade is just like usury; whereas Allah permitteth trading and forbiddeth usury. He unto whom an admonition from his Lord cometh, and (he) refraineth (in obedience thereto), he shall keep (the profits of) that which is past, and his affair (henceforth is with Allah. As for him who returneth (to usury) — Such are rightful owners of the Fire. They will abide therein.

276. Allah hath blighted usury and made almsgiving fruitful. Allah loveth not the impious and guilty.

277. Lo! those who believe and do good works and establish worship and pay the poor-due, their reward is with their Lord and there shall no fear come upon them neither shall they grieve.

278. O ye who believe! Observe your duty to Allah, and give up what remaineth (due to you) from usury, if ye are (in truth) believers.

279. And if ye do not, then be warned of war (against you) from Allah and His messenger. And if ye repent, then ye have your principal (without interest). Wrong not, and ye shall not be wronged.

280. And if the debtor is in straitened circumstances, then (let there be) postponement to (the time of) ease; and that ye remit the debt as almsgiving would be better for you if ye did but know.

281. And guard yourselves against a day in which ye will be brought back to Allah. Then every soul will be paid in full then which it hath earned, and they will not be wronged.

282. O ye who believe! When ye contract a debt for a fixed term, record it in writing. Let a scribe record it in writing between you in (terms of) equity. No scribe should refuse to write as Allah hath taught him, so let him write, and let him who incurreth the debt dictate, and let him observe his duty to Allah his Lord, and diminish naught thereof. But if he who oweth the debt of low understanding, or weak, or unable himself to dictate, then let the guardian of his interests dictate in (terms of) equity. And call to witness, from among your men, two witnesses. And if two men be not (at hand) then a man and two women, of such as ye approve as witnesses, so that if the one erreth (through forgetfulness) the other will remember. And the witnesses must not refuse when they are summoned. Be not averse to writing down (the contract) whether it be small or great, with (record of) the term thereof. That is more suitable in the sight of Allah and more sure for testimony, and the best way of avoiding doubt between you; save only in the case when it is actual merchandise which ye transfer among yourselves from hand to hand. In that case it is no sin for you if ye write it not. And have witnesses when ye sell one to another, and let no harm be done to scribe or witness. If ye do (harm to them) lo! it is a sin in you. Observe your duty to Allah. Allah is teaching you. And Allah is Knower of all things.

283. If ye be on a journey and cannot find a scribe, then a pledge in hand (shall suffice). And if one of you entrusteth to another let him who is trusted deliver up that which is entrusted to him (according to the pact between them) and let him observe his duty to Allah his Lord. Hide not testimony. He who hideth it, verily his heart is sinful. Allah is Aware of what ye do.

284. Unto Allah (belongeth) whatsoever is in the heavens and whatsoever is in the earth; and whether ye make known what is in your minds or hide it, Allah will bring you to account

for it. He will forgive whom He will and He will punish whom He will. Allah is Able to do all things.

285. The messenger believeth in that which hath been revealed unto him from his Lord and (so do) the believers. Each one believeth in Allah and His angels and His scriptures and His messengers—We make no distinction between any of His messengers—and they say: We hear, and we obey. (Grant us) Thy forgiveness, our Lord. Unto Thee is the journeying.

286. Allah tasketh not a soul beyond its scope. For it (is only) that which it hath earned, and against it (only) that which it hath deserved. Our Lord! Condemn us not if we forget, or miss the mark! Our Lord! Lay not on us such a burden as Thou lay on those before us! Our Lord! Impose not on us that which we have not the strength to bear! Pardon us, absolve us and have mercy on us, Thou, our Protector, and give us victory over the disbelieving folk.

SÛRAH 3

Ali 'Imrân takes its title from v. 32, where "the family of 'Imrân" (the father of Moses) occurs as a generic name for all the Hebrew prophets from Moses to John the Baptist and Jesus Christ. This, with the mention of the mother of Mary as "the wife of "Imrân" (v.34), and the words "sister of Aaron" addressed to Mary (19:28), have given rise to a charge of anachronism—absurd because the whole of the rest of the Koran is against it—by Muir and other non-Muslim writers, who say that the Prophet confused Mary, the mother of Jesus, with Miriam, the sister of Moses. Most Muslims believe, on the authority of the Koran, that the grandfather of Jesus Christ was named 'Imrân', which may also have been the name of the father of Moses. In Sûrah 19:28, where Mary is addressed as "sister of Aaron", they hold the ancestral sense to be the more probable, while denying that there is any reason to suppose that the Virgin Mary had not a brother named Aaron.

If vv. 1 to 34 were, as tradition states, revealed on the occasion of the deputation from the Christians of Najrân, which took place in the tenth year of the Hijrah ("the year of deputations," as it is called), then they are of much later date than the rest of the sûrah, but it seems possible that they were only recited by the Prophet on that occasion, having been revealed before.

The Jews have become bolder and more bitter in opposition which, as Nöldeke points out, cannot have been the case, after the signal victory of Badr, until after the Muslims suffered a reverse at Uhud; a battle to which vv. 120 to 188 largely refer.

In the third year of the Hijrah the Meccans came against Al-Madînah, with an army of 3000 men to avenge their defeat at Badr in the previous year, and to wipe out the Muslims. The Prophet, against his own first plan, which was to defend Al-Madînah, at the insistence of his companions, went out to meet them on Mt. Uhud, posting his men carefully. He led an army of 1000 men, a third of whom under Abdullah ibn Ubeyy (the "Hypocrite" leader) deserted him before the battle, and said afterwards that they did not think there would be any fighting that day. The battle began well for the Muslims but was changed to something near defeat by the disobedience of a band of fifty archers placed to guard a certain point. Seeing the Muslims winning, they feared that they might lose their share of the spoils, and ran to join the others, leaving a way open for the Meccan cavalry. The idolaters then rallied and inflicted considerable loss upon the Muslims, the Prophet himself being wounded in the struggle. A cry arose that the Prophet had been slain, and the Muslims were in despair till someone recognized the Prophet and cried out that he was living. The Muslims then rallied to his side, and retired in some sort of order. The army of Qureysh also retired after the battle.

In this battle the wives of the leaders of Qureysh, who had been brought with the army to give courage by their presence and their chanting, mutilated the Muslim slain, making necklaces and bracelets of ears and noses. Hind, the wife of Abû Sufyân, plucked out the liver of the Prophet's uncle, Hamzah, publicly, and tried to eat it. The Prophet, when he saw the condition of the slain, was moved to vow reprisals. But he was relieved of his vow by a revelation, and mutilation was forbidden to the Muslims.

On the day after the battle of Mt. Uhud, the Prophet again went out with such of the army as survived, in order that Qureysh might hear that he was in the field and haply be deterred from any project of attacking Al-Madînah in its weakened state. On that occasion many wounded men went out with him. Tradition tells how a friendly nomad met the Muslims and afterwards met the army of Qureysh. Questioned by Abû Sufyân, he said that the Prophet was seeking vengeance with an overwhelming force; and that report determined Abû Sufyân to march back to Mecca.

The period of revelation is the third and fourth years of the Hijrah.

THE FAMILY OF 'IMRÂN

Revealed at Al-Madînah

In the name of Allah, the Beneficent, the Merciful.

1. Alif. Lâm. Mîm.

2. Allah! There is no God save Him, the Alive, the Eternal.

3. He hath revealed unto thee (Muhammad) the Scripture with truth, confirming that which was (revealed) before it, even as He revealed the Torah and the Gospel.

4. Aforetime, for a guidance to mankind; and hath revealed the Criterion (of right and wrong). Lo! those who disbelieve the revelations of Allah, theirs will be a heavy doom. Allah is mighty. Able to Requite (the wrong).

5. Lo! nothing in the earth or in the heavens is hidden from Allah.

6. He it is who fashioneth you in the wombs as pleaseth Him. There is no God save Him, the Almighty, the Wise.

7. He it is Who hath revealed unto thee (Muhammad) the Scripture wherein are clear revelations—They are substance of the Book—and others (which are) allegorical. But those in whose hearts is doubt pursue, forsooth, that which is allegorical seeking (to cause) dissension by seeking to explain it. None knoweth its explanation save Allah. And those who are of sound instruction say: We believe therein, the whole is from our Lord; but only men of understanding really heed.

8. Our Lord! Cause not our hearts to stray after Thou hast guided us, and bestow upon us mercy from Thy Presence. Lo! Thou, only Thou, art the Bestower.

9. Our Lord! it is Thou Who gatherest mankind together to a Day of which there is no doubt. Lo! Allah faileth not to keep the tryst.

10. (On that day) neither the riches nor the progeny of those who disbelieve will aught avail them with Allah. They will be fuel for fire.

11. Like Pharaoh's folk and those who were before them, they disbelieved Our revelations and so Allah seized them for their sins. And Allah is severe in punishment.

12. Say (O Muhammad) unto those who disbelieve: Ye shall be overcome and gathered unto Hell, an evil resting-place.

13. There was a token for you in two hosts which met: one army fighting in the way of Allah, and another disbelieving, whom they saw as twice their number, clearly, with their very eyes. Thus Allah strengtheneth with His succour whom He will. Lo! herein verily is a lesson for those who have eyes.

14. Beautified for mankind is love of the joys (that come) from women and offspring, and stored-up heaps of gold and silver, and horses branded (with their mark), and cattle and land. That is comfort of the life of the world. Allah! With Him is a more excellent abode.

15. Say: Shall I inform you of something better than that? For those who keep from evil, with their Lord, are Gardens underneath which rivers flow wherein they will abide, and pure companions, and contentment from Allah. Allah is Seer of His bondmen.

16. Those who say: Our Lord! Lo! we believe. So forgive us our sins and guard us from the punishment of Fire.

17. The steadfast, and the truthful, and the obedient, those who spend (and hoard not), those who pray for pardon in the watches of the night.

18. Allah (Himself) is witness that there is no God save Him. And the angels and the men of learning (too are witness). Maintaining His creation in justice, there is no God save Him, the Almighty, the Wise.

19. Lo! religion with Allah (is) The Surrender (to His Will and Guidance). Those who (formerly) received the Scripture differed only after knowledge came unto them, through transgression among themselves. Whoso disbelieveth the revelations of Allah (will find that) lo! Allah is swift at reckoning.

20. And if they argue with thee, (O Muhammad), say: I have surrendered my purpose to Allah and (so have) those who follow me. And say unto those who have received the Scripture and those who read not: Have ye (too) surrendered? If they surrender, then truly they are rightly guided, and if they turn away, then it is thy duty only to convey the message (unto them). Allah is Seer of (His) bondmen.

21. Lo! those who disbelieve the revelations of Allah, and slay the Prophets wrongfully, and slay those of mankind who enjoin equity: promise them a painful doom.

22. Those are they whose works have failed in the world and the Hereafter; and they have no helpers.

23. Hast thou not seen how those who have received a portion of the Scripture invoke the Scripture of Allah (in their disputes) that it may judge between them; then a faction of them turn away, being opposed (to it)?

24. That is because they say: The Fire will not touch us save for a certain number of days. That which they used to invent hath deceived them regarding their religion.

25. How (will it be with them) when We have brought them

41

all together to a Day of which there is no doubt, when every soul will be paid in full what it hath earned, and they will not be wronged.

26. Say: O Allah! Owner of Sovereignty! Thou givest sovereignty unto whom Thou wilt, and Thou withdrawest sovereignty from whom Thou wilt. Thou exaltest whom Thou wilt and Thou abasest whom Thou wilt. In Thy hand is the good. Lo! Thou art Able to do all things.

27. Thou causest the night to pass into the day, and Thou causest the day to pass into the night. And Thou bringest forth the living from the dead, and Thou bringest forth the dead from the living. And Thou givest sustenance to whom Thou choosest, without stint.

28. Let not the believers take disbelievers for their friends in preference to believers. Whoso doeth that hath no connection with Allah unless (it be) that ye but guard yourselves against them, taking (as it were) security. Allah biddeth you beware (only) of Himself. Unto Allah is the journeying.

29. Say, (O Muhammad): Whether ye hide that which is in your breasts or reveal it, Allah knoweth it. He knoweth that which is in the heavens and that which is in the earth, and Allah is Able to do all things.

30. On the day when every soul will find itself confronted with all that it hath done of good and all that it hath done of evil (every soul) will long that there might be a mighty space of distance between it and that (evil). Allah biddeth you beware of Him. And Allah is full of pity for (His) bondmen.

31. Say, (O Muhammad, to mankind): If ye love Allah, follow me; Allah will love you and forgive you your sins. Allah is Forgiving, Merciful.

32. Say: Obey Allah and the messenger. But if they turn away, lo! Allah loveth not the disbelievers (in His guidance).

33. Lo! Allah preferred Adam and Noah and the Family of Abraham and the Family of 'Imrân above (all His) creatures.

34. They were descendants one of another. Allah is Hearer, Knower.

35. (Remember) when the wife of 'Imrân said: My Lord! I have vowed unto Thee that which is in my belly as a consecrated (offering). Accept it from me. Lo! Thou, only Thou, art the Hearer, the Knower.

36. And when she was delivered she said: My Lord! Lo! I am delivered of a female — Allah knew best of what she was delivered — the male is not as the female; and lo! I have named her Mary, and lo! I crave Thy protection for her and for her offspring from Satan the outcast.

42

37. And her Lord accepted her with full acceptance and vouchsafed to her a goodly growth; and made Zachariah her guardian. Whenever Zachariah went into the sanctuary where she was, he found that she had food. He said: O Mary! Whence cometh unto thee this (food)? She answered: It is from Allah. Allah giveth without stint to whom He will.

38. Then Zachariah prayed unto his Lord and said: My Lord! Bestow upon me of Thy bounty goodly offspring. Lo! Thou art the Hearer of Prayer.

39. And the angels called to him as he stood praying in the sanctuary: Allah giveth thee glad tidings of (a son whose name is) John, (who cometh) to confirm a word from Allah, lordly, chaste, a Prophet of the righteous.

40. He said: My Lord! How can I have a son when age hath overtaken me already and my wife is barren? (The angel) answered: So (it will be). Allah doeth what He will.

41. He said: My Lord! Appoint a token for me. (The angel) said: The token unto thee (shall be) that thou shalt not speak unto mankind three days except by signs. Remember thy Lord much, and praise (Him) in the early hours of night and morning.

42. And when the angels said: O Mary! Lo! Allah hath chosen thee and made thee pure; and hath preferred thee above (all) the women of creation.

43. O Mary! Be obedient to thy Lord, prostrate thyself and bow with those who bow (in worship).

44. This is of the tidings of things hidden. We reveal it unto thee (Muhammad). Thou wast not present with them when they threw their pens (to know) which of them should be the guardian of Mary, nor wast thou present with them when they quarrelled (thereupon).

45. (And remember) when the angels said: O Mary! Lo! Allah giveth thee glad tidings of a word from Him, whose name is the Messiah, Jesus, son of Mary, illustrious in the world and the Hereafter, and one of those brought near (unto Allah).

46. He will speak unto mankind in his cradle and in his manhood, and he is of the righteous.

47. She said: My Lord! How can I have a child when no mortal hath touched me? He said: So (it will be). Allah createth what He will. If He decreeth a thing, He saith unto it only: Be! and it is.

48. And He will teach him the Scripture and wisdom, and the Torah and the Gospel.

49. And will make him a messenger unto the Children of Israel, (saying): Lo! I come unto you with a sign from your Lord.

Lo! I fashion for you out of clay the likeness of a bird, and I breathe into it and it is a bird, by Allah's leave. I heal him who was born blind, and the leper, and I raise the dead, by Allah's leave. And I announce unto you what ye eat and what ye store up in your houses. Lo! herein verily is a portent for you, if ye are to be believers.

50. And (I come) confirming that which was before me of the Torah, and to make lawful some of that which was forbidden unto you. I come unto you with a sign from your Lord, so keep your duty to Allah and obey me.

51. Lo! Allah is my Lord and your Lord, so worship Him. That is a straight path.

52. But when Jesus became conscious of their disbelief, he cried: Who will be my helpers in the cause of Allah? The disciples said: We will be Allah's helpers. We believe in Allah, and bear thou witness that we have surrendered (unto Him).

53. Our Lord! We believe in that which Thou hast revealed and we follow him whom Thou hast sent. Enroll us among those who witness (to the truth).

54. And they (the disbelievers) schemed, and Allah schemed (against them): and Allah is the best of schemers.

55. (And remember) when Allah said: O Jesus! Lo! I am gathering thee and causing thee to ascend unto Me, and am cleansing thee of those who disbelieve and am setting those who follow thee above those who disbelieve until the Day of Resurrection. Then unto Me ye will (all) return, and I shall judge between you as to that wherein ye used to differ.

56. As for those who disbelieve I shall chastise them with a heavy chastisement in the world and the Hereafter; and they will have no helpers.

57. And as for those who believe and do good works; He will pay them their wages in full. Allah loveth not wrong-doers.

58. This (which) We recite unto thee is a revelation and a wise reminder.

59. Lo! the likeness of Jesus with Allah is as the likeness of Adam. He created him of dust, then He said unto him: Be! and he is.

60. (This is) the truth from thy Lord (O Muhammad), so be not thou of those who waver.

61. And whoso disputeth with thee concerning him, after the knowledge which hath come unto thee, say (unto him): Come! We will summon our sons and your sons, and our women and your women, and ourselves and yourselves, then we will pray humbly (to our Lord) and (solemnly) invoke the curse of Allah upon those who lie.

62. Lo! This verily is the true narrative. There is no God save Allah, and lo! Allah is the Mighty, the Wise.

63. And if they turn away, then lo! Allah is Aware of (who are) the corrupters.

64. Say: O People of the Scripture! Come to an agreement between us and you: that we shall worship none but Allah, and that we shall ascribe no partner unto Him, and that none of us shall take others for lords beside Allah. And if they turn away, then say: Bear witness that we are they who have surrendered (unto Him).

65. O People of the Scripture! Why will ye argue about Abraham, when the Torah and the Gospel were not revealed till after him ? Have ye then no sense?

66. Lo! ye are those who argue about that whereof ye have some knowledge: Why then argue ye concerning that whereof ye have no knowledge? Allah knoweth. Ye know not.

67. Abraham was not a Jew, nor yet a Christian; but he was an upright man who had surrendered (to Allah), and he was not of the idolaters.

68. Lo! those of mankind who have the best claim to Abraham are those who followed him, and this Prophet and those who believe (with him): and Allah is the Protecting Friend of the believers.

69. A party of the People of the Scripture long to make you go astray; and they make none to go astray except themselves, but they perceive not.

70. O People of the Scripture! Why disbelieve ye in the revelations of Allah, when ye (yourselves) bear witness (to their truth)?

71. O People of the Scripture! Why confound ye truth with falsehood and knowingly conceal the truth?

72. And a party of the People of the Scripture say: Believe in that which hath been revealed, unto those who believe at the opening of the day, and disbelieve at the end thereof, in order that they may return.

73. And believe not save in one who followeth your religion—Say (O Muhammad): Lo! the guidance is Allah's guidance—that any one is given the like of that which was given unto you or that they may argue with you in the presence of their Lord. Say (O Muhammad): Lo! the bounty is in Allah's hand. He bestoweth it on whom He will. Allah is All-Embracing, All-Knowing.

74. He selecteth for His mercy whom He will. Allah is of Infinite Bounty.

75. Among the People of the Scripture there is he who, if thou trust him with a weight of treasure, will return it to thee.

And among them there is he who, if thou trust him with a piece of gold, will not return it to thee unless thou keep standing over him. That is because they say: We have no duty to the Gentiles. They speak a lie concerning Allah knowingly.

76. Nay, but (the chosen of Allah is) he who fulfilleth his pledge and wardeth off (evil); for lo! Allah loveth those who ward off (evil).

77. Lo! those who purchase a small gain at the cost of Allah's covenant and their oaths, they have no portion in the Hereafter. Allah will neither speak to them nor look upon them on the Day of Resurrection, nor will He make them grow. Theirs will be a painful doom.

78. And lo! there is a party of them who distort the Scripture with their tongues, that ye may think that what they say is from the Scripture, when it is not from the Scripture. And they say: It is from Allah, when it is not from Allah; and they speak a lie concerning Allah knowingly.

79. It is not (possible) for any human being unto whom Allah had given the Scripture and wisdom and the Prophethood that he should afterwards have said unto mankind: Be slaves of me instead of Allah; but (what he said was): Be ye faithful servants of the Lord by virtue of your constant teaching of the Scripture and of your constant study thereof.

80. And he commanded you not that ye should take the angels and the Prophets for lords. Would he command you to disbelieve after ye had surrendered (to Allah)?

81. When Allah made (His) covenant with the Prophets, (He said): Behold that which I have given you of the Scripture and knowledge. And afterward there will come unto you a messenger, confirming that which ye possess. Ye shall believe in him and ye shall help him. He said: Do ye agree, and will ye take up My burden (which I lay upon you) in this (matter)? They answered: We agree. He said: Then bear ye witness. I will be a witness with you.

82. Then whosoever after this shall turn away: they will be miscreants.

83. Seek they other than the religion of Allah, when unto Him submitteth whosoever is in the heavens and the earth, willingly, or unwillingly, and unto Him they will be returned.

84. Say (O Muhammad): We believe in Allah and that which is revealed unto us and that which was revealed unto Abraham and Ishmael and Isaac and Jacob and the tribes, and that which was vouchsafed unto Moses and Jesus and the Prophets from their Lord. We make no distinction between any of them, and unto Him we have surrendered.

85. And whoso seeketh as religion other than the Surrender (to Allah) it will not be accepted from him, and he will be a loser in the Hereafter.

86. How shall Allah guide a people who disbelieved after their belief and (after) they bore witness that the messenger is true and after clear proofs (of Allah's sovereignty) had come unto them. And Allah guideth not wrongdoing folk.

87. As for such, their guerdon is that on them rests the curse of Allah and of Angels and of men combined.

88. They will abide therein. Their doom will not be lightened, neither will they be reprieved.

89. Save those who afterward repent and do right. Lo! Allah is Forgiving, Merciful.

90. Lo! those who disbelieve after their (profession of) belief, and afterward grow violent in disbelief: their repentance will not be accepted. And such are those who are astray.

91. Lo! those who disbelieve, and die in disbelief, the (whole) earth full of gold would not be accepted from such a one if it were offered as a ransom (for his soul). Theirs will be a painful doom and they will have no helpers.

92. Ye will not attain unto piety until ye spend of that which ye love. And whatsoever ye spend, Allah is aware thereof.

93. All food was lawful unto the children of Israel, save that which Israel forbade himself, (in days) before the Torah was revealed. Say: Produce the Torah and read it (unto us) if ye are truthful.

94. And whoever shall invent a falsehood after that concerning Allah, such will be wrong-doers.

95. Say: Allah speaketh truth. So follow the religion of Abraham, the upright. He was not of the idolaters.

96. Lo! the first Sanctuary appointed for mankind was that at Becca, a blessed place, a guidance to the peoples;

97. Wherein are plain memorials (of Allah's guidance); the place where Abraham stood up to pray; and whosoever entereth it is safe. And pilgrimage to the House is a duty unto Allah for mankind, for him who can find a way thither. As for him who disbelieveth, (let him know that) lo! Allah is Independent of (all) creatures.

98. Say: O People of the Scripture! Why disbelieve ye in the revelations of Allah, when Allah (Himself) is Witness of what ye do?

99. Say: O people of the Scripture! Why drive ye back believers from the way of Allah, seeking to make it crooked, when ye are witnesses (to Allah's guidance)? Allah is not

unaware of what ye do.

100. O ye who believe! If ye obey a party of those who have received the Scripture they will make you disbelievers after your belief.

101. How can ye disbelieve, when Allah's revelations are recited unto you, and His messenger is in your midst? He who holdeth fast to Allah, he indeed is guided unto a right path.

102. O ye who believe! Observe your duty to Allah with right observance, and die not save as those who have surrendered (unto Him).

103. And hold fast, all of you together, to the cable of Allah, and do not separate. And remember Allah's favour unto you: how ye were enemies and He made friendship between your hearts so that ye became as brothers by His grace; and (how) ye were upon the brink of an abyss of fire, and He did save you from it. Thus Allah maketh clear His revelations unto you, that haply ye may be guided.

104. And there may spring from you a nation who invite to goodness, and enjoin right conduct and forbid indecency. Such are they who are successful.

105. And be ye not as those who separated and disputed after the clear proofs had come unto them. For such there is an awful doom.

106. On the day when (some) faces will be whitened and (some) faces will be blackened; and as for those whose faces have been blackened, it will be said unto them: Disbelieved ye after your (profession of) belief? Then taste the punishment for that ye disbelieved.

107. As for those whose faces have been whitened, lo! in the mercy of Allah they dwell for ever.

108. These are revelations of Allah. We recite them unto thee in truth. Allah willeth no injustice to (His) creatures.

109. Unto Allah belongeth whatsoever is in the heavens and whatsoever is in the earth; and unto Allah all things are returned.

110. Ye are the best community that hath been raised up for mankind. Ye enjoin right conduct and forbid indecency; and ye believe in Allah. And if the People of the Scripture had believed it had been better for them. Some of them are believers; but most of them are evil-livers.

111. They will not harm you save a trifling hurt, and if they fight against you they will turn and flee. And afterward they will not be helped.

112. Ignominy shall be their portion wheresoever they are

found save (where they grasp) a rope from Allah and a rope from men. They have incurred anger from their Lord, and wretchedness is laid upon them. That is because they used to disbelieve the revelations of Allah, and slew the Prophets wrongfully. That is because they were rebellious and used to transgress.

113. They are not all alike. Of the People of the Scripture there is a staunch community who recite the revelations of Allah in the night season, falling prostrate (before Him).

114. They believe in Allah and the Last Day, and enjoin right conduct and forbid indecency, and vie one with another in good works. They are of the righteous.

115. And whatever good they do, they will not be denied the meed thereof. Allah is Aware of those who ward off (evil).

116. Lo! the riches and the progeny of those who disbelieve will not avail them aught against Allah; and such are rightful owners of the Fire. They will abide therein.

117. The likeness of that which they spend in this life of the world is as the likeness of a biting, icy wind which smiteth the harvest of a people who have wronged themselves, and devastateth it. Allah wronged them not, but they did wrong themselves.

118. O ye who believe! Take not for intimates others than your own folk, who would spare no pains to ruin you; they love to hamper you. Hatred is revealed by (the utterance of) their mouths, but that which their breasts hide is greater. We have made plain for you the revelations if ye will understand.

119. Lo! ye are those who love them though they love you not, and ye believe in all the Scripture. When they fall in with you they say: We believe; but when they go apart they bite their finger tips at you, for rage. Say: Perish in your rage! Lo! Allah is Aware of what is hidden in (your) breasts.

120. If a lucky chance befall you, it is evil unto them, and if disaster strike you they rejoice thereat. But if ye persevere and keep from evil their guile will never harm you. Lo! Allah is Surrounding what they do.

121. And remember when thou settedst forth at daybreak from thy housefolk to assign to the believers their positions for the battle, Allah was Hearer, Knower.

122. When two parties of you almost fell away, and Allah was their Protecting Friend. In Allah do believers put their trust.

123. Allah had already given you the victory at Badr, when ye were contemptible. So observe your duty to Allah in order that ye may be thankful.

124. And when thou didst say unto the believers: Is it not

sufficient for you that your Lord should support you with three thousand angels sent down (to your help)?

125. Nay, but if ye persevere, and keep from evil, and (the enemy) attack you suddenly, your Lord will help you with five thousand angels sweeping on.

126. Allah ordained this only as a message of good cheer for you, and that thereby your hearts might be at rest— Victory cometh only from Allah, the Mighty, the Wise—

127. That He may cut off a part of those who disbelieve, or overwhelm them so that they retire, frustrated.

128. It is no concern at all of thee (Muhammad) whether He relent toward them or punish them; for they are evil-doers.

129. Unto Allah belongeth whatsoever is in the heavens and whatsoever is in the earth. He forgiveth whom he will, and punisheth whom He will. Allah is Forgiving, Merciful.

130. O ye who believe! Devour not usury, doubling and quadrupling (the sum lent). Observe your duty to Allah, that ye may be successful.

131. And ward off (from yourselves) the Fire prepared for disbelievers.

132. And obey Allah and the messenger, that ye may find mercy.

133. And vie one with another for forgiveness from your Lord, and for a Paradise as wide as are the heavens and the earth, prepared for those who ward off (evil).

134. Those who spend (of that which Allah gath given them) in ease and in adversity, those who control their wrath and are forgiving toward mankind; Allah loveth the good.

135. And those who, when they do an evil thing or wrong themselves, remember Allah and implore forgiveness for their sins—Who forgiveth sins save Allah only?—and will not knowingly repeat (the wrong) they did.

136. The reward of such will be forgiveness from their Lord, and Gardens underneath which rivers flow, wherein they will abide for ever—a bountiful reward for workers!

137. Systems have passed away before you. Do but travel in the land and see the nature of the consequence for those who did deny (the messengers).

138. This is a declaration for mankind, a guidance and an admonition unto those who ward off (evil).

139. Faint not nor grieve, for ye will overcome them if ye are (indeed) believers.

140. If ye have received a blow, the (disbelieving) people have received a blow the like thereof. These are (only) the vicissitudes which We cause to follow one another for mankind,

to the end that Allah may know those who believe and may choose witnesses from among you; and Allah loveth not wrong-doers.

141. And that Allah may prove those who believe, and may blight the disbelievers.

142. Or deemed ye that ye would enter Paradise while yet Allah knoweth not those of you who really strive, nor knoweth those (of you) who are steadfast?

143. And verily ye used to wish for death before ye met it (in the field). Now ye have seen it with your eyes!

144. Muhammad is but a messenger, messengers (the like of whom) have passed away before him. Will it be that, when he dieth or is slain, ye will turn back on your heels? He who turneth back doth no hurt to Allah, and Allah will reward the thankful.

145. No soul can ever die except by Allah's leave and at a term appointed. Whoso desireth the reward of the world, We bestow on him thereof; and whoso desireth the reward of the Hereafter, We bestow on him thereof. We shall reward the thankful.

146. And with how many a prophet have there been a number of devoted men who fought (beside him). They quailed not for aught that befell them in the way of Allah, nor did they weaken, nor were they brought low. Allah loveth the steadfast.

147. Their cry was only that they said: Our Lord! Forgive us for our sins and wasted efforts, make our foothold sure, and give us victory over the disbelieving folk.

148. So Allah gave them the reward of the world and the good reward of the Hereafter. Allah loveth those whose deeds are good.

149. O ye who believe! If ye obey those who disbelieve, they will make you turn on your heels, and ye turn back as losers.

150. But Allah is your Protector, and He is the best of helpers.

151. We shall cast terror into the hearts of those who disbelieve because they ascribe unto Allah partners, for which no warrant hath been revealed. Their habitation is the Fire, and hapless the abode of the wrong-doers.

152. Allah verily made good His promise unto you when ye routed them by His leave, until (the moment) when your courage failed you, and ye disagreed about the order and ye disobeyed, after He had shown you that for which ye long. Some of you desired the world, and some of you desired the Hereafter. Therefore He made you flee from them, that He might try you. Yet now He hath forgiven you. Allah is a Lord of Kindness to believers.

153. When ye climbed (the hill) and paid no heed to anyone, while the messenger, in your rear, was calling you (to fight). Therefore He rewarded you grief for (his) grief, that (He might teach) you not to sorrow either for that which ye missed or for that which befell you. Allah is Informed of what ye do.

154. Then, after grief, He sent down security for you. As slumber did it overcome a party of you, while (the other) party, who were anxious on their own account, thought wrongly of Allah, the thought of ignorance. They said: Have we any part in the cause? Say (O Muhammad): The cause belongeth wholly to Allah. They hide within themselves (a thought) which they reveal not unto thee, saying: Had we had any part in the cause we should not have been slain here. Say: Even though ye had been in your houses, those appointed to be slain would have gone forth to the places where they were to lie. (All this hath been) in order that Allah might try what is in your breasts and prove what is in your hearts. Allah is Aware of what is hidden in the breasts (of men).

155. Lo! those of you who turned back on the day when the two hosts met, Satan alone it was who caused them to backslide, because of some of that which they have earned. Now Allah hath forgiven them: Lo! Allah is Forgiving Clement.

156. O ye who believe! Be not as those who disbelieved and said of their brethren who went abroad in the land or were fighting in the field: If they had been (here) with us they would not have died or been killed; that Allah may make it anguish in their hearts. Allah giveth life and causeth death; and Allah is Seer of what ye do.

157. And what though ye be slain in Allah's way or die therein? Surely pardon from Allah and mercy are better than all that they amass.

158. What though ye be slain or die, when unto Allah ye are gathered?

159. It was by the mercy of Allah that thou wast lenient with them (O Muhammad), for if thou hadst been stern and fierce of heart they would have dispersed from round about thee. So pardon them and ask forgiveness for them and consult with them upon the conduct of affairs. And when thou art resolved, then put thy trust in Allah. Lo! Allah loveth those who put their trust (in Him).

160. If Allah is your helper none can overcome you, and if He withdraw His help from you, who is there who can help you? In Allah let believers put their trust.

161. It is not for any Prophet to deceive (mankind). Whoso

deceiveth will bring his deceit with him on the Day of Resurrection. Then every soul will be paid in full what it hath earned; and they will not be wronged.

162. Is one who followeth the pleasure of Allah as one who hath earned condemnation from Allah, whose habitation is the Fire, a hapless journey's end?

163. There are degrees (of grace and reprobation) with Allah, and Allah is Seer of what ye do.

164. Allah verily hath shown grace to the believers by sending unto them a messenger of their own who reciteth unto them His revelations, and causeth them to grow, and teacheth them the Scripture and wisdom; although before (he came to them) they were in flagrant error.

165. And was it so, when a disaster smote you, though ye had smitten (them with a disaster) twice (as great), that ye said: How is this? Say (unto them, O Muhammad): It is from yourselves. Lo! Allah is Able to do all things.

166. That which befell you, on the day when the two armies met, was by permission of Allah; that He might know the true believers.

167. And that He might know the hypocrites, unto whom it was said: Come, fight in the way of Allah, or defend yourselves. They answered: If we knew aught of fighting we would follow you. On that day they were nearer disbelief than faith. They utter with their mouths a thing which is not in their hearts. Allah is best aware of what they hide.

168. Those who, while they sat at home, said of their brethren (who were fighting for the cause of Allah): If they had been guided by us they would not have been slain. Say (unto them, O Muhammad): Then avert death from yourselves if ye are truthful.

169. Think not of those, who are slain in the way of Allah, as dead. Nay, they are living. With their Lord they have provision.

170. Jubilant (are they) because of that which Allah hath bestowed upon them of His bounty, rejoicing for the sake of those who have not joined them but are left behind: that there shall no fear come upon them neither shall they grieve.

171. They rejoice because of favour from Allah and kindness, and that Allah wasteth not the wage of the believers.

172. As for those who heard the call of Allah and His messenger after the harm befell them (in the fight); for such of them as do right and ward off (evil), there is great reward.

173. Those unto whom men said: Lo! the people have gathered against you, therefore fear them. (The threat of

danger) but increased the faith of them and they cried: Allah is sufficient for us! Most Excellent is He in Whom we trust!

174. So they returned with grace and favour from Allah, and no harm touched them. They followed the good pleasure of Allah, and Allah is of infinite bounty.

175. It is only the devil who would make (men) fear his partisans. Fear them not; fear Me, if ye are true believers.

176. Let not their conduct grieve thee, who run easily to disbelief, for lo! they injure Allah not at all. It is Allah's will to assign them no portion in the Hereafter, and theirs will be an awful doom.

177. Those who purchase disbelief at the price of faith harm Allah not at all, but theirs will be a painful doom.

178. And let not those who disbelieve imagine that the rein We give them bodeth good unto their souls. We only give them rein that they may grow in sinfulness. And theirs will be a shameful doom.

179. It is not (the purpose) of Allah to leave you in your present state till He shall separate the wicked from the good. And it is not (the purpose of) Allah to let you know the unseen. But Allah chooseth of His messengers whom He will, (to receive knowledge thereof.) So believe in Allah and His messengers. If ye believe and ward off (evil), yours will be a vast reward.

180. And let not those who hoard up that which Allah hath bestowed upon them of His bounty think that it is better for them. Nay, it is worse for them. That which they hoard will be their collar on the Day of Resurrection. Allah's is the heritage of the heavens and the earth, and Allah is Informed of what ye do.

181. Verily Allah heard the saying of those who said, (when asked for contributions to the war): "Allah, forsooth, is poor, and we are rich!" We shall record their saying with their slaying of the Prophets wrongfully and We shall say: Taste ye the punishment of burning!

182. This is on account of that which your own hands have sent before (you to the judgement). Allah is no oppressor of (His) bondmen.

183. (The same are) those who say: Lo! Allah hath charged us that we believe not in any messenger until he bring us an offering which fire (from heaven) shall devour. Say (unto them, O Muhammad): Messengers came unto you before me with miracles, and with that (very miracle) which ye describe. Why then did ye slay them? (Answer that) if ye are truthful!

184. And if they deny thee, even so did they deny messengers who were before thee, who came with miracles and

with the Psalms and with the Scripture giving light.

185. Every soul will taste of death. And ye will be paid on the Day of Resurrection only that which ye have fairly earned. Whoso is removed from the Fire and is made to enter Paradise, he indeed is triumphant. The life of this world is but comfort of illusion.

186. Assuredly ye will be tried in your property and in your persons, and ye will hear much wrong from those who were given the Scripture before you, and from the idolaters. But if ye persevere and ward off (evil), then that is of the steadfast heart of things.

187. And (remember) when Allah laid a charge on those who had received the Scripture (He said): Ye are to expound it to mankind and not to hide it. But they flung it behind their backs and bought thereby a little gain. Verily evil is that which they have gained thereby.

188. Think not that those who exult in what they have given, and love to be praised for what they have not done—Think not, they are in safety from the doom. A painful doom is theirs.

189. Unto Allah belongeth the Sovereignty of the heavens and the earth. Allah is Able to do all things.

190. Lo! In the creation of the heavens and the earth and (in) the difference of night and day are tokens (of His sovereignty) for men of understanding.

191. Such as remember Allah, standing, sitting, and reclining, and consider the creation of the heavens and the earth, (and say): Our Lord! Thou createdst not this in vain. Glory be to Thee! Preserve us from the doom of Fire.

192. Our Lord! Whom Thou causest to enter the Fire: him indeed Thou hast confounded. For evil-doers there will be no helpers.

193. Our Lord! Lo! we have heard a crier calling unto Faith: "Believe ye in your Lord!" So we believed. Our Lord! Therefore forgive us our sins, and remit from us our evil deeds, and make us die the death of the righteous.

194. Our Lord! And give us that which Thou hast promised to us by Thy messengers. Confound us not upon the Day of Resurrection. Lo! Thou breakest not the tryst.

195. And their Lord hath heard them (and He saith): Lo! I suffer not the work of any worker, male or female, to be lost. Ye proceed one from another. So those who fled and were driven forth from their homes and suffered damage for My cause, and fought and were slain, verily I shall remit their evil deeds from them and verily I shall bring them into Gardens

underneath which rivers flow—A reward from Allah. And with Allah is the fairest of rewards.

196. Let not the vicissitude (of the success) of those who disbelieve, in the land, deceive thee (O Muhammad).

197. It is but a brief comfort. And afterward their habitation will be hell, an ill abode.

198. But those who keep their duty to their Lord, for them are Gardens underneath which rivers flow, wherein they will be safe for ever. A gift of welcome from their Lord. That which Allah hath in store is better for the righteous.

199. And lo! of the People of the Scripture there are some who believe in Allah and that which is revealed unto you and that which was revealed unto them, humbling themselves before Allah. They purchase not a trifling gain at the price of the revelations of Allah. Verily their reward is with their Lord, and lo! Allah is swift to take account.

200. O ye who believe! Endure, outdo all others in endurance, be ready, and observe your duty to Allah, in order that ye may succeed.

SÛRAH 4

An-Nisâ, "Women", is so-called because it deals largely with women's rights. The period of revelation is the months following the battle of Uhud, or, as Nöldeke, a careful critic, puts it, "between the end of the third year and the end of the fifth year" of the Prophet's reign at Al-Madînah ("The War of the Trench") by the allied tribes, which took place in the fifth year, I should rather say, between the end of the third year and the beginning of the fifth year.

Many Muslims were killed at the Battle of Uhud, hence the concern for orphans and widows in the opening verses which lead on to a declaration of some rights of women of which they were deprived among the pagan Arabs. The defection of the Hypocrites—as the lukewarm or purely time-serving adherents were called—had been the chief cause of the reverse at Uhud; and after that reverse some of the Jewish tribes, who had till then observed the letter of their treaty with the Prophet, became avowed supporters of the enemy, even going so far as to declare that the old Arab idolatry was preferable to Al-Islâm as a religion, and giving help and information to Qureysh, so that in the end the Muslims were obliged to make war on them. Both the Hypocrites and the rebellious Jews are dealt with incidently in this sûrah, the former at some length. There is a reference to Christian beliefs in vv. 171-2.

The period of revelation is the fourth year of the Hijrah.

WOMEN

Revealed at Al-Madînah

In the name of Allah, the Beneficent, the Merciful.

1. O mankind! Be careful of your duty to your Lord Who created you from a single soul and from it created its mate and from them twain hath spread abroad a multitude of men and women. Be careful of your duty toward Allah in Whom ye claim (your rights) of one another, and towards the wombs (that bore you). Lo! Allah hath been a Watcher over you.

2. Give unto orphans their wealth. Exchange not the good for the bad (in your management thereof) nor absorb their wealth into your own wealth. Lo! that would be a great sin.

3. And if ye fear that ye will not deal fairly by the orphans, marry of the women, who seem good to you, two or three or four; and if ye fear that ye cannot do justice (to so many) then one (only) or (the captives) that your right hands possess. Thus it is more likely that he will not do injustice.

4. And give unto the women, (whom ye marry) free gift of their marriage portions; but if they of their own accord remit unto you a part thereof, then ye are welcome to absorb it (in your wealth).

5. Give not unto the foolish (what is in) your (keeping of their) wealth, which Allah hath given you to maintain; but feed and clothe them from it, and speak kindly unto them.

6. Prove orphans till they reach the marriageable age; then, if ye find them of sound judgement, deliver over unto them their fortune; and devour it not by squandering and in haste lest they should grow up. Whoso (of the guardians) is rich, let him abstain generously (from taking of the property of orphans); and whoso is poor let him take thereof in reason (for his guardship). And when ye deliver up their fortune unto orphans, have (the transaction) witnessed in their presence. Allah sufficeth as a Reckoner.

7. Unto the men (of a family) belongeth a share of that which parents and near kindred leave, and unto the women a share of that which parents and near kindred leave, whether it be little or much-a legal share.

8. And when kinsfolk and orphans and the needy are present at the division (of the heritage), bestow on them therefrom and speak kindly unto them.

9. And let those who fear (in their behaviour toward orphans) who if they left behind them weak offspring would be afraid for them. So let them mind their duty to Allah, and

speak justly.

10. Lo! those who devour the wealth of orphans wrongfully, they do but swallow fire into their bellies, and they will be exposed to burning flame.

11. Allah chargeth you concerning (the provision for) your children: to the male the equivalent of the portion of two females, and if there be women more than two, then theirs is two-thirds of the inheritance, and if there be one (only) then the half. And to his parents a sixth of the inheritance, if he have a son; and if he have no son and his parents are his heirs, then his mother appertaineth the third; and if he have brethren, then to his mother appertaineth the sixth, after any legacy he may have bequeathed, or debt (hath been paid). Your parents or your children: Ye know not which of them is nearer unto you in usefulness. It is an injunction from Allah. Lo! Allah is Knower, Wise.

12. And unto you belongeth a half of that which your wives leave, if they have no child; but if they have a child then unto you the fourth of that which they leave, after any legacy they may have bequeathed, or debt (they may have contracted, hath been paid). And unto them belongeth the fourth of that which ye leave if ye have no child, but if ye have a child then the eighth of that which ye leave, after any legacy ye may have bequeathed, or debt (ye may have contracted, hath been paid). And if a man or a woman have a distant heir (having left neither parent nor child), and he (or she) have a brother or a sister (only on the mother's side) then to each of them twain (the brother and the sister) the sixth, and if they be more than two, then they shall be sharers in the third, after any legacy that may have been bequeathed or debt (contracted) not injuring (the heirs by willing away more than a third of the heritage) hath been paid. A commandment from Allah. Allah is Knower, Indulgent.

13. These are the limits (imposed by) Allah. Whose obeyeth Allah and His messenger, He will make him enter Gardens underneath which rivers flow, where such will dwell for ever. That will be the great success.

14. And whose disobeyeth Allah and His messenger and transgresseth His limits, He will make him enter Fire, where such will dwell for ever; his will be a shameful doom.

15. As for those of your women who are guilty of lewdness, call of witness four of you against them. And if they testify (to the truth of the allegation) then confine them to the houses until death take them or (until) Allah appoint for them a way (through new legislation).

16. And as for the two of you who are guilty thereof, punish them both. And if they repent and improve, then let them be. Lo! Allah is Relenting, Merciful.

17. Forgiveness is only incumbent on Allah toward those who do evil in ignorance (and) then turn quickly (in repentance) to Allah. These are they toward whom Allah relenteth. Allah is ever Knower, Wise.

18. The forgiveness is not for those who do ill deeds until, when death attendeth upon one of them, he saith: Lo! I repent now; nor yet for those who die while they are disbelievers. For such We have prepared a painful doom.

19. O ye who believe! It is not lawful for you forcibly to inherit the women (of your deceased kinsmen), nor (that) ye should put constraint upon them that ye may take away a part of that which ye have given them, unless they be guilty of flagrant lewdness. But consort with them in kindness, for if ye hate them it may happen that ye hate a thing wherein Allah hath placed much good.

20. And if ye wish to exchange one wife for another and ye have given unto one of them a sum of money (however great), take nothing from it. Would ye take it by the way of calumny and open wrong?

21. How can ye take it (back) after one of you hath gone in unto the other, and they have taken a strong pledge from you?

22. And marry not those women whom your fathers married, except what hath already happened (of that nature) in the past. Lo! it was ever lewdness and abomination, and an evil way.

23. Forbidden unto you are your mothers, and your daughters, and your sisters, and your father's sisters, and your mother's sisters, and your brother's daughters and your sister's daughters, and your foster-mothers, and your foster-sisters, and your mothers-in-law, and your step-daughters who are under your protection (born) of your women unto whom ye have gone in—but if ye have not gone in unto them, then it is no sin for you (to marry their daughters)—and the wives of your sons who (spring) from your own loins. And (it is forbidden unto you) that ye should have two sisters together; except what hath already happened (of that nature) in the past. Lo! Allah is ever Forgiving, Merciful.

24. And all married women (are forbidden unto you) save those (captives) whom your right hands possess. It is a decree of Allah for you. Lawful unto you are all beyond those mentioned, so that ye seek them with your wealth in honest wedlock, not debauchery. And those of whom ye seek content

(by marrying them), give unto them their portions as a duty.
And there is no sin for you in what ye do by mutual agreement
after the duty (hath been done). Lo! Allah is ever Knower,
Wise.

25. And whoso is not able to afford to marry free, believing
women, let them marry from the believing maids whom your
right hands possess. Allah knoweth best (concerning) your
faith. Ye (proceed) one from another; so wed them by
permission of their folk, and give unto them their portions in
kindness, they being honest, not debauched nor of loose
conduct. And if when they are honourably married they
commit lewdness they shall incur the half of the punishment
(prescribed) for free women (in that case). This is for him among
you who feareth to commit sin. But to have patience would
be better for you. Allah is Forgiving, Merciful.

26. Allah would explain to you and guide you by the
examples of those who were before you, and would turn to
you in mercy. Allah is Knower, Wise.

27. And Allah would turn to you in mercy; but those who
follow vain desires would have you go tremendously astray.

28. Allah would make the burden light for you, for man
was created weak.

29. O ye who believe! Squander not your wealth among
yourselves in vanity, except it be a trade by mutual consent,
and kill not one another. Lo! Allah is ever Merciful unto you.

30. Whoso doeth that through aggression and injustice, We
shall cast him into Fire, and that is ever easy for Allah.

31. If ye avoid the great (things) which ye are forbidden, We
will remit from you your evil deeds and make you enter at a
noble gate.

32. And covet not the thing in which Allah hath made some
of you excel others. Unto men a fortune from that which they
have earned, and unto women a fortune from that which they
have earned. (Envy not one another) but ask Allah of His
bounty. Lo! Allah is ever Knower of all things.

33. And unto each We have appointed heirs of that which
parents and near kindred leave; and as for those with whom
your right hands have made a covenant, give them their due.
Lo! Allah is ever Witness over all things.

34. Men are in charge of women, because Allah hath made
the one of them to excel the other, and because they spend of
their property (for the support of women). So good women are
the obedient, guarding in secret what Allah hath guarded. As
for those from whom ye fear rebellion, admonish them and
banish them to beds apart, and scourge them. Then if they obey

you, seek not a way against them. Lo! Allah is ever High Exalted, Great.

35. And if ye fear a breach betweem them twain (the man and the wife), appoint an arbiter from his folk and an arbiter from her folk. If they desire amendment Allah will make them of one mind. Lo! Allah is ever knower, Aware.

36. And serve Allah. Ascribe no things as partner unto Him. (Show) kindness unto parents, and unto near kindred, and orphans, and the needy, and unto the neighbour who is of kin (unto you) and the neighbour who is not of kin, and the fellow-traveller and the wayfarer and (the slaves) whom your right hands possess. Lo! Allah loveth not such as are proud and boastful.

37. Who hoard their wealth and enjoin avarice on others, and hide that which Allah hath bestowed upon them of His bounty. For disbelievers We prepare a shameful doom.

38. And (also) those who spend their wealth in order to be seen of men, and believe not in Allah nor the Last Day. whoso taketh Satan for a comrade, a bad comrade hath he.

39. What have they (to fear) if they believe in Allah and the Last Day and spend (aright) of that which Allah hath bestowed upon them, when Allah is ever Aware of them (and all they do)?

40. Lo! Allah wrongeth not even of the weight of an ant; and if there is a good deed, He will double it and will give (the doer) from His presence an immense reward.

41. But how (will it be with them) when We bring of every people a witness, and We bring thee (O Muhammad) a witness against these?

42. On that day those who disbelieved and disobeyed the messenger will wish that they were level with the ground, and they can hide no fact from Allah.

43. O ye who believe! Draw not near unto prayer when ye are drunken, till ye know that which ye utter, nor when ye are polluted, save when journeying upon the road, till ye have bathed. And if ye be ill, or on a journey, or one of you cometh from the closet, or ye have touched women, and ye find not water, then go to high clean soil and rub your faces and your hands (therewith). Lo! Allah is Benign, Forgiving.

44. Seest thou not those unto whom a portion of the scripture hath been given, how they purchase error, and seek to make you (Muslims) err from the right way?

45. Allah knoweth best (who are) your enemies. Allah is sufficient as a friend, and Allah is sufficient as a Helper.

46. Some of those who are Jews change words from their

context and say: "We hear and disobey; hear thou as one who heareth not" and "Listen to us!" distorting with their tongues and slandering religion. If they had said: "We hear and we obey; hear thou, and look at us," it had been better for them, and more upright. But Allah hath cursed them for their disbelief, so they believe not, save a few.

47. O ye unto whom the Scripture hath been given! Believe in what We have revealed confirming that which ye possess, before We destroy countenances so as to confound them, or curse them as We cursed the Sabbath breakers (of old time). The commandment of Allah is always executed.

48. Lo! Allah forgiveth not that a partner should be ascribed unto Him. He forgiveth (all) save that to whom He will. Whoso ascribeth partners to Allah, he hath indeed invented a tremendous sin.

49. Hast thou not seen those who praise themselves for purity? Nay, Allah purifieth whom He will, and they will not be wronged even the hair upon a date-stone.

50. See, how they invent lies about Allah! That of itself is flagrant sin.

51. Hast thou not seen those unto whom a portion of the Scripture hath been given, how they believe in idols and false deities, and how they say of those (idolaters) who disbelieve: "These are more rightly guided than those who believe?"

52. Those are they whom Allah hath cursed, and he whom Allah hath cursed, thou (O Muhammad) wilt find for him no helper.

53. Or have they even a share in the Sovereignty? Then in that case, they would not give mankind even the speck on a date-stone.

54. Or are they jealous of mankind because of that which Allah of His bounty hath bestowed upon them? For We bestowed upon the house of Abraham (of old) the Scripture and Wisdom, and We bestowed on them a mighty kingdom.

55. And of them were (some) who believed therein and of them were (some) who disbelieved therein. Hell is sufficient for (their) burning.

56. Lo! Those who disbelieve our revelations, We shall expose them to the Fire. As often as their skins are consumed We shall exchange them for fresh skins that they may taste the torment. Lo! Allah is ever Mighty, Wise.

57. And as for those who believe and do good works, We shall make them enter Gardens underneath which rivers flow — to dwell therein for ever; there for them are pure companions — and We shall make them enter plenteous shade.

58. Lo! Allah commandeth you that ye restore deposits to their owners, and, if ye judge between mankind, that ye judge justly. Lo! comely is this which Allah admonisheth you. Lo! Allah is ever Hearer, Seer.

59. O ye who believe! Obey Allah, and obey the messenger and those of you who are in authority; and if ye have a dispute concerning any matter, refer it to Allah and the messenger if ye are (in truth) believers in Allah and the Last Day. That is better and more seemly in the end.

60. Hast thou not seen those who pretend that they believe in that which is revealed unto thee and that which was revealed before thee, how they would go for judgement (in their disputes) to false deities when they have been ordered to abjour them? Satan would mislead them far astray.

61. And when it is said unto them: Come unto that which Allah hath revealed and unto the messenger, thou seest the hypocrites turn from thee with aversion.

62. How would it be if a misfortune smote them because of that which their own hands have sent before (them)? Then would they come unto thee, swearing by Allah that they were seeking naught but harmony and kindness.

63. Those are they, the secrets of whose hearts Allah knoweth. So oppose them and admonish them, and address them in plain terms about their souls.

64. We sent no messenger save that he should be obeyed by Allah's leave. And if, when they had wronged themselves, they had but come unto thee and asked forgiveness of Allah, and asked forgiveness of the messenger, they would have found Allah forgiving, Merciful.

65. But nay, by thy Lord, they will not believe (in truth) until they make thee judge of what is in dispute between them and find within themselves no dislike of that which thou decidest, and submit with full submission.

66. And if We had decreed for them: Lay down your lives or go forth from your dwellings, but few of them would have done it; though if they did what they are exhorted to do it would be better for them, and more strengthening.

67. And then We should bestow upon them from Our presence an immense reward.

68. And should guide them unto a straight path.

69. Whoso obeyeth Allah and the messenger, they are with those unto whom Allah hath shown favour, of the Prophets and the saints and the martyrs and righteous. The best of company are they!

70. Such is the bounty of Allah, and Allah sufficeth as

Knower.

71. O ye who believe! Take your precautions, then advance the proven ones, or advance all together.

72. Lo! among you there is he who loitereth; and if disaster overtook you, he would say: Allah hath been gracious unto me since I was not present with them.

73. And if a bounty from Allah befell you, he would surely cry, as if there had been no love between you and him: Oh, would that I had been with them, then should I have achieved a great success!

74. Let those fight in the way of Allah who sell the life of this world for the other. Whoso fighteth in the way of Allah, be he slain or be he victorious, on him We shall bestow a vast reward.

75. How should ye not fight for the cause of Allah and of the feeble among men and of the women and the children who are crying: Our Lord! Bring us forth from out this town of which the people are oppressors! Oh, give us from Thy presence some protecting friend! Oh, give us from Thy presence some defender!

76. Those who believe do battle for the cause of Allah; and those who disbelieve do battle for the cause of idols. So fight the minions of the devil. Lo! the devil's strategy is ever weak.

77. Hast thou not seen those unto whom it was said: Withhold your hands, establish worship and pay the poor-due, but when fighting was prescribed for them behold! a party of them fear mankind even as their fear of Allah or with greater fear, and say: Our Lord! Why hast thou ordained fighting for us? If only Thou wouldst give us respite yet a while! Say (unto them, O Muhammad): The comfort of this world is scant; the Hereafter will be better for him who wardeth off (evil); and ye will not be wronged the down upon a date-stone.

78. Wheresoever ye may be, death will overtake you, even though ye were in lofty towers. Yet if a happy thing befalleth them they say: This is from Allah; and if an evil thing befalleth them they say: This is of thy doing (O Muhammad). Say (unto them): All is from Allah. What is amiss with these people that they come not nigh to understand a happening?

79. Whatever of good befalleth thee (O man) it is from Allah, and whatever of ill befalleth thee it is from thyself. We have sent thee (Muhammad) as a messenger unto mankind and Allah is sufficient as witness.

80. Whoso obeyeth the messenger obeyeth Allah, and whoso turneth away: We have not sent thee as a warder over them.

81. And they say: (It is) obedience; but when they have gone

forth from thee a party of them spend the night in planning other than what thou sayest. Allah recordeth what they plan by night. So oppose them and put thy trust in Allah. Allah is sufficient as Trustee.

82. Will they not then ponder on the Qur'ân? If it had been from other than Allah they would have found therein much incongruity.

83. And if any tidings, whether of safety or fear, come unto them, they noise it abroad, whereas if they had referred it to the messenger and such of them as are in authority, those among them who are able to think out the matter would have known it. If it had not been for the grace of Allah and His mercy ye would have followed Satan, save a few (of you).

84. So fight (O Muhammad) in the way of Allah — Thou art not taxed (with the responsibility for anyone) except for thyself — and urge on the believers. Peradventure Allah will restrain the might of those who disbelieve. Allah is stronger in might and stronger in inflicting punishment.

85. Whoso interveneth in a good cause will have the reward thereof, and whoso interveneth in an evil cause will bear the consequence thereof. Allah overseeth all things.

86. When ye are greeted with a greeting, greet ye with a better than it or return it. Lo! Allah taketh count of all things.

87. Allah! There is no God save Him. He gathereth you all unto a Day of Resurrection whereof there is no doubt. Who is more true in statement than Allah?

88. What aileth you that ye are become two parties regarding the hypocrites when Allah cast them back (to disbelief) because of what they earned? Seek ye to guide him whom Allah hath sent astray? He whom Allah sendeth astray, for him thou (O Muhammad) canst not find a road.

89. They long that ye should disbelieve even as they disbelieve, that ye may be upon a level (with them). So choose not friends from them till they forsake their homes in the way of Allah; if they turn back (to enmity) then take them and kill them wherever ye find them, and choose no friend nor helper from among them.

90. Except those who seek refuge with a people between whom and you there is a covenant, or (those who) come unto you because their hearts forbid them to make war on you or make war on their own folk. Had Allah willed He could have given them power over you so that assuredly they would have fought you. So, if they hold aloof from you and wage not war against you and offer you peace, Allah alloweth you no way against them.

91. Ye will find others who desire that they should have security from you, and security from their own folk. So often as they are returned to hostility they are plunged therein. If they keep not aloof from you nor offer you peace nor hold their hands, then take them and kill them wherever ye find them. Against such We have given you clear warrant.

92. It is not for a believer to kill a believer unless (it be) by mistake. He who hath killed a believer by mistake must set free a believing slave, and pay the blood-money to the family of the slain, unless they remit it as a charity. If he (the victim) be of a people hostile unto you, and he is a believer, then (the penance is) to set free a believing slave. And if he cometh of a folk between whom and you there is a covenant, then the blood-money must be paid unto his folk and (also) a believing slave must be set free. And whoso hath not the wherewithal must fast two consecutive months. A penance from Allah. Allah is Knower, Wise.

93. Whoso slayeth a believer of a set purpose, his reward is Hell for ever. Allah is wroth against him and He hath cursed him and prepared for him an awful doom.

94. O ye who believe! When ye go forth (to fight) in the way of Allah, be careful to discriminate, and say not unto one who offereth you peace: "Thou are not a believer," seeking the chance profits of this life (so that ye may despoil him). With Allah are plenteous spoils. Even thus (as he now is) were ye before; but Allah hath since then been gracious unto you. Therefore take care to discriminate. Allah is ever informed of what ye do.

95. Those of the believers who sit still, other than those who have a (disabling) hurt, are not on an equality with those who strive in the way of Allah with their wealth and lives. Allah hath conferred on those who strive with their wealth and lives a rank above the sedentary. Unto each Allah hath promised good but He hath bestowed on those who strive a great reward above the sedentary;

96. Degrees of rank from Him, and forgiveness and mercy. Allah is every Forgiving, Merciful.

97. Lo! as for those whom the angels take (in death) while they wrong themselves, (the angels) will ask: In what were ye engaged? They will say: We were oppressed in the land. (The angels) will say: Was not Allah's earth spacious that ye could have migrated therein? As for such, their habitation will be hell, an evil journey's end;

98. Except the feeble men, and the women, and the children, who are unable to devise a plan and are not shown a way.

99. As for such, it may be that Allah will pardon them: Allah is ever Clement, Forgiving.

100. Whoso migrateth for the cause of Allah will find much refuge and abundance in the earth, and whoso forsaketh his home, a fugitive unto Allah and His messenger, and death overtaketh him, his reward is then incumbent on Allah. Allah is ever Forgiving, Merciful.

101. And when ye go forth in the land, it is no sin for you to curtail (your) worship if ye fear that those who disbelieve may attack you. In truth the disbelievers are an open enemy to you.

102. And when thou (O Muhammad) art among them and arrangest (their) worship for them, let only a party of them stand with thee (to worship) and let them take their arms. Then when they have performed their prostrations let them fall to the rear and let another party come that hath not worshipped and let them worship with thee, and let them take their precaution and their arms. Those who disbelieve long for you to neglect your arms and your baggage that they may attack you once for all. It is no sin for you to lay aside your arms, if rain impedeth you or ye are sick. But take your precaution. Lo! Allah prepareth for the disbelievers shameful punishment.

103. When ye have performed the act of worship, remember Allah, standing, sitting and reclining. And when ye are in safety observe proper worship. Worship at fixed hours hath been enjoined on the believers.

104. Relent not in pursuit of the enemy. If ye are suffering, Lo! they suffer even as ye suffer and ye hope from Allah that for which they cannot hope. Allah is ever Knower, Wise.

105. Lo! We reveal unto thee the Scripture with the truth, that thou mayst judge between mankind by that which Allah showeth thee. And be not thou a pleader for the treacherous.

106. And seek forgiveness of Allah. Lo! Allah is ever Forgiving, Merciful.

107. And plead not on behalf of (people) who deceive themselves. Lo! Allah loveth not one who is treacherous and sinful.

108. They seek to hide from men and seek not to hide from Allah. He is with them when by night they hold discourse displeasing unto Him. Allah ever surroundeth what they do.

109. Lo! ye are they who pleaded for them in the life of the world. But who will plead with Allah for them on the Day of Resurrection, or who will then be their defender?

110. Yet whoso doeth evil or wrongeth his own soul, then

seeketh pardon of Allah, will find Allah Forgiving, Merciful.

111. Whoso committeth sin committeth it only against himself. Allah is ever Knower, Wise.

112. And whoso committeth a delinquency or crime, then throweth (the blame) thereof upon the innocent, hath burdened himself with falsehood and a flagrant crime.

113. But for the grace of Allah upon thee (Muhammad), and His mercy, a party of them had resolved to mislead thee, but they will mislead only themselves and they will hurt thee not at all. Allah revealeth unto thee the Scripture and wisdom, and teacheth thee that which thou knewest not. The grace of Allah toward thee hath been infinite.

114. There is no good in much of their secret conferences save (in) him who enjoineth almsgiving and kindness and peace-making among the people. Whoso doeth that, seeking the good pleasure of Allah, We shall bestow on him a vast reward.

115. And whoso opposeth the messenger after the guidance (of Allah) hath been manifested upon him, and followeth other than the believer's way, We appoint for him that unto which he himself hath turned, and expose him unto hell—a hapless journey's end!

116. Lo! Allah pardoneth not that partners should be ascribed unto him. He pardoneth all save that to whom He will. Whoso ascribeth partners unto Allah hath wandered far astray.

117. They invoke in His stead only females, they pray to none else than Satan, a rebel.

118. Whom Allah cursed, and he said: Surely I will take of Thy bondmen an appointed portion.

119. And surely I will read them astray, and surely I will arouse desires in them, and surely I will command them and they will cut the cattle's ears, and surely I will command them and they will change Allah's creation. Whoso chooseth Satan for a patron instead of Allah is verily a loser and loss is manifest.

120. He promiseth them and stirreth up desires in them, and Satan promiseth them only to beguile.

121. For such, their habitation will be hell, and they will find no refuge therefrom.

122. But as for those who believe and do good works We shall bring them into gardens underneath which rivers flow, wherein they will abide for ever. It is a promise for Allah in truth; and who can be more truthful than Allah in utterance?

123. It will not be in accordance with your desires, nor the

desires of the people of the Scripture. He who doeth wrong will have the recompense thereof, and will not find against Allah any protecting friend or helper.

124. And whoso doeth good works, whether of male of female, and he (or she) is a believer, such will enter paradise and they will not be wronged the dint in a date-stone.

125. Who is better in religion than he who surrendereth his purpose to Allah while doing good (to men) and followeth the tradition of Abraham, the upright? Allah (Himself) chose Abraham for friend.

126. Unto Allah belongeth whatsoever is in the heavens and whatsoever is in the earth. Allah ever surroundeth all things.

127. They consult the concerning women. Say: Allah giveth you decree concerning them, and the Scripture which hath been recited unto you (giveth decree), concerning female or orphans unto whom ye give not that which is ordained for them though ye desire to marry them, and (concerning) the weak among children, and that ye should deal justly with orphans. Whatever good ye do, lo! Allah is ever Aware of it.

128. If a woman feareth ill-treatment from her husband, or desertion, it is no sin for them twain if they make terms of peace between themselves. Peace is better. But greed hath been made present in the minds (of men) If ye do good and keep from evil, lo! Allah is ever informed of what ye do.

129. Ye will not be able to deal equally between (your) wives, however much ye wish (to do so). But turn not altogether away (from one), leaving her as in suspense. If ye do good and keep from evil, lo! Allah is ever Forgiving, Merciful.

130. But if they separate, Allah will compensate each out of His abundance. Allah is ever All-Embracing, All-Knowing.

131. Unto Allah belongeth whatsoever is in the heavens and whatsoever is in the earth. And We charged those who received the Scripture before you, and (We charge) you, that ye keep your duty toward Allah. And if ye disbelieve, lo! unto Allah belongeth whatsoever is in the heavens and whatsoever is in the earth, and Allah is ever Absolute, Owner of Praise.

132. Unto Allah belongeth whatsoever is in the heavens and whatsoever is in the earth. And Allah is sufficient as Defender.

133. If He will, He can remove you, O people, and produce others (in your stead). Allah is Able to do that.

134. Whoso desireth the reward of the world, (let him know that) with Allah is the reward of the world and the Hereafter. Allah is ever Hearer, Seer.

135. O ye who believe! Be ye staunch in justice, witnesses for

Allah, even though it be against yourselves or (your) parents
or (your) kindred, whether (the case be of) a rich man or a poor
man, for Allah is nearer unto both (than ye are). So follow not
passion lest ye lapse (from truth), and if ye lapse or fall away,
then lo! Allah is ever informed of what ye do.

136. O ye who believe! Believe in Allah and His messenger
and the Scripture which He hath revealed unto His messenger,
and the Scripture which He revealed aforetime. Whoso
disbelieveth in Allah and His angels and His scriptures and
His messengers and the Last Day, he verily hath wandered far
astray.

137. Lo! those who believe, then disbelieve and then (again)
believe, then disbelieve, and then increase in disbelief, Allah
will never pardon them, nor will He guide them unto a way.

138. Bear unto the hypocrites the tidings that for them there
is a painful doom.

139. Those who choose disbelievers for their friends
instead of believers! Do they look for power at their hands?
Lo, all power appertaineth to Allah.

140. He hath already revealed unto you in the Scripture that,
when ye hear the revelations of Allah rejected and derided, (ye)
sit not with them (who disbelieve and mock) until they engage
in some other conversation. Lo! in that case (if ye stayed) ye
would be like unto them. Lo! Allah will gather hypocrites and
disbelievers, all together, into hell.

141. Those who wait upon occasion in regard to you and,
if a victory cometh unto you from Allah, say: Are we not with
you? and if the disbelievers meet with a success say: Had we
not the mastery of you, and did we not protect you from the
believers? — Allah will judge between you at the Day of
Resurrection, and Allah will not give the disbelievers any way
(of success) against the believers.

142. Lo! the hypocrites seek to beguile Allah, but it is Allah
who beguileth them. When they stand up to worship they
perform it languidly and to be seen of men, and are mindful
of Allah but little.

143. Swaying between this (and that), (belonging) neither to
these nor to those. He whom Allah causeth to go astray, thou
(O Muhammad) wilt not find a way for him.

144. O ye who believe! Choose not disbelievers for (your)
friends in place of believers. Would ye give Allah a clear
warrant against you?

145. Lo! the hypocrites (will be) in the lowest deep of the fire,
and thou wilt find no helper for them.

146. Save those who repent and amend and hold fast of

Allah and make their religion pure for Allah (only). Those are with the believers. And Allah will bestow on the believers an immense reward.

147. What concern hath Allah for your punishment if ye are thankful (for His mercies) and believe (in Him)? Allah was ever Responsive, Aware.

148. Allah loveth not the utterance of harsh speech save by one who hath been wronged. Allah is ever Hearer, Knower.

149. If ye do good openly or keep it secret, or forgive evil, lo! Allah is Forgiving, Powerful.

150. Lo! those who disbelieve in Allah and His messengers, and seek to make distinction between Allah and His messengers, and say: We believe in some and disbelieve in others, and seek to choose a way in between.

151. Such are disbelievers in truth; and for disbelievers We prepare a shameful doom.

152. But those who believe in Allah and His messengers and make no distinction between any of them, unto them Allah will give their wages; and Allah was ever Forgiving, Merciful.

153. The People of the Scripture ask of thee that thou shouldst cause an (actual) Book to descend upon them from heaven. They asked a greater thing of Moses aforetime, for they said: Show us Allah plainly. The storm of lightning seized them for their wickedness. Then (even after that) they chose the calf (for worship) after clear proofs (of Allah's Sovereignty) had come unto them. And We forgave them that! and We bestowed on Moses evident authority.

154. And We caused the Mount to tower above them at (the taking of) their covenant: and We bade them: Enter the gate, prostrate! and we bade them: Transgress not the Sabbath! and We took from them a firm covenant.

155. Then because of their breaking of their covenant, and their disbelieving in the revelations of Allah, and their slaying of the Prophets wrongfully, and their saying: Our hearts are hardened—Nay, but Allah hath set a seal upon them for their disbelief, so that they believe not save a few—

156. And because of their disbelief and of their speaking against Mary a tremendous calumny.

157. And because of their saying: We slew the Messiah Jesus son of Mary, Allah's messenger—They slew him not nor crucified, but it appeared so unto them; and lo! those who disagree concerning it are in doubt thereof; they have no knowledge thereof save pursuit of a conjecture; they slew him not for certain.

158. But Allah took him up unto Himself. Allah was ever Mighty, Wise.

159. There is not one of the People of the Scripture but will believe in him before his death, and on the Day of Resurrection he will be a witness against them—

160. Because of the wrongdoing of the Jews We forbade them good things which were (before) made lawful unto them, and because of their much hindering from Allah's way.

161. And of their taking usury when they were forbidden it, and of their devouring people's wealth by false pretences. We have prepared for those of them who disbelieve a painful doom.

162. But those of them who are firm in knowledge and the believers believe in that which is revealed unto thee, and that which was revealed before thee, especially the diligent in prayer and those who pay the poor-due, the believers in Allah and the Last Day. Upon these We shall bestow immense reward.

163. Lo! We inspire thee as We inspired Noah and the prophets after him, as We inspired Abraham and Ishmael and Isaac and Jacob and the tribes, and Jesus and Job and Jonah and Aaron and Solomon, and as We imparted unto David the Psalms.

164. And messengers We have mentioned unto thee before the messengers We have not mentioned unto thee; and Allah spake directly unto Moses.

165. Messengers of good cheer and of warning, in order that mankind might have no argument against Allah after the messengers. Allah was ever Mighty, Wise.

166. But Allah (Himself) testifieth concerning that which He hath revealed unto thee; in His knowledge hath He revealed it; and the Angels also testify. And Allah is sufficient witness.

167. Lo! those who disbelieve and hinder (others) from the way of Allah, they verily have wandered far astray.

168. Lo! those who disbelieve and deal in wrong. Allah will never forgive them, neither will He guide them unto a road.

169. Except the road of hell, wherein they will abide for ever. And that is ever easy for Allah.

170. O mankind! The messenger hath come unto you with the truth from your Lord. Therefore believe; (it is) better for you. But if he disbelieve, still, lo! unto Allah belongeth whatsoever is in the heavens and the earth. Allah is ever Knower, Wise.

171. O People of the Scripture! Do not exaggerate in your religion nor utter aught concerning Allah save the truth. The

Messiah, Jesus son of Mary, was only a messenger of Allah, and His word which He conveyed unto Mary, and a spirit from Him. So believe in Allah and His messengers, and say not "Three" — Cease! (it is) better for you! — Allah is only One God. Far is it removed from His Transcendant Majesty that he should have a son. His is all that is in the heavens and all that is in the earth. And Allah is sufficient as Defender.

172. The Messiah will never scorn to be a slave unto Allah, nor will the favoured angels. Whoso scorneth His service and is proud, all such will He assemble unto him.

173. Then, as for those who believed and did good works, unto them will He pay their wages in full, adding unto them of His bounty; and as for those who were scornful and proud, them will He punish with a painful doom. And they will not find for them, against Allah, any protecting friend or helper.

174. O mankind! Now hath a proof from your Lord come unto you, and We have sent down unto you a clear light.

175. As for those who believe in Allah, and hold fast unto Him, them He will cause to enter into His mercy and grace, and will guide them unto Him by a straight road.

176. They ask thee for a pronouncement. Say: Allah hath pronounced for you concerning distant kindred. If a man die childless and he have a sister, hers is half the heritage, and he would have inherited from her had she died childless. And if there be two sisters, then theirs are two-thirds of the heritage, and if they be brethren, men and women, unto the male is the equivalent of the share of two females. Allah expoundeth unto you, so that ye err not. Allah is Knower of all things.

SÛRAH 5

Al Mâ'idah, "The Table Spread", derives its name from vv. 112 ff., where it is told how the disciples of Jesus asked that a table spread with food might be sent down from Heaven, and their prayer was granted, a passage in which some have seen an allusion to the Eucharist. Many authorities regard it as the last sûrah in order of revelation, and Rodwell has so placed it in his chronological arrangement; but the claim can only be established in the case of verse 3, which announces the completion of their religion for the Muslims, and the choice for them of Al-Islâm (the Surrender to Allah) as their religion. That verse is undoubtedly the latest of the whole Koran. It was revealed during the Prophet's last pilgrimage ("The Farewell Pilgrimage", as it is called) to Mecca, and spoken by him in the course of his address to the assembled thousands at 'Arafât, when all Arabia had embraced Al-Islâm, only a little while before his death. It is possible that, as Nöldeke supposes, two other verses near to it are of the same date, but the remainder of the revelations contained in this sûrah belong rather to the period between the fourth and seventh years of the Hijrah. Its subject is observance of religious duties. The followers of former prophets had failed through breaking their covenant, and so the Muslims are adjured to keep their covenant with God and all their obligations watchfully, because God's covenant is only with those who do right. There is more mention of the Christians here than in the former sûrahs, from which some writers infer that this sûrah must have been revealed at the time when the Prophet was at war with certain Christian tribes belonging to the Eastern Roman Empire. But there is no evidence for that either in tradition or in the text itself.

The period of revelation is between the fifth and tenth years of the Hijrah.

THE TABLE SPREAD

Revealed at Al-Madînah

In the name of Allah, the Beneficent, the Merciful.

1. O ye who believe! Fulfil your undertakings. The beast of cattle is made lawful unto you (for food) except that which is announced unto you (herein), game being unlawful when ye are on pilgrimage. Lo! Allah ordaineth that which pleaseth Him.

2. O ye who believe! Profane not Allah's monuments nor the Sacred Month nor the offerings nor the garlands, nor those repairing to the Sacred House, seeking the grace and pleasure of Allah. But when ye have left the sacred territory, then go hunting (if ye will). And let not your hatred of a folk who (once) stopped your going to the Inviolable Place of Worship seduce you to transgress; but help ye one another unto righteousness and pious duty. Help not one another unto sin and transgression, but keep your duty to Allah. Lo! Allah is severe in punishment.

3. Forbidden unto you (for food) are carrion and blood and swine-flesh, and that which hath been dedicated unto any other than Allah, and the strangled, and the dead through beating, and the dead through falling from a height, and that which hath been killed by (the goring of) horns, and the devoured of wild beasts, saving that which he make lawful (by the death-stroke), and that which hath been immolated unto idols. And (forbidden is it) that ye swear by the divining arrows. This is an abomination. This day are those who disbelieve in despair of (ever harming) your religion; so fear

them not, fear Me! This day have I perfected your religion for you and completed My favour unto you, and have chosen for you as religion AL-ISLÂM. Whoso is forced by hunger, not by will, to sin: (for him) lo! Allah is Forgiving, Merciful.

4. They ask thee (O Muhammad) what is made lawful for them. Say: (all) good things are made lawful for you, And those beasts and birds of prey which ye have trained as hounds are trained, ye teach them that Allah taught you; so eat of that which they catch for you and mention Allah's name upon it, and observe your duty to Allah. Lo! Allah is swift to take account.

5. This day are (all) good things made lawful for you. The food of those who have received the Scripture is lawful for you, and your food is lawful for them. And so are the virtuous women of the believers and the virtuous women of those who received the Scripture before you (lawful for you) when ye give them their marriage portions and live with them in honour, not in fornication, nor taking them as secret concubines. Whoso denieth the faith, his work is vain and he will be among the losers in the Hereafter.

6. O ye who believe! When ye rise up for prayer, wash your faces and your hands up to the elbows, and lightly rub your heads and (wash) your feet up to the ankles. And if ye are unclean, purify yourselves. And if ye are sick or on a journey, or one of you cometh from the closet, or ye have had contact with women, and ye find not water, then go to clean, high ground and rub your faces and your hands with some of it. Allah would not place a burden on you, but He would purify you and would perfect His grace upon you, that ye may give thanks.

7. Remember Allah's grace upon you and His covenant by which He bound you when ye said: We hear and we obey; and keep your duty to Allah. Lo! Allah knoweth what is in the breasts (of men).

8. O ye who believe! Be steadfast witnesses for Allah in equity, and let not hatred of any people seduce you that ye deal not justly. Deal justly, that is nearer to your duty. Observe your duty to Allah. Lo! Allah is Informed of what ye do.

9. Allah hath promised those who believe and do good works: Theirs will be forgiveness and immense reward.

10. And they who disbelieve and deny Our revelations, such are rightful owners of hell.

11. O ye who believe! Remember Allah's favour unto you, how many people were minded to stretch out their hands against you but He withheld their hands from you; and keep your duty to Allah. In Allah let believers put their trust.

12. Allah made a covenant of old with the Children of Israel and We raised among them twelve chieftains, and Allah said: Lo! I am with you. If ye establish worship and pay the poor-due, and believe in My messengers and support them, and lend unto Allah a kindly loan, surely I shall remit your sins, and surely I shall bring you into gardens underneath which rivers flow. Whoso among you disbelieveth after this will go astray from a plain road.

13. And because of their breaking their covenant, We have cursed them and made hard their hearts. They change words from their context and forget a part of that whereof they were admonished. Thou wilt not cease to discover treachery from all save a few of them. But bear with them and pardon them. Lo! Allah loveth the kindly.

14. And with those who say: "Lo! we are Christians," We made a covenant, but they forgot a part of that whereof they were admonished. Therefore We have stirred up enmity and hatred among them till the Day of Resurrection, when Allah will inform them of their handiwork.

15. O people of the Scripture! Now hath Our messenger come unto you, expounding unto you much of that which ye used to hide in the Scripture, and forgiving much. Now hath come unto you light from Allah and a plain Scripture.

16. Whereby Allah guideth him who seeketh His good pleasure unto paths of peace. He bringeth them out of darkness unto light by His decree, and guideth them unto a straight path.

17. They indeed have disbelieved who say: Lo! Allah is the Messiah son of Mary. Say: Who then can do aught against Allah if he had willed to destroy the Messiah son of Mary, and his mother and everyone on earth? Allah's is the Sovereignty of the heavens and the earth and all that is between them. He createth what He will. And Allah is Able to do all things.

18. The Jews and Christians say: We are sons of Allah and His loved ones. Say: Why then doth He chastise you for your sins? Nay, ye are but mortals of His creating. He forgiveth whom He will, and chastiseth whom He will. Allah's is the Sovereignty of the heavens and the earth and all that is between them, and unto Him is the journeying.

19. O people of the Scripture! Now hath Our messenger come unto you to make things plain after an interval (of cessation) of the messengers, lest ye should say: There came not unto us a messenger of cheer nor any warner. Now hath a messenger of cheer and a warner come unto you. Allah is Able to do all things.

20. And (remember) when Moses said unto his people: O

my people! Remember Allah's favour unto you, how He placed among you Prophets, and He made you kings, and gave you that (which) He gave not to any (other) of (His) creatures.

21. O my people! Go into the holy land which Allah hath ordained for you. Turn not in flight, for surely ye turn back as losers.

22. They said: O Moses! Lo! a giant people (dwell) therein, and lo! we go not in till they go forth from thence. When they go forth, then we will enter (not till then).

23. Then outspake two of those who feared (their Lord, men) unto whom Allah had been gracious: Enter in upon them by the gate, for if ye enter by it, lo! ye will be victorious. So put your trust (in Allah) if ye are indeed believers.

24. They said: O Moses! We will never enter (the land) while they are in it. So go thou and thy Lord and fight! We will sit here.

25. He said: My Lord! I have control of none but myself and my brother, so distinguish between us and the wrongdoing folk.

26. (Their Lord) said: For this the land will surely by forbidden them for forty years that they will wander in the earth, bewildered. So grieve not over the wrongdoing folk.

27. But recite unto them with truth the tale of the two sons of Adam, how they offered each a sacrifice, and it was accepted from the one of them and it was not accepted from the other. (The one) said: I will surely kill thee. (The other) answered: Allah accepteth only from those who ward off (evil).

28. Even if thou stretch out thy hand against me to kill me, I shall not stretch out my hand against thee to kill thee, lo! I fear Allah, the Lord of the Worlds.

29. Lo! I would rather thou shouldst bear the punishment of the sin against me and thine own sin and become one of the owners of the Fire. That is the reward of evildoers.

30. But (the other's) mind imposed on him the killing of his brother, so he slew him and became one of the losers.

31. Then Allah sent a raven scratching up the ground, to show him how to hide his brother's naked corpse. He said: Woe unto me! Am I not able to be as this raven and so hide my brother's naked corpse? And he became repentant.

32. For that cause We decreed for the Children of Israel that whosoever killeth a human being for other than manslaughter or corruption in the earth, it shall be as if he had killed all mankind, and whoso saveth the life of one, it shall be as if he had saved the life of all mankind. Our messengers came unto them of old with clear proofs (of Allah's sovereignty), but

afterwards lo! many of them became prodigals in the earth.

33. The only reward of those who make war upon Allah and His messenger and strive after corruption in the land will be that they will be killed or crucified, or have their hands and feet on alternate sides cut off, or will be expelled out of the land. Such will be their degradation in the world, and in the Hereafter theirs will be an awful doom.

34. Save those who repent before ye overpower them. For know that Allah is Forgiving, Merciful.

35. O ye who believe! Be mindful of your duty to Allah, and seek the way of approach unto Him, and strive in His way in order that ye may succeed.

36. As for those who disbelieve, lo! if all that is in the earth were theirs, and as much again therewith, to ransom them from the doom on the Day of Resurrection, it would not be accepted from them. Theirs will be a painful doom.

37. They will wish to come forth from the Fire, but they will not come forth from it. Theirs will be a lasting doom.

38. As for the thief, both male and female, cut off their hands. It is the reward of their own deeds, an exemplary punishment from Allah. Allah is Mighty, Wise.

39. But whoso repenteth after his wrongdoing and amendeth, lo! Allah will relent toward him. Lo! Allah is Forgiving, Merciful.

40. Knowest thou not that unto Allah belongeth the Sovereignty of the heavens and the earth? He punisheth whom He will, and forgiveth whom He will. Allah is Able to do all things.

41. O Messenger! Let not them greive thee who vie one with another in the race to disbelief, of such as say with their mouths: "We believe," but their hearts believe not, and of the Jews: listeners for the sake of falsehood, listeners on behalf of other folk who come not unto thee, changing words from their context and saying: If this be given unto you, receive it, but if this be not given unto you, then beware! He whom Allah doometh unto sin, thou (by thine efforts) wilt avail him naught against Allah. Those are they for whom the will of Allah is that He cleanse not their hearts. Theirs in the world will be ignominy, and in the Hereafter an awful doom.

42. Listeners for the sake of falsehood! Greedy for illicit gain! If then they have recourse unto thee (Muhammad) judge between them or disclaim jurisdiction. If thou disclaimest jurisdiction, then they cannot harm thee at all. But if thou judgest, judge between them with equity. Lo! Allah loveth the equitable.

43. How come they unto thee for judgement when they have the Torah, wherein Allah hath delivered judgement (for

them)? Yet even after they turn away. Such (folk) are not believers.

44. Lo! We did reveal the Torah, wherein is guidance and a light, by which the Prophets who surrendered (unto Allah) judged the Jews, and the rabbis and the priests (judged) by such of Allah's Scripture as they were bidden to observe, and thereunto were they witnesses. So fear not mankind, but fear Me. And barter not My revelations for a little gain. Whoso judgeth not by that which Allah hath revealed: such are disbelievers.

45. And We prescribed for them therein: The life for the life, and the eye for the eye, and the nose for the nose, and the ear for the ear, and the tooth for the tooth, and for wounds retaliation. But whoso forgoeth it (in the way of charity) it shall be expiation for him. Whoso judgeth not by that which Allah hath revealed: such are wrongdoers.

46. And We caused Jesus, son of Mary, to follow in their footsteps, confirming that which was (revealed) before him, and We bestowed on him the Gospel wherein is guidance and a light, confirming that which was (revealed) before it in the Torah—a guidance and an admonition unto those who ward off (evil).

47. Let the People of the Gospel judge by that which Allah hath revealed therein. Whoso judgeth not by that which Allah hath revealed: such are evil-livers.

48. And unto thee have We revealed the Scripture with the truth, confirming whatever Scripture was before it, and a watcher over it. So judge between them by that which Allah hath revealed, and follow not their desires away from the truth which hath come unto thee. For each We have appointed a divine law and a traced-out way. Had Allah willed He could have made you one community. But that He may try you by that which He hath given you (He hath made you as ye are). So vie one with another in good works. Unto Allah ye will all return, and He will then inform you of that wherein ye differ.

49. So judge between them by that which Allah hath revealed, and follow not their desires, but beware of them lest they seduce thee from some part of that which Allah hath revealed unto thee. And if they turn away, then know that Allah's will is to smite them for some sin of theirs. Lo! many of mankind are evil-livers.

50. Is it a judgement of the time of (pagan) ignorance that they are seeking? Who is better than Allah for judgement to a people who have certainty (in their belief)?

51. O ye who believe! Take not the Jews and Christians for friends. They are friends one to another. He among you who

taketh them for friends is (one) of them. Lo! Allah guideth not wrongdoing folk.

52. And thou seest those in whose heart is a disease race toward them, saying: We fear lest a change of fortune befall us. And it may happen that Allah will vouchsafe (unto thee) the victory, or a commandment from His presence. Then will they repent of their secret thoughts.

53. Then will the believers say (unto the people of the Scripture): Are these they who swore by Allah their most binding oaths that they were surely with you? Their works have failed, and they have become the losers.

54. O ye who believe! Whoso of you becometh a renegade from his religion, (know that in his stead) Allah will bring a people whom He loveth and who love Him, humble toward believers, stern toward disbelivers, striving in the way of Allah, and fearing not the blame of any blamer. Such is the grace of Allah which He giveth unto whom He will. Allah is All-Embracing, All-Knowing.

55. Your friend can only be Allah; and His messenger and those who believe, who establish worship and pay the poor-due, and bow down (in prayer).

56. And whoso taketh Allah and His messenger and those who believe for friend (will know that), lo! the party of Allah, they are the victorious.

57. O ye who believe! Choose not for friends such of those who received the scripture before you, and of the disbelievers, as make a jest and sport of your religion. But keep your duty to Allah if ye are true believers.

58. And when ye call to prayer they take it for a jest and sport. That is because they are a folk who understand not.

59. Say: O, People of the Scripture! Do ye blame us for aught else than that we believe in Allah and that which is revealed unto us and that which was revealed aforetime, and because most of you are evil-livers?

60. Shall I tell thee of a worse (case) than theirs for retribution with Allah? Worse (is the case of him) whom Allah hath cursed, him on whom His wrath hath fallen! Worse is he of whose sort Allah hath turned some to apes and swine, and who serveth idols. Such are in worse plight and further astray from the plain road.

61. When they come unto you (Muslims), they say: We believe, but they came in unbelief and they went out in the same; and Allah knoweth best what they were hiding.

62. And thou seest many of them vying one with another in sin and transgression and their devouring of illicit gain. Verily evil is what they do.

63. Why do not the rabbis and the priests forbid their evil-speaking and their devouring of illicit gain. Verily evil is their handiwork.

64. The Jews say: Allah's hand is fettered. Their hands are fettered and they are accursed for saying so. Nay, but both His hands are spread out wide in bounty. He bestoweth as He will. That which hath been revealed unto thee from thy Lord is certain to increase the contumacy and disbelief of many of them, and We have cast among them enmity and hatred till the Day of Resurrection. As often as they light a fire for war, Allah extinguisheth it. Their effort is for corruption in the land, and Allah loveth not corrupters.

65. If only of the People of the Scripture would believe and ward off (evil), surely We should remit their sins from them and surely We should bring them into Gardens of Delight.

66. If they had observed the Torah and the Gospel and that which was revealed unto them from their Lord, they would surely have been nourished from above them and from beneath their feet. Among them there are people who are moderate, but many of them are of evil conduct.

67. O Messenger! Make known that which hath been revealed unto thee from thy Lord, for if thou do it not, thou will not have conveyed His message. Allah will protect thee from mankind. Lo! Allah guideth not the disbelieving folk.

68. Say: O People of the Scripture! Ye have naught (of guidance) till ye observe the Torah and the Gospel and that which was revealed unto you from your Lord. That which is revealed unto thee (Muhammad) from thy Lord is certain to increase the contumacy and disbelief of many of them. But grieve not for the disbelieving folk.

69. Lo! those who believe, and those who are Jews and Sabaeans, and Christians—Whosoever believeth in Allah and the Last Day and doeth right—there shall no fear come upon them neither shall they grieve.

70. We made a covenant of old with the Children of Israel and We sent unto them messengers. As often as a messenger came unto them with that which their souls desired not (they became rebellious). Some (of them) they denied and some they slew.

71. They thought no harm would come of it, so they were wilfully blind and deaf. And afterward Allah turned (in mercy) toward them. Now (even after that) are many of them wilfully blind and deaf. Allah is Seer of what they do.

72. They surely disbelieve who say: Lo! Allah is the Messiah, son of Mary. The Messiah (himself) said: O Children of Israel, worship Allah, my Lord and your Lord. Lo! whoso ascribeth partners unto Allah, for him Allah hath forbidden Paradise. His abode is the Fire. For evil-doers there will be no helpers.

73. They surely disbelieve who say: Lo! Allah is the third of three; when there is no God save the One God. If they desist not from so saying a painful doom will fall on those of them who disbelieve.

74. Will they not rather turn unto Allah and seek forgiveness of Him? For Allah is Forgiving, Merciful.

75. The Messiah, son of Mary, was no other than a messenger, messengers (the like of whom) had passed away before him. And his mother was a saintly woman. And they both used to eat (earthly) food. See how We make the revelations clear for them, and see how they are turned away!

76. Say: Serve ye in place of Allah that which possesseth for you neither hurt nor use? Allah it is Who is the Hearer, the Knower.

77. Say: O People of the Scripture! Stress not in your religion other than the truth, and follow not the vain desires of folk who erred of old and led many astray, and erred from a plain road.

78. Those of the children of Israel who went astray were cursed by the tongue of David, and of Jesus, son of Mary. That was because they rebelled and used to transgress.

79. They restrained not one another from the wickedness they did. Verily evil was that they used to do!

80. Thou seest many of them making friends with those who disbelieve. Surely ill for them is that which they themselves send on before them: that Allah will be wroth with them and in the doom they will abide.

81. If they believed in Allah and the Prophet and that which is revealed unto him, they would not choose them for their friends. But many of them are of evil conduct.

82. Thou wilt find the most vehement of mankind in hostility to those who believe (to be) the Jews and the idolaters. And thou wilt find the nearest of them in affection to those who believe (to be) those who say: Lo! We are Christians. That is because there are among them priests and monks, and because they are not proud.

83. When they listen to that which hath been revealed unto the messenger, thou seest their eyes overflow with tears because of their recognition of the Truth. They say: Our Lord, we believe. Inscribe us as among the witnesses.

84. How should we not believe in Allah and that which hath come unto us of the Truth. And (how should we not) hope that our Lord will bring us in along with righteous folk?

85. Allah hath rewarded them for that their saying—Gardens underneath which rivers flow, wherein they will abide for ever. That is the reward of the good.

86. But those who disbelieve and deny Our revelations, they

are owners of hell-fire.

87. O ye who believe! Forbid not the good things which Allah hath made lawful for you, and transgress not. Lo! Allah loveth not transgressors.

88. Eat of that which Allah hath bestowed on you as food lawful and good, and keep your duty to Allah in Whom ye are believers.

89. Allah will not take you to task for that which is unintentional in your oaths, but He will take you to task for the oaths which ye swear in earnest. The expiation thereof is the feeding of ten of the needy with the average of that where with ye feed your own folk, or the clothing of them, or the liberation of a slave, and for him who findeth not (the wherewithal to do so) then a three days' fast. This is the expiation of your oaths when ye have sworn; and keep your oaths. Thus Allah expoundeth unto you His revelations in order that ye may give thanks.

90. O ye who believe! Strong drink and games of chance and idols and divining arrows are only an infamy of Satan's handiwork. Leave it aside in order that ye may succeed.

91. Satan seeketh only to cast among you enmity and hatred by means of strong drink and games of chance, and to turn you from remembrance of Allah and from (His) worship. Will ye then have done?

92. Obey Allah and obey the messenger, and beware! But if ye turn away, then know that the duty of Our messenger is only plain conveyance (of the message).

93. There shall be no sin (imputed) unto those who believe and do good works for what they may have eaten (in the past). So be mindful of your duty (to Allah), and do good works; and again: be mindful of your duty, and believe; and once again: be mindful of your duty, and do right; Allah loveth the good.

94. O ye who believe! Allah will surely try you somewhat (in the matter) of the game which ye take with your hands and your spears, that Allah may know him who feareth Him in secret. Whoso transgresseth after this, for him there is a painful doom.

95. O ye who believe! Kill no wild game while ye are on the pilgrimage. Whoso of you killeth it of set purpose he shall pay its forfeit in the equivalent of that which he hath killed, of domestic animals, the judge to be two men among you known for justice, (the forfeit) to be brought as an offering to the Ka'bah; or, for expiation, he shall feed poor persons, or the equivalent thereof in fasting, that he may taste the evil consequences of his deed. Allah forgiveth whatever (of this kind) may have happened in the past, but whoso relapseth,

Allah will take retribution from him. Allah is Mighty, Able to Requite (the wrong).

96. To hunt and to eat the fish of the sea is made lawful for you, a provision for you and for seafarers; but to hunt on land is forbidden you so long as ye are on the pilgrimage. Be mindful of your duty to Allah, unto Whom ye will be gathered.

97. Allah hath appointed the Ka'bah, the Sacred House, a standard for mankind, and the Sacred Month and the offerings and the garlands. That is so that ye may know that Allah knoweth whatsoever is in the heavens and whatsoever is in the earth, and that Allah is Knower of all things.

98. Know that Allah is severe in punishment, but that Allah (also) is Forgiving, Merciful.

99. The duty of the messenger is only to convey (the message). Allah knoweth what ye proclaim and what ye hide.

100. Say: The evil and the good are not alike even though the plenty of the evil attract thee. So be mindful of your duty to Allah, O men of understanding, that ye may succeed.

101. O ye who believe! Ask not of things which, if they were made known unto you, would trouble you; but if ye ask of them when the Qur'ân is being revealed, they will be made known unto you. Allah pardoneth this, for Allah is Forgiving, Clement.

102. A folk before you asked (for such disclosures) and then disbelieved therein.

103. Allah hath not appointed anything in the nature of a *Barhirah* or a *Sâ'ibah* or a *Wasîlah* or a *Hâmi*, but those who disbelieve invent a lie against Allah. Most of them have no sense.

104. And when it is said unto them: Come unto that which Allah hath revealed and unto the messenger, they say: Enough for us is that wherein we found our fathers. What! Even though their fathers had no knowledge whatsoever, and no guidance?

105. O ye who believe! Ye have charge of your own souls. He who erreth cannot injure you if ye are rightly guided. Unto Allah ye will all return; and then He will inform you of what ye used to do.

106. O ye who believe! Let there be witnesses between you when death draweth nigh unto one of you, at the time of bequest—two witnesses, just men from among you, or two others from another tribe, in case ye are compaigning in the land and the calamity of death befall you. Ye shall empanel them both after the prayer, and, if ye doubt, they shall be made to swear by Allah (saying): We will not take a bribe, even though it were (on behalf of) a near kinsman nor will we

hide the testimony of Allah, for then indeed we should be of the sinful.

107. But then, if it is afterwards ascertained that both of them merit (the suspicion of) sin, let two others take their place of those nearly concerned, and let them swear by Allah, (saying): Verily our testimony is truer than their testimony and we have not transgressed (the bounds of duty), for then indeed we should be of the evildoers.

108. Thus it is more likely that they will bear true witness of fear that after their oath the oath (of others) will be taken. So be mindful of your duty (to Allah) and hearken. Allah guideth not the froward folk.

109. In the day when Allah gathereth together the messengers, and saith: What was your response (from mankind)? they say: We have no knowledge, Lo! Thou, only Thou art the Knower of Things Hidden.

110. Then Allah saith: O Jesus, son of Mary! Remember My favour unto thee and unto thy mother; how I strengthened thee with the holy Spirit, so that thou spakest unto mankind in the cradle as in maturity; and how I taught thee the Scripture and Wisdom and the Torah and the Gospel; and how thou didst shape of clay as it were the likeness of a bird by My permission, and didst blow upon it and it was a bird by My permission, and thou didst heal him who was born blind and the leper by My permission; and how thou didst raise the dead by My permission; and how I restrained the Children of Israel from (harming) thee when thou camest unto them with clear proofs, and those of them who disbelieved exclaimed: This is naught else than mere magic;

111. And when I inspired the disciples, (saying): Believe in Me and in My messenger, they said: We believe. Bear witness that we have surrendered (unto Thee).

112. When the disciples said: O Jesus, son of Mary! Is thy Lord able to send down for us a table spread with food from heaven? He said: Observe your duty to Allah, if ye are true believers.

113. (They said:) We wish to eat thereof, that we may satisfy our hearts and know that thou hast spoken truth to us, and that thereof we may be witnesses.

114. Jesus, son of Mary, said: O Allah, Lord of us! Send down for us a table spread with food from heaven, that it may be a feast for us, for the first of us and for the last of us, and a sign from Thee. Give us sustenance, for Thou art the Best of Sustainers.

115. Allah said: Lo! I send it down for you. And whoso disbelieveth of you afterward, him surely will I punish with a punishment wherewith I have not punished any of (My) creatures.

116. And when Allah saith: O Jesus, son of Mary! Didst thou say unto mankind: Take me and my mother for two gods beside Allah? he saith: Be glorified! It was not mine to utter that to which I had no right. If I used to say it, then Thou knewest it. Thou knowest what is in my mind, and I know not what is in Thy mind. Lo! Thou, only Thou art the Knower of Things Hidden.

117. I spake unto them only that which Thou commandedst me, (saying): Worship Allah, my Lord and your Lord. I was a witness of them while I dwelt among them, and when Thou tookest me Thou wast the Watcher over them. Thou art Witness over all things.

118. If Thou punish them, lo! they are Thy slaves, and if Thou forgive them (lo! they are Thy slaves). Lo! Thou, only Thou art the Mighty, the Wise.

119. Allah saith: This is a day in which their truthfulness profiteth the truthful, for theirs are Gardens underneath which rivers flow, wherein they are secure for ever. Allah taking pleasure in them and they in Him. That is the great triumph.

120. Unto Allah belongeth the Sovereignty of the heavens and the earth and whatsoever is therein, and He is Able to do all things.

SÛRAH 6

Al-An'âm " Cattle", takes its name from a word in v. 137, repeated in vv. 139, 140, where cattle are mentioned in connection with superstitious practices condemned by Al-Islâm.

With the possible exception of nine verses, which some authorities—e.g. Ibn Salâmah—ascribe to the Madînah period, the whole of this sûrah belongs to the year before the Hijrah. It is related, on the authority of Ibn 'Abbâs, that it was revealed in a single visitation. It is placed here on account of the subject, vindication of the Divine Unity, which fitly follows on the subjects of the previous sûrahs. The note of certain triumph is remarkable in the circumstances of its revelation, when the Prophet, after thirteen years of effort, saw himself obliged to flee from Mecca and seek help from strangers.

A late Meccan Sûrah.

CATTLE

Revealed at Mecca

In the name of Allah, the Beneficent, the Merciful.

1. Praise be to Allah, Who hath created the heavens and the earth, and hath appointed darkness and light. Yet those who disbelieve ascribe rivals unto their Lord.

2. He it is Who hath created you from clay, and hath decreed a term for you. A term is fixed with Him. Yet still ye doubt!

3. He is Allah in the heavens and in the earth. He knoweth both your secret and your utterance, and He knoweth what ye earn.

4. Never came there unto them a revelation of the revelations of Allah but they did turn away from it.

5. And they denied the truth when it came unto them. But there will come unto them the tidings of that which they used to deride.

6. See they not how many a generation We destroyed before them, whom We had established in the earth more firmly than We have established you, and We shed on them abundant showers from the sky, and made the rivers flow beneath them. Yet We destroyed them for their sins, and created after them another generation.

7. Had We sent down unto thee (Muhammad) (actual) writing upon parchment, so that they could feel it with their hands, those who disbelieve would have said: This is naught else than mere magic.

8. They say: Why hath not an angel been sent down unto him? If We sent down an angel, then the matter would be judged; no further time would be allowed them (for reflection).

9. Had We appointed an angel (Our messenger), We assuredly had made him (as) a man (that he might speak to men); and (thus) obscured for them (the truth) they (now) obscure.

10. Messengers (of Allah) have been derided before thee, but that whereat they scoffed surrounded such of them as did deride.

11. Say (unto the disbelievers): Travel in the land, and see the nature of the consequence for the rejecters!

12. Say: Unto whom belongeth whatsoever is in the heavens and the earth? Say: Unto Allah. He hath prescribed for Himself mercy, that He may bring you all together to a Day whereof there is no doubt. Those who ruin their own souls will not believe.

13. Unto Him belongeth whatsoever resteth in the night and the day. He is the Hearer, the Knower.

14. Say: Shall I choose for a protecting friend other than Allah, the Originator of the heavens and the earth, who feedeth

and is never fed? Say: I am ordered to be the first to surrender (unto Him). And be not thou (O Muhammad) of the idolaters.

15. Say: I fear, if I rebel against my Lord, the retribution of an Awful Day.

16. He from whom (such retribution) is averted on that day, (Allah) hath in truth had mercy on him. That will be the signal triumph.

17. If Allah touch thee with affliction, there is none that can relieve therefrom save Him, and if He touch thee with good fortune (there is none that can impair it); for He is Able to do all things.

18. He is the Omnipotent over His slaves, and He is the Wise, the Knower.

19. Say (O Muhammad): What thing is of most weight in testimony? Say: Allah is witness between you and me. And this Qur'ân hath been inspired in me, that I may warn therewith you and whomsoever it may reach. Do ye in sooth bear witness that there are gods beside Allah? Say: I bear no such witness. Say: He is only One God. Lo! I am innocent of that which ye associate (with Him).

20. Those unto whom We gave the Scripture recognise (this Revelation) as they recognise their sons. Those who ruin their own sons will not believe.

21. Who doth greater wrong than he who inventeth a lie against Allah and denieth His revelations? Lo! the wrongdoers will not be successful.

22. And on the day We gather them together We shall say unto those who ascribed partners (unto Allah): Where are (now) those partners of your make-believe?

23. Then will they have no contention save that they will say: By Allah, our Lord, we never were idolaters.

24. See how they lie against themselves, and (how) the thing which they devised hath failed them!

25. Of them are some who listen unto thee, but We have placed upon their hearts veils, lest they should understand, and in their ears a deafness. If they saw every token they would not believe therein; to the point that, when they come unto thee to argue with thee, the disbelievers say: This is naught else than fables of the men of old.

26. And they forbid (men) from it and avoid it, and they ruin none save themselves, though they perceive not.

27. If thou couldst see when they are set before the Fire and say: Oh, would that we might return! Then would we not deny the revelations of our Lord but we would be of the believers!

28. Nay, but that hath become clear unto them which before they used to hide. And if they were sent back they would return

unto that which they are forbidden. Lo! they are liars.

29. And they say: There is naught save our life of the world, and we shall not be raised (again).

30. If thou couldst see when they are set before their Lord! He will say: Is not this real? They will say: Yea, verily, by our Lord! He will say: Taste now the retribution for that ye used to disbelieve.

31. They indeed are losers who deny their meeting with Allah until, when the hour cometh on them suddenly, they cry: Alas for us, that we neglected it! They bear upon their backs their burdens. Ah, evil is that which they bear!

32. Naught is the life of the world save a pastime and a sport. Better far is the abode of the Hereafter for those who keep their duty (to Allah). Have ye then no sense?

33. We know well how their talk grieveth thee, though in truth they deny not thee (Muhammad) but evildoers flout the revelations of Allah.

34. Messengers indeed have been denied before thee, and they were patient under the denial and the persecution till Our succour reached them. There is none to alter the decisions of Allah. Already there hath reached thee (somewhat) of the tidings of the messengers (We sent before).

35. And if their aversion is grievous unto thee, then, if thou canst, seek a way down into the earth or a ladder unto the sky that thou mayst bring unto them a portent (to convince them all)!—If Allah willed, He could have brought them all together to the guidance—So be not thou among the foolish ones.

36. Only those can accept who hear. As for the dead, Allah will raise them up; then unto Him they will be returned.

37. They say: Why hath no portent been sent down upon him from his Lord? Say: Lo! Allah is Able to send down a portent. But most of them know not.

38. There is not an animal in the earth, nor a flying creature flying on two wings, but they are peoples like unto you. We have neglected nothing in the Book (of Our decrees). Then unto their Lord they will be gathered.

39. Those who deny our revelations are deaf and dumb in darkness. Whom Allah will He sendeth astray, and whom He will He placeth on a straight path.

40. Say: Can ye see yourselves, if the punishment of Allah come upon you or the Hour come upon you, calling upon other than Allah? Do ye then call (for help) to any other than Allah? (Answer that) if ye are truthful.

41. Nay, but unto Him ye call, and He removeth that because of which ye call unto Him, if He will, and ye forget whatever

partners ye ascribed unto Him.

42. We have sent already unto peoples that were before thee, and We visited them with tribulation and adversity, in order that they might grow humble.

43. If only, when our disaster came on them, they had been humble! But their hearts were hardened and the devil made all that they used to do seem fair unto them!

44. Then, when they forgot that whereof they had been reminded, We opened unto them the gates of all things till, even as they were rejoicing in that which they were given, We seized them unawares, and lo! they were dumbfounded.

45. So of the people who did wrong the last remnant was cut off. Praise be to Allah, Lord of the Worlds!

46. Say: Have ye imagined, if Allah should take away your hearing and your sight and seal your hearts, who is the God who could restore it to you save Allah? See how We display the revelations unto them? Yet still they turn away.

47. Say: Can ye see yourselves, if the punishment of Allah come upon you unawares or openly. Would any perish save wrongdoing folk?

48. We send not the messengers save as bearers of good news and warners. Whoso believeth and doeth right, there shall no fear come upon them neither shall they grieve.

49. But as for those who deny Our revelations, torment will afflict them for that they used to disobey.

50. Say (O Muhammad, to the disbelievers): I say not unto you (that) I possess the treasures of Allah, nor that I have knowledge of the Unseen; and I say not unto you: Lo! I am an angel. I follow only that which is inspired in me. Say: Are the blind man and the seer equal? Will ye not then take thought.

51. Warn hereby those who fear (because they know) that they will be gathered unto their Lord, for whom there is no protecting friend nor intercessor beside Him, that they may ward off (evil).

52. Repel not those who call upon their Lord at morn and evening, seeking His Countenance. Thou art not accountable for them in aught, nor are they accountable for thee in aught, that thou shouldst repel them and be of the wrongdoers.

53. And even so do We try some of them by others, that they say: Are these they whom Allah favoureth among us? Is not Allah best aware of the thanksgivers?

54. And when those who believe in Our revelations come unto thee, say: Peace be unto you! Your Lord hath prescribed for Himself mercy, that whoso of you doeth evil and repenteth afterward thereof and doeth right, (for him) lo! Allah is

Forgiving, Merciful.

55. Thus do We expound the revelations that the way of the unrighteous may be manifest.

56. Say: I am forbidden to worship those on whom ye call instead of Allah. Say: I will not follow your desires, for then should I go astray and I should not be of the rightly guided.

57. Say: I am (relying) on clear proof from my Lord, while ye deny Him. I have not that for which ye are impatient. The decision is for Allah only. He telleth the truth and He is the Best of Deciders.

58. Say: If I had that for which ye are impatient, then would the case (ere this) have been decided between me and you. Allah is best aware of the wrongdoers.

59. And with Him are the keys of the invisible. None but He knoweth them. And He knoweth what is in the land and the sea. Not a leaf falleth but He knoweth it, not a grain amid the darkness of the earth, naught of wet or dry but (it is noted) in a clear record.

60. He it is Who gathereth you at night and knoweth that which ye commit by day. Then He raiseth you again to life therein, that the term appointed (for you) may be accomplished. And afterward unto Him is your return. Then He will proclaim unto you what ye used to do.

61. He is the Omnipotent over His slaves. He sendeth guardians over you until, when death cometh unto one of you, Our messengers receive him, and they neglect not.

62. Then are they restored unto Allah, their Lord, the Just. Surely His is the judgement. And He is the most swift of reckoners.

63. Say: Who delivereth you from the darkness of the land and the sea? Ye call upon Him humbly and in secret, (saying): If we are delivered from this (fear) we truly will be of the thankful.

64. Say: Allah delivereth you from this and from all affliction. Yet ye attribute partners unto Him.

65. Say: He is able to send punishment upon you from above you or from beneath your feet, or to bewilder you with dissension and make you taste the tyranny one of another. See how We display the revelations so that they may understand.

66. Thy people (O Muhammad) have denied it, though it is the Truth. Say: I am not put in charge of you.

67. For every announcement there is a term, and ye will come to know.

68. And when thou seest those who meddle with Our revelations, withdraw from them until they meddle with

another topic. And if the devil cause thee to forget, sit not, after the remembrance, with the congregation of wrongdoers.

69. Those who ward off (evil) are not accountable for them in aught, but the Reminder (must be given them) that haply they (too) may ward off (evil).

70. And forsake those who take their religion for a pastime and a jest, and whom the life of the world beguileth. Remind (mankind) hereby lest a soul be destroyed by what it earneth. It hath beside Allah no friend nor intercessor, and though it offer every compensation it will not be accepted from it. Those are they who perish by their own deserts. For them is drink of boiling water and a painful doom, because they disbelieved.

71. Say: Shall we cry, instead of unto Allah, unto that which neither profiteth us nor hurteth us, and shall we turn back after Allah hath guided us, like one bewildered whom the devils have infatuated in the earth, who hath companions who invite him to the guidance (saying): Come unto us? Say: Lo! the guidance of Allah is Guidance, and we are ordered to surrender to the Lord of the Worlds.

72. And to establish worship and ward off (evil), and He it is unto Whom ye will be gathered.

73. He it is Who created the heavens and the earth in truth. In that day when He saith: Be! it is. His word is the truth, and His will be the Sovereignty on the day when the trumpet is blown. Knower of the invisible and the visible, He is the Wise, the Aware.

74. (Remember) when Abraham said unto his father Azar: Takest thou idols for gods? Lo! I see thee and thy folk in error manifest.

75. Thus did We show Abraham the kingdom of the heavens and the earth that he might be of those possessing certainty.

76. When the night grew dark upon him he beheld a star. He said: This is my Lord. But when it set, he said: I love not things that set.

77. And when he saw the moon uprising, he exclaimed: This is my Lord. But when it set, he said: Unless my Lord guide me, I surely shall become one of the folk who are astray.

78. And when he saw the sun uprising, he cried: This is my Lord! This is greater! And when it set he exclaimed: O my people! Lo! I am free from all that ye associate (with Him).

79. Lo! I have turned my face toward Him Who created the heavens and the earth, as one by nature upright, and I am not of the idolaters.

80. His people argued with him. He said: Dispute ye with me concerning Allah when He hath, guided me? I fear not at all that which ye set beside Him unless my Lord willeth. My Lord includeth all things in His knowledge. Will ye not then remember?

81. How should I fear that which ye set beside Him, when ye fear not to set up beside Allah that for which He hath revealed unto you no warrant? Which of the two factions hath more right to safety? (Answer me that) if ye have knowledge.

82. Those who believe and obscure not their belief by wrong-doing, theirs is safety; and they are rightly guided.

83. That is Our argument. We gave it unto Abraham against his folk. We raise unto degrees of wisdom whom We will. Lo! thy Lord is Wise, Aware.

84. And we bestowed upon him Isaac and Jacob; each of them We guided; and Noah did We guide aforetime; and of his seed (We guided) David and Solomon and Job and Joseph and Moses and Aaron. Thus do We reward the good.

85. And Zachariah and John and Jesus and Elias. Each one (of them) was of the righteous.

86. And Ishmael and Elisha and Jonah and Lot. Each one of them did We prefer above (Our) creatures.

87. With some of their forefathers and their offspring and their brethren; and We chose them and guided them unto a straight path.

88. Such is the guidance of Allah wherewith He guideth whom He will of His bondmen. But if they had set up (for worship) aught beside Him, (all) that they did would have been in vain.

89. Those are they unto whom We gave the Scripture and command and prophethood. But if these disbelieve therein, then indeed We shall entrust it to a people who will not be disbelievers therein.

90. Those are they whom Allah guideth, so follow their guidance. Say (O Muhammad, unto mankind): I ask of you no fee for it. Lo! it is naught but a Reminder to (His) creatures.

91. And they measure not the power of Allah its true measure when they say: Allah hath naught revealed unto a human being. Say (unto the Jews who speak thus): Who revealed the Book which Moses brought, a light and guidance for mankind, which ye have put on parchments which ye show, but ye hide much (thereof), and by which ye were taught that which ye knew not yourselves nor (did) your fathers (know it)? Say: Allah. Then leave them to their play of cavilling.

92. And this is a blessed Scripture which We have revealed, confirming that which (was revealed) before it, that thou mayst

warn the Mother of Villages and those around her. Those who believe in the Hereafter believe herein, and they are careful of their worship.

93. Who is guilty of more wrong than he who forgeth a lie against Allah, or saith: I am inspired, when he is not inspired in aught; and who saith: I will reveal the life of that which Allah hath revealed? If thou couldst see, when the wrongdoers reach the pangs of death and the angels stretch their hands out, saying: Deliver up your souls. This day ye are awarded doom of degradation for that ye spake concerning Allah other than the truth, and scorned His portents.

94. Now have ye come unto Us solitary as We did create you at the first, and ye have left behind you all that We bestowed upon you, and We behold not with you those your intercessors, of whom ye claimed that they possessed a share in you. Now is the bond between you severed, and that which ye presumed hath failed you.

95. Lo! Allah (it is) who splitteth the grain of corn and the date-stone (for sprouting). He bringeth forth the living from the dead, and is the bringer-forth of the dead from the living. Such is Allah. How then are ye perverted?

96. He is the Cleaver of the Daybreak, and He hath appointed the night for stillness, and the sun and the moon for reckoning. That is the measuring of the Mighty, the Wise.

97. And He it is Who hath set for you the stars that ye may guide your course by them amid the darkness of the land and the sea. We have detailed Our revelations for a people who have knowledge.

98. And He it is Who hath produced you from a single being, and (hath given you) a habitation and a repository. We have detailed Our revelations for a people who have understanding.

99. He it is Who sendeth down water from the sky, and therewith We bring forth buds of every kind; We bring forth the green blade from which we bring forth the thick-clustered grain; and from the date-palm, from the pollen thereof, spring pendant bunches; and (We bring forth) gardens of grapes, and the olive and the pomegranate, alike and unlike. Look upon the fruit thereof, when they bear fruit, and upon its ripening. Lo! herein verily are portents for a people who believe.

100. Yet they ascribe as partners unto Him the jinn, although He did create them, and impute falsely, without knowledge, sons and daughters unto Him. Glorified be He and high exalted above (all) that they ascribe (unto Him).

101. The Originator of the heavens and the earth! How can He have a child, when there is for Him no consort, when He

created all things and is Aware of all things?

102. Such is Allah, your Lord. There is no God save Him, the Creator of all things, so worship Him. And He taketh care of all things.

103. Vision comprehendeth Him not, but He comprehendeth (all) vision. He is the Subtle, the Aware.

104. Proofs have come unto you from your Lord, so whoso see h, it is for his own good, and whoso is blind is blind to his own hurt. And I am not a keeper over you.

105. Thus do We display Our revelations that they may say (unto thee, Muhammad): "Thou hast studied," and that We may make (it) clear for people who have knowledge.

106. Follow that which is inspired in thee from thy Lord; there is no God save Him; and turn away from the idolaters.

107. Had Allah willed, they had not been idolatrous. We have not set thee as a keeper over them, nor art thou responsible for them.

108. Revile not those unto whom they pray beside Allah lest they wrongfully revile Allah through ignorance. Thus unto every nation have We made their deed seem fair. Then unto their Lord is their return, and He will tell them what they used to do.

109. And they swear a solemn oath by Allah that if there come unto them a portent they will believe therein. Say: Portents are with Allah and (so is) that which telleth you that if such came unto them they would not believe.

110. We confound their hearts and their eyes. As they believed not therein at the first, We let them wander blindly on in their contumacy.

111. And though We should send down the angels unto them, and the dead should speak unto them, and We should gather against them all things in array, they would not believe unless Allah so willed. Howbeit, most of them are ignorant.

112. Thus have We appointed unto every Prophet an adversary—devils of humankind and jinn who inspire in one another plausible discourse through guile. If thy Lord willed, they would not do so; so leave them alone with their devising.

113. That the hearts of those who believe not in the Hereafter may incline thereto, and that they may take pleasure therein, and that they may earn what they are earning.

114. Shall I seek other than Allah for judge, when He it is who hath revealed unto you (this) Scripture, fully explained? Those unto whom We gave the Scripture (aforetime) know that it is revealed from thy Lord in truth. So be not thou (O

Muhammad) of the waverers.

115. Perfected is the Word of thy Lord in truth and justice. There is naught that can change His words. He is the Hearer, the Knower.

116. If thou obeyedst most of those on earth they would mislead thee far from Allah's way. They follow naught but an opinion, and they do but guess.

117. Lo! thy Lord, He Knoweth best who erreth from His way; and He knoweth best (who are) the rightly guided.

118. Eat of that over which the name of Allah hath been mentioned, if ye are believers in His revelations.

119. How should ye not eat of that over which the name of Allah hath been mentioned, when He hath explained unto you that which is forbidden unto you, unless ye are compelled thereto. But lo! many are led astray by their own lusts through ignorance. Lo! thy Lord, He is best aware of the transgressors.

120. Forsake the outwardness of sin and the inwardness thereof. Lo! those who garner sin will be awarded that which they have earned.

121. And eat not of that whereon Allah's name hath not been mentioned, for lo! it is abomination. Lo! the devils do inspire their minions to dispute with you. But if ye obey them, ye will be in truth idolaters.

122. Is he who was dead and We have raised him unto life, and set for him a light wherein he walketh among men, as him whose similitude is in utter darkness whence he cannot emerge? Thus is their conduct made fair seeming for the disbelievers.

123. And thus have We made in every city great ones of its wicked ones, that they should plot therein. They do but plot against themselves, though they perceive not.

124. And when a token cometh unto them, they say: We will not believe till we are given that which Allah's messengers are given. Allah knoweth best with whom to place His message. Humiliation from Allah and heavy punishment will smite the guilty for their scheming.

125. And whomsoever it is Allah's will to guide, He expandeth his bosom unto the Surrender, and whomsoever it is His Will to send astray, He maketh his bosom close and narrow as if he were engaged in sheer ascent. Thus Allah layeth ignominy upon whose who believe not.

126. This is the path of thy Lord, a straight path. We have detailed Our revelations for a people who take heed.

127. For them is the abode of peace with their Lord. He will be their Protecting Friend because of what they used to

do.

128. In the day when He will gather them together (He will say): O ye assembly of the jinn! Many of humankind did ye seduce. And their adherents among humankind will say: Our Lord! We enjoyed one another, but now we have arrived at the appointed term which Thou appointedst for us. He will say: Fire is your home. Abide therein for ever, save him whom Allah willeth (to deliver). Lo! thy Lord is Wise, Aware.

129. Thus We let some of the wrongdoers have power over others because of what they are wont to earn.

130. O ye assembly of the jinn and humankind! Came there not unto you messengers of your own who recounted unto you My tokens and warned you of the meeting of this your Day? They will say: We testify against ourselves. And the life of the world beguiled them. And they testify against themselves that they were disbelievers.

131. This is because thy Lord destroyeth not the townships arbitrarily while their people are unconscious (of the wrong they do).

132. For all there will be ranks from what they did. Thy Lord is not unaware of what they do.

133. Thy Lord is the Absolute, the Lord of Mercy. If He will, He can remove you and can cause what He will to follow after you, even as He raised you from the seed of other folk.

134. Lo! that which ye are promised will surely come to pass, and ye cannot escape.

135. Say (O Muhammad): O my people! Work according to your power. Lo! I too am working. Thus ye will come to know for which of us will be the happy sequel. Lo! the wrongdoers will not be successful.

136. They assign unto Allah, of the crops and cattle which He created, a portion, and they say: "This is Allah's" — in their make-believe — "and this is for (His) partners in regard to us." Thus that which (they assign) unto His partners in them reacheth not Allah and that which (they assign) unto Allah goeth to their (so-called) partners. Evil is their ordinance.

137. Thus have their (so-called) partners (of Allah) made the killing of their children to seem fair unto many of the idolaters, that they may ruin them and make their faith obscure for them. Had Allah willed (it otherwise), they had not done so. So leave them alone with their devices.

138. And they say: Such cattle and crops are forbidden. No one is to eat of them save whom We will — in their make-believe — cattle whose backs are forbidden, cattle over which they mention not the name of Allah. (All that is) a lie against

Him. He will repay them for that which they invent.

139. And they say: That which is in the bellies of such cattle is reserved for our males and is forbidden to our wives; but if it be born dead, then they (all) may be partakers thereof. He will reward them for their attribution (of such ordinances unto Him), He is Wise, Aware.

140. They are losers who besottedly have slain their children without knowledge, and have forbidden that which Allah bestowed upon them, inventing a lie against Allah. They indeed have gone astray and are not guided.

141. He it is Who produceth gardens trellised and untrellised, and the date-palm, and crops of divers flavour, and the olive and the pomegranate, like and unlike. Eat ye of the fruit thereof when it fruiteth, and pay the due thereof upon the Harvest day, and be not prodigal. Lo! Allah loveth not the prodigals.

142. And of the cattle (He produceth) some for burdens, some for food. Eat of that which Allah hath bestowed upon you, and follow not the footsteps of the devil, for lo! he is an open foe to you.

143. Eight pairs: Of the sheep twain, and of the goats twain. Say: Hath He forbidden the two males or the two females, or that which the wombs of the two females contain? Expound to me (the case) with knowledge, if ye are truthful.

144. And of the camels twain and of the oxen twain. Say: Hath He forbidden the two males or the two females, or that which the wombs of the two females contain; or were ye by to witness when Allah commanded you (all) this? Then who doth greater wrong than he who deviseth a lie concerning Allah, that he may lead mankind astray without knowledge. Lo! Allah guideth not wrongdoing folk.

145. Say: I find not in that which is revealed unto me aught prohibited to an eater that he eat thereof, except it be carrion, or blood poured forth, or swineflesh—for that verily is foul—or the abomination which was immolated to the name of other than Allah. But whoso is compelled (thereto), neither craving nor transgressing, (for him) lo! your Lord is Forgiving, Merciful.

146. Unto those who are Jews We forbade every animal with claws. And of the oxen and the sheep forbade We unto them the fat thereof save that upon the backs or the entrails, or that which is mixed with the bone. That We awarded them for their rebellion. And lo! We verily are truthful.

147. So if they give the lie to thee (Muhammad), say: Your Lord is a lord of all-embracing mercy, and His wrath will never be withdrawn from guilty folk.

148. They who are idolaters will say: Had Allah willed, we had not ascribed (unto Him) partners neither had our fathers, nor had we forbidden aught. Thus did those who were before them give the lie (to Allah's messengers) till they tasted of the fear of Us. Say: Have ye any knowledge that ye can adduce for Us? Lo! ye follow naught but an opinion, Lo! ye do but guess.

149. Say—For Allah's is the final argument—Had He willed He could indeed have guided all of you.

150. Say: Come, bring your witnesses who can bear witness that Allah forbade (all) this. And if they bear witness, do not thou bear witness with them. Follow thou not the whims of those who deny Our revelations, those who believe not in the Hereafter and deem (others) equal with their Lord.

151. Say: Come, I will recite unto you that which your Lord hath made a sacred duty for you: that ye ascribe nothing as partner unto Him and that ye do good to parents, and that ye slay not your children because of penury—We provide for you and for them—and that ye draw not nigh to lewd things whether open or concealed. And that ye slay not the life which Allah hath made sacred, save in the course of justice. This He had commanded you, in order that ye may discern.

152. And approach not the wealth of the orphan save with that which is better, till he reach maturity. Give full measure and full weight, in justice. We task not any soul beyond its scope. And if ye give your word, do justice thereunto, even though it be (against) a kinsman; and fulfil the convenant of Allah. This He commandeth you that haply ye may remember.

153. And (He commandeth you, saying): This is My straight path, so follow it. Follow not other ways, lest ye be parted from His way. This hath He ordained for you, that ye may ward off (evil).

154. Again, We gave the Scripture unto Moses, complete for him who would do good, an explanation of all things, a guidance and a mercy, that they might believe in the meeting with their Lord.

155. And this is a blessed Scripture which We have revealed. So follow it and ward off (evil), that ye may find mercy.

156. Lest ye should say: The scripture was revealed only to two sects before us, and we in sooth were unaware of what they read.

157. Or lest ye should say: If the Scripture had been revealed unto us, we surely had been better guided than are they. Now hath there come unto you a clear proof from your Lord, a guidance and a mercy; and who doeth greater wrong

than he who denieth the revelations of Allah, and turneth away from them? We award unto those who turn away from Our revelations an evil doom because of their aversion.

158. Wait they, indeed, for nothing less than that the angels should come unto them, or thy Lord should come, or there should come one of the portents from thy Lord? In the day when one of the portents from thy Lord cometh, its belief availeth naught a soul which theretofore believed not, nor in its belief earned good (by works). Say: Wait ye! Lo! We (too) are waiting.

159. Lo! As for those who sunder their religion and become schismatics, no concern at all hast thou with them. Their case will go to Allah, Who then will tell them what they used to do.

160. Whoso bringeth a good deed will receive tenfold the like thereof, while whoso bringeth an ill deed will be awarded but the like thereof; and they will not be wronged.

161. Say: Lo! As for me, my Lord hath guided me unto a straight path, a right religion, the community of Abraham, the upright, who was no idolater.

162. Say: Lo! my worship and my sacrifice and my living and my dying are for Allah, Lord of the Worlds.

163. He hath no partner. This am I commanded, and I am first of those who surrender (unto Him).

164. Say: Shall I seek another than Allah for Lord, when He is Lord of all things? Each soul earneth only on its own account, nor doth any laden bear another's load. Then unto your Lord is your return and He will tell you that wherein ye differed.

165. He it is who hath placed you as viceroys of the earth and hath exalted some of you in rank above others, that He may try you by (the test of) that which He hath given you. Lo! Thy Lord is swift in prosecution, and lo! He is Forgiving, Merciful.

SÛRAH 7

Al-A'râf, "The Heights", takes its name from a word in v. 46," And on the Heights are men who know them all by their marks." The best authorities assign the whole of it to about the same period as Sûrah 6, *i.e.* the Prophet's last year in Mecca, though some consider vv. 163-167 to have been revealed at Al-Madînah. The subject may be said to be the opponents of God's will and purpose, from Satan onward, through the history of Divine Guidance.

A late Meccan Sûrah.

THE HEIGHTS

Revealed at Mecca

In the name of Allah, the Beneficent, the Merciful.

1. Alif. Lâm. Mîm. Sâd.

2. (It is) a Scripture that is revealed unto thee (Muhammad) — so let there be no heaviness in thy heart therefrom — that thou mayest warn thereby, and (it is) a Reminder unto believers.

3. (Saying): Follow that which is sent down unto you from your Lord, and follow no protecting friends beside Him. Little do ye recollect!

4. How many a township have We destroyed! As a raid by night, or while they slept at noon, Our terror came unto them.

5. No plea had they, when Our terror came unto them, save that they said: Lo! We were wrongdoers.

6. Then verily We shall question those unto whom (Our message) hath been sent, and verily We shall question the messengers.

7. Then verily We shall narrate unto them (the event) with knowledge, for We were not absent (when it came to pass).

8. The weighing on that day is the true (weighing). As for those whose scale is heavy, they are the successful.

9. And as for those whose scale is light: those are they who lose their souls because they disbelieved Our revelations.

10. And We have given you (mankind) power in the earth, and appointed for you therein a livelihood. Little give ye thanks!

11. And We created you, then fashioned you, then told the angels: Fall ye prostrate before Adam! And they fell prostrate, all save Iblîs, who was not of those who make prostration.

12. He said: What hindered thee that thou didst not fall prostrate when I bade thee? (Iblîs) said: I am better than him. Thou createdst me of fire while him Thou didst create of mud.

13. He said: Then go down hence! It is not for thee to show pride here, so go forth! Lo! thou art of those degarded.

14. He said: Reprieve me till the day when they are raised (from the dead).

15. He said: Lo! thou art of those reprieved.

16. He said: Now, because thou hast sent me astray, verily I shall lurk in ambush for them on Thy Right Path.

17. Then I shall come upon them from before them and from behind them and from their right hands and from their left hands, and Thou wilt not find most of them beholden (unto Thee).

18. He said: Go forth from hence, degraded, banished. As for such of them as follow thee, surely I will fill hell with all of

you.

19. And (unto man): O Adam! Dwell thou and thy wife in the Garden and eat from whence ye will, but come not nigh this tree lest ye become wrongdoers.

20. Then Satan whispered to them that he might manifest unto them that which was hidden from them of their shame, and he said: Your Lord forbade you from this tree only lest ye should become angels or become of the immortals.

21. And he swore unto them (saying): Lo! I am a sincere adviser unto you.

22. Thus did he lead them on with guile. And when they tasted of the tree their shame was manifest to them and they began to hide (by heaping) on themselves some of the leaves of the Garden. And their Lord called them, (saying): Did I not forbid you from that tree and tell you: Lo! Satan is an open enemy to you?

23. They said: Our Lord! We have wronged ourselves. If Thou forgive us not and have not mercy on us, surely we are of the lost!

24. He said: Go down (from hence), one of you a foe unto the other. There will be for you on earth a habitation and provision for a while.

25. He said: There shall ye live, and there shall ye die, and thence shall ye be brought forth.

26. O Children of Adam! We have revealed unto you raiment to conceal your shame, and splendid vesture, but the raiment of restraint from evil, that is best. This is of the revelations of Allah, that they may remember.

27. O Children of Adam! Let not Satan seduce you as he caused your (first) parents to go forth from the Garden and tore off from them their robe (of innocence) that he might manifest their shame to them. Lo! He seeth you, he and his tribe, from whence ye see him not. Lo! We have made the devils protecting friends for those who believe not.

28. And when they do some lewdness they say: We found our fathers doing it and Allah hath enjoined it on us. Say: Allah, verily, enjoineth not lewdness. Tell ye concerning Allah that which ye know not?

29. Say: My Lord enjoineth justice. And set your faces, upright (toward Him) at every place of worship and call upon Him, making religion pure for Him (only). As He brought you into being, so return ye (unto Him).

30. A party hath He led aright, while error hath just hold over (another) party, for lo! they choose the devils for protecting friends instead of Allah and deem that they are rightly guided.

31. O Children of Adam! Look to your adornment at every

place of worship, and eat and drink, but be not prodigal. Lo! he loveth not the prodigals.

32. Say: Who hath forbidden the adornment of Allah which He hath brought forth for His bondmen, and the good things of His providing? Say: Such, on the Day of Resurrection, will be only for those who believed during the life of the world. Thus do We detail Our revelations for people who have knowledge.

. 33. Say: My Lord forbiddeth only indecencies, such of them as are apparent and such as are within, and sin and wrongful oppression, and that ye associate with Allah that for which no warrant hath been revealed, and that ye tell concerning Allah that which ye know not.

34. And every nation hath its term, and when its term cometh, they cannot put it off an hour nor yet advance (it).

35. O Children of Adam! If messengers of your own come unto you who narrate unto you My revelations, then whosoever refraineth from evil and amendeth—there shall no fear come upon them neither shall they grieve.

36. But they who deny Our revelations and scorn them—such are rightful owners of Fire; they will abide therein.

37. Who doeth greater wrong than he who inventeth a lie concerning Allah or denieth Our tokens. (For such) their appointed portion of the Book (of destiny) reacheth them till, when Our messengers come to gather them, they say: Where (now) is that to which ye cried beside Allah? They say: They have departed from us. And they testify against themselves that they were disbelievers.

38. He saith: Enter into the Fire among nations of the jinn and humankind who passed away before you. Every time a nation entereth, it curseth its sister (nation) till, when they have all been made to follow one another thither, the last of them saith unto the first of them: Our Lord! These led us astray, so give them double torment of the Fire. He saith: For each one there is double (torment), but ye know not.

39. And the first of them saith unto the last of them: Ye were no whit better than us, so taste the doom for which ye used to earn.

40. Lo! they who deny Our revelations and scorn them, for them the gates of Heaven will not be opened nor will they enter the Garden until the camel goeth through the needle's eye. Thus do We requite the guilty.

41. Theirs will be a bed of Hell, and over them coverings (of Hell). Thus do We requite wrongdoers.

42. But (as for) those who believe and do good works—We tax not any soul beyond its scope—Such are rightful owners

of the Garden. They abide therein.

43. And We remove whatever rancour maybe in theirs hearts. Rivers flow beneath them. And they say: The praise to Allah, Who hath guided us to this. We could not truly have been led aright if Allah had not guided us. Verily the messengers of our Lord did bring the Truth. And it is cried unto them: This is the Garden. Ye inherit it for what ye used to do.

44. And the dwellers of the Garden cry unto the dwellers of the Fire: We have found that which our Lord promised us (to be) the Truth. Have ye (too) found that which your Lord promised the Truth? They say: Yea, verily. And a crier in between them crieth: The curse of Allah is on evildoers.

45. Who debar (men) from the path of Allah and would have it crooked, and who are disbelievers in the Last Day.

46. Between them is a veil. And on the Heights are men who know them all by their marks. And they call unto the dwellers of the Garden: Peace be unto you! They enter it not although they hope (to enter).

47. And when their eyes are turned toward the dwellers of the Fire, they say: Our Lord! Place us not with the wrongdoing folk.

48. And the dwellers on the Heights call unto men whom they know by their marks, (saying): What did your multitude and that in which ye took your pride avail you?

49. Are these they of whom ye swore that Allah would not show them mercy? (Unto them it hath been said): Enter the Garden. No fear shall come upon you nor is it ye who will grieve.

50. And the dwellers of the Fire cry out unto the dwellers of the Garden; Pour on us some water or some of that wherewith Allah hath provided you. They say: Lo! Allah hath forbidden both to disbelievers (in His guidance).

51. Who took their religion for a sport and pastime, and whom the life of the world beguiled. So this day We have forgotten them even as they forgot the meeting of this Day and as they used to deny Our tokens.

52. Verily We have brought them a Scripture which We expound with knowledge, a guidance and a mercy for a people who believe.

53. Await they aught save the fulfilment thereof? On the day when the fulfilment thereof cometh, those who were before forgetful thereof will say: The messengers of our Lord did bring the Truth? Have we any intercessors, that they may intercede for us? Or can we be returned (to life on earth), that we may act otherwise than we used to act? They have lost their souls,

and that which they devised hath failed them.

54. Lo! your Lord is Allah Who created the heavens and the earth in six Days, then mounted He the Throne. He covereth the night with the day, which is in haste to follow it, and hath made the sun and the moon and the stars subservient by His command. His verily is all creation and commandment. Blessed be Allah, the Lord of the Worlds!

55. (O mankind!) Call upon your Lord humbly and in secret. Lo! He loveth not aggressors.

56. Work not confusion in the earth after the fair ordering (thereof), and call on Him in fear and hope. Lo! the mercy of Allah is nigh unto the good.

57. And He it is Who sendeth the winds as tidings heralding His mercy, till, when they bear a cloud heavy (with rain), We lead it to a dead land, and then cause water to descend thereon and thereby bring forth fruits of every kind. Thus bring We forth the dead. Haply ye may remember.

58. As for the good land, its vegetation cometh forth by permission of its Lord; while as for that which is bad, only evil cometh forth (from it). Thus do We recount the tokens for people who give thanks.

59. We sent Noah (of old) unto his people, and he said: O my people! Serve Allah. Ye have no other God save Him. Lo! I fear for you the retribution of an Awful Day.

60. The chieftains of his people said: Lo! we see thee surely in plain error.

61. He said: O My people! There is no error in me, but I am a messenger from the Lord of the Worlds.

62. I convey unto you the messages of my Lord and give good counsel unto you, and know from Allah that which ye know not.

63. Marvel ye that there should come unto you a Reminder from your Lord by means of a man among you, that he may warn you, and that ye may keep from evil, and that haply ye may find mercy.

64. But they denied him, so We saved him and those with him in the ship, and We drowned those who denied Our tokens. Lo! they were blind folk.

65. And unto (the tribe of) A'âd (We sent) their brother, Hûd. He said: O my people! Serve Allah. Ye have no other God save Him. Will ye not ward off (evil)?

66. The chieftains of his people, who were disbelieving, said: Lo! we surely see thee in foolishness, and lo! we deem thee of the liars.

67. He said: O my people! There is no foolishness in me, but

I am a messenger from the Lord of the Worlds.

68. I convey unto you the messages of my Lord and am for you a true advisor.

69. Marvel ye that there should come unto you a Reminder from your Lord by means of a man among you, that he may warn you? Remember how He made you viceroys after Noah's folk, and gave you growth of stature. Remember (all) the bounties of your Lord, that haply ye may be successful.

70. They said: Hast come unto us that we should serve Allah alone, and forsake what our fathers worshipped? Then bring upon us that wherewith thou threatenest us if thou art of the truthful!

71. He said: Terror and wrath from your Lord have already fallen on you. Would ye wrangle with me over names which ye have named, ye and your fathers, for which no warrant from Allah hath been revealed? Then await (the consequence), lo! I (also) am of those awaiting (it).

72. And We saved him and those with him by a mercy from Us. and We cut the root of those who denied Our revelations and were not believers.

73. And to (the tribe of) Thamûd (We sent) their brother Sâlih. He said: O my people! Serve Allah. Ye have no other God save Him. A wonder from your Lord hath come unto you. Lo! this is the camel of Allah, a token unto you; so let her feed in Allah's earth, and touch her not with hurt lest painful torment seize you.

74. And remember how He made you viceroys after A'âd and gave you station in the earth. Ye choose castles in the plains and hew the mountains into dwellings. So remember (all) the bounties of Allah and do not evil, making mischief in the earth.

75. The chieftains of his people, who were scornful, said unto those whom they despised, unto such of them as believed: Know ye that Sâlih is one sent from his Lord? They said: Lo! In that wherewith he hath been sent we are believers.

76. Those who were scornful said: Lo! in that which ye believe we are disbelievers.

77. So they hamstrung the she-camel, and they flouted the commandment of their Lord, and they said: O Sâlih! Bring upon us that thou threatenest if thou art indeed of those sent (from Allah).

78. So the earthquake seized them, and morning found them prostrate in their dwelling-place.

79. And Sâlih turned from them and said: O my people! I delivered my Lord's message unto you and gave you good advice, but ye love not good advisors.

80. And Lot! (Remember) when he said unto his folk: Will ye commit abomination such as no creature ever did before you?

81. Lo! ye come with lust unto men instead of women. Nay, but ye are wanton folk.

82. And the answer of his people was only that they said (one to another): Turn them out of your township. They are folk, forsooth, who keep behind.

83. And We rescued him and his household, save his wife, who was of those who stayed behind.

84. And We rained a rain upon them. See now the nature of the consequence for evildoers!

85. And unto Midian (We sent) their brother, Shu'eyb. He said: O my people! Serve Allah. Ye have no other God save Him. Lo! a clear proof hath come unto you from your Lord; so give full measure and full weight and wrong not mankind in their goods, and work not confusion in the earth after the fair ordering thereof. That will be better for you, if ye are believers.

86. Lurk not on every road to threaten (wayfarers), and to turn away from Allah's path him who believeth in Him, and to seek to make it crooked. And remember, when ye were but few, how He did multiply you. And see the nature of the consequence for the corrupters!

87. And if there is a party of you which believeth in that wherewith I have been sent, and there is a party which believeth not, then have patience until Allah judge between us. He is the best of all who deal in judgement.

88. The chieftains of his people, who were scornful, said: Surely we will drive thee out, O Shu'eyb, and those who believe with thee, from our township, unless ye return to our religion. He said: Even though we hate it?

89. We should have invented a lie against Allah if we returned to your religion after Allah hath rescued us from it. It is not for us to return to it unless Allah should (so) will. Our Lord comprehendeth all things in knowledge. In Allah do we put our trust. Our Lord! Decide with truth between us and our folk, for Thou art the best of those who make decision.

90. But the chieftains of his people, who were disbelieving, said: If ye follow Shu'eyb, then truly ye shall be the losers.

91. So the earthquake seized them, and morning found them prostrate in their dwelling-place.

92. Those who denied Shu'eyb became as though they had not dwelt there. Those who denied Shu'eyb, they were the losers.

93. So he turned from them and said: O my people! I

delivered my Lord's messages unto you and gave you good advice; then how can I sorrow for a people that rejected (truth)?

94. And We sent no prophet unto any township but We did afflict its folk with tribulation and adversity that haply they might grow humble.

95. Then changed We the evil plight for good till they grew affluent and said: Tribulation and distress did touch our fathers. Then We seized them unawares, when they perceived not.

96. And if the people of the townships had believed and kept from evil, surely We should have opened for them blessings from the sky and from the earth. But (unto every messenger) they gave the lie, and so We seized them on account of what they used to earn.

97. Are the people of the townships then secure from the coming of Our wrath upon them as a night-raid while they sleep?

98. Or are the people of the townships then secure from the coming of Our wrath upon them in the daytime while they play?

99. Are they then secure from Allah's scheme? None deemeth himself secure from Allah's scheme save folk that perish.

100. Is it not an indication to those who inherit the land after its people (who thus reaped the consequence of evil-doing) that, if We will, We can smite them for their sins and print upon their hearts so that they hear not?

101. Such were the townships. We relate some tidings of them unto thee (Muhammad). Their messengers verily came unto them with clear proofs (of Allah's Sovereignty), but they could not believe because they had before denied. Thus doth Allah print upon the hearts of disbelievers (that they hear not).

102. We found no (loyalty to any) covenant in most of them. Nay, most of them We found wrongdoers.

103. Then, after them, We sent Moses with our tokens unto Pharaoh and his chiefs, but they repelled them. Now, see the nature of the consequence for the corrupters!

104. Moses said: O Pharaoh! Lo! I am a messenger from the Lord of the Worlds.

105. Approved upon condition that I speak concerning Allah nothing but the truth. I come unto you (lords of Egypt) with a clear proof from your Lord. So let the Children of Israel go with me.

106. (Pharaoh) said: If thou comest with a token, then produce it, if thou art of those who speak the truth.

107. Then he flung down his staff and lo! it was a serpent manifest.

108. And he drew forth his hand (from his bosom), and lo! it was white for the beholders.

109. The chiefs of Pharaoh's people said: Lo! this is some knowing wizard.

110. Who would expel you from your land. Now what do ye advise?

111. They said (unto Pharaoh): Put him off (a while)—him and his brother—and send into the cities summoners.

112. To bring each knowing wizard unto thee.

113. And the wizards came to Pharaoh, saying: Surely there will be a reward for us if we are victors.

114. He answered: Yea, and surely ye shall be of those brought near (to me).

115. They said: O Moses! Either throw (first) or let us be the first throwers?

116. He said: Throw! And when they threw they cast a spell upon the people's eyes, and overawed them, and produced a mighty spell.

117. And We inspired Moses (saying): Throw thy staff! And lo! it swallowed up their lying show.

118. Thus was the Truth vindicated and that which they were doing was made vain.

119. Thus were they there defeated and brought low.

120. And the wizards fell down prostrate.

121. Crying: We believe in the Lord of the Worlds.

122. The Lord of Moses and Aaron.

123. Pharaoh said: Ye believe in Him before I give you leave! Lo! this is the plot that ye have plotted in the city that ye may drive its people hence. But ye shall come to know!

124. Surely I shall have your hands and feet cut off upon alternate sides. Then I shall crucify you every one.

125. They said: Lo! We are about to return unto our Lord!

126. Thou takest vengeance on us only forasmuch as we believed the tokens of our Lord when they came unto us. Our Lord! Vouchsafe unto us steadfastness and make us die as men who have surrendered (unto Thee).

127. The chiefs of Pharaoh's people said: (O King), wilt thou suffer Moses and his people to make mischief in the land, and flout thee and thy gods? He said: We will slay their sons and spare their women, for lo! we are in power over them.

128. And Moses said unto his people: Seek help in Allah and endure. Lo! the earth is Allah's. He giveth it for an inheritance to whom He will. And lo! the sequel is for those who keep their

duty (unto Him).

129. They said: We suffered hurt before thou camest unto us, and since thou hast come unto us. He said: It may be that your Lord is going to destroy your adversary and make you viceroys in the earth, that He may see how ye behave.

130. And We straitened Pharaoh's folk with famine and the dearth of fruits, that peradventure they might heed.

131. But whenever good befell them, they said: This is ours; and whenever evil smote them they ascribed it to the evil auspices of Moses and those with him. Surely their evil auspice was only with Allah. But most of them knew not.

132. And they said: Whatever portent thou bringest wherewith to bewitch us, we shall not put faith in thee.

133. So We sent them the flood and the locusts and the vermin and the frogs and the blood — a succession of clear signs. But they were arrogant and became guilty.

134. And when the terror fell on them they cried: O Moses! Pray for us unto thy Lord, because He hath a covenant with thee. If thou removest the terror from us we verily will trust thee and will let the Children of Israel go with thee.

135. But when We did remove from them the terror for a term which they must reach, behold! they broke their covenant.

136. Therefore We took retribution from them; therefore We drowned them in the sea: because they denied Our revelations and were heedles of them.

137. And We caused the folk who were despised to inherit the eastern parts of the land and the western parts thereof which We had blessed. And the fair word of the Lord was fulfilled for the Children of Israel because of their endurance; and We annihilated (all) that Pharaoh and his folk had done and that they had contrived.

138. And We brought the Children of Israel across the sea, and they came unto a people who were given up to idols which they had. They said: O Moses! Make for us a god even as they have gods. He said: Lo! ye are a folk who know not.

139. Lo! as for these, their way will be destroyed and all that they are doing is in vain.

140. He said: Shall I seek for you a god other than Allah when He hath favoured you above (all) creatures?

141. And (remember) when We did deliver you from Pharaoh's folk who were afflicting you with dreadful torment, slaughtering your sons and sparing your women. That was a tremendous trial from your Lord.

142. And when We did appoint for Moses thirty nights (of

solitude), and added to them ten, and he completed the whole time appointed by his Lord of forty nights, and Moses said unto his brother: Take my place among the people. Do right, and follow not the way of mischief-makers.

143. And when Moses came to Our appointed tryst and his Lord had spoken unto him, he said: My Lord! Show me (Thyself), that I may gaze upon Thee. He said: Thou wilt not see Me, but gaze upon the mountain! If it stand still in its place, see Me. And when his Lord revealed (His) glory to the mountain He sent it crashing down. And Moses fell down senseless. And when he woke he said: Glory unto Thee! I turn unto Thee repentant, and I am the first of (true) believers.

144. He said: O Moses! I have preferred thee above mankind by My messages and by My speaking (unto thee). So hold that which I have given thee, and be among the thankful.

145. And We wrote for him, upon the tablets, the lesson to be drawn from all things and the explanation of all things, then (bade him): Hold it fast; and command thy people (saying): Take the better (course made clear) therein. I shall show thee the abode of evil-livers.

146. I shall turn away from My revelations those who magnify themselves wrongfully in the earth, and if they see each token believe it not, and if they see the way of righteousness choose it not for (their) way, and if they see the way of error choose it for (their) way. That is because they deny Our revelations and are used to disregard them.

147. Those who deny Our revelations and the meeting of the Hereafter, their works are fruitless. Are they requited aught save what they used to do?

148. And the folk of Moses, after (he had left them), chose a calf (for worship), (made) out of their ornaments, of saffron hue, which gave a lowing sound. Saw they not that it spake not unto them or guided them in any way? They chose it, and became wrongdoers.

149. And when they feared the consequences thereof and saw that they had gone astray, they said: Unless our Lord have mercy on us and forgive us, we verily are of the lost.

150. And when Moses returned unto his people, angry and grieved, he said: Evil is that (course) which ye took after I had left you. Would ye hasten on the judgement of your Lord? And he cast down the tablets, and he seized his brother by the head, dragging him toward him. He said: Son of my mother! Lo! the folk did judge me weak and almost killed me. Oh, make not mine enemies to triumph over me and place me not among the evildoers!

151. He said: My Lord! Have mercy on me and on my brother; bring us into Thy mercy, Thou the Most Merciful of all who show mercy.

152. Lo! those who chose the calf (for worship), terror from their Lord and humiliation will come upon them in the life of the world. Thus do We requite those who invent a lie.

153. But those who do ill deeds and afterward repent and believe — lo! for them, afterward, Allah is Forgiving, Merciful.

154. Then, when the anger of Moses abated, he took up the tablets, and in their inscription there was guidance and mercy for all those who fear their Lord.

155. And Moses chose of his people seventy men for Our appointed tryst and, when the trembling came on them, he said: My Lord! If thou hadst willed Thou hadst destroyed them long before, and me with them, Wilt thou destroy us for that which the ignorant among us did? It is but Thy trial (of us). Thou sendest whom Thou wilt astray and guidest whom Thou wilt. Thou art our Protecting Friend, therefore forgive us and have mercy on us, Thou, the Best of all who show forgiveness.

156. And ordain for us in this world that which is good, and in the Hereafter (that which is good), Lo! We have turned unto Thee. He said: I smite with My punishment whom I will, and My mercy embraceth all things, therefore I shall ordain it for those who ward off (evil) and pay the poor-due, and those who believe Our revelations.

157. Those who follow the messenger, the Prophet who can neither read nor write, whom they will find described in the Torah and the Gospel (which are) with them. He will enjoin on them that which is right and forbid them that which is wrong. He will make lawful for them all good things and prohibit for them only the foul; and he will relieve them of their burden and the fetter that they used to wear. Then those who believe in him, and honour him, and help him, and follow the light which is sent down with him: they are the successful.

158. Say (O Muhammad): O mankind! Lo! I am the messenger of Allah to you all — (the messenger of) Him unto whom belongeth the Sovereignty of the heavens and the earth. There is no God save Him. He quickeneth and He giveth death. So believe in Allah and His messenger, the Prophet who can neither read nor write, who believeth in Allah and in His words and follow him that haply ye may be led aright.

159. And of Moses' folk there is a community who lead with truth and establish justice therewith.

160. We divided them into twelve tribes, nations: and We inspired Moses, when his people asked him for water, saying:

Smite with thy staff the rock! And there gushed forth therefrom twelve springs, so that each tribe knew their drinking-place. And we caused the white cloud to overshadow them and sent down for them the manna and the quails (saying): Eat of the good things wherewith We have provided you. They wronged Us not, but they were wont to wrong themselves.

161. And when it was said unto them: Dwell in this township and eat therefrom whence ye will, and say "Repentance," and enter the gate prostrate; We shall forgive you your sins; We shall increase (reward) for the right-doers.

162. But those of them who did wrong changed the word which had been told them for another saying, and We sent down upon them wrath from heaven for their wrong-doing.

163. Ask them (O Muhammad) of the township that was by the sea, how they did break the sabbath, how their big fish came unto them visibly upon their sabbath day and on a day when they did not keep sabbath came they not unto them. Thus did We try them for that they were evil-livers.

164. And when a community among them said: Why preach ye to a folk whom Allah is about to destroy and punish with an awful doom, they said: In order to be free from guilt before your Lord, and that haply they may ward off (evil).

165. And when they forgot that whereof they had been reminded, We rescued those who forbade wrong, and visited those who did wrong with dreadful punishment because they were evil-livers.

166. So when they took pride in that which they had been forbidden, We said unto them: Be ye apes despised and loathed!

167. And (remember) when thy Lord proclaimed that He would raise against them till the Day of Resurrection those who would lay on them a cruel torment. Lo! verily thy Lord is swift in prosecution and lo! verily He is Forgiving, Merciful.

168. And We have sundered them in the earth as (separate) nations. Some of them are righteous, and some far from that. And We have tried them with good things and evil things that haply they might return.

169. And a generation hath succeeded them who inherited the Scriptures. They grasp the goods of this low life (as the price of evil-doing) and say: It will be forgiven us. And if there came to them (again) the offer of the like, they would accept it (and would sin again). Hath not the covenant of the Scripture been taken on their behalf that they should not speak aught concerning Allah save the truth? And they have studied that which is therein. And the abode of the Hereafter is better, for

those who ward off (evil). Have ye then no sense?

170. And as for those who make (men) keep the Scripture, and establish worship—lo! We squander not the wages of reformers.

171. And when We shook the Mount above them as it were a covering, and they supposed that it was going to fall upon them (and We said): Hold fast that which We have given you, and remember that which is therein, that ye may ward off (evil).

172. And (remember) when thy Lord brought forth from the Children of Adam, from their reins, their seed, and made them testify of themselves, (saying): Am I not your Lord? They said: Yea. verily. We testify. (That was) lest ye should say at the Day of Resurrection: Lo! of this we were unaware.

173. Or lest ye should say: (It is) only (that) our fathers ascribed partners to Allah of old and we were (their) seed after them. Wilt Thou destroy us on account of that which those who follow falsehood did?

174. Thus We detail Our revelations that haply they may return.

175. Recite unto them the tale of him to whom We gave Our revelations, but he sloughed them off so Satan overtook him and he became of those who lead astray.

176. And had We willed We could have raised him by their means, but he clung to the earth and followed his own lust. Therefore his likeness is as the likeness of a dog; if thou attackest him he panteth with his tongue out, and if thou leavest, him he panteth with his tongue out. Such is the likeness of the people who deny Our revelations. Narrate unto them the history (of the men of old), that haply they may take thought.

177. Evil as an example are the folk who denied Our revelations, and were wont to wrong themselves.

178. He who Allah leadeth, he indeed is led aright, while he whom Allah sendeth astray—they indeed are losers.

179. Already have we urged unto hell many of the jinn and humankind, having hearts wherewith they understand not, and having eyes wherewith they see not and having ears wherewith they hear not. These are as the cattle—nay but they are worse! These are the neglectful.

180. Allah's are the fairest names. Invoke Him by them. And leave the company of those who blaspheme His names. They will be requited what they do.

181. And of those whom We created there is a nation who guide with the truth and establish justice therewith.

182. And those who deny Our revelations—step by step We lead them on from whence they know not.

183. I give them rein (for) lo! My scheme is strong.

184. Have they not bethought them (that) there is no madness in their comrade? He is but a plain warner.

185. Have they not considered the dominion of the heavens and the earth, and what things Allah hath created, and that it may be that their own term draweth nigh? In what fact after this will they believe?

186. Those whom Allah sendeth astray, there is no guide for them. He leaveth them to wander blindly on in their contumacy.

187. They ask thee of the (destined) Hour, when will it come to port. Say: Knowledge thereof is with my Lord only. He alone will manifest it as its proper time. It is heavy in the heavens and the earth. It cometh not to you save unawares. They question thee as if thou couldst be well informed thereof. Say: Knowledge thereof is with Allah only, but most of mankind know not.

188. Say: For myself I have no power to benefit, nor power to hurt, save that which Allah willeth. Had I knowledge of the unseen I should have abundance of wealth, and adversity would not touch me. I am but a warner, and a bearer of good tidings unto folk who believe.

189. He it is who did create you from a single soul, and therefrom did make his mate that he might take rest in her. And when he covered her she bore a light burden, and she passed (unnoticed) with it, but when it became heavy they cried unto Allah, their Lord saying: if thou givest unto us aright we shall be of the thankful.

190. But when He gave unto them aright, they ascribed unto Him partners in respect of that which He had given them. High is He exalted above all that they associate (with Him).

191. Attribute they as partners to Allah those who created naught, but are themselves created.

192. And cannot give them help, nor can they help themselves?

193. And if ye call them to the Guidance, they follow you not. Whether ye call them or are silent is all one to them.

194. Lo! those on whom ye call beside Allah are slaves like unto you. Call on them now, and let them answer you, if ye are truthful!

195. Have they feet wherewith they walk, or have they hands wherewith they hold, or have they eyes wherewith they see or have they ears wherewith they hear? Say: Call upon your (so called) partners (of Allah), and then contrive against me, spare me not!

196. Lo! my Protecting Friend is Allah who revealeth the

115

Scripture. He befriendeth the righteous.

197. They on whom ye call beside Him have no power to help you, nor can they help themselves.

198. And if ye (Muslims) call them to the Guidance they hear not; and thou (Muhammad) seest them looking toward thee, but they see not.

199. Keep to forgiveness (O Muhammad), and enjoin kindness, and turn away from the ignorant.

200. And if a slander from the devil wound thee, then seek refuge in Allah. Lo! He is Hearer, Knower.

201. Lo! those who ward off (evil) when a glamour from the devil troubleth them, they do but remember (Allah's Guidance) and behold them seers!

202. Their brethren plunge them further into error and cease not.

203. And when thou bringest not a verse for them they say: Why hast thou not chosen it? say: I follow only that which is inspired in 'me from my Lord. This (Qur'ân) is insight from your Lord, and a guidance and a mercy for a people that believe.

204. And when the Qur'ân is recited, give ear to it and pay heed, that ye may obtain mercy.

205. And do thou (O Muhammad) remember thy Lord within thyself humbly and with awe, below thy breath, at morn and evening. And be thou not of the neglectful.

206. Lo! those who are with my Lord are not too proud to do Him service, but they praise Him and adore Him.

SÛRAH 8

Al-Anfâl, "The spoils", takes its name from the first verse by which it is proclaimed that property in war belongs "to Allah and His messenger"—that is to say, to the theocratic State, to be used for the common weal. The date of the revelation of this sûrah is established, from the nature of the contents, as the time that elapsed between the battle of Badr and the division of the spoils—a space of only one month—in the second year of the Hijrah. The concluding verses are of later date and lead up to the subject of sûrah 9.

A Meccan caravan was returning from Syria, and its leader, Abû Sufyân, fearing an attack from Al-Madînah sent a camel-rider on to Mecca with a frantic appeal for help; which must have come too late, considering the distances, if as some writers even among Muslims have alleged, the Prophet had always intended to attack the caravan. Ibn Ishâq (*apud* Ibn Hishâm) when treating of the Tabûk expedition, says that the

116

Prophet announced the destination on that occasion, whereas it was his custom to hide his real objective. Was not the real objective hidden in this first campaign? It is a fact that he only advanced when the army sent to protect the caravan, or rather (it is probable) to punish the Muslims for having plundered it, was approaching Al-Madînah. His little army of three hundred and thirteen men, ill-armed and roughly equipped, traversed the desert for three days till, when they halted near the water of Badr, they had news that the army of Qureysh was approaching on the other side of the valley. Then rain fell—heavily upon Qureysh so that they could not advance further on account of the muddy state of the ground, lightly on the Muslims, who were able to advance to the water and secure it. At the same time Abû Sufyân, the leader of the caravan, which was also heading for the water of Badr, was warned by one of his scouts of the advance of the Muslims and turned back to the coast-plain. Before the battle against what must have appeared to all men overwhelming odds, the Prophet gave the Ansâr, the men of Al-Madînah, whose oath of allegiance had not included fighting in the field, the chance of returning if they wished; but they were only hurt by the suggestion that they could possibly forsake him. On the other hand, several of Qureysh, including the whole Zuhri clan, returned to Mecca when they heard the caravan was safe, having no grudge otherwise against the Prophet and his followers, whom they regarded as men who had been wronged.

Still the army of Qureysh outnumbered the Muslims by more than two to one, and was much better mounted and equipped, so that their leaders counted on an easy victory. When the Prophet saw them streaming down the sandhills, he cried: "O Allah! Here are Qureysh with all their chivalry and pomp, who oppose Thee and deny Thy messenger. O Allah! Thy help which Thou hast promised me! O Allah! make them bow this day!"

The Muslims were successful in the single combats with which Arab battles opened. But the mêlée at first went hard against them; and the Prophet stood and prayed under the shelter which they had put up to screen him from the sun, and cried: "O Allah! If this little company is destroyed, there will be none left in the land to worship Thee." Then he fell into a trance and, when he spoke again, he told Abû Bakr, who was with him, that the promised help had come. Thereupon he went out to encourage his people. Taking up a handful of gravel, he ran towards Qureysh and flung it at them, saying: "The faces are confounded!" on which the tide of battle turned in favour of the Muslims. The leader of Qureysh and several of their greatest men were killed, many were taken prisoner, and their baggage and camels were captured by the Muslims. It was indeed a day to be remembered in the early history of Al-Islâm, and there was great rejoicing in Al-Madînah. But the Muslims are warned in this sûrah that it is only the beginning of their struggle against heavy odds. In fact, in the following year at Mt. Uhud (referred to in Sûr. 3), the enemy came against them with an army of three thousand, and in the fifth year of the Hijrah, an allied army of the pagan clans, amounting to 10,000 besieged Al-Madînah in the "War of the Trench" (see Sûr. 33, "The Clans").

The date of revelation is the second year of the Hijrah for the most part. Some good Arabic authorities hold that vv. 30-40, or some of them, were revealed at Mecca just before the Hijrah.

SPOILS OF WAR

Revealed at Al-Madînah

In the name of Allah, the Beneficent, the Merciful.

1. They ask thee (O Muhammad) of the spoils of war. Say: The spoils of war belong to Allah and the messenger, so keep your duty to Allah, and adjust the matter of your difference, and obey Allah and His messenger, if ye are (true) believers.

2. They only are the (true) believers whose hearts feel fear when Allah is mentioned, and when the revelations of Allah are recited unto them they increase their faith, and who trust in their Lord.

3. Who establish worship and spend of that We have bestowed on them.

4. Those are they who are in truth believers. For them are grades (of honour) with their Lord, and pardon, and a bountiful provision.

5. Even as thy Lord caused thee (Muhammad) to go forth from thy home with the Truth, and lo! a party of the believers were averse (to it).

6. Disputing with thee of the Truth after it had been made manifest, as if they were being driven to death visible.

7. And when Allah promised you one of the two bands (of the enemy) that it should be yours, and ye longed that other than the armed one might be yours. And Allah willed that He should cause the Truth to triumph by His words, and cut the root of the disbelievers.

8. That He might cause the Truth to triumph and bring

118

vanity to naught, however much the guilty might oppose.

9. When ye sought help of your Lord and He answered you (saying): I will help you with a thousand of the angels, rank on rank.

10. Allah appointed it only as good tidings, and that your hearts thereby might be at rest. Victory cometh only by the help of Allah. Lo! Allah is Mighty, Wise.

11. When He made the slumber fall upon you as a reassurance, from Him and sent down water from the sky upon you, that thereby He might purify you, and remove from you the fear of Satan, and make strong your hearts and firm (your) feet thereby.

12. When thy Lord inspired the angels, (saying): I am with you. So make those who believe stand firm. I will throw fear into the hearts of those who disbelieve. Then smite the necks and smite of them each finger.

13. That is because they opposed Allah and His messenger. Whoso opposeth Allah and His messenger, (for him) lo! Allah is severe in punishment.

14. That (is the award), so taste it, and (know) that for disbelievers is the torment of the Fire.

15. O ye who believe! When ye meet those who disbelieve in battle, turn not your backs to them.

16. Whoso on that day turneth his back to them, unless manoeuvring for battle or intent to join a company, he truly hath incurred wrath from Allah, and his habitation will be hell, a hapless journey's end.

17. Ye (Muslims) slew them not, but Allah slew them. And thou (Muhammad) threwest not when thou didst throw, but Allah threw, that He might test the believers by a fair test from Him. Lo! Allah is Hearer, Knower.

18. That (is the case); and (know) that Allah (it is) who maketh weak the plan of disbelievers.

19. (O Qureysh!) If ye sought a judgement, now hath the judgement come unto you. And if ye cease (from persecuting the believers) it will be better for you, but if ye return (to the attack) We also shall return. And your host will avail you naught, however numerous it be, and (know) that Allah is with the believers (in His guidance).

20. O ye who believe! Obey Allah and His messenger, and turn not away from him when ye hear (him speak).

21. Be not as those who say, We hear, and they hear not.

22. Lo! the worst of beasts in Allah's sight are the deaf, the dumb, who have no sense.

23. Had Allah known of any good in them He would have

119

made them hear, but had He made them hear they would have turned away, averse.

24. O ye who believe; Obey Allah, and the messenger when He calleth you to that which quickeneth you, and know that Allah cometh in between the man and his own heart, and that He it is unto Whom ye will be gathered.

25. And guard yourselves against a chastisement which cannot fall exclusively on those of you who are wrongdoers, and know that Allah is severe in punishment.

26. And remember, when ye were few and reckoned feeble in the land, and were in fear lest men would extirpate you how He gave you refuge, and strengthened you with His help, and made provision of good things for you, that haply ye might be thankful.

27. O ye who believe! Betray not Allah and His messenger, nor knowingly betray your trusts.

28. And know that your possessions and your children are a test, and that with Allah is immense reward.

29. O ye who believe! If ye keep your duty to Allah, He will give you discrimination (between right and wrong) and will rid you of your evil thoughts and deeds, and will forgive you. Allah is of infinite bounty.

30. And when those who disbelieve plot against thee (O Muhammad) to wound thee fatally, or to kill thee or to drive thee forth; they plot, but Allah (also) plotteth; and Allah is the best of plotters.

31. And when Our revelations are recited unto them they say: We have heard. If we wish we can speak the like of this. Lo! this is naught but fables of the men of old.

32. And when they said: O Allah! If this be indeed the truth from Thee, then rain down stones on us or bring on us some painful doom!

33. But Allah would not punish them while thou wast with them, nor will He punish them while they seek forgiveness.

34. What (plea) have they that Allah should not punish them, when they debar (His servants) from the Inviolable Place of Worship, though they are not its fitting guardians. Its fitting guardians are those only who keep their duty to Allah. But most of them know not.

35. And their worship at the (holy) House is naught but whistling and hand-clapping. Therefore (it is said unto them): Taste of the doom because ye disbelieve.

36. Lo! those who disbelieve spend their wealth in order that they may debar (men) from the way of Allah. They will spend it, then it will become an anguish for them, then they will be

conquered. And those who disbelieve will be gathered unto hell.

37. That Allah may separate the wicked from the good. The wicked will He place piece upon piece, and heap them all together, and consign them unto hell. Such verily are the losers.

38. Tell those who disbelieve that if they cease (from persecution of believers) that which is past will be forgiven them; but if they return (thereto) then the example of the men of old hath already gone (before them, for a warning).

39. And fight them until persecution is no more, and religion is all for Allah. But if they cease, then lo! Allah is Seer of what they do.

40. And if they turn away, then know that Allah is your Befriender—a transcendent Patron, a transcendent Helper!

41. And know that whatever ye take as spoils of war, lo! a fifth thereof is for Allah, and for the messenger and for the kinsman (who hath need) and orphans and the needy and the wayfarer, if ye believe in Allah and that which We revealed unto Our slave on the Day of Discrimination, the day when the two armies met. And Allah is Able to do all things.

42. When ye were on the near bank (of the valley) and they were on the yonder bank, and the caravan was below you (on the coast plain). And had ye trusted to meet one another ye surely would have failed to keep the tryst, but (it happened, as it did, without the forethought of either of you) that Allah might conclude a thing that must be done; that he who perished (on that day) might perish by a clear proof (of His sovereignty) and he who survived might survive by a clear proof (of His sovereignty). Lo! Allah in truth is Hearer, Knower.

43. When Allah showed them unto thee (O Muhammad) in thy dream as few in number, and if He had shown them to thee as many, ye (Muslims) would have faltered and would have quarrelled over the affair. But Allah saved (you). Lo! He knoweth what is in the breasts (of men).

44. And when He made you (Muslims), when ye met (them), see them with your eyes as few, and lessened you in their eyes, (it was) that Allah might conclude a thing that must be done. Unto Allah all things are brought back.

45. O ye who believe! When ye meet an army, hold firm and think of Allah much, that ye may be successful.

46. And obey Allah and His messenger, and dispute not one with another: lest ye falter and your strength depart from you; but be steadfast! Lo! Allah is with the steadfast.

47. Be not as those who came forth from their dwellings

boastfully and to be seen of men, and debar (men) from the way of Allah, while Allah is surrounding all they do.

48. And when Satan made their deeds seem fair to them and said: No one of mankind can conquer you this day, for I am your protector. But when the armies came in sight of one another, he took flight, saying: Lo! I am guiltless of you. Lo! I see that which ye see not. Lo! I fear Allah. And Allah is severe in punishment.

49. When the hypocrites and those in whose hearts is a disease said: Their religion hath deluded these. Whoso putteth his trust in Allah (will find that) lo! Allah is Mighty, Wise.

50. If thou couldst see how the angels receive those who disbelieve, smiting their faces and their backs and (saying): Taste the punishment of burning!

51. This is for that which your own hands have sent before (to the Judgement), and (know) that Allah is not a tyrant to His slaves).

52. (Their way is) as the way of Pharaoh's folk and those before them; they disbelieved the revelations of Allah, and Allah took them in their sins. Lo! Allah is Strong, severe in punishment.

53. That is because Allah never changeth the grace He hath bestowed on any people until they first change that which is in their hearts, and (that is) because Allah is Hearer, Knower.

54. (Their way is) as the way of Pharaoh's folk and those before them; they denied the revelations of their Lord, so We destroyed them in their sins. And We drowned the folk of Pharaoh. All were evil-doers.

55. Lo! the worst of beasts in Allah's sight are the ungrateful who will not believe.

56. Those of them with whom thou madest a treaty, and then at every opportunity they break their treaty, and they keep not duty (to Allah).

57. If thou comest on them in the war, deal with them so as to strike fear in those who are behind them, that haply they may remember.

58. And if thou fearest treachery from any folk, then throw back to them (their treaty) fairly, Lo! Allah loveth not the treacherous.

59. And let not those who disbelieve suppose that they can outstrip (Allah's purpose) Lo! they cannot escape.

60. Make ready for them all thou canst of (armed) force and of horses tethered, that thereby ye may dismay the enemy of Allah and your enemy, and others beside them whom ye know not. Allah knoweth them. Whatsoever ye spend in the way of

Allah it will be repaid to you in full, and ye will not be wronged.

61. And if they incline to peace, incline thou also to it, and trust in Allah. Lo! He is the Hearer, the Knower.

62. And if they would deceive thee, then lo! Allah is sufficient for thee. He it is Who supporteth thee with His Help and with the believers.

63. And (as for the believers) hath attuned their hearts. If thou hadst spent all that is in the earth thou couldst not have attuned their hearts, but Allah hath attuned them. Lo! He is Mighty, Wise.

64. O Prophet! Allah is Sufficient for thee and those who follow thee of the believers.

65. O Prophet! Exhort the believers to fight. If there be of you twenty steadfast they shall overcome two hundred, and if there be of you a hundred steadfast they shall overcome a thousand of those who disbelieve, because they (the disbelievers) are a folk without intelligence.

66. Now hath Allah lightened your burden, for He knoweth that there is a weakness in you. So if there be of you a steadfast hundred they shall overcome two hundred, and if there be of you a thousand (steadfast) they shall overcome two thousand by permission of Allah. Allah is with the steadfast.

67. It is not for any Prophet to have captives until he hath made slaughter in the land. Ye desire the lure of this world and Allah desireth (for you) the Hereafter, and Allah is Mighty, Wise.

68. Had it not been for an ordinance of Allah which had gone before, an awful doom had come upon you on account of what ye took.

69. Now enjoy what ye have won, as lawful and good, and keep your duty to Allah. Lo! Allah is Forgiving, Merciful.

70. O Prophet! Say unto those captives who are in your hands: If Allah knoweth any good in your hearts He will give you better than that which hath been taken from you, and will forgive you. Lo! Allah is Forgiving, Merciful.

71. And if they would betray thee, they betrayed Allah before, and He gave (thee) power over them. Allah is Knower, Wise.

72. Lo! those who believed and left their homes and strove with their wealth and their lives for the cause of Allah, and those who took them in and helped them; these are protecting friends one of another. And those who believed but did not leave their homes, ye have no duty to protect them till they leave their homes; but if they seek help from you in the matter

of religion then it it your duty to help (them) except against a folk between whom and you there is a treaty. Allah is Seer of what ye do.

73. And those who disbelieve are protectors one of another — If ye do not so, there will be confusion in the land, and great corruption.

74. Those who believed and left their homes and strove for the cause of Allah, and those who took them in and helped them — these are the believers in truth. For them is pardon, and a bountiful provision.

75. And those who afterwards believed and left their homes and strove along with you, they are of you; and those who are akin are nearer one to another in the ordinance of Allah. Lo! Allah is Knower of all things.

SÛRAH 9

At-Taubah, "Repentance" takes its name from v. 104. It is often called Al-Barâ'at (The Immunity), from the first word. It is the only sûrah which is without the *Bi'smi'llâhi'r-Rahîm* ("In the name of Allah the Beneficent, the Merciful") which is generally considered to be on account of the stern commandments against idolaters which it contains. vv 1-12, forming the proclamation of immunity from obligation toward the idolaters, were revealed after the pilgrims had started for Mecca in the ninth year of the Hijrah and sent by special messenger to Abû Bakr, leader of the pilgrimage, to be read out by Ali to the multitudes at Mecca. It signified the end of idolatry in Arabia. The Christian Byzantine Empire had begun to move against the growing Muslim power, and this sûrah contains mention of a greater war to come, and instructions with regard to it. vv. 38-39 refer to the Tabûk campaign, and especially to those Arab tribes who failed to join the Muslims in that campaign. The "Hypocrites", as the half-hearted supporters of Al-Islâm were called, had long been a thorn in the side of the Muslims. They had even at one time gone the length in dissent of forming a congregation and building a mosque of their own surreptitiously. On the Prophet's return from Tabûk they invited him to visit that mosque. This is referred to in vv. 107 ff.

The date of revelation is the ninth year of the Hijrah.

REPENTANCE

Revealed at Al-Madînah

1. Freedom from obligation (is proclaimed) from Allah and His messenger toward those of the idolaters with whom ye

made a treaty.

2. Travel freely in the land four months, and know that ye cannot escape Allah and that Allah will confound the disbelievers (in His guidance).

3. And a proclamation from Allah and His messenger to all men on the day of the Greater Pilgrimage that Allah is free from obligation to the idolaters, and (so is) His messenger. So, if ye repent, it will be better for you; but if ye are averse, then know that ye cannot escape Allah. Give tidings (O Muhammad) of a painful doom to those who disbelieve.

4. Excepting those of the idolaters with whom ye (Muslims) have a treaty, and who have since abated nothing of your right nor have supported anyone against you. (As for these), fulfil their treaty to them till their term. Lo! Allah loveth those who keep their duty (unto Him).

5. Then, when the sacred months have passed, slay the idolaters wherever ye find them, and take them (captive), and besiege them, and prepare for them each ambush. But if they repent and establish worship and pay the poor-due, then leave their way free. Lo! Allah is Forgiving, Merciful.

6. And if anyone of the idolaters seeketh thy protection (O Muhammad), then protect him so that he may hear the word of Allah, and afterward convey him to his place of safety. That is because they are a folk who know not.

7. How can there be a treaty with Allah and with His messenger for the idolaters save those with whom ye made a treaty at the Inviolable Place of Worship? So long as they are true to you, be true to them. Lo! Allah loveth those who keep their duty.

8. How (can there be any treaty for the others) when, if they have the upper hand of you, they regard not pact nor honour in respect of you? They satisfy you with their mouths the while their hearts refuse. And most of them are wrongdoers.

9. They have purchased with the revelations of Allah a little gain, so they debar (men) from His way. Lo! evil is that which they are wont to do.

10. And they observe toward a believer neither pact nor honour. These are they who are transgressors.

11. But if they repent and establish worship and pay the poor due, then are they your brethren in religion. We detail Our revelations for a people who have knowledge.

12. And if they break their pledge after their treaty (hath been made with you) and assail your religion, then fight the heads of disbelief—Lo! they have no binding oaths—in order that they may desist.

13. Will ye not fight a folk who broke their solemn pledges, and purposed to drive out the messenger and did attack you first? What! Fear ye them? Now Allah hath more right that ye should fear Him, if ye are believers.

14. Fight them! Allah will chastise them at your hands, and He will lay them low and give you victory over them, and he will heal the breasts of folk who are believers.

15. And He will remove the anger of their hearts. Allah relenteth toward whom He will. Allah is Knower, Wise.

16. Or deemed ye that ye would be left (in peace) when Allah yet knoweth not those of you who strive, choosing for familiar none save Allah and His messenger and the believers? Allah is Informed of what ye do.

17. It is not for the idolaters to tend Allah's sanctuaries, bearing witness against themselves of disbelief. As for such, their works are vain and in the Fire they will abide.

18. He only shall tend Allah's sanctuaries who believeth in Allah and the Last day and observeth proper worship and payeth the poor-due and feareth none save Allah. For such (only) is it possible that they can be of the rightly guided.

19. Count ye the slaking of a pilgrim's thirst and tendance of the Inviolable Place of Worship as (equal to the worth of him) who believeth in Allah and the Last Day, and striveth in the way of Allah? They are not equal in the sight of Allah. Allah guideth not wrong-doing folk.

20. Those who believe, and have left their homes and striven with their wealth and their lives in Allah's way are of much greater worth in Allah's sight. These are they who are triumphant.

21. Their Lord giveth them good tidings of mercy from Him, and acceptance, and Gardens where enduring pleasure will be theirs.

22. There they will abide for ever. Lo! with Allah there is immense reward.

23. O ye who believe! Choose not your fathers nor your brethren for friends if they take pleasure in disbelief rather than faith. Whoso of you taketh them for friends, such are wrong-doers.

24. Say: If your fathers, and your sons, and your brethren, and your wives, and your tribe, and the wealth ye have acquired, and merchandise for which ye fear that there will be no sale, and dwelling ye desire are dearer to you than Allah and His messenger and striving in His way: then wait till Allah bringeth His command to pass. Allah guideth not wrong-doing folk.

25. Allah hath given you victory on many fields and on the

day of Huneyn, when ye exulted in your multitude but it availed you naught, and the earth, vast as it is, was straitened for you: then ye turned back in flight.

26. Then Allah sent His peace of reassurance down upon His messenger and upon the believers, and sent down hosts ye could not see, and punished those who disbelieved. Such is the reward of disbelievers.

27. Then afterward Allah will relent toward whom He will; for Allah is Forgiving, Merciful.

28. O ye who believe! The idolaters only are unclean. So let them not come near the Inviolable Place of Worship after this their year. If ye fear poverty (from the loss of their merchandise) Allah shall preserve you of His bounty if He will. Lo! Allah is Knower, Wise.

29. Fight against such of those who have been given the Scripture as believe not in Allah not the Last Day, and forbid not that which Allah hath forbidden by His messenger, and follow not the religion of truth, until they pay the tribute readily, being brought low.

30. And the Jews say: Ezra is the son of Allah, and the Christians say: The Messiah is the son of Allah. That is their saying with their mouths. They imitate the saying of those who disbelieved of old. Allah (Himself) fighteth against them. How perverse are they.

31. They have taken as lords beside Allah their rabbis and their monks and the Messiah son of Mary, when they were bidden to worship only One God. There is no god save Him. Be He glorified from all that they ascribe as partner (unto Him)!

32. Fain would they put out the light of Allah with their mouths, but Allah disdaineth (aught) save that he shall perfect His light, however much the disbelievers are averse.

33. He it is who hath sent His messenger with the guidance and the Religion of Truth, that He may cause it to prevail over all religion, however much the idolaters may be averse.

34. O ye who believe! Lo! many of the (Jewish) rabbis and the (Christian) monks devour the wealth of mankind wantonly and debar (men) from the way of Allah. They who hoard up gold and silver and spend it not in the way of Allah, unto them give tidings (O Muhammad) of a painful doom.

35. On the day when it will (all) be heated in the fire of hell, and their foreheads and their flanks and their backs will be branded therewith (and it will be said unto them): Here is that which ye hoarded for yourselves. Now taste of what ye used to hoard.

36. Lo! the number of the months with Allah is twelve months by Allah's ordinance in the day that He created the heavens and the earth. Four of them are sacred: that is the right religion. So wrong not yourselves in them. And wage war on all the idolaters as they are waging war on all of you. And know that Allah is with those who keep their duty (unto Him).

37. Postponement (of a sacred month) is only an excess of disbelief whereby those who disbelieve are misled, they allow it one year and forbid it (another) year, that they may make up the number of the months which Allah hath hallowed, so that they allow that which Allah hath forbidden. The evil of their deeds is made fair-seeming unto them. Allah guideth not the disbelieving folk.

38. O ye who believe! What aileth you that when it is said unto you: Go forth in the way of Allah, ye are bowed down to the ground with heaviness. Take ye pleasure in the life of the world rather than in the Hereafter? The comfort of the life of the world is but little in the Hereafter.

39. If ye go not forth He will afflict you with a painful doom, and will choose instead of you a folk other than you. Ye cannot harm Him at all. Allah is Able to do all things.

40. If ye help him not, still Allah helped him when those who disbelieve drove him forth, the second of two; when they two, were in the cave, when he said unto his comrade: Grieve not. Lo! Allah is with us. Then Allah caused His peace of reassurance to descend upon him and supported him with hosts ye cannot see, and made the word of those who disbelieved the nethermost, while Allah's word it was that became the uppermost. Allah is Mighty, Wise.

41. Go forth, light-armed and heavy-armed, and strive with your wealth and your lives in the way of Allah! That is best for you if ye but knew.

42. Had it been a near adventure and an easy journey they had followed thee, but the distance seemed too far for them. Yet will they swear by Allah (saying): If we had been able we would surely have set out with you. They destroy their souls and Allah knoweth that they verily are liars.

43. Allah forgive thee (O Muhammad)! Wherefor didst thou grant them leave ere those who told the truth were manifest to thee and thou didst know the liars?

44. Those who believe in Allah and the Last Day ask no leave of thee lest they should strive with their wealth and their lives. Allah is Aware of those who keep their duty (unto Him).

45. They alone ask leave of thee who believe not in Allah and the Last Day, and whose hearts feel doubt, so in their doubt

they waver.

46. And if they had wished to go forth they would assuredly have made ready some equipment, but Allah was averse to their being sent forth, and held them back and (it was said unto them): Sit ye with the sedentary!

47. Had they gone forth among you they had added to you naught save trouble and had hurried to and fro among you, seeking to cause sedition among you, and among you there are some who would have listened to them. Allah is Aware of evil-doers.

48. Aforetime they sought to cause sedition and raised difficulties for thee till the Truth came and decree of Allah was made manifest, though they were loth.

49. Of them is he who saith: Grant me leave (to stay at home) and tempt me not. Surely it is into temptation that they (thus) have fallen. Lo! hell is all around the disbelievers.

50. If good befalleth thee (O Muhammad) it afflicteth them, and if calamity befalleth thee, they say: We took precaution, and they turn away well pleased.

51. Say: Naught befalleth us save that which Allah hath decreed for us. He is our Protecting Friend. In Allah let believers put their trust!

52. Say: Can ye await for us aught save one of two good things (death or victory in Allah's way)? while we await for you that Allah will afflict you with a doom from Him or at our hands. Await then! Lo! we are awaiting with you.

53. Say: Pay (your contribution), willingly or unwillingly, it will not be accepted from you. Lo! ye were ever froward folk.

54. And naught preventeth that their contributions should be accepted from them save that they have disbelieved in Allah and in His messenger, and they come not to worship save as idlers, and pay not (their contribution) save reluctantly.

55. So let not their riches nor their children please thee (O Muhammad). Allah thereby intendeth but to punish them in the life of the world and that their souls shall pass away while they are disbelievers.

56. And they swear by Allah that they are in truth of you, when they are not of you, but they are folk who are afraid.

57. Had they but found a refuge, or caverns, or a place to enter, they surely had resorted thither swift as runaways.

58. And of them is he who defameth thee in the matter of the alms. If they are given thereof they are content, and if they are not given thereof, behold! they are enraged.

59. (How much more seemly) had they been content with that which Allah and His messenger had given them and had

said: Allah sufficeth us. Allah will give us of His bounty, and (also) His messenger. Unto Allah we are suppliants.

60. The alms are only for the poor and the needy, and those who collect them, and those whose hearts are to be reconciled, and to free the captives and the debtors, and for the cause of Allah, and (for) the wayfarers; a duty imposed by Allah. Allah is Knower, Wise.

61. And of them are those who vex the Prophet and say: He is only a hearer. Say: A hearer of good for you, who believeth in Allah and is true to the believers, and a mercy for such of you as believe. Those who vex the messenger of Allah, for them there is a painful doom.

62. They swear by Allah to you (Muslims) to please you, but Allah, with His messenger, hath more right that they should please Him if they are believers.

63. Know they not that whoso opposeth Allah and His messenger, his portion verily is hell, to abide therein? That is the extreme abasement.

64. The hypocrites fear lest a sûrah should be revealed concerning them, proclaiming what is in their hearts. Say: Scoff (your fill)! Lo! Allah is disclosing what ye fear.

65. And if thou ask them (O Muhammad) they will say: We did but talk and jest. Say: Was it at Allah and His revelations and His messenger that ye did scoff?

66. Make no excuse. Ye have disbelieved after your (confession of) belief. If We forgive a party of you, a party of you We shall punish because they have been guilty.

67. The hypocrites, both men and women, proceed one from another. They enjoin the wrong, and they forbid the right, and they withhold their hands (from spending for the cause of Allah). They forget Allah, so He hath forgotten them. Lo! the hypocrites, they are the transgressors.

68. Allah promiseth the hypocrites, both men and women, and the disbelievers fire of hell for their abode. It will suffice them. Allah curseth them, and theirs is lasting torment.

69. Even as those before you were mightier than you in strength, and more affluent than you in wealth and children. They enjoyed their lot awhile, so ye enjoy your lot awhile even as those before you did enjoy their lot awhile. And ye prate even as they prated. Such are they whose works have perished in the world and the Hereafter. Such are they who are the losers.

70. Hath not the fame of those before them reached them — the folk of Noah, A'âd, Thamûd, the folk of Abraham, the dwellers of Midian and the disasters (which befell them)? Their messengers (from Allah) came unto them with proofs (of Allah's sovereignty). So Allah surely wronged them not, but

they did wrong themselves.

71. And the believers, men and women, are protecting friends one of another; they enjoin the right and forbid the wrong, and they establish worship and they pay the poor-due, and they obey Allah and His messenger. As for these, Allah will have mercy on them. Lo! Allah is Mighty, Wise.

72. Allah promiseth to the believers, men and women, Gardens underneath which rivers flow, wherein they will abide—blessed dwellings in Gardens of Eden. And—greater (far)!—acceptance from Allah. That is the supreme triumph.

73. O Prophet! Strive against the disbelievers and the hypocrites! Be harsh with them. Their ultimate abode is hell, a hapless journey's-end.

74. They swear by Allah that they said nothing (wrong), yet they did say the word of disbelief, and did disbelieve after their Surrender (to Allah). And they purposed that which they could not attain, and they sought revenge only that Allah by His messenger should enrich them of His bounty. If they repent it will be better for them; and if they turn away, Allah will afflict them with a painful doom in the world and the Hereafter, and they have no protecting friend nor helper in the earth.

75. And of them is he who made a covenant with Allah (saying): If he gives us of His bounty We will give alms and become of the righteous.

76. Yet when He gave them of His bounty, they hoarded it and turned away, averse.

77. So He hath made the consequence (to be) hypocrisy in their hearts until the day when they shall meet Him, because they broke their word to Allah that they promised Him, and because they lied.

78. Know they not that Allah knoweth both their secret and the thought that they confide, and that Allah is the Knower of Things Hidden?

79. Those who point at such of the believers as give the alms willingly and such as can find naught to give but their endeavours, and deride them—Allah (Himself) derideth them. Theirs will be a painful doom.

80. Ask forgiveness for them (O Muhammad), or ask not forgiveness for them; though thou ask forgiveness for them seventy times Allah will not forgive them. That is because they disbelieved in Allah and His messenger, and Allah guideth not wrongdoing folk.

81. Those who were left behind rejoiced at sitting still behind the messenger of Allah, and were averse to striving with their

wealth and their lives in Allah's way. And they said: Go not forth in the heat! Say: The heat of hell is more intense of heat, if they but understood.

82. Then let them laugh a little: they will weep much, as the reward of what they used to earn.

83. If Allah bring thee back (from the campaign) unto a party of them and they ask of thee leave to go out (to fight), then say unto them: Ye shall never more go out with me nor fight with me against a foe. Ye were content with sitting still the first time. So sit still, with the useless.

84. And never (O Muhammad) pray for one of them who dieth, nor stand by his grave. Lo! they disbelieved in Allah and His messenger, and they died while they were evil-doers.

85. Let not their wealth nor their children please thee! Allah purposeth only to punish them thereby in the world, and that their souls shall pass away while they are disbelievers.

86. And when a sûrah is revealed (which saith): Believe in Allah and strive along with His messenger, the men of wealth among them still ask leave of thee and say: Suffer us to be with those who sit (at home).

87. They are content that they should be with the useless and their hearts are sealed, so that they apprehend not.

88. But the messenger and those who believe with him strive with their wealth and their lives. Such are they for whom are the good things. Such are they who are the successful.

89. Allah hath made ready for them Gardens underneath which rivers flow, wherein they will abide. That is the supreme triumph.

90. And those among the wandering Arabs who had an excuse came in order that permission might be granted them. And those who lied to Allah and His messenger sat at home. A painful doom will fall on those of them who disbelieve.

91. Not unto the weak nor unto the sick nor unto those who can find naught to spend is any fault (to be imputed though they stay at home) if they are true to Allah and His messenger. Not unto the good is there any road (of blame). Allah is Forgiving, Merciful.

92. Nor unto those whom, when they came to thee (asking) that thou shouldest mount them, thou didst tell: I cannot find whereon to mount you. They turned back with eyes flowing with tears, for sorrow that they could not find the means to spend.

93. The road (of blame) is only against those who ask for

leave of thee (to stay at home) when they are rich. They are content to be with the useless. Allah hath sealed their hearts so that they know not.

94. They will make excuse to you (Muslims) when ye return unto them. Say: Make no excuse, for we shall not believe you. Allah hath told us tidings of you. Allah and His messenger will see your conduct, and then ye will be brought back unto Him who knoweth the invisible as well as the visible, and He will tell you that ye used to do.

95. They will swear by Allah unto you, when ye return unto them, that ye may let them be. Let them be, for lo! they are unclean, and their abode is hell as the reward for what they used to earn.

96. They swear unto you, that ye may accept them. Though ye accept them, Allah verily accepteth not wrongdoing folk.

97. The wandering Arabs are more hard in disbelief and hypocrisy, and more likely to be ignorant of the limits which Allah hath revealed unto His messenger. And Allah is Knower, Wise.

98. And of the wandering Arabs there is he who taketh that which he expendeth (for the cause of Allah), as a loss, and awaiteth (evil) turns of fortune for you (that he may be rid of it). The evil turn of fortune will be theirs. Allah is Hearer, Knower.

99. And of the wandering Arabs there is he who believeth in Allah and the Last Day, and taketh that which he expendeth and also the prayers of the messenger as acceptable offerings in the sight of Allah. Lo! verily it is an acceptable offering for them. Allah will bring them into His mercy. Lo! Allah is Forgiving, Merciful.

100. And the first to lead the way, of the Muhâjirîn and the Ansâr, and those who followed them in goodness — Allah is well pleased with them and they are well pleased with Him, and He hath made ready for them Gardens underneath which rivers flow, wherein they will abide for ever. That is the supreme triumph.

101. And among those around you of the wandering Arabs there are hypocrites, and among the townspeople of Al-Madînah (there are some who) persist in hypocrisy whom thou (O Muhammad) knowest not. We, We know them, and We shall chastise them twice; then they will be relegated to a painful doom.

102. And (there are) others who have acknowledged their faults. They mixed a righteous action with another that was bad. It may be that Allah will relent toward them. Lo! Allah

is Relenting, Merciful.

103. Take alms of their wealth, wherewith thou mayst purify them and mayst make them grow, and pray for them. Lo! thy prayer is an assuagement for them. Allah is Hearer, Knower.

104. Know they not that Allah is He Who accepteth repentance from His bondmen and taketh the alms, and that Allah is He Who is the Relenting, The Merciful.

105. And say (unto them): Act! Allah will behold your actions, and (so will) His messenger and the believers, and ye will be brought back to the Knower of the invisible and the visible, and He will tell you what ye used to do.

106. And (there are) others who await Allah's decree, whether He will punish them or will forgive them. Allah is Knower, Wise.

107. And as for those who chose a place of worship out of opposition and disbelief, and in order to cause dissent among the believers, and as an outpost for those who warred against Allah and His messenger aforetime, they will surely swear: We purposed naught save good. Allah beareth witness that they verily are liars.

108. Never stand (to pray) there. A place of worship which was founded upon duty (to Allah) from the first day is more worthy that thou shouldst stand (to pray) therein, wherein are men who love to purify themselves. Allah loveth the purifiers.

109. Is he who founded his building upon duty to Allah and His good pleasure better; or he who founded his building on the brink of a crumbling, overhanging precipice so that it toppled with him into the fire of hell? Allah guideth not wrongdoing folk.

110. The building which they built will never cease to be a misgiving in their hearts unless their hearts be torn to pieces. Allah is Knower, Wise.

111. Lo! Allah hath bought from the believers their lives and their wealth because the Garden will be theirs: they shall fight in the way of Allah and shall slay and be slain. It is a promise which is binding on Him in the Torah and the Gospel and the Qur'ân. Who fulfilleth His covenant better than Allah? Rejoice then in your bargain that ye have made, for that is the supreme triumph.

112. (Triumphant) are those who turn repentant (to Allah), those who serve (Him), those who praise (Him); those who fast; those who bow down, those who fall prostrate (in worship), those who enjoin the right and who forbid the wrong and those who keep the limits (ordained) of Allah—And give glad tidings

to believers!

113. It is not for the Prophet, and those who believe, to pray for the forgiveness of idolaters even though they may be near of kin (to them) after it hath become clear that they are people of hell-fire.

114. The prayer of Abraham for the forgiveness of his father was only because of a promise he had promised him, but when it had become clear unto him that he (his father) was an enemy to Allah he (Abraham) disowned him. Lo! Abraham was soft of heart, long-suffering.

115. It was never Allah's (part) that he should send a folk astray after He had guided them until He had made clear unto them what they should avoid. Lo! Allah is Aware of all things.

116. Lo! Allah! Unto Him belongeth the sovereignty of the heavens and the earth. He quickeneth and He giveth death. And ye have, instead of Allah, no protecting friend nor helper.

117. Allah hath turned in mercy to the Prophet, and to the Muhâjirîn and the Ansâr who followed him in the hour of hardship. After the hearts of a party of them had almost swerved aside, then turned He unto them in mercy: Lo! He is Full of Pity, Merciful for them.

118. And to the three also (did He turn in mercy) who were left behind, when the earth, vast as it is, was straitened for them, and their own souls were straitened for them till they bethought them that there is no refuge from Allah save toward Him. Then turned He unto them in mercy that they (too) might turn (repentant unto Him). Lo! Allah! He is the Relenting, the Merciful.

119. O ye who believe! Be careful of your duty to Allah, and be with the truthful.

120. It is not for the townsfolk of Al-Madînah and for those around them of the wandering Arabs to stay behind the messenger of Allah and prefer their lives to his life. That is because neither thirst nor toil nor hunger afflicteth them in the way of Allah, nor step they any step that angereth the disbelievers, nor gain they from the enemy a gain, but a good deed is recorded for them therefore. Lo! Allah loseth not the wages of the good.

121. Nor spend they any spending, small or great, nor do they cross a valley, but it is recorded for them, that Allah may repay them the best of what they used to do.

122. And the believers should not all go out to fight. Of every troop of them, a party only should go forth, that they (who are left behind) may gain sound knowledge in religion, and that they may warn their folk when they return to them, so that they

may beware.

123. O ye who believe! Fight those of the disbelievers who are near to you, and let them find harshness in you, and know that Allah is with those who keep their duty (unto Him).

124. And whenever a sûrah is revealed there are some of them who say: Which one of you hath thus increased in faith? As for those who believe, it hath increased them in faith and they rejoice (therefore).

125. But as for those in whose hearts is disease, it only addeth wickedness to their wickedness, and they die while they are disbelievers.

126. See they not that they are tested once or twice in every year? Still they turn not in repentance, neither pay they heed.

127. And whenever a sûrah is revealed, they look one at another (as who should say): Doth anybody see you? Then they turn away. Allah turneth away their hearts because they are a folk who understand not.

128. There hath come unto you a messenger, (one) of yourselves, unto whom aught that ye are overburdened is grievous, full of concern for you, for the believers full of pity, merciful.

129. Now, if they turn away (O Muhammad) say: Allah sufficeth me. There is no God save Him. In Him have I put my trust, and He is Lord of the Tremendous Throne.

SÛRAH 10

Derives its title from v. 99. "If only there had been a community (of those that were) destroyed of old that believed and profited by its belief as did the folk of Jonah!" As is the case with nearly all the Meccan Sûrahs, the date of revelation is uncertain, on account of the dearth of historical allusion. All that can with certainty be said is, that it belongs to the latest group of Meccan Sûrahs, and must therefore have been revealed at some time during the last four years before the Hijrah.

A late Meccan Sûrah, with the exception of three verses revealed at Al-Madînah.

JONAH

Revealed at Mecca

In the name of Allah, the Beneficent, the Merciful.

1. Alif, Lâm Râ. These are verses of the Wise Scripture.

2. Is it a wonder for mankind that We have inspired a man among them, saying: Warn mankind and bring unto those who

believe the good tidings that they have a sure footing with their Lord? The disbelievers say: Lo! this is a mere wizard.

3. Lo! your Lord is Allah Who created the heavens and the earth in six Days, then He established Himself upon the Throne, directing all things. There is no intercessor (with Him) save after His permission. That is Allah, your Lord, so worship Him: Oh, will ye not remind?

4. Unto Him is the return of all of you; it is a promise of Allah in truth. Lo! He produceth creation, then reproduceth it, that He may reward those who believe and do good works with equity; while, as for those who disbelieve, theirs will be a boiling drink and painful doom because they disbelieved.

5. He it is who appointed the sun a splendour and the moon a light, and measured for her stages, that ye might know the number of years, and the reckoning. Allah created not (all) that save in truth. He detaileth the revelations for people who have knowledge.

6. Lo! in the difference of day and night and all that Allah hath created in the heavens and the earth are portents, verily, for folk who ward off (evil).

7. Lo! those who expect not the meeting with Us but desire the life of the world and feel secure therein, and those who are neglectful of Our revelations.

8. Their home will be the Fire because of what they used to earn.

9. Lo! those who believe and do good works, their Lord guideth them by their faith. Rivers will flow beneath them in the Gardens of Delight.

10. Their prayer therein will be: Glory be to Thee, O Allah! and their greeting therein will be: Peace. And the conclusion of their prayer will be: Praise be to Allah, Lord of the Worlds.

11. If Allah were to hasten on for men the ill (that they have earned) as they would hasten on the good, their respite would already have expired. But We suffer those who look not for the meeting with Us to wander blindly on in their contumacy.

12. And if misfortune touch a man he crieth unto Us, (while reclining) on his side, or sitting or standing, but when We have relieved him of the misfortune he goeth his way as though he had not cried unto us because of a misfortune that afflicted him. Thus is what they do made (seeming) fair unto the prodigal.

13. We destroyed the generations before you when they did wrong; and their messengers (from Allah) came unto them with clear proofs (of His Sovereignty) but they would not believe. Thus do We reward the guilty folk.

14. Then We appointed you viceroys in the earth after

them, that We might see how ye behave.

15. And when Our clear revelations are recited unto them, they who look not for the meeting with Us say: Bring a Lecture other than this, or change it. Say (O Muhammad): It is not for me to change it of my own accord. I only follow that which is inspired in me. Lo! if I disobey my Lord I fear the retribution of an awful Day.

16. Say: If Allah had so willed I should not have recited it to you nor would He have made it known to you. I dwelt among you a whole lifetime before it (came to me). Have ye then no sense?

17. Who doeth greater wrong than he who inventeth a lie concerning Allah and denieth His revelations? Lo! the guilty never are successful.

18. They worship beside Allah that which neither hurteth them nor profiteth them, and they say: These are our intercessors with Allah. Say: Would ye inform Allah of (something) that He knoweth not in the heavens or in the earth? Praised be He and high exalted above all that ye associate (with Him)!

19. Mankind were but one community; then they differed; and had it not been for a word that had already gone forth from thy Lord it had been judged between them in respect of that wherein they differ.

20. And they will say: If only a portent were sent down upon him from his Lord! Then say (O Muhammad): The Unseen belongeth to Allah. So wait! Lo, I am waiting with you.

21. And when We cause mankind to taste of mercy after some adversity which had afflicted them, behold! they have some plot against Our revelations. Say: Allah is more swift in plotting. Lo! Our messengers write down that which ye plot.

22. He it is who maketh you to go on the land and the sea till, when ye are in the ships and they sail with them with a fair breeze and they are glad therein, a storm-wind reacheth them and the wave cometh unto them from every side and they deem that they are overwhelmed therein; (then) they cry unto Allah, making their faith pure for Him only; if Thou deliver us from this, we truly will be of the thankful.

23. Yet when He hath delivered them, behold! they rebel in the earth wrongfully. O mankind! Your rebellion is only against yourselves. (Ye have) enjoyment of the life of the world; then unto Us is your return and We shall proclaim unto you what ye used to do.

24. The similitude of the life of the world is only as water

which We send down from the sky then the earth's growth
of that which men and cattle eat mingleth with it till, when
the earth hath taken on her ornaments and is embellished,
and her people deem that they are masters of her, Our
commandment cometh by night or by day and we make it as
reaped corn as if it had not flourished yesterday. Thus do We
expound the revelations for people who reflect.

25. And Allah summoneth to the abode of peace, and
leadeth whom He will to a straight path.

26. For those who do good is the best (reward) and more
(thereto). Neither dust nor ignominy cometh near their faces.
Such are rightful owners of the Garden; they will abide
therein.

27. And those who earn ill deeds, (for them) requital of
each ill deed by the like thereof; and ignomity overtaketh
them—They have no protector from Allah—as if their faces
had been covered with a cloak of darkest night. Such are
rightful owners of the Fire; they will abide therein.

28. On the day when We gather them all together, then We
say unto those who ascribed partners (unto Us): Stand back,
ye and your (pretended) partners (of Allah)! And We separate
them, the one from the other, and their (pretended) partners
say: It was not us ye worshipped.

29. Allah sufficeth as a witness between us and you that
we were unaware of your worship.

30. There doth every soul experience that which it did
aforetime and they are returned unto Allah, their rightful
Lord, and that which they used to invent hath failed them.

31. Say (unto them, O Muhammad): Who provideth for you
from the sky and the earth, or Who owneth hearing and sight;
and Who bringeth forth the living from the dead and
bringeth forth the dead from the living; and Who directeth
the course? They will say: Allah. Then say: Will ye not then
keep your duty (unto Him)?

32. Such then is Allah, your rightful Lord. After the Truth
what is there saving error? How then are ye turned away!

33. Thus is the Word of thy Lord justified concerning those
who do wrong: that they believe not.

34. Say: Is there of your partners (whom ye ascribe unto
Allah) one that produceth Creation and then reproduceth it?
Say : Allah produceth Creation, then reproduceth it. How then,
are ye misled!

35. Say: Is there of your partners (whom ye ascribe unto
Allah) one that leadeth to the Truth? Say: Allah leadeth to the
Truth. Is He Who leadeth to the truth more deserving that He
should be followed, or he who findeth not the way unless he

(himself) be guided. What aileth you? How judge ye?

36. Most of them follow naught but conjecture. Assuredly conjecture can by no means take the place of truth. Lo! Allah is Aware of what they do.

37. And this Qur'ân is not such as could ever be invented in despite of Allah; but it is a confirmation of that which was before it and an exposition of that which is decreed for mankind—Therein is no doubt—from the Lord of the Worlds.

38. Or say they: He hath invented it? Say: Then bring a sûrah like unto it, and call (for help) on all ye can besides Allah, if ye are truthful.

39. Nay, but they denied that, the knowledge whereof they could not compass, and whereof the interpretation (in events) hath not yet come unto them. Even so did those before them deny. Then see what was the consequence for the wrongdoers!

40. And of them is he who believeth therein, and of them is he who believeth not therein, and thy Lord is best aware of the corruters.

41. And if they deny thee, say: Unto me my work, and unto you your work. Ye are innocent of what I do and I am innocent of what ye do.

42. And of them are some who listen unto thee. But canst thou make the deaf to hear even though they apprehend not?

43. And of them is he who looketh toward thee. But canst thou guide the blind even though they see not?

44. Lo! Allah wrongeth not mankind in aught; but mankind wrong themselves.

45. And on the day when He shall gather them together, (when it will seem) as though they had tarried but an hour of the day, recognising one another, those will verily have perished who denied the meeting with Allah and were not guided.

46. Whether We let thee (O Muhammad) behold something of that which We promise them or (whether We) cause thee to die, still unto Us is their return, and Allah, moreover, is Witness over what they do.

47. And for every nation there is a messenger. And when their messenger cometh (on the Day of judgement) it will be judged between them fairly, and they will not be wronged.

48. And they say; When will this promise be fulfilled, if ye are truthful?

49. Say: I have no power to hurt or benefit myself, save that which Allah willeth. For every nation there is an appointed time. When their time cometh, then they cannot put it off an hour, nor hasten (it).

50. Say: Have ye thought: When His doom cometh unto

you as a raid by night, or in the (busy) day; what is there of it that the guilty ones desire to hasten?

51. Is it (only) then, when it hath befallen you, that ye will believe? What! (Believe) now, when (until now) ye have been hastening it on (through disbelief)?

52. Then will it be said unto those who dealt unjustly: Taste the torment of eternity. Are ye requited aught save what ye used to earn?

53. And they ask thee to inform them (saying): Is it true? Say: Yea, by my Lord verily it is true, and ye cannot escape.

54. And if each soul that doeth wrong had all that is in the earth it would seek to ransom itself therewith; and they will feel remorse within them, when they see the doom. But it hath been judged between them fairly and they are not wronged.

55. Lo! verily all that is in the heavens and the earth is Allah's. Lo! verily Allah's promise is true. But most of them know not.

56. He quickeneth and giveth death, and unto Him ye will be returned.

57. O mankind! There hath come unto you an exhortation from your Lord, a balm for that which is in the breasts, a guidance and a mercy for believers.

58. Say: In the bounty of Allah and in His mercy; therein let them rejoice. It is better than what they hoard.

59. Say: Have ye considered what provision Allah hath sent down for you, how ye have made of it lawful and unlawful? Say: Hath Allah permitted you, or do ye invent a lie concerning Allah?

60. And what think those who invent a lie concerning Allah (will be their plight) upon the Day of Resurrection? Lo! Allah truly is Bountiful toward mankind, but most of them give not thanks.

61. And thou (Muhammad) art not occupied with any business and thou recitest not a Lecture from this (Scripture), and ye (mankind) perform no act, but We are Witness of you when ye are engaged therein. And not an atom's weight in the earth or in the sky escapeth your Lord, nor what is less than that or greater than that, but it is (written) in a clear Book.

62. Lo! verily the friends of Allah are (those) on whom fear (cometh) not, nor do they grieve.

63. Those who believe and keep their duty (to Allah).

64. Theirs are good tidings in the life of the world and in the Hereafter—There is no changing the Words of Allah—that is the Supreme Triumph.

65. And let not their speech grieve thee (O Muhammad). Lo! power belongeth wholly to Allah. He is the Hearer, the

Knower.

66. Lo! is it not unto Allah that belongeth whosoever is in the heavens and whosoever is in the earth? Those who follow aught instead of Allah follow not (His) partners. They follow only a conjecture, and they do but guess.

67. He it is who hath appointed for you the night that ye should rest therein and the day giving sight. Lo! herein verily are portents for a folk that heed.

68. They say: Allah hath taken (unto Him) a son—Glorified be He! He hath no needs! His is all that is in the heavens and all that is in the earth. Ye have no warrant for this. Tell ye concerning Allah that which ye know not?

69. Say: Verily those who invent a lie concerning Allah will not succeed.

70. This world's portion (will be theirs) then unto Us is their return, Then We make them taste a dreadful doom because they used to disbelieve.

71. Recite unto them the story of Noah, when he told his people: O my people! If my sojourn (here) and my reminding you by Allah's revelations are an offence unto you, in Allah have I put my trust, so decide upon your course of action, you and your partners. Let not your course of action be in doubt, for you. Then have at me, give me no respite.

72. But if ye are averse I have asked of you no wage. My wage is the concern of Allah only, and I am commanded to be of those who surrender (unto Him).

73. But they denied him, so We saved him and those with him in the ship, and made them viceroys (in the earth), while We drowned those who denied Our revelations. See then the nature of the consequence for those who had been warned.

74. Then, after him, We sent messengers unto their folk, and they brought them clear proofs. But they were not ready to believe in that which they before denied. Thus print We on the hearts of the transgressors.

75. Then, after them, We sent Moses and Aaron unto Pharaoh and his chiefs with Our revelations, but they were arrogant and were a guilty folk.

76. And when the Truth from Our presence came unto them, they said: Lo! this is mere magic.

77. Moses said: Speak ye (so) of the Truth when it hath come unto you? Is this magic? Now magicians thrive not.

78. They said: Hast thou come unto us to pervert us from that (faith) in which we found our fathers, and that you two may own the place of greatness in the land? We will not believe you two.

79. And Pharaoh said: Bring every cunning wizard unto

me.

80. And when the wizards came, Moses said unto them: Cast your cast!

81. And when they had cast, Moses said: That which ye have brought is magic. Lo! Allah will make it vain. Lo! Allah upholdeth not the work of mischief makers.

82. And Allah will vindicate the Truth by His words, however much the guilty be averse.

83. But none trusted Moses, save some scions of his people (and they were) in fear of Pharaoh and their chiefs, that they would persecute them. Lo! Pharaoh was verily a tyrant in the land, and lo! he verily was of the wanton.

84. And Moses said: O my people! If ye have believed in Allah then put trust in Him, if ye have indeed surrendered (unto Him)!

85. They said: In Allah we put trust. Our Lord! Oh, make us not a lure for the wrong-doing folk.

86. And, of Thy mercy, save us from the folk that disbelieve.

87. And We inspired Moses and his brother; (saying) Appoint houses for your people in Egypt and make your houses oratories, and establish worship. And give good news to the believers.

88. And Moses said: Our Lord! Lo! thou hast given Pharaoh and his chiefs splendour and riches in the life of the world. Our Lord! that they may lead men astray from Thy way, our Lord! Destroy their riches and harden their hearts so that they believe not till they see the painful doom.

89. He said: Your prayer is heard. Do ye twain keep to the straight path, and follow not the road of those who have no knowledge.

90. And We brought the Children of Israel across the sea, and Pharaoh with his hosts pursued them in rebellion and transgression, till, when the (fate of) drowning overtook him, he exclaimed: I believe that there is no God save Him in whom the Children of Israel believe, and I am of those who surrender (unto Him).

91. What! Now! When hitherto thou hast rebelled and been of the wrong-doers?

92. But this day We save thee in thy body that thou mayest be a portent for those after thee. Lo! most of mankind are heedless of Our portents.

93. And We verily did allot unto the Children of Israel a fixed abode, and did provide them with good things; and they differed not until knowledge came unto them. Lo! thy Lord will judge between them on the Day of Resurrection concerning that

wherein they used to differ.

94. And if thou (Muhammad) art in doubt concerning that which We reveal unto thee, then question those who read the Scripture (that was) before thee. Verily the Truth from my Lord hath come unto thee. So be not thou of the waverers.

95. And be not thou of those who deny the revelations of Allah, for then wert thou of the losers.

96. Lo! those for whom the word of thy Lord (concerning sinners) hath effect will not believe.

97. Though every token come unto them, till they see the painful doom.

98. If only there had been a community (of all those that were destroyed of old) that believed and profited by its belief as did the folk of Jonah! When they believed We drew off from them the torment of disgrace in the life of the world and gave them comfort for a while.

99. And if thy Lord willed, all who were in the earth would have believed together. Wouldst thou (Muhammad) compel men until they are believers?

100. It is not for any soul to believe save by the permission of Allah. He hath sent uncleanness upon those who have no sense.

101. Say: Behold what is in the heavens and the earth! But revelations and warnings avail not folk who will not believe.

102. What expect they save the like of the days of those who passed away before them? Say: Expect then! I am with you among the expectant.

103. Then shall We save Our messengers and the believers, in like manner (as of old). It is incumbent upon Us to save believers.

104. Say (O Muhammad): O mankind! If ye are in doubt of my religion, then (know that) I worship not those whom ye worship instead of Allah, but I worship Allah who causeth you to die, and I have been commanded to be of the believers.

105. And, (O Muhammad) set thy purpose resolutely for religion, as a man by nature upright, and be not of those who ascribe partners (to Allah).

106. And cry not, beside Allah, unto that which cannot profit thee nor hurt thee, for if thou didst so then wert thou of the wrong-doers.

107. If Allah afflicteth thee with some hurt, there is none who can remove it save Him; and if He desireth good for thee, there is none who can repel His bounty. He striketh with it whom He will of his bondmen. He is the Forgiving, the Merciful.

108. Say: O mankind! Now hath the Truth from your Lord come unto you. So whosoever is guided, is guided only for (the good of) his soul, and whosoever erreth erreth only against it. And I am not a warder over you.

109. And (O Muhammad) follow that which is inspired in thee, and forbear until Allah give judgement. And He is the Best of Judges.

SÛRAH 11

Takes its name from v. 50, which begins the story of Hûd, of the tribe of A'âd, one of the prophets of Arabia who is not mentioned in the Hebrew Scriptures. The Sûrah also contains the stories of two other Arab prophets, Sâlih, of the tribe of Thamûd, and Shu'eyb of Midian (identified with Jethro), which, with those of Noah and Moses, are quoted as part of the history of Divine Revelation, the truth of which is here vindicated, in a manner supplementary to Sûrah 10.

A late Meccan Sûrah, except v. 114 f., revealed at Al-Madînah.

HÛD

Revealed at Mecca

In the name of Allah, the Beneficent, the Merciful.

1. Alif. Lâm. Râ. (This is) a Scripture the revelations whereof are perfected and then expounded. (It cometh) from One Wise, Informed.

2. (Saying): Serve none but Allah. Lo! I am unto you from Him a warner and a bringer of good things.

3. And (bidding you): Ask pardon of your Lord and turn to Him repentant. He will cause you to enjoy a fair estate until a time appointed. He giveth His bounty unto every bountiful one. But if ye turn away, lo! (then) I fear for you the retribution of an awful Day.

4. Unto Allah is your return, and He is able to do all things.

5. Lo! now they fold up their breasts that they may hide (their thoughts) from Him. At the very moment when they cover themselves with their clothing, Allah knoweth that which they keep hidden and that which they proclaim. Lo! He is Aware of what is in the breasts (of men).

6. And there is not a beast in the earth but the sustenance thereof dependeth on Allah. He knoweth its habitation and its repository. All is in a clear record.

7. And He it is Who created the heavens and the earth in

six Days—and His Throne was upon the water—that He might try you, which of you is best in conduct. Yet if thou (O Muhammad) sayest: Lo! ye will be raised again after death! those who disbelieve will surely say: This is naught but mere magic.

8. And if We delay for them the doom until a reckoned time, they will surely say: What withholdeth it? Verily on the day when it cometh unto them, it cannot be averted from them, and that which they derided will surround them.

9. And if We cause man to taste some mercy from Us and afterward withdraw it from him, lo! he is despairing, thankless.

10. And if We cause him to taste grace after some misfortune that had befallen him, he saith: The ills have gone from me. Lo! he is exultant, boastful.

11. Save those who persevere and do good works. Theirs will be forgiveness and a great reward.

12. A likely thing, that thou wouldst forsake aught of that which hath been revealed unto thee, and that thy breast should be straitened for it, because they say: Why hath not a treasure been sent down for him, or an angel come with him? Thou art but a warner, and Allah is in charge of all things.

13. Or they say: He hath invented it. Say: Then bring ten sûrahs, the like thereof, invented, and call on everyone ye can beside Allah, if ye are truthful!

14. And if they answer not your prayer, then know that it is revealed only in the knowledge of Allah; and that there is no God save Him. Will ye then be (of) those who surrender?

15. Whoso desireth the life of the world and its pomp, We shall repay them their deeds herein, and therein they will not be wronged.

16. Those are they for whom is naught in the Hereafter save the Fire. (All) that they contrive here is vain and (all) that they are wont to do is fruitless.

17. Is he (to be counted equal with them) who relieth on a clear proof from his Lord, and a witness from Him reciteth it, and before it was the Book of Moses, an example and a mercy? Such believe therein, and whoso disbelieveth therein of the clans, the Fire is his appointed place. So be not thou in doubt concerning it. Lo! It is the Truth from thy Lord; but most of mankind believe not.

18. Who doeth greater wrong than he who inventeth a lie concerning Allah? Such will be brought before their Lord, and the witnesses will say: These are they who lied concerning their Lord. Now the curse of Allah is upon wrong-doers.

19. Who debar (men) from the way of Allah and would have

it crooked, and who are disbelievers in the Hereafter.

20. Such will not escape in the earth, nor have they any protecting friends beside Allah. For them the torment will be double. They could not bear to hear, and they used not to see.

21. Such are they who have lost their souls, and that which they used to invent hath failed them.

22. Assuredly in the Hereafter they will be the greatest losers.

23. Lo! those who believe and do good works and humble themselves before their Lord: such are rightful owners of the Garden; they will abide therein.

24. The similitude of the two parties is as the blind and the deaf and the seer and the hearer. Are they equal in similitude? Will ye not then be admonished?

25. And We sent Noah unto his folk (and he said): Lo! I am a plain warner unto you.

26. That ye serve none, save Allah. Lo! I fear for you the retribution of a painful Day.

27. The chieftains of his folk, who disbelieved, said: We see thee but a mortal like us, and we see not that any follow thee save the most abject among us, without reflection. We behold in you no merit above us—nay, we deem you liars.

28. He said: O my people! Bethink you, if I rely on a clear proof from my Lord and there hath come unto me a mercy from His presence, and it hath been made obscure to you, can we compel you to accept it when ye are averse thereto?

29. And O my people! I ask of you no wealth therefore. My reward is the concern only of Allah, and I am not going to thrust away those who believe—Lo! they have to meet their Lord—but I see you a folk that are ignorant.

30. And, O my people! who would deliver me from Allah if I thrust them away? Will ye not then reflect?

31. I say not unto you: "I have the treasures of Allah" nor "I have knowledge of the Unseen", nor say I: "Lo! I am an angel!" Nor say I unto those whom your eyes scorn that Allah will not give them good—Allah knoweth best what is in their hearts—Lo! then indeed I should be of the wrong-doers.

32. They said: O Noah! Thou hast disputed with us and multiplied disputation with us; now bring upon us that wherewith thou threatenest us, if thou art of the truthful.

33. He said: Only Allah will bring it upon you if He will, and ye can by no means escape.

34. My counsel will not profit you if I were minded to advise you, if Allah's will is to keep you astray. He is your Lord and unto Him ye will be brought back.

35. Or say they (again): He hath invented it? Say: If I have invented it, upon me be my crimes, but I am innocent of (all) that ye commit.

36. And it was inspired in Noah, (saying): No one of thy folk will believe save him who hath believed already. Be not distressed because of what they do.

37. Build the ship under Our Eyes and by Our inspiration, and speak not unto Me on behalf of those who do wrong. Lo! they will be drowned.

38. And he was building the ship, and every time that chieftains of his people passed him, they made mock of him. He said: Though ye make mock of us, yet we mock at you even as ye mock.

39. And ye shall know to whom a punishment that will confound him cometh, and upon whom a lasting doom will fall.

40. (Thus it was) till, when Our commandment came to pass and the oven gushed forth water, We said: Load therein two of every kind, a pair (the male and female), and thy household, save him against whom the word hath gone forth already, and those who believe. And but a few were they who believed with him.

41. And he said: Embark therein! In the name of Allah be its course and its mooring. Lo! my Lord is Forgiving, Merciful.

42. And it sailed with them amid waves like mountains, and Noah cried unto his son—and he was standing aloof—O my son! Come ride with us, and be not with the disbelievers.

43. He said: I shall betake me to some mountain that will save me from the water. (Noah) said: This day there is none that saveth from the commandment of Allah save him on whom He hath had mercy. And the wave came in between them, so he was among the drowned.

44. And it was said: O earth! Swallow thy water and, O sky! be cleared of clouds! And the water was made to subside. And the commandment was fulfilled. And it (the ship) came to rest upon (the mount) Al-Jûdî and it was said: A far removal for wrongdoing folk!

45. And Noah cried unto his Lord and said: My Lord! Lo! my son is of my household! Surely Thy promise is the Truth and Thou art the Most Just of Judges.

46. He said: O Noah! Lo! he is not of thy household; lo! he is of evil conduct, so ask not of Me that whereof thou hast no knowledge. I admonish thee lest thou be among the ignorant.

47. He said: My Lord! Lo! in Thee do I seek refuge (from the sin) that I should ask of Thee that whereof I have no knowledge. Unless Thou forgive me and have mercy on me I shall be among

the lost.

48. It was said (unto him): O Noah! Go thou down (from the mountain) with peace from Us and blessings upon thee and some nations (that will spring) from those with thee. (There will be other) nations whom We shall give enjoyment a long while and then a painful doom from Us will overtake them.

49. This is of the tidings of the Unseen which We inspire in thee (Muhammad). Thou thyself knewest it not, nor did thy folk (know it) before this. Then have patience. Lo! the sequel is for those who ward off (evil).

50. And unto (the tribe of) A'âd (We sent) their brother, Hûd. He said: O my people! Serve Allah! Ye have no other God save Him. Lo! ye do but invent!

51. O my people! I ask of you no reward for it. Lo! my reward is the concern only of Him who made me. Have ye then no sense?

52. And, O my people! Ask forgiveness of your Lord, then turn unto Him repentant; He will cause the sky to rain abundance on you and will add unto you strength to your strength. Turn not away, guilty!

53. They said: O Hûd! Thou hast brought us no clear proof and we are not going to forsake our gods on thy (mere) saying, and we are not believers in thee.

54. We say naught save that one of our gods hath possessed thee in an evil way. He said: I call Allah to witness, and do ye (too) bear witness, that I am innocent of (all) that ye ascribe as partners (to Allah).

55. Beside Him. So (try to) circumvent me, all of you, give me no respite.

56. Lo! I have put my trust in Allah, my Lord and your Lord. Not an animal but He doth grasp it by the forelock! Lo! my Lord is on a straight path.

57. And if ye turn away, still I have conveyed unto you that wherewith I was sent unto you, and my Lord will set in place of you a folk other than you. Ye cannot injure Him at all. Lo! my Lord is Guardian over all things.

58. And when Our commandment came to pass We saved Hûd and those who believed with him by a mercy from Us; We saved them from a harsh doom.

59. And such were A'âd. They denied the revelations of their Lord and flouted His messengers and followed the command of every forward potentate.

60. And a curse was made to follow them in the world and on the Day of Resurrection. Lo! A'âd disbelieved in their Lord.

A far removal for A'âd, the folk of Hûd!

61. And unto (the tribe of) Thamûd (We sent) their brother Sâlih. He said: O my people! Serve Allah, Ye have no other God save Him. He brought you forth from the earth and hath made you husband it. So ask forgiveness of Him and turn unto Him repentant. Lo, my Lord is Nigh, Responsive.

62. They said: O Sâlih! Thou hast been among us hitherto as that wherein our hope was placed. Lo! we verily are in grave doubt concerning that to which thou callest us.

63. He said: O my people! Bethink you: if I am (acting) on clear proof from my Lord and there hath come unto me a mercy from Him, who will save me from Allah if I disobey Him? Ye would add to me naught save perdition.

64. O my people! This is the camel of Allah, a token unto you, so suffer her to feed in Allah's earth, and touch her not with harm lest a near torment seize you.

65. But they hamstrung her, and then he said: Enjoy life in your dwelling-place three days! This is a threat that will not be belied.

66. So, when Our commandment came to pass, We saved Sâlih, and those who believed with him, by a mercy from Us, from the ignominy of that day. Lo, thy Lord! He is the Strong, the Mighty.

67. And the (Awful) Cry overtook those who did wrong, so that morning found them prostrate in their dwellings.

68. As though they had not dwelt there. Lo! Thamûd disbelieved in their Lord. A far removal for Thamûd!

69. And Our messengers came unto Abraham with good news. They said: Peace! He answered: Peace! and delayed not to bring a roasted calf.

70. And when he saw their hands reached not to it, he mistrusted them and conceived a fear of them. They said: Fear not! Lo! we are sent unto the folk of Lot.

71. And his wife, standing by, laughed when We gave her good tidings (of the birth) of Isaac, and, after Isaac, of Jacob.

72. She said: Oh, woe is me! Shall I bear a child when I am an old woman, and this my husband is an old man? Lo! this is a strange thing.

73. They said: Wonderest thou at the commandment of Allah? The mercy of Allah and His blessings be upon you, O people of the house! Lo! He is Owner of Praise, Owner of Glory!

74. And when the awe departed from Abraham, and the glad news reached him, he pleaded with Us on behalf of the folk of Lot.

75. Lo! Abraham was mild, imploring, penitent.

76. (It was said) O Abraham! Forsake this! Lo! thy Lord's commandment hath gone forth, an lo! there cometh unto them a doom which cannot be repelled.

77. And when Our messengers came unto Lot, he was distressed and knew not how to protect them. He said: This is a distressful day.

78. And his people came unto him, running towards him — and before then they used to commit abominations — He said: O my people! Here are my daughters! They are purer for you. Beware of Allah, and degrade me not in (the person of) my guests. Is there not among you any upright man?

79. They said: Well thou knowest that we have no right to thy daughters, and well thou knowest what we want.

80. He said: Would that I had strength to resist you or had some strong support (among you)!

81. (The messengers) said: O Lot! Lo! we are messengers of thy Lord; they shall not reach thee. So travel with thy people in a part of the night, and let not one of you turn round — (all) save thy wife. Lo! that which smiteth them will smite her (also). Lo! their trust is (for) the morning: Is not the morning nigh?

82. So when Our commandment came to pass We overthrew (that township) and rained upon it stones of clay, one after another.

83. Marked with fire in the providence of thy Lord (for the destruction of the wicked). And they are never far from the wrongdoers.

84. And unto Midian (We sent) their brother Shu'eyb. He said: O my people! Serve Allah. Ye have no other God save Him! And give not short measure and short weight. Lo! I see you well-to-do, and lo! I fear for you the doom of a besetting Day.

85. O my people! Give full measure and full weight in justice, and wrong not people in respect of their goods. And do not evil in the earth, causing corruption.

86. That which Allah leaveth with you is better for you if ye are believers; and I am not a keeper over you.

87. They said: O Shu'eyb! Doth thy way of prayer command thee that we should forsake that which our fathers (used to) worship, or that we (should leave off) doing what we will with our own property. Lo! thou art the mild, the guide to right behaviour.

88. He said: O my people! Bethink you: if I am (acting) on a clear proof from my Lord and He sustaineth me with fair sustenance from Him (how can I concede aught to you)? I desire

not to do behind your backs that which I ask you not to do. I desire naught save reform so far as I am able. My welfare is only in Allah. In Him I trust and unto Him I turn (repentant).

89. And, O my people! Let not the schism with me cause you to sin so that there befall you that which befell the folk of Noah and the folk of Hûd, and the folk of Sâlih; and the folk of Lot are not far off from you.

90. Ask pardon of your Lord and then turn unto Him (repentant). Lo! My Lord is Merciful, Loving.

91. They said: O Shu'eyb! We understand not much of that thou tellest, and lo! we do behold thee weak among us. But for thy family, we should have stoned thee, for thou art not strong against us.

92. He said: O my people! Is my family more to be honoured by you than Allah? And ye put Him behind you, neglected! Lo! my Lord surroundeth what ye do.

93. And, O my people! Act according to your power, lo, I (too) am acting. Ye will soon know on whom there cometh a doom that will abase him, and who it is that lieth. And watch! Lo! I am a watcher with you.

94. And when Our commandment came to pass We saved Shu'eyb and those who believed with Him by a mercy from Us; and the (Awful) Cry seized those who did injustice, and morning found them prostrate in their dwellings.

95. As though they had not dwelt there. A far removal for Midian, even as Thamûd had been removed afar!

96. And verily We sent Moses with Our revelations and a clear warrant.

97. Unto Pharaoh and his chiefs, but they did follow the command of Pharaoh, and the command of Pharaoh was no right guide.

98. He will go before his people on the Day of Resurrection and will lead them to the Fire for watering-place. Ah, hapless is the watering-place (whither they are) led.

99. A curse is made to follow them in the world and on the Day of Resurrection. Hapless is the gift (that will be) given (them).

100. That is (something) of the tidings of the townships (which were destroyed of old). We relate it unto thee (Muhammad). Some of them are standing and some (already) reaped.

101. We wronged them not, but they did wrong themselves; and their gods on whom they call beside Allah availed them naught when came thy Lord's command; they added to them

naught save ruin.

102. Even thus is the grasp of thy Lord when he graspeth the townships while they are doing wrong. Lo! His grasp is painful, very strong.

103. Lo! herein verily there is a portent for those who fear the doom of the Hereafter. That is a day unto which mankind will be gathered, and that is a day that will be witnessed.

104. And We defer it only as a term already reckoned.

105. On the day when it cometh no soul will speak except by His permission; some among them will be wretched, (others) glad.

106. As for those who will be wretched (on that day) they will be in the Fire; sighing and wailing will be their portion therein.

107. Abiding there so long as the heavens and the earth endure save for that which thy Lord willeth. Lo! thy Lord is Doer of what He will.

108. And as for those who will be glad (that day) they will be in the Garden, abiding there so long as the heavens and the earth endure save for that which thy Lord willeth: a gift unfailing.

109. So be not thou in doubt concerning that which these (folk) worship. They worship only as their fathers worshipped aforetime. Lo! We shall pay them their whole due unabated.

110. And We verily gave unto Moses the Scripture, and there was strife thereupon; and had it not been for a Word that had already gone forth from thy Lord, the case would have been judged between them, and lo! they are in grave doubt concerning it.

111. And lo! unto each thy Lord will verily repay his works in full. Lo! He is Informed of what they do.

112. So tread thou the straight path as thou art commanded, and those who turn (unto Allah) with thee, and transgress not. Lo! He is Seer of what ye do.

113. And incline not toward those who do wrong lest the Fire touch you, and ye have no protecting friends against Allah, and afterward ye would not be helped.

114. Establish worship at the two ends of the day and in some watches of the night. Lo! good deeds annul ill deeds. This is a reminder for the mindful.

115. And have patience, (O Muhammad), for lo! Allah loseth not the wages of the good.

116. If only there had been among the generations before you men possessing a remnant (of good sense) to warn (their

people) from corruption in the earth, as did a few of those whom We saved from them! The wrongdoers followed that by which they were made sapless, and were guilty.

117. In truth thy Lord destroyed not the townships tyrannously while their folk were doing right.

118. And if thy Lord had willed, He verily would have made mankind one nation, yet they cease not differing.

119. Save him on whom thy Lord hath mercy; and for that He did create them. And the Word of thy Lord hath been fulfilled:Verily I shall fill hell with the jinn and mankind together.

120. And all that We relate unto thee of the story of the messengers is in order that thereby We may make firm thy heart. And herein hath come unto thee the Truth and an exhortation and a reminder for believers.

121. And say unto those who believe not: Act according to your power. Lo! we (too) are acting.

122. And wait! Lo! we (too) are waiting.

123. And Allah's is the Invisible of the heavens and the earth, and unto Him the whole matter will be returned. So worship Him and put thy trust in Him. Lo! thy Lord is not unaware of what ye (mortals) do.

SÛRAH 12

Yûsuf takes its name from its subject which is the life-story of Joseph. It differs from all other sûrahs in having only one subject. The differences from the Bible narrative are striking. Jacob is here a Prophet, who is not deceived by the story of his son's death, but is distressed because, through a suspension of his clairvoyance, he cannot see what has become of Joseph. The real importance of the narrative, its psychic burden, is emphasised throughout, and the manner of narration, though astonishing to Western readers, is vivid.

Tradition says that it was recited by the Prophet at Mecca to the first converts from Yathrib (Al-Madînah), *i.e.* in the second year before the Hijrah; but that, as Nöldeke points out, does not mean that it was not revealed till then, but that it had been revealed by then.

A late Meccan Sûrah.

JOSEPH

Revealed at Mecca

In the name of Allah, the Beneficent, the Merciful.

1. Alif. Lâm. Râ. These are verses of the Scripture that maketh plain.

154

2. Lo! We have revealed it, a Lecture in Arabic, that ye may understand.

3. We narrate unto thee (Muhammad) the best of narratives in that We have inspired in thee this Qur'ân, though aforetime thou wast of the heedless.

4. When Jospeh said unto his father: O my father! Lo! I saw in a dream elevan planets and the sun and the moon, I saw them prostrating themselves unto me.

5. He said: O my dear son! Tell not thy brethren of thy vision, lest they plot a plot against thee. Lo! Satan is for man an open foe.

6. Thus thy Lord will prefer thee and will teach thee the interpretation of events, and will perfect His grace upon thee and upon the family of Jacob as He perfected it upon thy forefathers, Abraham and Isaac. Lo! thy Lord is Knower, Wise.

7. Verily in Joseph and his brethren are signs (of Allah's Sovereignty) for the inquiring.

8. When they said: Verily Joseph and his brother are dearer to our father than we are, many though we be. Lo! our father is in plain aberration.

9. (One said): Kill Joseph or cast him to some (other) land, so that your father's favour may be all for you; and (that) ye may afterward be righteous folk.

10. One among them said: Kill not Joseph but, if ye must be doing, fling him into the depth of the pit; some caravan will find him.

11. They said: O our father! Why wilt thou not trust us with Joseph, when lo! we are good friends to him?

12. Send him with us tomorrow that he may enjoy himself and play. And lo! we shall take good care of him.

13. He said: Lo! in truth it saddens me that ye should take him with you, and I fear lest the wolf devour him while ye are heedless of him.

14. They said: If the wolf should devour him when we are (so strong) a band, then surely we should have already perished.

15. Then, when they led him off, and were of one mind that they should place him in the depth of the pit, We inspired in him: Thou wilt tell them of this deed of theirs when they know (thee) not.

16. And they came weeping to their father in the evening.

17. Saying: O our father! We went racing one with another, and left Joseph by our things, and the wolf devoured him, and thou believest not our sayings even when we speak the truth.

18. And they came with false blood on his shirt. He said:

Nay, but your minds have beguiled you into something. (My course is) comely patience. And Allah it is Whose help is to be sought in that (predicament) which ye describe.

19. And there came a caravan, and they sent their water-drawer. He let down his pail (into the pit). He said: Good luck! Here is a youth. And they hid him as a treasure, and Allah was Aware of what they did.

20. And they sold him for a low price, a number of silver coins; and they attached no value to him.

21. And he of Egypt who purchased him said unto his wife: Receive him honourably. Perchance he may prove useful to us or we may adopt him as a son. Thus We established Joseph in the land that We might teach him the interpretation of events. And Allah was predominant in his career, but most of mankind know not.

22. And when he reached his prime We gave him wisdom and knowledge. Thus We reward the good.

23. And she, in whose house he was, asked of him an evil act. She bolted the doors and said: Come! He said: I seek refuge in Allah! Lo! he is my lord, who hath treated me honourably. Wrongdoers never prosper.

24. She verily desired him, and he would have desired her if it had not been that he saw the argument of his Lord. Thus it was, that We might ward off from him evil and lewdness. Lo! he was of Our chosen slaves.

25. And they raced with one another to the door, and she tore his shirt from behind, and they met her lord and master at the door. She said: What shall be his reward, who wisheth evil to thy folk, save prison or a painful doom?

26. (Joseph) said: She it was who asked of me an evil act. And a witness of her own folk testified: If his shirt is torn from before, then she speaketh truth and he is of the liars.

27. And if his shirt is torn from behind, then she hath lied and he is of the truthful.

28. So when he saw his shirt torn from behind, he said: Lo! this is of the guile of you women. Lo! the guile of you is very great.

29. O Joseph! Turn away from this, and thou, (O woman), ask forgiveness for thy sin. Lo! thou art of the sinful.

30. And women in the city said: The ruler's wife is asking of her slave-boy an ill deed. Indeed he has smitten her to the heart with love. We behold her in plain aberration.

31. And when she heard of their sly talk, she sent to them and prepared for them a cushioned couch (to lie on at the feast) and gave to every one of them a knife and said (to Joseph):

Come out unto them! And when they saw him they exalted him and cut their hands, exclaiming: Allah Blameless! This is not a human being. This is no other than some gracious angel.

32. She said: This is he on whose account ye blamed me. I asked of him an evil act, but he proved continent, but if he do not my behest he verily shall be imprisoned, and verily shall be of those brought low.

33. He said: O my Lord! Prison is more dear than that unto which they urge me, and if Thou fend not off their wiles from me I shall incline into them and become of the foolish.

34. So his Lord heard his prayer and fended off their wiles from him. Lo! he is Hearer, Knower.

35. And it seemed good to them (the men-folk) after they had seen the signs (of his innocence) to imprison him for a time.

36. And two young men went to prison with him. One of them said: I dreamed that I was pressing wine. The other said: I dreamed that I was carrying upon my head bread whereof the birds were eating. Announce unto us the interpretation, for we see thee of those good (at interpretation).

37. He said: The food which ye are given (daily) shall not come unto you but I shall tell you the interpretation ere if cometh unto you. This is of that which my Lord hath taught me. Lo! I have forsaken the religion of folk who believe not in Allah and are disbelievers in the Hereafter.

38. And I have followed the religion of my fathers, Abraham and Isaac and Jacob. It never was for us to attribute aught as partner to Allah. This is of the bounty of Allah unto us (the seed of Abraham) and unto mankind; but most men give not thanks.

39. O my two fellow-prisoners! Are divers lords better, or Allah the One, the Almighty?

40. Those whom ye worship beside Him are but names which ye have named, ye and your fathers. Allah hath revealed no sanction for them. The decision rests with Allah only, Who hath commanded you that ye worship none save Him. This is the right religion, but most men know not.

41. O my two fellow-prisoners! As for one of you, he will pour out wine for his lord to drink; and as for the other, he will be crucified so that the birds will eat from his head. Thus is the case judged concerning which ye did inquire.

42. And he said unto him of the twain who he knew would be released: Mention me in the presence of thy lord. But Satan caused him to forget to mention it to his lord, so he (Joseph) stayed in prison for some years.

43. And the king said: Lo! I saw in a dream seven fat kine

which seven lean were eating, and seven green ears of corn and other (seven) dry. O notables! Expound for me my vision, if ye can interpret dreams.

44. They answered: Jumbled dreams! And we are not knowing in the interpretation of dreams.

45. And he of the two who was released, and (now) at length remembered, said: I am going to announce unto you the interpretation, therefore send me forth.

46. (And when he came to Joseph in the prison, he exclaimed): Joseph! O thou truthful one! Expound for us the seven fat kine which seven lean were eating and the seven green ears of corn and other (seven) dry, that I may return unto the people, so that they may know.

47. He said: Ye shall sow seven years as usual, but that which ye reap, leave it in the ear, all save a little which ye eat.

48. Then after that will come seven hard years which will devour all that ye have prepared for them, save a little of that which ye have stored.

49. Then, after that, will come a year when the people will have plenteous crops and when they will press (wine and oil).

50. And the king said: Bring him unto me. And when the messenger came unto him, he (Joseph) said: Return unto thy lord and ask him what was the case of the women who cut their hands. Lo! my lord knoweth their guile.

51. He (the king) (then sent for those women and) said: What happened when ye asked an evil act of Joseph? They answered: Allah Blameless! We know no evil of him. Said the wife of the ruler: Now the truth is out. I asked of him an evil act, and he is surely of the truthful.

52. (Then Joseph said: I asked for) this, that he (my lord) may know that I betrayed him not in secret, and that surely Allah guideth not the snare of the betrayers.

53. I do not exculpate myself. Lo! the (human) soul enjoineth unto evil, save that whereon my Lord hath mercy. Lo! my Lord is Forgiving, Merciful.

54. And the king said: Bring him unto me that I may attach him to my person. And when he had talked with him he said: Lo! thou art today in our presence established and trusted.

55. He said: Set me over the storehouses of the land. Lo! I am a skilled custodian.

56. Thus gave We power to Joseph in the land. He was the owner of it where he pleased. We reach with Our mercy whom We will. We lose not the reward of the good.

57. And the reward of the Hereafter is better, for those who believe and ward off (evil).

58. And Joseph's brethren came and presented themselves before him, and he knew them but they knew him not.

59. And when he provided them with their provision he said: Bring unto me a brother of yours from your father. See ye not that I fill up the measure and I am the best of hosts?

60. And if ye bring him not unto me, then there shall be no measure for you with me, nor shall ye draw near.

61. They said: We will try to win him from his father: that we will surely do.

62. He said unto his young men: Place their merchandise in their saddlebags, so that they may know it when they go back to their folk, and so will come again.

63. So when they went back to their father they said: O our father! The measure is denied us, so send with us our brother that we may obtain the measure, surely we will guard him well.

64. He said: Can I entrust him to you save as I entrusted his brother to you aforetime? Allah is better at guarding, and He is the Most Merciful of those who show mercy.

65. And when they opened their belongings they discovered that their merchandise had been returned to them. They said: O our father! What (more) can we ask? Here is our merchandise returned to us. We shall get provision for our folk and guard our brother, and we shall have the extra measure of a camel (load). This (that we bring now) is a light measure.

66. He said: I will not send him with you till ye give me an undertaking in the name of Allah that ye will bring him back to me, unless ye are surrounded. And when they gave him their undertaking he said: Allah is the Warden over what we say.

67. And he said: O my sons! Go not in by one gate; go in by different gates. I can naught avail you as against Allah. Lo! the decision rests with Allah only. In Him do I put my trust, and in Him let all the trusting put their trust.

68. And when they entered in the manner which their father had enjoined, it would have naught availed them as against Allah; it was but a need of Jacob's soul which he thus satisfied, and lo! he was a lord of knowledge because We had taught him; but most of mankind know not.

69. And when they sent in before Joseph, he took his brother unto himself, saying: Lo! I, even I, am thy brother, therefore sorrow not for what they did.

70. And when he provided them with their provision, he put the drinking-cup in his brother's saddlebag, and then a crier cried: O camel-riders! Ye are surely thieves!

71. They cried, coming toward them: What is it ye have lost?

72. They said: We have lost the king's cup, and he who bringeth it shall have a camel-load, and I (said Joseph) am answerable for it.

73. They said: By Allah, well ye know we came not to do evil in the land, and are no thieves.

74. They said: And what shall be the penalty for it, if ye prove liars?

75. They said: The penalty for it! He in whose bag (the cup) is found, he is the penalty for it. Thus we requite wrongdoers.

76. Then he (Joseph) began the search with their bags before his brother's bag, then he produced it from his brother's bag. Thus did We contrive for Joseph. He could not have taken his brother according to the king's law unless Allah willed. We raise by grades (of mercy) whom We will, and over every lord of knowledge there is one more knowing.

77. They said: If he stealeth, a brother of his stole before. But Joseph kept it secret in his soul and revealed it not unto them. He said (within himself): Ye are in worse case and Allah knoweth best (the truth of) what which ye allege.

78. They said: O ruler of the land! Lo! he hath an aged father, so take one of us instead of him. Lo! we behold thee of those who do kindness.

79. He said: Allah forbid that we should seize save him with whom we found our property; then truly we should be wrongdoers.

80. So, when they despaired of (moving) him, they conferred together apart. The eldest of them said: Know ye not how your father took an undertaking from you in Allah's name and how ye failed in the case of Joseph aforetime? Therefore I shall not go forth from the land until my father giveth leave or Allah judgeth for me. He is the Best of Judges.

81. Return unto your father and say: O our father! Lo! thy son hath stolen. We testify only to that which we know; we are not guardians of the Unseen.

82. Ask the township where we were, and the caravan with which we travelled hither. Lo! we speak the truth.

83. (And when they came unto their father and had spoken thus to him) he said: Nay, but your minds have beguiled you into something. (My course is) comely patience! It may be that Allah will bring them all unto me. Lo! He, only He , is the Knower, the Wise.

84. And he turned away from them and said: Alas, my grief for Joseph! And his eyes were whitened with sorrow that he was suppressing.

85. They said: By Allah, thou wilt never cease remembering Joseph till thy health is ruined or thou art of those who perish!

86. He said: I expose my distress and anguish only unto Allah, and I know from Allah that which ye know not.

87. Go, O my sons, and ascertain concerning Joseph and his brother, and despair not of the Spirit of Allah. Lo! none despaireth of the Spirit of Allah save disbelieving folk.

88. And when they came (again) before him (Joseph) they said: O ruler! Misfortune hath touched us and our folk, and we bring but poor merchandise, so fill for us the measure and be charitable unto us. Lo! Allah will requite the charitable.

89. He said: Know ye what ye did unto Joseph and his brother in your ignorance?

90. They said: Is it indeed thou who art Joseph? He said: I am Joseph and this is my brother. Allah hath shown us favour. Lo! he who wardeth off (evil) and endureth (findeth favour); for verily Allah loseth not the wages of the kindly.

91. They said: By Allah, verily Allah hath preferred thee above us, and we were indeed sinful.

92. He said: Have no fear this day! May Allah forgive you, and He is the Most Merciful of those who show mercy.

93. Go with this shirt of mine and lay it on my father's face, he will become (again) a seer; and come to me with all your folk.

94. When the caravan departed their father had said: Truly I am conscious of the breath of Joseph, though ye call me dotard.

95. (Those around him) said: By Allah, lo! thou art in thine old aberration.

96. Then, when the bearer of glad tidings came, he laid it on his face and he became a seer once more. He said: Said I not unto you that I know from Allah that which ye know not?

97. They said: O our father! Ask forgiveness of our sins for us, for lo! we were sinful.

98. He said: I shall ask forgiveness for you of my Lord. Lo! He is the Forgiving, the Merciful. He said: I shall ask forgiveness.

99. And when they came in before Joseph, he took his parents unto him, and said: Come into Egypt safe, if Allah will!

100. And he placed his parents on the dais and they fell down before him prostrate, and he said: O my father! This is the interpretation of my dream of old. My Lord hath made it true, and He hath shown me kindness, since He took me out of the prison and hath brought you from the desert after Satan had made strife between me and my brethren. Lo! my Lord is tender unto whom He will. He is the Knower, the Wise.

101. O my Lord! Thou hast given me (something) of

sovereignty and hast taught me (something) of the interpretation of events—Creator of the heavens and the earth! Thou art my Protecting Friend in the world and the Hereafter. Make me to die submissive (unto Thee), and join me to the righteous.

102. This is of the tidings of the Unseen which We inspire in thee (Muhammad). Thou wast not present with them when they fixed their plan and they were scheming.

103. And though thou try much, most men will not believe.

104. Thou askest them no fee for it. It is naught else than a reminder unto the peoples.

105. How many a portent is there in the heavens and the earth which they pass by with face averted!

106. And most of them believe not in Allah except that they attribute partners (unto Him).

107. Deem they themselves secure from the coming on them of a pall of Allah's punishment, or the coming of the Hour suddenly while they are unaware?

108. Say: This is my Way: I call on Allah with sure knowledge, I and whosoever followeth me—Glory be to Allah!—and I am not of the idolaters.

109. We sent not before thee (any messengers save men whom We inspired from among the folk of the townships—Have they not travelled in the land and seen the nature of the consequence for those who were before them? And verily the abode of the Hereafter, for those who ward off (evil), is best. Have ye then no sense?—

110. Till, when the messengers despaired and thought that they were denied, then came unto them Our help, and whom We would was saved. And our wrath cannot be warded from the guilty.

111. In their history verily there is a lesson for men of understanding. It is no invented story but a confirmation of the existing (Scripture) and a detailed explanation of everything, and a guidance and a mercy for folk who believe.

SÛRAH 13

Ar-Ra'd, "The Thunder", take its name from a word in v. 13. The subject is Divine Guidance in relation to the law of consequences, it being explained here, as elsewhere in the Koran, that there is no partiality or aversion on the part of God, but that reward and punishment are the result of obeying or rejecting natural (or Divine) laws. According to some ancient authorities, it is Meccan Sûrah with the exception of two verses revealed at Al-Madînah; according to others, a Madînan Sûrah with the exception of two verses revealed at Mecca. The very fact of such wholesale difference of opinion favours the Meccan attribution because there could be no such doubt about a complete Madînan Sûrah, owing to the great number of witnesses. The Madînan ascription may have arisen from the recognition of some verses by those witnesses as having been revealed at Al-Madînah on certain occasion.

A late Meccan Sûrah for the most part.

THE THUNDER

Revealed at Mecca

In the name of Allah, the Beneficent, the Merciful.

1. Alif. Lâm. Mîm. Râ. These are verses of the Scripture. That which is revealed unto thee from thy Lord is the Truth, but most of mankind believe not.

2. Allah it is Who raised up the heavens without visible supports, then mounted the Throne, and compelled the sun and the moon to be of service, each runneth unto an appointed term; He ordereth the course; He detaileth the revelations, that haply ye may be certain of the meeting with your Lord.

3. And He it is who spread out the earth and placed therein firm hills and flowing streams, and of all fruits he placed therein two spouses (male and female). He covereth the night with the day. Lo! herein verily are portents for people who take thought.

4. And in the Earth are neighbouring tracts, vineyards and ploughed lands, and date-palms, like and unlike, which are watered with one water. And We have made some of them to excel others in fruit. Lo! herein verily are portents for people who have sense.

5. And if thou wondered, then wondrous is their saying: When we are dust, are we then forsooth (to be raised) in a new creation? Such are they who disbelieve in their Lord; such have carcans on their necks; such are rightful owners of the Fire, they will abide therein.

6. And they bid thee hasten on the evil rather than the good, when examplary punishments have indeed occurred before them. But lo! thy Lord is rich in pardon for mankind despite their wrong, and lo! thy Lord is strong in punishment.

7. Those who disbelieve say: If only some portent were sent down upon him from his Lord! Thou art a warner only, and for every folk a guide.

8. Allah knoweth that which every female beareth and that which the wombs absorb and that which they grow. And

everything with Him is measured.

9. He is the Knower of the Invisible and the Visible, the Great, the High Exalted.

10. Alike of you is he who hideth the saying and he who noiseth it abroad, he who lurketh in the night and he who goeth freely in the daytime.

11. For him are angels ranged before him and behind him, who guard him by Allah's command. Lo! Allah changeth not the condition of a folk until they (first) change that which is in their hearts; and if Allah willeth misfortune for a folk there is none that can repel it, nor have they a defender beside Him.

12. He it is Who showeth you the lightning, a fear and a hope, and raiseth the heavy clouds.

13. The thunder hymneth His praise and (so do) the angels for awe of Him. He launcheth the thunderbolts and smiteth with them whom He will while they dispute (in doubt) concerning Allah, and He is mighty in wrath.

14. Unto Him is the real prayer. Those unto whom they pray beside Allah respond to them not at all, save as (is the response to) one who stretcheth forth his hands toward water (asking) that it may come unto his mouth, and it will never reach it. The prayer of disbelievers goeth (far) astray.

15. And unto Allah falleth prostrate whosoever is in the heavens and the earth, willingly or unwillingly, as do their shadows in the morning and the evening hours.

16. Say (O Muhammad): Who is Lord of the heavens and the earth? Say: Allah! Say: Take ye then (others) beside Him for protectors, which, even for themselves, have neither benefit nor hurt? Say: Is the blind man equal to the seer, or is darkness equal to light? Or assign they unto Allah partners who created the like of His creation so that the creation (which they made and His creation) seemed alike to them? Say: Allah is the Creator of all things, and He is the One, the Almighty.

17. He sendeth down water from the sky, so that valleys flow according to their measure, and the flood beareth (on its surface) swellings foam—from that which they smelt in the fire in order to make ornaments and tools riseth a foam like unto it—thus Allah coineth (the similitude of) the true and the false. Then, as for the foam, it passeth away as scum upon the banks, while, as for that which is of use to mankind, it remaineth in the earth. Thus Allah coineth the similitudes.

18. For those who answered Allah's call is bliss; and for those who answered not His call, if they had all that is in the earth, and therewith the like thereof, they would proffer it as ransom.

Such will have a woeful reckoning and their habitation will be hell, a dire abode.

19. Is he who knoweth that what is revealed unto thee from thy Lord is the truth like him who is blind? But only men of understanding heed.

20. Such as keep the pack of Allah, and break not the covenant.

21. Such as unite that which Allah hath commanded should be joined and fear their Lord, and dread a woeful reckoning.

22. Such as persevere in seeking their Lord's countenance and are regular in prayer and spend of that which We bestow upon them secretly and openly, and overcome evil with good. Theirs will be the sequel of the (heavenly) Home.

23. Gardens of Eden which they enter, along with all who do right of their fathers and their helpmates and their seed. The angels enter unto them from every gate.

24. (Saying): Peace be unto you because ye persevered. Ah, passing sweet will be the sequel of the (heavenly) Home.

25. And those who break the covenant of Allah after ratifying it, and sever that which Allah hath commanded should be joined, and make mischief in the earth; theirs is the curse and theirs the ill abode.

26. Allah enlargeth livelihood for whom He will, and straiteneth (it for whom He will); and they rejoice in the life of the world, whereas the life of the world is but brief comfort as compared with the Hereafter.

27. Those who disbelieve say: If only a portent were sent down upon him from his Lord! Say: Lo! Allah sendeth whom He will astray, and guideth unto Himself all who turn (unto Him).

28. Who have believed and whose hearts have rest in the remembrance of Allah. Verily in the remembrance of Allah do hearts find rest!

29. Those who believe and do right: Joy is for them, and bliss (their) journey's end.

30. Thus We send thee (O Muhammad) unto a nation, before whom other nations have passed away, that thou mayst recite unto them that which We have inspired in thee, while they are disbelievers in the Beneficent. Say: He is my Lord; there is no God save Him. In Him do I put my trust and unto Him is my recourse.

31. Had it been possible for a Lecture to cause the mountains to move, or the earth to be torn asunder or the dead to speak, (this Qur'ân would have done so). Nay but Allah's is the whole command. Do not those who believe know that, had Allah willed, He could have guided all mankind? As for those who

disbelieve, disaster ceaseth not to strike them because of what they do, or it dwelleth near their home until the threat of Allah come to pass. Lo! Allah faileth not to keep the tryst.

32. And verily messengers (of Allah) were mocked before thee, but long I bore with those who disbelieved. At length I seized them, and how (awful) was My punishment!

33. Is He who is aware of the deserts of every soul (as he who is aware of nothing)? Yet they ascribe unto Allah partners. Say: Name them. Is it that ye would inform Him of something which He knoweth not in the earth? Or is it but a way of speaking? Nay, but their contrivance is made seeming fair for those who disbelieve and they are kept from the right road. He whom Allah sendeth astray, for him there is no guide.

34. For them is torment in the life of the world, and verily the doom of the Hereafter is more painful, and they have no defender from Allah.

35. A similitude of the Garden which is promised unto those who keep their duty (to Allah): Underneath it rivers flow; its food is everlasting and its shade; this is the reward of those who keep their duty, while the reward of disbelievers is the fire.

36. Those unto whom We gave the Scripture rejoice in that which is revealed unto thee. And of the clans there are those who deny some of it. Say: I am commanded only that I serve Allah and ascribe unto Him no partner. Unto Him I cry, and unto Him is my return.

37. Thus have We revealed it, a decisive utterance in Arabic; and if thou shouldst follow their desires after that which hath come unto thee of knowledge, then truly wouldst thou have from Allah no protecting friend nor defender.

38. And verily We sent messengers (to mankind) before thee, and We appointed for them wives and offspring and it was not (given) to any messenger that he should bring a portent save by Allah's leave. For everything there is a time prescribed.

39. Allah effaceth what he will, and establisheth (what He will), and with Him is the source of ordinance.

40. Whether We let thee see something of that which We have promised them, or make thee die (before its happening), thine is but conveyance (of the message), Ours the reckoning.

41. See they not how We visit the land, reducing it of its outlying parts? (When) Allah doometh there is none that can postpone His doom, and He is swift at reckoning.

42. Those who were before them plotted; but all plotting is Allah's. He knoweth that which each soul earneth. The

disbelievers will come to know for whom will be the sequel of the (heavenly) Home.

43. They who disbelieve say: Thou art no messenger (of Allah). Say: Allah, and whosoever hath true knowledge of the Scripture, is sufficient witness between me and you.

SÛRAH 14

Ibrâhîm, so-called from Abraham's prayer in vv. 35-41, at the time when he was establishing his son Ishmael, the ancestor of the Arabs, in the "uncultivable valley" of Mecca. Otherwise the subject of the sûrah is the same as that of other Meccan Sûrahs revealed during the last three years before the Hijrah. The reference in v. 46 to the plot of the idolaters makes it probable that it is among the last of the Meccan revelations.

A late Meccan Sûrah; except vv. 28-30, revealed at Al-Madînah.

ABRAHAM

Revealed at Mecca

In the name of Allah, the Beneficent, the Merciful.

1. Alif. Lâm. Râ. (This is) a Scripture which We have revealed unto thee (Muhammad) that thereby thou mayst bring forth mankind from darkness unto light, by the permission of their Lord, unto the path of the Mighty, the Owner of Praise.

2. Allah, unto Whom belongeth whatsoever is in the heavens and whatsoever is in the earth. And woe unto the disbelievers from an awful doom.

3. Those who love the life of the world more than the Hereafter, and debar (men) from the way of Allah and would have it crooked: such are far astray.

4. And We never sent a messenger save with the language of his folk, that he might make (the message) clear for them. Then Allah sendeth whom He will astray, and guideth whom He will. He is the Mighty, the wise.

5. We verily sent Moses with Our revelations, saying: Bring thy people forth from darkness unto light. And remind them of the days of Allah. Lo! therein are revelations for each steadfast, thankful (heart).

6. And (remind them) how Moses said unto his people: Remember Allah's favour unto you when He delivered you from Pharaoh's folk who were afflicting you with dreadful torment, and were slaying your sons and sparing your women; that was a tremendous trial from your Lord.

7. And when your Lord proclaimed: If ye give thanks, I will give you more; but if ye are thankless, lo! My punishment is dire.

8. And Moses said: Though ye and all who are in the earth prove thankless, lo! Allah verily is Absolute, Owner of Praise.

9. Hath not the history of those before you reached you: the folk of Noah, and (the tribes of) A'âd and Thamûd, and those after them? None save Allah knoweth them. Their messengers came unto them with clear proofs, but they thrust their hands into their mouths, and said: Lo! we disbelieve in that wherewith ye have been sent, and lo! we are in grave doubt concerning that to which ye call us.

10. Their messengers said: Can there be doubt concerning Allah, the Creator of the heavens and the earth? He calleth you that He may forgive you your sins and reprieve you unto an appointed term. They said: Ye are but mortals like us, who would fain turn us away from what our fathers used to worship. Then bring some clear warrants.

11. Their messengers said unto them: We are but mortals like you, but Allah giveth grace unto whom He will of His slaves. It is not ours to bring you a warrant unless by the permission of Allah. In Allah let believers put their trust!

12. How should we not put our trust in Allah when He hath shown us our ways? We surely will endure that hurt ye do us. In Allah let the trusting put their trust!

13. And those who disbelieved said unto their messengers: Verily we will drive you out from our land, unless ye return to our religion. Then their Lord inspired them, (saying): Verily We shall destroy the wrong-doers.

14. And verily We shall make you to dwell in the land after them. This is for them who feareth My Majesty and feareth My threats.

15. And they sought help (from their Lord) and every forward potentate was brought to naught.

16. Hell is before him, and he is made to drink a festering water.

17. Which he sippeth but can hardly swallow, and death cometh unto him from every side while yet he cannot die, and before him is a harsh doom.

18. A similitude of those who disbelieve in their Lord: Their works are as ashes which the wind bloweth hard upon a stormy day. They have no control of aught that they have earned. That is the extreme failure.

19. Hast thou not seen that Allah hath created the heavens and the earth with truth? If He will, He can remove you and

bring (in) some new creation.

20. And that is no great matter for Allah.

21. They all come forth unto their Lord. Then those who were despised say unto those who were scornful: We were unto you a following, can ye then avert from us aught of Allah's doom? They say: Had Allah guided us, we should have guided you. Whether we rage or patiently endure is (now) all one for us; we have no place of refuge.

22. And Satan saith, when the matter hath been decided: Lo! Allah promised you a promise of truth; and I promised you, then failed you. And I have no power over save that I called unto you and ye obeyed me. So blame me not, but blame yourselves. I cannot help you, nor can ye help me. Lo! I disbelieved in that which ye before ascribed to me. Lo! for wrong-doers is a painful doom.

23. And those who believed and did good works are made to enter Gardens underneath which rivers flow, therein abiding by permission of their Lord, their greeting therein: Peace!

24. Seest thou not how Allah coineth a similitude: A goodly saying, as a goodly tree, its root set firm, its branches reaching into heaven.

25. Giving its fruit at every season by permission of its Lord? Allah cointeth the similitudes for mankind in order that they may reflect.

26. And the similitude of a bad saying is as a bad tree, uprooted from upon the earth, possessing no stability.

27. Allah confirmeth those who believe by a firm saying in the life of the world and in the Hereafter, and Allah sendeth wrong-doers astray. And Allah doeth what He will.

28. Hast thou not seen those who have the grace of Allah in exchange for thanklessness and let their people down to the Abode of Loss.

29. (Even to) hell? They are exposed thereto. A hapless end!

30. And they set up rivals to Allah that they may mislead (men) from His way. Say: Enjoy life (while ye may) for lo! your journey's end will be the Fire.

31. Tell My bondmen who believe to establish worship and spend of that which We have given them, secretly and publicly, before a day cometh wherein there will be neither traffick nor befriending.

32. Allah is He Who created the heavens and the earth, and causeth water to descend from the sky, thereby producing fruits as food for you, and maketh the ships to be of service unto you, that they may run upon the sea at His command, and hath made of service unto you the rivers.

33. And maketh the sun and the moon, constant in their courses, to be of service unto you, and hath made of service unto you the night and the day.

34. And He giveth you of all ye ask of Him, and if ye would count the bounty of Allah ye cannot reckon it. Lo! man is verily a wrong-doer, an ingrate.

35. And when Abraham said: My Lord! Make safe this territory, and preserve me and my sons from serving idols.

36. My Lord! Lo! they have led many of mankind astray. But whoso followeth me, he verily is of me. And whoso disobeyeth me—Still Thou art Forgiving, Merciful.

37. Our Lord! Lo! I have settled some of my posterity in an uncultivable valley near unto Thy holy House, our Lord! that they may establish proper worship; so incline some hearts of men that they may yearn toward them, and provide Thou them with fruits in order that they may be thankful.

38. Our Lord! Lo! Thou knowest that which we hide and that which we proclaim. Nothing in the earth or in the heaven is hidden from Allah.

39. Praise be to Allah Who hath given me, in my old age, Ishmael and Isaac! Lo! my Lord is indeed the Hearer of Prayer.

40. My Lord! Make me to establish proper worship, and some of my posterity (also); our Lord! and accept the prayer.

41. Our Lord! Forgive me and my parents and believers on the day when the account is cast.

42. Deem not that Allah is unaware or what the wicked do. He but giveth them a respite, till a day when eyes will stare (in terror).

43. As they come hurrying on in fear, their heads upraised, their gaze returning not to them, and their hearts as air.

44. And warn mankind of a day when the doom will come upon them, and those who did wrong will say: Our Lord! Reprieve us for a little while. We will obey Thy call and will follow the messengers. (It will be answered): Did ye not swear before that there would be no end for you?

45. And (have ye not) dwelt in the dwellings of those who wronged themselves (of old) and (hath it not) become plain to you how We dealt with them, and made examples for you?

46. Verily they have plotted their plot, and their plot is with Allah, though their plot were one whereby the mountains should be moved.

47. So think not that Allah will fail to keep His promise to His messengers. Lo! Allah is Mighty, Able to Requite (the wrong).

48. On the day when the earth will be changed to other than

the earth, and the heavens (also will be changed) and they will come forth unto Allah, the One, the Almighty.

49. Thou wilt see the guilty on that day linked together in chains.

50. Their raiment of pitch, and the Fire covering their faces.

51. That Allah may repay each soul what it hath earned. Lo! Allah is swift at reckoning.

52. This is a clear message for mankind in order that they may be warned thereby, and that they may know that He is only One God, and that men of understanding may take heed.

SÛRAH 15

Al-Hijr (which I take to be a place-name) is so called from vv. 80-84, where the fate of the dwellers at that place is described. The date of revelation is earlier than that of any of the Meccan Sûrahs, which precede it in the arrangement of the Book, though the subject and the tone are similar, which accounts for its position. Nöldeke places it in his middle group of Meccan Sûrahs, that is (as far as one can judge from the inclusions), those revealed after the eighth year and before the third year before the Hijrah, and in so doing confirms the judgement of the best Muslim authorities, though some Muslim authorities would place it among the earliest revelations.

It belongs to the middle group of Meccan Sûrahs.

AL-HIJR

Revealed at Mecca

In the name of Allah, the Beneficent, the Merciful.

1. Alif. Lâm. Râ. These are verses of the Scripture and a plain Reading.

2. It may be that those Who disbelieve wish ardently that they were Muslims.

3. Let them eat and enjoy life, and let (false) hope beguile them. They will come to know!

4. And We destroyed no township but there was a known decree for it.

5. No nation can outstrip its term nor can they lag behind.

6. And they say: O thou unto whom the Reminder is revealed, lo! thou art indeed a madman!

7. Why bringest thou not angels unto us, if thou art of the truthful?

8. We send not down the angels save with the Fact, and in that case (the disbelievers) would not be tolerated.

9. Lo! We, even We, reveal the reminder, and lo! We

verily are its Guardian.

10. We verily sent (messengers before thee among the factions of the men of old.

11. And never came there unto them a messenger but they did mock him.

12. Thus do We make it traverse the hearts of the guilty.

13. They believe not therein though the example of the men of old hath gone before.

14. And even if We opened unto them a gate of Heaven and they kept mounting through it.

15. They would say: Our sight is wrong—nay, but we are folk bewitched.

16. And verily in the heaven We have set mansions of the stars, and We have beautified it for beholders.

17. And We have guarded it from every outcast devil.

18. Save him who stealeth the hearing, and them doth a clear flame pursue.

19. And the earth have We spread out; and placed therein firm hills, and caused each seemly thing to grow therein.

20. And We have given unto you livelihoods therein, and unto those for whom ye provide not.

21. And there is not a thing but with Us are the stores thereof. And we send it not down save in appointed measure.

22. And We send the winds fertilising, and cause water to descend from the sky, and give it you to drink. It is not ye who are the holders of the store thereof.

23. Lo! and it is We even, We who quicken and give death, and We are the inheritor.

24. And verily We know the eager among you and verily we know the laggards.

25. Lo! thy Lord will gather them together. Lo! He is Wise, Aware.

26. Verily we created man of potter's clay of black mud altered.

27. And the jinn did We create aforetime of essential fire.

28. And (remember) when thy Lord said unto the angels: Lo! I am creating a mortal out of potter's clay of black mud altered.

29. So, when I have made him and have breathed into him of My spirit, do ye fall down, prostrating yourselves unto him.

30. So the angels fell prostrate all of them together.

31. Save Iblîs. He refused to be among the prostrate.

32. He said; O Iblîs! What aileth thee that thou art not among the prostrate?

33. He said: Why should I prostrate myself unto a mortal

whom Thou hast created out of potter's clay of black mud altered?

34. He said: Then go thou forth from hence, for verily thou art outcast.

35. And lo! the curse shall be upon thee till the day of judgement.

36. He said: My Lord! Reprieve me till the day when they are raised.

37. He said: Then lo! thou art of those reprieved.

38. Till an appointed time.

39. He said: My Lord! Because Thou has sent me astray I verily shall adorn the path of error for them in the earth, and shall mislead them every one.

40. Save such of them as are Thy perfectly devoted slaves.

41. He said: This is a right course incumbent upon Me.

42. Lo! as for My slaves, thou hast no power over any of them save such of the forward as follow thee.

43. And lo! for all such, hell will be the promised place.

44. It hath seven gates, and each gate hath an appointed portion.

45. Lo! those who ward off (evil) are among gardens and watersprings.

46. (And it is said unto them): Enter them in peace, secure.

47. And We remove whatever rancour may be in their breasts. As brethren, face to face, (they rest) on couches raised.

48. Toil cometh not unto them there, nor will they be expelled from thence.

49. Announce, (O Muhammad) unto My slaves that verily I am the Forgiving, the Merciful.

50. And that My doom is the dolorous doom.

51. And tell them of Abraham's guests.

52. (How) when they came in unto him, and said: Peace. He said: Lo! we are afraid of you.

53. They said: Be not afraid! Lo! we bring thee good tidings of a boy possessing wisdom.

54. He said: Bring ye me good tidings (of a son) when did age hath overtaken me? Of what then can ye bring good tidings?

55. They said: We bring thee good tidings in truth. So be not thou of the despairing.

56. He said: And who despaireth of the mercy of his Lord save those who are astray?

57. He said: And afterward what is your business, O ye messengers (of Allah)?

58. They said: We have been sent unto a guilty folk.

59. (All) save the family of Lot!. Them we shall deliver

every one.

60. Except his wife, of whom we had decreed that she should be of those who stay behind.

61. And when the messengers came unto the family of Lot.

62. He said: Lo! ye are folk unknown (to me).

63. They said: Nay, but we bring thee that concerning which they keep disputing.

64. And bring thee the Truth, and lo! we are truth-tellers.

65. So travel with thy household in a portion of the night, and follow thou their backs. Let none of you turn round, but go whither ye are commanded.

66. And We made plain the case to him, that the root of them (who did wrong) was to be cut at early morn.

67. And the people of the city came rejoicing at the news (of new arrivals).

68. He said: Lo! they are my guest Affront me not!

69. And keep your duty to Allah, and shame me not!

70. They said: Have we not forbidden you from (entertaining) anyone?

71. He said: Here are my daughters, if ye must be doing (so).

72. By thy life (O Muhammad) they moved blindly in the frenzy of approaching death.

73. Then the (Awful) Cry overtook them at the sunrise.

74. And We utterly confounded them and We rained upon them stones of heated clay.

75. Lo! therein verily are portents for those who read the signs.

76. And lo! it is upon a road still uneffaced.

77. Lo! therein is indeed a portent for believers.

78. And the dwellers in the wood indeed were evil-doers.

79. So We took vengeance on them; and lo! they both are on a high road plain to see.

80. And the dwellers in Al-Hijr indeed denied (Our) messengers.

81. And We gave them Our revelations but they were averse to them.

82. And they used to hew out dwellings from the hills, (wherein they dwelt) secure.

83. But the (Awful) Cry overtook them at the morning hour.

84. And that which they were wont to count as gain availed them not.

85. We created not the heavens and the earth and all that is between them save with truth, and lo! the Hour is surely coming. So forgive, O Muhammad with a gracious forgive-

ness.

86. Lo! Thy Lord! He is the All-Wise Creator.

87. We have given thee seven of the oft-repeated (verses) and the great Qur'ân.

88. Strain not thine eyes toward that which We cause some wedded pairs among them to enjoy, and be not grieved on their account and lower thy wing (in tenderness) for the believers.

89. And say: Lo! I even I, am a plain warner.

90. Such as We send down for those who make division.

91. Those who break the Qur'ân into parts.

92. Them, by the Lord, We shall question, every one.

93. Of what they used to do.

94. So proclaim that which thou art commanded, and withdraw from the idolaters.

95. Lo! We defend thee from the scoffers.

96. Who set some other god along with Allah. But they will come to know.

97. Well know We that thy bosom is at times oppressed by what they say.

98. But hymn the praise of thy Lord, and be of those who make prostration (unto Him).

99. And serve thy Lord till the inevitable cometh unto thee.

SÛRAH 16

An-Nahl, "The Bee", takes its name from v. 68, where the activities of the Bee are mentioned as a type of duty and of usefulness. It calls attention to God's providence for creation, and to His guidance to mankind as a necessary part of it, and warns disbelievers in that guidance of a folly in rejecting it as great as would be the rejection of food and drink. The sûrah is ascribed to the last Meccan group, though some ancient authorities regard the ascription as valid only for vv. 1-40, and consider the whole latter portion as revealed at Al-Madînah. The only verse in the sûrah which is self-evidently of Madînan revelation is v. 110, where the fugitives from persecution are said to have fought; for in the Meccan period fighting was unlawful for the Muslims, though many of them fled from persecution, taking refuge in Abyssinia.

A late Meccan Sûrah, with the exception of v. 110, which must have been revealed at Al-Madînah not earlier than the year 2 A.H., and possibly many other verses toward the end.

THE BEE

Revealed at Mecca

In the name of Allah, the Beneficent, the Merciful.

1. The commandment of Allah will come to pass, so seek not ye to hasten it. Glorified and Exalted be He above all that they associate (with Him).

2. He sendeth down the angels with the Spirit of His command unto whom He will of His bondmen, (saying): Warn mankind that there is no god save Me, so keep your duty unto Me.

3. He hath created the heavens and the earth with truth. High be He exalted above all that they associate (with Him).

4. He hath created man from a drop of fluid, yet behold! he is an open opponent.

5. And the cattle hath He created, whence ye have warm clothing and uses, and whereof ye eat.

6. And wherein is beauty for you, when ye bring them home, and when ye take them out to pasture.

7. And they bear your loads for you unto a land ye could not reach save with great trouble to yourselves. Lo! your Lord is Full of Pity, Merciful.

8. And horses and mules and asses (hath He created) that ye may ride them, and for ornament. And He createth that which ye know not.

9. And Allah's is the direction of the way, and some (roads) go not straight. And had He willed He would have led you all aright.

10. He it is Who sendeth down water from the sky, whence ye have drink, and whence are trees on which ye send your beasts to pasture.

11. Therewith He causeth crops to grow for you, and the olive and the date-palm and grapes and all kinds of fruit. Lo! herein is indeed a portent for people who reflect.

12. And he hath constrained the night and the day and the sun and the moon to be of service unto you, and the stars are made subservient by His command. Lo! herein indeed are portents for people who have sense.

13. And whatsoever He hath created for you in the earth of divers hues, lo! therein is indeed a portent for people who take heed.

14. And He it is Who hath constrained the sea to be of service that ye eat fresh meat from thence, and bring forth from thence ornaments which ye wear. And thou seest the ships ploughing it that ye (mankind) may seek of His bounty, and that haply ye may give thanks.

15. And He hath cast into the earth firm hills that it quake not with you, and streams and roads that ye may find a way.

16. And landmarks (too), and by the star they find a way.

17. Is He then Who createth as him who createth not? Will ye not then remember?

18. And if ye would count the favour of Allah ye cannot reckon it. Lo! Allah is indeed Forgiving, Merciful.

19. And Allah knoweth that which ye keep hidden and that which ye proclaim.

20. Those unto whom they cry beside Allah created naught, but are themselves created.

21. (They are) dead, not living. And they know not when they will be raised.

22. Your God is One God. But as for those who believe not in the Hereafter their hearts refuse to know, for they are proud.

23. Assuredly Allah knoweth that which they keep hidden and that which they proclaim. Lo! He loveth not the proud.

24. And when it is said unto them: What hath your Lord revealed? they say: (Mere) fables of the men of old.

25. That they may bear their burdens undiminished on the Day of Resurrection, with somewhat of the burdens of those whom they mislead without knowledge. Ah! evil is that which they bear!

26. Those before them plotted, so Allah struck at the foundations of their building, and then the roof fell down upon them from above them, and the doom came on them whence they knew not.

27. Then on the Day of Resurrection He will disgrace them and will say: Where are My partners, for whose sake ye opposed (My Guidance)? Those who have been given knowledge will say: Disgrace this day and evil are upon the disbelievers.

28. Whom the angels cause to die while they are wronging themselves. Then will they make full submission (saying): We used not to do any wrong. Nay! Surely Allah is Knower of what ye used to do.

29. So enter the gates of hell, to dwell therein for ever. Woeful indeed will be the lodging of the arrogant.

30. And it is said unto those who ward off (evil): What hath your Lord revealed? They say: Good. For those who do good in this world there is a good (reward) and the home of the Hereafter will be better. Pleasant indeed will be the home of those who ward off (evil) —

31. Gardens of Eden which they enter, underneath which rivers flow, wherein they have what they will. Thus Allah repayeth those who ward off (evil).

32. Those whom the angels cause to die (when they are) good. They say: Peace be unto you! Enter the Garden because

of what ye used to do.

33. Await they aught save that the angels should come unto them or thy Lord's command should come to pass? Even so did those before them. Allah wronged them not, but they did wrong themselves.

34. So that the evil of what they did smote them, and that which they used to mock surrounded them.

35. And the idolaters say: Had Allah willed, we had not worshipped aught beside Him, we and our fathers, nor had we forbidden aught without (command from) Him. Even so did those before them. Are the messengers charged with aught save plain conveyance (of the message)?

36. And verily We have raised in every nation a messenger, (proclaiming): Serve Allah and shun false gods. Then some of them (there were) whom Allah guided, and some of them (there were) upon whom error had just hold. Do but travel in the land and see the nature of the consequences for the deniers!

37. Even if thou (O Muhammad) desirest their right guidance, still Allah assuredly will not guide him who misleadeth. Such have no helpers.

38. And they swear by Allah their most binding oaths (that) Allah will not raise up him who dieth. Nay, but it is a promise (binding) upon Him in truth, but most of mankind know not.

39. That he may explain unto them that wherein they differ, and that those who disbelieved may know that they were liars.

40. And Our word unto a thing, when We intend it, is only that We say unto it: Be! and it is.

41. And those who became fugitives for the cause of Allah after they had been oppressed, We verily shall give them goodly lodging in the world, and surely the reward of the Hereafter is greater, if they but knew;

42. Such as are steadfast and put their trust in Allah.

43. And We sent not (as Our messengers) before thee other than men whom We inspired—Ask the followers of the Remembrance if ye know not!—

44. With clear proofs and writings; and We have revealed unto thee the Remembrance that thou mayst explain to mankind that which hath been revealed for them, and that haply they may reflect.

45. Are they who plan ill deeds then secure that Allah will not cause the earth to swallow them, or that the doom will not come on them whence they know not?

46. Or that he will not seize them in their going to and fro so that there be no escape for them?

47. Or that He will not seize them with a gradual wasting?

Lo! thy Lord is indeed Full of Pity, Merciful.

48. Have they not observed all things that Allah hath created, how their shadows incline to the right and to the left, making prostration unto Allah, and they are lowly?

49. And unto Allah maketh prostration whatsoever is in the heavens and whatsoever is in the earth of living creatures, and the angels (also), and they are not proud.

50. They fear their Lord above them, and do what they are bidden.

51. Allah hath said: Choose not two gods. There is only One god. So of Me, Me only, be in awe.

52. Unto Him belongeth whatsoever is in the heavens and the earth, and religion is His for ever. Will ye then fear any other than Allah?

53. And whatever of comfort ye enjoy it is from Allah. Then, when misfortune reacheth you, unto Him ye cry for help.

54. And afterward, when He hath rid you of the misfortune, behold! a set of you attribute partners to their Lord,

55. So as to deny that which We have given them. Then enjoy life (while ye may), for ye will come to know.

56. And they assign a portion of that which We have given them unto what they know not. By Allah! but ye will indeed be asked concerning (all) that ye used to invent.

57. And they assign unto Allah daughters—Be He Glorified!—and unto themselves what they desire;

58. When if one of them receiveth tidings of the birth of a female, his face remaineth darkened, and he is wroth inwardly.

59. He hideth himself from the folk because of the evil of that whereof he hath had tidings, (asking himself): Shall he keep it in contempt, or bury it beneath the dust. Verily evil is their judgement.

60. For those who believe not in the Hereafter is an evil similitude, and Allah's is the Sublime Similitude. He is the Mighty, the Wise.

61. If Allah were to take mankind to task for their wrong-doing, he would not leave hereon a living creature, but He reprieveth them to an appointed term, and when their term cometh they cannot put (it) off an hour nor (yet) advance (it).

62. And they assign unto Allah that which they (themselves) dislike, and their tongues expound the lie that the better portion will be theirs. Assuredly theirs will be the Fire, and they will be abandoned.

63. By Allah, We verily sent messengers unto the nations before thee, but the devil made their deeds fair-seeming unto them. So he is their patron this day, and theirs will be a painful

doom.

64. And we have revealed the Scripture unto thee only that thou mayst explain unto them that wherein they differ, and (as) a guidance and a mercy for a people who believe.

65. Allah sendeth down water from the sky and therewith reviveth the earth after her death. Lo! herein is indeed a portent for a folk who hear.

66. And lo! in the cattle there is a lesson for you. We give you to drink of that which is in their bellies, from betwixt the refuse and the blood, pure milk palatable to the drinkers.

67. And of the fruits of the date-palm, and grapes, whence ye derive strong drink and (also) good nourishment. Lo! therein, is indeed a portent for people who have sense.

68. And thy Lord inspired the bee, saying: Choose thou habitations in the hills and in the trees and in that which they thatch;

69. Then eat of all fruits and follow the ways of thy Lord, made smooth (for thee). There cometh forth from their bellies a drink diverse of hues, wherein is healing for mankind. Lo! herein is indeed a portent for people who reflect.

70. And Allah createth you, then causeth you to die, and among you is he who is brought back to the most abject of life, so that he knoweth nothing after (having had) knowledge. Lo! Allah is Knower, Powerful.

71. And Allah hath favoured some of you above others in provision. Now those who are more favoured will be by no means hand over their provision to those (slaves) whom their right hands possess, so that they may be equal with them in respect thereof. Is it then the grace of Allah that they deny?

72. And Allah hath given you wives of your own kind and hath given you, from your wives, sons and grandsons, and hath made provision of good things for you. Is it then in vanity that they believe and in the grace of Allah that they disbelieve?

73. And they worship beside Allah that which owneth no provision whatsoever for them from the heavens or the earth, nor have they (whom they worship) any power.

74. So coin not similitudes for Allah. Lo! Allah knoweth; ye know not.

75. Allah coineth a similitude: (on the one hand) a (mere) chattel slave, who hath control of nothing, and (on the other hand) one on whom We have bestowed a fair provision from Us, and he spendeth thereof secretly and openly. Are they equal? Praise be to Allah! But most of them know not.

76. And Allah coineth a similitude: Two men, one of them dumb, having control of nothing, and he is a burden on his

owner; whithersoever he directeth him to go, he bringeth no good. Is he equal with one who enjoineth justice and followeth a straight path (of conduct)?

77. And unto Allah belongeth the Unseen of the heavens and the earth, and the matter of the Hour (of Doom) is but as a twinkling of the eye, or it is nearer still. Lo! Allah is Able to do all things.

78. And Allah brought you forth from the wombs of your mothers knowing nothing, and gave you hearing and sight and hearts that haply ye might give thanks.

79. Have they not seen the birds obedient in mid-air? None holdeth them save Allah. Lo! herein, verily, are portents for a people who believe.

80. And Allah hath given you in your houses an abode, and hath given you (also), of the hides of cattle, houses which ye find light (to carry) on the day of migration and on the day of pitching camp; and of their wool and their fur and their hair, caparison and comfort for a while.

81. And Allah hath given you, of that which He hath created, shelter from the sun; and hath given you places of refuge in the mountains, and hath given you coats to ward off the heat from you, and coats (of armour) to save you from your own foolhardiness. Thus doth He perfect His favour unto you, in order that ye may surrender (unto Him).

82. Then, if they turn away, thy duty (O Muhammad) is but plain conveyance (of the message).

83. They know the favour of Allah and then deny it. Most of them are ingrates.

84. And (bethink you of) the day when We raise up of every nation a witness, then there is no leave for disbelievers, nor are they allowed to make amends.

85. And when those who did wrong behold the doom it will not be made light for them, nor will they be reprieved.

86. And when those who ascribed partners to Allah behold those partners of theirs, they will say: Our Lord! these are our partners unto whom we used to cry instead of Thee. But they will fling to them the saying: Lo! ye verily are liars!

87. And they proffer unto Allah submission on that day, and all that they used to invent hath failed them.

88. For those who disbelieve and debar (men) from the way of Allah, We add doom to doom because they wrought corruption.

89. And (bethink you of) the day when We raise in every nation a witness against them of their own folk, and We bring thee (Muhammad) as a witness against these. And We reveal

the Scripture unto thee as an exposition of all things, and a guidance and a mercy and good tidings for those who have surrendered (to Allah).

90. Lo! Allah enjoineth justice and kindness, and giving to kinsfolk, and forbiddeth lewdness and abomination and wickedness. He exhorteth you in order that ye take heed.

91. Fulfil the covenant of Allah when ye have covenanted, and break not your oaths after the assertion of them, and after ye have made Allah surety over you. Lo! Allah knoweth what ye do.

92. And be not like unto her who unravelleth the thread, after she hath made it strong, to thin filaments, making your oaths a deceit between you because of a nation being more numerous than (another) nation. Allah only trieth you thereby, and He verily will explain to you on the Day of Resurrection that wherein ye differed.

93. Had Allah willed He could have made you (all) one nation, but He sendeth whom He will astray and guideth whom He will, and ye will indeed be asked of what ye used to do.

94. Make not your oaths a deceit between you, lest a foot should slip after being firmly planted and ye should taste evil forasmuch as ye debarred (men) from the way of Allah, and yours should be an awful doom.

95. And purchase not a small gain at the price of Allah's covenant. Lo! that which Allah hath is better for you, if ye did but know.

96. That which ye have wasteth away, and that which Allah hath remaineth. And verily We shall pay those who are steadfast a recompense in proportion to the best of what they used to do.

97. Whosoever doeth right, whether male or female, and is a believer, him verily We shall quicken with good life, and We shall pay them a recompense in proportion to the best of what they used to do.

98. And when thou recitest the Qur'ân, seek refuge in Allah from Satan the outcast.

99. Lo! he hath no power over those who believe and put trust in their Lord.

100. His power is only over those who make a friend of him, and those who ascribe partners unto Him (Allah).

101. And when We put a revelation in place of (another) revelation, — and Allah knoweth best what He revealeth — they say: Lo! thou art but inventing. Most of them know not.

102. Say: The holy Spirit hath revealed it from thy Lord with truth, that it may confirm (the faith of) those who believe, and

as guidance and good tidings for those who have surrendered (to Allah).

103. And We know well that they say: Only a man teacheth him. The speech of him at whom they falsely hint is outlandish, and this is clear Arabic speech.

104. Lo! those who disbelieve the revelations of Allah, Allah guideth them not and theirs will be a painful doom.

105. Only they invent falsehood who believe not Allah's revelations, and (only) they are the liars.

106. Whoso disbelieveth in Allah after his belief — save him who is forced thereto and whose heart is still content with Faith — but whoso findeth ease in disbelief: On them is wrath from Allah. Theirs will be an awful doom.

107. That is because they have chosen the life of the world rather than the Hereafter, and because Allah guideth not the disbelieving folk.

108. Such are they whose hearts and ears and eyes Allah hath sealed. And such are the heedless.

109. Assuredly in the Hereafter they are the losers.

110. Then lo! thy Lord — for those who become fugitives after they had been persecuted, and then fought and were steadfast — lo! thy Lord afterward is (for them) indeed Forgiving, Merciful.

111. On the Day when every soul will come pleading for itself, and every soul will be repaid what it did, and they will not be wronged.

112. Allah coineth a similitude: a township that dwelt secure and well content, its provision coming to it in abundance from every side, but it disbelieved in Allah's favours, so Allah made it experience the garb of dearth and fear because of what they used to do.

113. And verily there had come unto them a messenger from among them, but they had denied him, and so the torment seized them while they were wrong-doers.

114. So eat of the lawful and good food which Allah hath provided for you, and thank the bounty of your Lord if it is Him ye serve.

115. He hath forbidden for you only carrion and blood and swine-flesh and that which hath been immolated in the name of any other than Allah; but he who is driven thereto, neither craving nor transgressing, lo! then Allah is Forgiving, Merciful.

116. And speak not, concerning that which your own tongues qualify (as clean or unclean), the falsehood: "This is lawful, and this is forbidden," so that ye invent a lie against Allah. Lo! those who invent a lie against Allah will not succeed.

117. A brief enjoyment (will be theirs); and theirs a painful doom.

118. And unto those who are Jews We have forbidden that which We have already related unto thee. And We wronged them not, but they were wont to wrong themselves.

119. Then lo! thy Lord—for those who do evil in ignorance and afterward repent and amend—lo! (for them) thy Lord is afterward indeed Forgiving, Merciful.

120. Lo! Abraham was a nation obedient to Allah, by nature upright, and he was not of the idolaters;

121. Thankful for His bounties; He chose him and He guided him unto a straight path.

122. And We gave him good in the world, and in the Hereafter he is among, the righteous.

123. And afterward We inspired thee (Muhammad, saying): Follow the religion of Abraham, as one by nature upright. He was not of the idolaters.

124. The Sabbath was appointed only for those who differed concerning it, and lo! thy Lord will judge between them on the Day of Resurrection concerning that wherein they used to differ.

125. Call unto the way of thy Lord with wisdom and fair exhortation, and reason with them in the better way. Lo! thy Lord is Best Aware of him who strayeth from His way, and He is Best Aware of those who go aright.

126. If ye punish, then punish with the like of that wherewith ye were afflicted. But if ye endure patiently, verily it is better for the patient.

127. Endure thou patiently (O Muhammad). Thine endurance is only by (the help of) Allah. Grieve not for them, and be not in distress because of that which they devise.

128. Lo! Allah is with those who keep their duty unto Him and those who are doers of good.

SÛRAH 17

Banî Isrâîl, "The Children of Israel", begins and ends with references to the Israelites. V.1 relates to the Prophet's vision in which he was carried by night upon a heavenly steed to the Temple of Jerusalem, whence he was caught up through the seven heavens to the very presence of God. The sûrah may be taken as belonging to the middle group of Meccan Sûrahs, except v. 81, or, according to other commentators, vv. 76-82, revealed at Al-Madînah.

THE CHILDREN OF ISRAEL

Revealed at Mecca

In the name of Allah, the Beneficent, the Merciful.

1. Glorified be He Who carried His servant by night from the Inviolable Place of Worship to the Far Distant Place of Worship the neighbourhood whereof We have blessed, that We might show him of Our tokens! Lo! He, only He, is the Hearer, the Seer.

2. We gave unto Moses the Scripture, and We appointed it a guidance for the Children of Israel, saying: Choose no guardian beside Me.

3. (They were) the seed of those whom We carried (in the ship) along with Noah. Lo! he was a grateful slave.

4. And We decreed for the Children of Israel in the Scripture: Ye verily will work corruption in the earth twice, and ye will become great tyrants.

5. So when the time for the first of the two came, We roused against you slaves of Ours of great might who ravaged (your) country, and it was a threat performed.

6. Then we gave you once again your turn against them, and We aided you with wealth and children and made you more in soldiery.

7. (Saying): If ye do good, ye do good for your own souls, and if ye do evil, it is for them (in like manner). So, when the time for the second (of the judgements) came (We roused against you others of Our slaves) to ravage you, and to enter the Temple even they entered it the first time, and to lay waste all that they conquered with an utter wasting.

8. It may be that your Lord will have mercy on you, but if ye repeat (the crime) We shall repeat (the punishment), and We have appointed hell a dungeon for the disbelievers.

9. Lo! this Qur'ân guideth unto that which is straightest, and giveth tidings unto the believers who do good works that theirs will be a great reward.

10. And that those who believe not in the Hereafter, for them We have prepared a painful doom.

11. Man prayeth for evil as he prayeth for good; for man was ever hasty.

12. And we appoint the night and the day two portents. Then We make dark the portent of the night, and We make the portent of the day sight-giving, that ye may seek bounty from your Lord, and that ye may know the computation of the years, and the reckoning; and everything had We expounded with a clear expounding.

13. And every man's augury have We fastened to his own neck, and We shall bring forth for him on the Day of Resurrection a book which he will find wide open.

14. (And it will be said unto him): Read thy book. Thy soul sufficeth as reckoner against thee this day.

15. Whosoever goeth right, it is only for (the good of) his own soul that he goeth right, and whosoever erreth, erreth only to its hurt. No laden soul can bear another's load, We never punish until We have sent a messenger.

16. And when We would destroy a township We send commandment to its folk who live at ease, and afterward they commit abomination therein, and so the Word (of doom) hath effect for it, and We annihilate it with complete annihilation.

17. How many generations have We destroyed since Noah! And Allah sufficeth as Knower and Beholder of the sins of His slaves.

18. Whoso desireth that (life) which hasteneth away, We hasten for him therein that We will for whom We please. And afterward We have appointed for him hell; he will endure the heat thereof, condemned, rejected.

19. And whoso desireth the Hereafter and striveth for it with the effort necessary, being a believer; for such, their effort findeth favour (with their Lord).

20. Each do We supply, both these and those, from the bounty of thy Lord. And the bounty of thy Lord can never be walled up.

21. See how We prefer one above another, and verily the Hereafter will be greater in degrees and greater in preferment.

22. Set not up with Allah any other god (O man) lest thou sit down reproved, forsaken.

23. Thy Lord hath decreed, that ye worship none save Him, and (that ye show) kindness to parents. If one of them or both of them attain to old age with thee, say not "Fie" unto them nor repulse them, but speak unto them a gracious word.

24. And lower unto them the wing of submission through mercy, and say: My Lord! Have mercy on them both as they did care for me when I was little.

25. Your Lord is best aware of what is in your minds. If ye are righteous, then lo! He was ever Forgiving unto those who turn (unto Him).

26. Give the kinsman his due, and the needy, and the wayfarer, and squander not (thy wealth) in wantonness.

27. Lo! the squanderers were ever brothers of the devils, and the devil was ever an ingrate to his Lord.

28. But if thou turn away from them, seeking mercy from thy Lord, for which thou hopest, then speak unto them a reasonable word.

29. And let not thy hand be chained to thy neck nor open it with a complete opening, lest thou sit down rebuked, denuded.

30. Lo! thy Lord enlargeth the provision for whom He will, and straiteneth (it for whom He will). Lo! He was ever Knower, Seer of His slaves.

31. Slay not your children, fearing a fall to poverty, We shall provide for them and for you. Lo! the slaying of them is great sin.

32. And come not near unto adultery. Lo! it is an abomination and an evil way.

33. And slay not the life which Allah hath forbidden save with right. Whoso is slain wrongfully, We have given power unto his heir, but let him not commit excess in slaying. Lo! he will be helped.

34. Come not near the wealth of the orphan save with that which is better till he come to strength; and keep the covenant. Lo! of the covenant it will be asked.

35. Fill the measure when ye measure, and weigh with a right balance; that is meet, and better in the end.

36. (O man), follow not that whereof thou hast no knowledge. Lo! the hearing and the sight and the heart—of each of these it will be asked.

37. And walk not in the earth exultant. Lo! thou canst not read the earth, nor canst thou stretch to the height of the hills.

38. The evil of all that is hateful in the sight of thy Lord.

39. This is (part) of that wisdom wherewith thy Lord hath inspired thee (O Muhammad). And set not up with Allah any other god, lest thou be cast into hell, reproved, abandoned.

40. Hath your Lord then distinguished you (O men of Mecca) by giving you sons, and hath chosen for Himself females from among the angels? Lo! verily ye speak an awful word!

41. We verily have displayed (Our warnings) in this Qur'ân that they may take heed, but it increaseth them in naught save aversion.

42. Say (O Muhammad, to the disbelievers): If there were other gods along with Him, as they say, then had they sought a way against the Lord of the Throne.

43. Glorified is He, and High Exalted above what they say!

44. The seven heavens and the earth and all that is therein praise Him, and there is not a thing but hymneth His praise; but ye understand not their praise. Lo! He is ever Clement, Forgiving.

45. And when thou recitest the Qur'ân We place between

thee and those who believe not in the Hereafter a hidden barrier.

46. And We place upon their hearts veils lest they should understand it, and in their ears a deafness; and when thou makest mention of thy Lord alone in the Qu'rân, they turn their backs in aversion.

47. We are best aware of what they wish to hear when they give ear to thee and when they take secret counsel, when the evil-doers say: Ye follow but a man bewitched.

48. See what similitudes they coin for thee, and thus are all astray, and cannot find a road!

49. And they say: When we are bones and fragments, shall we, forsooth, be raised up as a new creation?

50. Say: Be ye stones or iron.

51. Or some created thing that is yet greater in your thoughts! Then they will say: Who shall bring us back (to life). Say: He Who created you at the first. Then will they shake their heads at thee, and say: When will it be? Say: It will perhaps be soon.

52. A day when He will call you and ye will answer with His praise, and ye will think that ye have tarried but a little while.

53. Tell My bondmen to speak that which is kindlier. Lo! the devil soweth discord among them. Lo! the devil is for man an open foe.

54. Your Lord is best aware of you. If He will, He will have mercy on you, or if He will, He will punish you. We have not sent thee (O Muhammad) as a warden over them.

55. And thy Lord is best aware of all who are in the heavens and the earth. And We preferred some of the Prophets above others, and unto David We gave the Psalms.

56. Say: Cry unto those (saints and angels) whom ye assume (to be gods) beside Him, yet they have no power to rid you of misfortune nor to change.

57. Those unto whom they cry seek the way of approach to their Lord, which of them shall be the nearest; they hope for His mercy and they fear His doom. Lo! the doom of thy Lord is to be shunned.

58. There is not a township but We shall destroy it ere the Day of Resurrection, or punish it with dire punishment. That is set forth in the Book (of Our decrees).

59. Naught hindereth Us from sending portents save that the folk of old denied them. And We gave Thamûd the she-camel — a clear portent — but they did wrong in respect of her. We send not portents save to warn.

60. And (it was a warning) When we told thee: Lo! thy Lord encompasseth mankind, and We appointed the vision which We showed thee as an ordeal for mankind, and (likewise) the Accursed Tree in the Qurân. We warn them, but it increaseth them in naught save gross impiety.

61. And when We said unto the angels: Fall down prostrate before Adam, and they fell prostrate all save Iblîs, he said: Shall I fall prostrate before that which Thou hast created of clay?

62. He said: Seest Thou this (creature) whom Thou hast honoured above me, if Thou give me grace until the Day of Resurrection I verily will seize his seed, save but a few.

63. He said: Go, and whosoever of them followeth thee—lo! hell will be your payment, ample payment.

64. And excite any of them whom thou canst with thy voice, and urge thy horse and foot against them, and be a partner in their wealth and children, and promise them. Satan promiseth them only to deceive.

65. Lo! My (faithful) bondmen—over them thou hast no power, and thy Lord sufficeth as (their) guardian.

66. (O mankind), your Lord is He Who driveth for you the ship upon the sea that ye may seek of His bounty. Lo! He was ever Merciful toward you.

67. And when harm toucheth you upon the sea, all unto whom ye cry (for succour) fail save Him (alone), but when He bringeth you safe to land, ye turn away, for man was ever thankless.

68. Feel ye then secure that He will not cause a slope of the land to engulf you, or send a sand-storm upon you, and then ye will find that ye have no protector?

69. Or feel ye secure that He will not return you to that (plight) a second time, and send against you a hurricane of wind and drown you for your thanklessness, and then ye will not find therein that ye have any avenger against Us?

70. Verily We have honoured the children of Adam. We carry them on the land and sea, and have made provision of good things for them, and have preferred them above many of those whom We created with a marked preferment.

71. On the day when We shall summon all men with their record, whoso is given his book in his right hand—such will read their book and they will not be wronged a shred.

72. Whoso is blind here will be blind in the Hereafter, and yet further from the road.

73. And they indeed strove hard to beguile thee (Muhammad) away from that wherewith We have inspired thee, that thou shouldst invent other than it against Us; and then would they have accepted thee as a friend.

74. And if We had not made thee wholly firm thou mightest almost have inclined unto them a little.

75. Then had We made thee taste a double (punishment) of living and a double (punishment) of dying, then hadst thou found no helper against Us.

76. And they indeed wished to scare thee from the land that they might drive thee forth from thence, and then they would have stayed (there) but a little after thee.

77. (Such was Our) method in the case of those whom We sent before thee (to mankind), and thou wilt not find for Our method aught of power to change.

78. Establish worship at the going down of the sun until the dark of night, and (the recital of) the Qur'ân at dawn. Lo! (the recital of) the Qur'ân at dawn is ever witnessed.

79. And some part of the night awake for it, a largess for thee. It may be that thy Lord will raise thee to a praised estate.

80. And say: My Lord! Cause me to come in with a firm incoming and to go out with a firm outgoing. And give me from Thy presence a sustaining Power.

81. And say: Truth hath come and falsehood hath vanished away. Lo! falsehood is ever bound to vanish.

82. And We reveal of the Qur'ân that which is a healing and a mercy for believers though it increase the evil-doers in naught save ruin.

83. And when We make life pleasant unto man, he turneth away and is averse; and when ill toucheth him he is in despair.

84. Say; Each one doth according to his rule of conduct, and thy Lord is best aware of him whose way is right.

85. They will ask thee concerning the spirit. Say: The spirit is by command of my Lord, and of knowledge ye have been vouchsafed but little.

86. And if We willed. We could withdraw that which We have revealed unto thee, then wouldst thou find no guardian for thee against Us in respect thereof.

87. (It is naught) save mercy from thy lord. Lo! His kindness unto thee was ever great.

88. Say: Verily, though mankind and the jinn should assemble to produce the like of this Qur'ân, they could not produce the like thereof though they were helpers one of another.

89. And verily We have displayed for mankind in this Qur'ân all kinds of similitudes, but most of mankind refuse aught save disbelief.

90. And they say: We will not put faith in thee till thou cause a spring to gush forth from the earth for us.

91. Or thou have a garden of date-palms and grapes, and cause rivers to gush forth therein abundantly.

92. Or thou cause the heaven to fall upon us piecemeal, as thou hast pretended, or bring Allah and the angels as a warrant.

93. Thou have a house of gold; or thou ascend up into heaven, and even then we will put no faith in thine ascension till thou bring down for us a book that we can read. Say (O Muhammad): My Lord be Glorified! Am I naught save a mortal messenger?

94. And naught prevented mankind from believing when the guidance came unto them save that they said: Hath Allah sent a mortal as (His) messenger?

95. Say: If there were in the earth angels walking secure, We had sent down for them from heaven an angel as messenger.

96. Say: Allah sufficeth for a witness between me and you. Lo! He is knower, Seer of His slaves.

97. And he whom Allah guideth, he is led aright; while, as for him whom He sendeth astray, for them thou wilt find no protecting friends beside Him, and We shall assemble them on the Day of Resurrection on their faces, blind, dumb, and deaf; their habitation will be hell; whenever it abateth, We increase the flame for them.

98. That is their reward because they disbelieved Our revelations and said: When we are bones and fragments shall we, forsooth, be raised up as a new creation?

99. Have they not seen that Allah who created the heavens and the earth is Able to create the like of them, and hath appointed for them an end whereof there is no doubt? But the wrong-doers refuse aught save disbelief.

100. Say (unto them): If ye possessed the treasures of the mercy of my Lord, ye would surely hold them back for fear of spending for man was ever grudging.

101. And verily We gave unto Moses nine tokens, clear proofs (of Allah's Sovereignty). Do but ask the Children of Israel how he came unto them, then Pharaoh said unto him: Lo! I deem thee one bewitched, O Moses.

102. He said: In truth thou knowest that none sent down these (portents) save the Lord of the heavens and the earth as proofs and lo! (for my part) I deem thee lost, O Pharaoh.

103. And he wished to scare them from the land, but We drowned him and those with him, all together.

104. And We said unto the Children of Israel after him: Dwell in the land; but when the promise of the Hereafter

cometh to pass we shall bring as a crowd gathered out of various nations.

105. With truth have We sent it down, and with truth hath it descended. And We have sent thee as naught else save a bearer of good tidings and a warner.

106. And (it is) a Qur'ân that We have divided, that thou mayest recite it unto mankind at intervals, and We have revealed it by (Successive) revelation.

107. Say: Believe therein or believe not, lo! those who were given knowledge before it, when it is read unto them, fall down prostrate on their faces, adoring.

108. Saying: Glory to our Lord! Verily the promise of our Lord must be fulfilled.

109. They fall down on their faces, weeping, and it increaseth humility in them.

110. Say (unto mankind): Cry unto Allah, or cry unto the Beneficent, unto whichsoever ye cry (it is the same). His are the most beautiful names. And thou (Muhammad) be not loud voiced in thy worship nor yet silent therein, but follow a way between.

111. And say: Praise be to Allah, Who hath not taken unto Himself a son, and Who hath no partner in the Sovereignty, nor hath He any protecting friend through dependence. And magnify Him with all magnificence.

SÛRAH 18

Al-Kahf, "The cave", takes its name from the story of the youths who took refuge from persecution in a cave (vv 10-27) and who were preserved there as if asleep for a long period — a story which is generally identified by Western writers (e.g. Gibbon) with the legend of the seven sleepers of Ephesus. But a strong tradition in the Muslim world asserts that this story and that of Dhû'l Qarneyn ("The Two-horned One"), vv. 83-99. possibly also that of Moses and the angel, vv. 61-82, were revealed to the prophet to enable him to answer the questions which the Jewish doctors of Yathrib had instructed the idolaters to ask him, as a test of Prophethood.

The questions were three: "Ask him," said the Rabbis, "of some youths who were of old, what was their fate, for they have a strange story; and ask him of a much-travelled man who reached the sunrise regions of the earth and the sun-set regions thereof, what was his history; and ask him of the Spirit, What it is."

The tormentors of the Prophet, who had been to Yathrib to get hints from the Jews, on their return to Mecca put these questions to the Prophet, after having told the people that it was to be a crucial test. The Prophet said that he would surely answer them upon the morrow, without adding "if God will," as though he could command God's revelation. As a reproof for that omission, the wished-for revelation was withheld from him for some days, and when it came included the rebuke contained in verse 24. There is no reason whatever to doubt the truth of the tradition which connects this chapter with three questions set by Jewish rabbis, and the answers must have been considered satisfying, or at least silencing, or the Jews would certainly have made fun of them when they were taunting the Prophet daily after his flight to Yathrib (Al-Madînah). That being so, it would seem rash to identify the story with that of the Christian Seven Sleepers; it must belong, as the story of the "Two-Horned One" actually does belong to rabbinical lore. The third of the questions is answered in Sûrah 17, vv.85 ff.

It belongs to the middle group of Meccan Sûrahs.

THE CAVE

Revealed at Mecca

In the name of Allah, the Beneficent, the Merciful.

1. Praise be to Allah Who hath revealed the Scripture unto His slave, and hath not placed therein any crookedness.

2. (But hath made it) straight, to give warning of stern punishment from Him, and to bring unto the believers who do good works the news that theirs will be a fair reward.

3. Wherein they will abide for ever.

4. And to warn those who say: Allah hath chosen a son.

5. (A thing) whereof they have no knowledge, nor (had) their fathers. Dreadful is the word that cometh out of their mouths. They speak naught but a lie.

6. Yet it may be, if they believe not in this statement, that thou (Muhammad) wilt torment thy soul with grief over their footsteps.

7. Lo! We have placed all that is in the earth as an ornament thereof that we may try them: which of them is best in conduct.

8. And lo! We shall make all that is thereon a barren mound.

9. Or deemest thou that the people of the cave and the Inscription are a wonder among Our portents?

10. When the young men fled for refuge to the cave and said: Our Lord! Give us mercy from Thy presence and shape for us right conduct in our plight.

11. Then we sealed up their hearing in the Cave for a number of years.

12. And afterward We raised them up that We might know which of the two parties would best calculate the time that they had tarried.

13. We narrate unto thee their story with truth. Lo! they were young men who believed in their Lord and We increased them in guidance.

14. And We made firm their hearts when they stood forth and said: Our Lord is the Lord of the heavens and the earth. We cry unto no god beside Him, for then should we utter an enormity.

15. These, our people have chosen (other) gods beside Him though they bring no clear warrant (vouchsafed) to them. And who doth greater wrong than he who inventeth a lie concerning Allah?

16. And when ye withdraw from them and that which they worship except Allah, then seek refuge in the Cave; your Lord will spread for you of His mercy and will prepare for you a pillow in your plight.

17. And thou mightest have seen the sun when it rose move away from their cave to the right and when it set go past them on the left, and they were in the cleft thereof. That was (one) of the portents of Allah. He whom Allah guideth, he indeed is led aright, and he whom He sendeth astray for him thou wilt not find a guiding friend.

18. And thou wouldst have deemed them waking though they were asleep, and we caused them to turn over to the right and the left and their dog stretching out his paws on the threshold. If thou hadst observed them closely thou hadst assuredly turned away from them in flight, and hadst been filled with awe of them.

19. And in like manner We awakened them that they might question one another. A speaker from among them said: How long have ye tarried? They said: We have tarried a day or some part of a day, (others) said: Your Lord best knoweth what ye have tarried. Now send one of you with this your silver coin unto the city, and let him see what food is purest there and bring you a supply thereof. Let him be courteous and let no man know of you.

20. For they, if they should come to know of you, will stone you or turn you back to their religion; then ye will never prosper.

21. And in like manner We disclosed them (to the people of the city) that they might know that the promise of Allah

is true, and that, as for the Hour, there is no doubt concerning it. When (the people of the city) disputed of their case among themselves, they said: Build over them a building; their Lord Knoweth best concerning them. Those who won their point said: We verily shall build a place of worship over them.

22. (Some) will say; they were three, their dog the fourth and (some) say: Five, their dog the sixth, guessing at random; and (some) say: Seven and their dog the eighth. Say (O Muhammad): My Lord is best aware of their number. None knoweth them save a few. So contend not concerning them except with an outward contending, and ask not any of them to pronounce concerning them.

23. And say not of anything: Lo! I shall do that tomorrow.

24. Except if Allah will. And remember thy Lord when thou forgettest, and say: It may be that my Lord guideth me unto a nearer way of truth than this.

25. And (it is said) they tarried in their Cave three hundred years and add nine.

26. Say: Allah is best aware how long they tarried. His is the invisible of the heavens and the earth. How clear of sight is He and keen of hearing! They have no protecting friend beside Him, and He maketh none to share in His government.

27. And recite that which hath been revealed unto thee of the Scripture of thy Lord. There is none who can change His words and thou wilt find no refuge beside Him.

28. Restrain thyself along with those who cry unto their Lord at morn and evening, seeking His countenance; and let not thine eyes overlook them, desiring the pomp of the life of the world; and obey not him whose heart We have made heedless of Our remembrance, who followeth his own lust and whose case hath been abondoned.

29. Say: (it is) the truth from the Lord of you (all). Then whosoever will, let him believe, and whosoever will, let him disbelieve. Lo! We have prepared for disbelievers Fire. Its tent encloseth them. If they ask for showers, they will be showered with water like the molten lead which burneth the faces. Calamitous the drink and ill the resting-place!

30. Lo! as for those who believe and do good works—Lo! We suffer not the reward of one whose work is goodly to be lost.

31. As for such, theirs they will be Gardens of Eden, wherein rivers flow beneath them; therein they will be given armlets of gold and will wear green robes of finest silk and gold embroidery, reclining upon thrones therein. Blest the reward, and fair the resting-place!

32. Coin for them a similitude. Two men, unto one whom We had assigned two gardens of grapes, and We had surrounded both with date-palms and had put between them tillage.

33. Each of the gardens gave its fruit and withheld naught thereof. And We caused a river to gush forth therein.

34. And he had fruit. And he said unto his comrade, when he spake with him: I am more than thee in wealth, and stronger in respect of men.

35. And he went into his garden, while he (thus) wronged himself. He said: I think not that all this will ever perish.

36. I think not that the Hour will ever come, and if indeed I am brought back unto my Lord I surely shall find better than this as a resort.

37. And his comrade, while he disputed with him, exclaimed; Disbelievest thou in Him Who created thee of dust, then of a drop (of seed) and then fashioned thee a man?

38. But He is Allah, my Lord, and I ascribe unto my Lord no partner.

39. If only, when thou enteredst thy garden, thou hadst said: That which Allah willeth (will come to pass)! There is no strength save in Allah. Though thou seest me as less than thee in wealth and children.

40. Yet it may be that my Lord will gave me better than thy garden, and will send on it a bolt from heaven, and some morning it will be a smooth hillside.

41. Or some morning the water thereof will be lost in the earth so that thou canst not make search for it.

42. And his fruit was beset (with destruction): then began he to wring his hands for all that he had spent upon it, when (now) it was all ruined on its trellises, and to say: Would that I had ascribed no partner to my Lord!

43. And he had no troop of men to help him as against Allah, nor could he save himself.

44. In this case is protection only from Allah, the True. He is best for reward, and best for consequence.

45. And coin for them the similitude of the life of the world as water which We send down from the sky, and the vegetation of the earth mingleth with it and then becometh dry twigs that the winds scatter. Allah is Able to do all things.

46. Wealth and children are an ornament of life of the world. But the good deeds which endure are better in thy Lord's sight for reward, and better in respect of hope.

47. And (bethink you of) the Day when We remove the hills and ye see the earth emerging and We gather them

together so as to leave not one of them behind.

48. And they are set before thy Lord in ranks (and it is said unto them): Now verily have ye come unto Us as We created you at the first. But ye thought that We had set no tryst for you.

49. And the Book is placed, and thou seest the guilty fearful of that which is therein, and they say: What kind of a book is this that leaveth not a small thing nor a great thing but hath counted it! And they find all that they did confronting them, and thy Lord wrongeth no one.

50. And (remember) when We said unto the angels: Fall prostrate before Adam, and they fell prostrate, all save Iblis. He was of the jinn, so he rebelled against his Lord's command. Will ye choose him and his seed for your protecting friends instead of Me, when they are an enemy unto you? Calamitous is the exchange for evil-doers!

51. I made them not to witness the creation of the heavens and the earth, nor their own creation; nor choose I misleaders for (My) helpers.

52. And (be mindful of) the Day when He will say: Call those partners of Mine whom ye pretended. Then they will cry unto them, but they will not hear their prayer, and We shall set a gulf of doom between them.

53. And the guilty behold the Fire and know that they are about to fall therein, and they find no way of escape thence.

54. And verily We have displayed for mankind in this Qur'ân all manner of similitudes, but man is more than anything contentious.

55. And naught hindereth mankind from believing when the guidance cometh unto them, and from asking forgiveness of their Lord, unless (it be that they wish) that the judgement of the men of old should come upon them or (that) they should be confronted with the Doom.

56. We send not the messengers save as bearers of good news and warners. Those who disbelieve contend with falsehood in order to refute the Truth thereby. And they take Our revelations and that wherewith they are threatened as a jest.

57. And who doth greater wrong than he who hath been reminded of the revelations of his Lord, yet turneth away from them and forgetteth what his hands send forward (to the Judgement)? Lo! on their hearts We have placed coverings so that they understand not, and in their ears a deafness. And though thou call them to the guidance, in that case they can never be led aright.

58. Thy Lord is the Forgiver, Full of Mercy. If He took them

to task (now) for what they earn, He would hasten on the doom for them; but theirs is an appointed term from which they will find no escape.

59. And (all) those townships! We destroyed them when they did wrong, and We appointed a fixed time for their destruction.

60. And when Moses said unto his servant: I will not give up until I reach the point where the two rivers meet, though I march on for ages.

61. And when they reached the point where the two met, they forgot their fish, and it took its way into the waters, being free.

62. And when they had gone further, he said unto his servant: Bring us our breakfast. Verily we have found fatigue in this our journey.

63. He said: Didst thou see, when we took refuge on the rock, and I forgot the fish—and none but Satan caused me to forget to mention it—it took its way into waters by a marvel.

64. He said: This is that which we have been seeking. So they retraced their steps again.

65. Then found they one of Our slaves, unto whom We had given mercy from Us, and had taught him knowledge from Our presence.

66. Moses said unto him: May I follow thee, to the end that thou mayst teach me right conduct of that which thou hast been taught?

67. He said: Lo! thou canst not bear with me.

68. How canst thou bear with that whereof thou canst not compass any knowledge?

69. He said: Allah willing, thou shalt find me patient and I shall not in aught gainsay thee.

70. He said: Well, if thou go with me, ask me not concerning aught till I myself mention of it unto thee.

71. So the twain set out till, when they were in the ship, he made a hole therein. (Moses) said: Hast thou made a hole therein to drown the folk thereof? Thou verily hast done a dreadful thing.

72. He said: Did I not tell thee thou couldst not bear with me?

73. (Moses) said: Be not wroth with me that I forgot, and be not hard upon me for my fault.

74. So the twain journeyed on till, when they met a lad, he slew him. (Moses) said: What! Hast thou slain an innocent soul who hath slain no man? Verily thou hast done a horrid thing.

75. He said: Did I not tell thee that thou couldst not bear with me?

76. (Moses) said: If I ask thee after this concerning aught, keep not company with me. Thou hast received an excuse from me.

77. So the twain journeyed on till, when they came unto the folk of a certain township, they asked its folk for food, but they refused to make them guests. And they found therein a wall upon the point of falling into ruin, and he repaired it. (Moses) said: If thou hadst wished, thou couldst have taken payment for it.

78. He said: This is the parting between thee and me! I will announce unto thee the interpretation of that thou couldst not bear with patience.

79. As for the ship, it belonged to poor people working on the river, and I wished to mar it, for there was a king behind them who is taking every ship by force.

80. And as for the lad, his parents were believers and we feared lest he should oppress them by rebellion and disbelief.

81. And We intended that their Lord should change him for them for one better in purity and nearer to mercy.

82. And as for the wall, it belonged to two orphan boys in the city, and there was beneath it a treasure belonging to them, and their father had been righteous, and thy Lord intended that they should come to their full strength and should bring forth their treasure as a mercy from their Lord; and I did not upon my own command. Such is the interpretation of that wherewith thou couldst not bear.

83. They will ask thee of Dhû'l-Qarneyn. Say: I shall recite unto you a remembrance of him.

84. Lo! We made him strong in the land and gave him unto everything a road.

85. And he followed a road.

86. Till, when he reached the setting-place of the sun, he found it setting in a muddy spring, and found a people thereabout: We said: O Dhû'l-Qarneyn! Either punish or show them kindness.

87. He said: As for him who doeth wrong, we shall punish him, and then he will be brought back unto his Lord, who will punish him with an awful punishment!

88. But as for him who believeth and doeth right, good will be his reward, and We shall speak unto him a mild command.

89. Then he followed a road.

90. Till, when he reached the rising-place of the sun, he found it rising on a people for whom We had appointed no shelter therefrom.

91. So (it was). And We knew all concerning him.

92. Then he followed a road.

93. Till, when he came between the two mountains, he found upon their hither side a folk that scarce could understand a saying.

94. They said: O Dhû'l-Qarneyn! Lo! Gog and Magog are spoiling the land. So may we pay thee tribute on condition that thou set a barrier between us and them?

95. He said: That wherein my Lord hath established me is better (than your tribute). Do but help me with strength (of men), I will set between you and them a bank.

96. Give me pieces of iron—till, when he had levelled up (the gap) between the cliffs, he said: Blow!—till, when he had made it a fire, he said: Bring me molten copper to pour thereon.

97. And (Gog and Magog) were not able to surmount, nor could they pierce (it).

98. He said: This is a mercy from my Lord; but when the promise of my Lord cometh to pass, He will lay it low, for the promise of my Lord is true.

99. And on that day We shall let some of them surge against others, and the Trumpet will be blown. Then We shall gather them together in one gathering.

100. On that day We shall present hell to the disbelievers, plain to view.

101. Those whose eyes were hoodwinked from My reminder, and who could not bear to hear.

102. Do the disbelievers reckon that they can choose My bondmen as protecting friends beside Me? Lo! We have prepared hell as a welcome for the disbelievers.

103. Say: Shall be inform you who will be the greatest losers by their works?

104. Those whose effort goeth astray in the life of the world, and yet they reckon that they do good work.

105. Those are they who disbelieve in the revelations of their Lord and in the meeting with Him. Therefore their works are vain, and on the Day of Resurrection We assign no weight to them.

106. That is their reward: hell, because they disbelieved, and made a jest of Our revelations and Our messengers.

107. Lo! those who believe and do good works, theirs are the Gardens of Paradise for welcome.

108. Wherein they will abide, with no desire to be removed from thence.

109. Say: Though the sea became ink for the Words of my Lord, verily the sea would be used up before the Words of my Lord were exhausted, even though We brought the like thereof

to help.

110. Say: I am only a mortal like you. My Lord inspireth in me that your God is only One God. And whoever hopeth for the meeting with his Lord, let him do rigtheous work, and make none sharer of the worship due unto his Lord.

SÛRAH 19

Maryam takes its name from v. 16 ff. That it is of quite early Meccan revelation is established by the following tradition:

In the fifth year of the Prophet's mission (the ninth before the Hijrah, or Flight, to Al-Madînah) a number of the poorer converts were allowed by the Prophet to emigrate to Abyssinia, a Christian country where they would not be subject to persecution for their worship of the One God. This is known as the first Hijrah. The rulers of Mecca sent ambassadors to ask the Negus for their extradition, accusing them of having left the religion of their own people without entering the Christian religion, and of having done wrong in their own country. The Negus (against the wish of the envoys) sent for the spokesmen of the refugees and, in the presence of the bishops of his realm, questioned them of their religion. Ja'far ibn Abî Tâlib, cousin of the Prophet, answered: (I translate from the account given by Ibn Ishâq.)

"We were folk immersed in ignorance, worshipping idols, eating carrion, given to lewdness, severing the ties of kinship, bad neighbours, the strong among us preying on the weak; thus were we till Allah sent to us a messenger of our own, whose lineage, honesty, trustworthiness and chastity we knew, and he called us to Allah that we should acknowledge His unity and worship Him and eschew all the stones and idols that we and our fathers used to worship beside Him; and ordered us to be truthful and to restore the pledge and observe the ties of kinship, and be good neighbours, and to abstain from things forbidden, and from blood, and forbade us lewdness and false speech, and to prey upon the wealth of orphans, and to accuse good women; and commanded us to worship Allah only, ascribing nothing unto Him as partner, and enjoined upon us prayer and legal alms and fasting. (And he enumerated for him the teachings of Islâm.)

"So we trusted him and we believed in him and followed that which he had brought from Allah, and we worshipped Allah only, and ascribed no thing as partner upon Him. And we refrained from that which was forbidden to us, and indulged in that which was made lawful for us. And our people became hostile to us and tormented us, and sought to turn us from our religion that they might bring us back to the worship of idols from the worship of Allah Most High, and that we might indulge in those iniquities which before we had deemed lawful.

"And when they persecuted and oppressed us, and hemmed us in, and kept us from the practice of our religion, we came forth to thy land, and chose thee above all others, and sought thy protection, and hoped that we should not be troubled in thy land, O King!

"Then the Negus asked him: Hast with thee aught of that which he brought from Allah? Ja'far answered: Yes. Then the Negus said: Relate it to me, and Ja'far recited to him the beginning of Kâf, Hâ, Yâ, A'în, Sad" — the Arabic letters with which this Sûrah begins, such letters being generally used instead of titles by the early Muslims. Therefore this Sûrah must have been revealed and well-known before the departure of the emigrants for Abyssinia.

An early Meccan Sûrah, with the possible exception of vv. 59 and 60, which, according to some authorities, were revealed at Al-Madînah.

MARY

Revealed at Mecca

In the name of Allah, the Beneficent, the Merciful.

1. Kâf. Hâ. Yâ. A'în. Sad.

2. A mention of the mercy of thy Lord unto His servant Zachariah.

3. When he cried unto his Lord a cry in secret,

4. Saying: My Lord! Lo! the bones of me wax feeble and my head is shining with grey hair, and I have never been unblest in prayer to Thee, my Lord.

5. Lo! I fear my kinsfolk after me, since my wife is barren. Oh, give me from Thy presence a successor.

6. Who shall inherit of me and inherit (also) of the house of Jacob. And make him, my Lord, accepting (unto Thee).

7. (It was said unto him): O Zachariah! Lo! We bring thee tidings of a son whose name is John. We have given the same name to none before (him).

8. He said: My Lord! How can I have a son when my wife is barren and I have reached infirm old age?

9. He said: So (it will be). Thy Lord saith: It is easy for Me, even as I created thee before, when thou wast naught.

10. He said: My Lord! Appoint for me some token. He said: Thy token is that thou, with no bodily defect, shalt not speak

unto mankind three nights.

11. Then he came forth unto his people from the sanctuary, and signified to them: Glorify your Lord at break of day and fall of night.

12. (And it was said unto his son): O John! Hold fast the Scripture. And We gave him wisdom when a child.

13. And compassion from Our presence, and purity; and he was devout.

14. And dutiful toward his parents. And he was not arrogant, rebellious.

15. Peace on him the day he was born, and the day he dieth and the day he shall be raised alive!

16. And make mention of Mary in the Scripture, when she had withdrawn from her people to a chamber looking East.

17. And had chosen seclusion from them. Then We sent unto her Our Spirit and it assumed for her the likeness of a perfect man.

18. She said: Lo! I seek refuge in the Beneficent One from thee, if thou art God-fearing.

19. He said: I am only a messenger of thy Lord, that I may bestow on thee a faultless son.

20. She said: How can I have a son when no mortal hath touched me, neither have I been unchaste?

21. He said: So (it will be). Thy Lord saith: It is easy for Me. And (it will be) that We may make of him a revelation for mankind and a mercy from Us, and it is a thing ordained.

22. And she conceived him, and she withdrew with him to a far place.

23. And the pangs of childbirth drove her unto the trunk of the palm tree. She said: Oh, would that I had died ere this and had become a thing of naught, forgotten!

24. Then (one) cried unto her from below her, saying: Grieve not! Thy Lord hath placed a rivulet beneath thee.

25. And shake the trunk of the palm-tree toward thee, thou wilt cause ripe dates to fall upon thee.

26. So eat and drink and be consoled. And if thou meetest any mortal, say: Lo! I have vowed a fast unto the Beneficent, and may not speak this day to any mortal.

27. Then she brought him to her own folk, carrying him. They said: O Mary! Thou hast come with an amazing thing.

28. Oh sister of Aaron! Thy father was not a wicked man nor was thy mother a harlot.

29. Then she pointed to him. They said: How can we talk to one who is in the cradle, a young boy?

30. He spake: Lo! I am the slave of Allah. He hath given me

the Scripture and hath appointed me a prophet.

31. And hath made me blessed wheresoever I may be, and hath enjoined upon me prayer and alms-giving so long as I remain alive.

32. And (hath made me) dutiful toward her who bore me, and hath not made me arrogant, unblest.

33. Peace on me the day I was born, and the day I die, and the day I shall be raised alive!

34. Such was Jesus, son of Mary: (this is) a statement of the truth concerning which they doubt.

35. If befitteth not (the Majesty of) Allah that He should take unto Himself a son. Glory be to Him! When He decreeth a thing He saith unto it only: Be! and it is.

36. And lo! Allah is my Lord and your Lord. So serve Him. That is the right path.

37. The sects among them differ: but woe unto the disbelievers from the meeting of an awful Day.

38. See and hear them on the Day they come unto Us! Yet the evildoers are today in error manifest.

39. And warn them of the Day of anguish when the case hath been decided. Now they are in a state of carelessness, and they believe not.

40. Lo! We inherit the earth and all who are thereon, and unto Us they are returned.

41. And make mention (O Muhammad) in the Scripture of Abraham. Lo! he was a saint, a Prophet.

42. When he said unto his father: O my father! Why worshippest thou that which heareth not nor seeth, nor can in aught avail thee?

43. O my father! Lo! there hath come unto me of knowledge that which came not unto thee. So follow me, and I will lead thee on a right path.

44. O my father! Serve not the devil. Lo! the devil is a rebel unto the Beneficent.

45. O my father! Lo! I fear lest a punishment from the Beneficent overtake thee so that thou become a comrade of the devil.

46. He said: Rejectest thou my gods, O Abraham? If thou cease not, I shall surely stone thee. Depart from me a long while!

47. He said: Peace be unto thee! I shall ask forgiveness of my Lord for thee. Lo! He was ever gracious unto me.

48. I shall withdraw from you and that unto which ye pray beside Allah, and I shall pray unto my Lord. It may be that, in prayer unto my Lord, I shall not be unblest.

49. So, when he had withdrawn from them and that which they were worshipping beside Allah, we gave him Isaac and Jacob. Each of them We made a prophet.

50. And We gave them of Our mercy, and assigned to them a high and true renown.

51. And make mention in the Scripture of Moses. Lo! he was chosen, and he was a messenger (of Allah), a prophet.

52. We called him from the right slope of the Mount, and brought him nigh in communion.

53. And We bestowed upon him of Our mercy his brother Aaron, a prophet (likewise).

54. And make mention in the Scripture of Ishmael. Lo! he was a keeper of his promise, and he was a messenger (of Allah), a prophet.

55. He enjoined upon his people worship and almsgiving, and was acceptable in the sight of his Lord.

56. And make mention in the scripture of Idrîs. Lo! he was a saint, a prophet.

57. And We raised him to high station.

58. These are they unto whom Allah showed favour from among the prophets, of the seed of Adam and of those whom We carried (in the ship) with Noah, and of the seed of Abraham and Israel, and from among those whom We guided and chose. When the revelations of the Beneficent were recited unto them, they fell down, adoring and weeping.

59. Now there hath succeeded them a later generation who have ruined worship and have followed lusts. But they will meet deception.

60. Save him who shall repent and believe and do right. Such will enter the Garden, and they will not be wronged in aught—

61. Gardens of Eden, which the Beneficent hath promised to His slaves in the Unseen. Lo! His promise is ever sure of fulfilment—

62. They hear therein no idle talk, but only Peace; and therein they have food for morn and evening.

63. Such is the Garden which We cause the devout among Our bondmen to inherit.

64. We (angels) come not down save by commandment of thy Lord. Unto Him belongeth all that is before us and all that is behind us and all that is between those two, and thy Lord was never forgetful—

65. Lord of the heavens and the earth and all that is between them! Therefore, worship thou Him and be thou steadfast in His service. Knowest thou one that can be named along with Him?

66. And man saith: When I am dead, shall I forsooth be brought forth alive?

67. Doth not man remember that We created him before, when he was naught?

68. And, by thy Lord, verily We shall assemble them and the devils, then We shall bring them, crouching, around hell.

69. Then We shall pluck out from every sect whichever of them was most stubborn in rebellion to the Beneficent.

70. And surely We are best aware of those most worthy to be burned therein.

71. There is not one of you but shall approach it. That is a fixed ordinance of thy Lord.

72. Then We shall rescue those who kept from evil, and leave the evil-doers crouching there.

73. And when Our clear revelations are recited unto them, those who disbelieve say unto those who believe: Which of the two parties (yours or ours) is better in position, and more imposing as an army?

74. How many a generation have We destroyed before them, who were more imposing in respect of gear and outward seeming!

75. Say: As for him who is in error, the Beneficent will verily prolong his span of life until, when they behold that which they were promised, whether it be punishment (in the world), or the Hour (of Doom), they will know who is worse in position and who is weaker as an army.

76. Allah increaseth in right guidance those who walk aright, and the good deeds which endure are better in thy Lord's sight for reward, and better for resort.

77. Hast thou seen him who disbelieveth in Our revelations and saith: Assuredly I shall be given wealth and children?

78. Hath he perused the Unseen, or hath he made a pact with the Beneficent?

79. Nay, but We shall record that which he saith and prolong for him a span of torment.

80. And We shall inherit from him that whereof he spake, and he will come unto Us, alone (without his wealth and children).

81. And they have chosen (other) gods beside Allah that they may be a power for them.

82. Nay, but they will deny their worship of them, and become opponents unto them.

83. Seest thou not that We have set the devils on the disbelievers to confound them with confusion?

84. So make no haste against them (O Muhammad). We do

but number unto them a sum (of days).

85. On the Day when We shall gather the righteous unto the Beneficent, a goodly company.

86. And drive the guilty unto Hell, a weary herd.

87. They will have no power of intercession, save him who hath made a covenant with his Lord.

88. And they say: The Beneficent hath taken unto Himself a son.

89. Assuredly ye utter a disastrous thing.

90. Whereby almost the heavens are torn, and the earth is split asunder and the mountains fall in ruins.

91. That ye ascribe unto the Beneficent a son.

92. When it is not meet for (the Majesty of) the Beneficent that He should choose a son.

93. There is none in the heavens and the earth but cometh unto the Beneficent as a slave.

94. Verily He knoweth them and numbereth them with (right) numbering.

95. And each one of them will come unto Him on the Day of Resurrection, alone.

96. Lo! those who believe and do good works, the Beneficent will appoint for them love.

97. And We make (this Scripture) easy in thy tongue, (O Muhammad) only that thou mayst bear good tidings therewith unto those who ward off (evil), and warn therewith the froward folk.

98. And how many a generation before them have We destroyed! Canst thou (Muhammad) see a single man of them, or hear from them the slightest sound?

SÛRAH 20

Tâ Hâ takes its name from the Arabic letters which form the first verse. As in the case of Sûrah 29, the early date of revelation is established by a strong tradition.

Omar ibn ul-Khattâb, who afterwards became Caliph, was among the bitterest opponents of Islâm in early days. He set out one day, sword in hand, with intention of killing he Prophet—"this Sabaean who has split the unity of Qureysh, calls their ideals foolish and their religion shameful, and blasphemes their gods"—when a friend who met him dissuaded him, reminding him that if he slew the Prophet he would have to reckon with the vengeance of a powerful clan: "Thinkest thou that the Banû 'Abd Munâf would let thee walk on the earth if thou hadst slain Muhammad?" for tribal pride survived religious difference. "Is it not better for thee to return to the folk of thine own house and keep them straight?" Omar asked: "Which of the folk of my house?" "Thy brother-in-law and cousin, Sa'îd ibn Zeyd, and thy sister, Fâtimah daughter of Al-Khattâb, for, by Allah, they are become Muslims and followers of Muhammad in his religion, so look thou to them." Then Omar returned, enraged against his sister and brother-in-law, and there was with them in the house Khabâb ibn 'Arit, having with him a leaf on which was written Tâ Hâ (this sûrah) which he was reading aloud to them. When they heard the noise of Omar's coming, Khabâb hid in a closet that they had in the house and Fâtimah took the leaf and hid it under her thigh. But Omar had heard the sound of Khabâb's reading as he drew near the house, and when he entered he said: "What was that mumbling which I heard?" They said: "Thou heardest nothing," Omar said: "Yea, by Allah! And I have already been informed that ye are become followers of Muhammad in his religion." Then he attacked his brother-in-law Sa'îd ibn Zeyd, but Fâtimah sprang to keep him off her husband and he struck and wounded her. And when he had done that, his sister and his brother-in-law said to him: "Yes, we are Muslims and we believe in Allah and his messenger, so do what thou wilt! "But when Omar saw the blood upon his sister he was sorry for what he had done, and he said to his sister: "Give me that leaf from which I heard you reading just now, that I may see what this is that Muhammad has brought,"And Omar was a scribe. When he said that, his sister said: "We fear to trust thee with it." He said: "Fear not!" and swore by his gods that he would return it to her when he had read it. And when he said that, she hoped for his conversion to Al-Islâm, but said: "O my brother, thou art unclean on account of thine idolatry and none may touch it save the purified." Then Omar went out and washed himself, and she gave him the leaf on which Tâ Hâ was written and he read it. And when he had read it he said: "How excellent are these words!" and praised it highly. And when he heard that, Khabâb came out to him and said: "O Omar, I hope that Allah has brought you in answer to the prayer of the Prophet, for only yesterday I heared him saying: O Allah! Strengthen Al-Islâm with Abûl-Hukm ibn Hishâm or Omar ibn Al-Khattâb; and Allah is Allah, O Omar!" At that he said: "O Khabâb direct me to Muhammad that I may go to him and make surrender."

The conversion of Omar took place in the fifth year of the Prophet's mission (ninth before the Hijrah) soon after the departure of the emigrants to Abyssinia. At that time this sûrah was already written down and in circulation.

An early Meccan Sûrah.

TÂ HÂ

Revealed at Mecca

In the name of Allah, the Beneficent, the Merciful.

1. Tâ Hâ

2. We have not revealed unto thee (Muhammad) this Qur'ân that thou shouldst be distressed,

3. But as a reminder unto him who feareth,

4. A revelation from Him Who created the earth and the high heavens.

5. The Beneficent One, Who is established on the Throne.

6. Unto Him belongeth whatsoever is in the heavens and whatsoever is in the earth, and whatsoever is between them, and whatsoever is beneath the sod.

7. And if thou speakest aloud, then lo! He knoweth the secret (thought) and (that which is yet) more hidden.

8. Allah! There is no God save Him. His are the most beautiful names.

9. Hath there come unto thee the story of Moses?

10. When he saw a fire and said unto his folk: Wait! Lo! I see a fire afar off. Peradventure I may bring you a brand therefrom or may find guidance at the fire.

11. And when he reached it, he was called by name: O Moses!

12. Lo! even I am thy Lord. So take off thy shoes, for lo! thou art in the holy valley of Tuwa.

13. And I have chosen thee, so hearken unto that which is inspired.

14. Lo! I, even I am Allah. There is no God save Me. So serve Me and establish worship for My remembrance.

15. Lo! the Hour is surely coming. But I will to keep it hidden, that every soul may be rewarded for that which it striveth (to achieve).

16. Therefore, let not him turn thee aside from (the thought of) it who believeth not therein but followeth his own desire, lest thou perish.

17. And what is that in thy right hand, O Moses?

18. He said: This is my staff whereon I lean and wherewith I beat down branches for my sheep, and wherein I find other uses.

19. He said: Cast it down, O Moses!

20. So he cast it down, and lo! it was a serpent gliding.

21. He said: Grasp it and fear not. We shall return it to its former state.

22. And thrust thy hand within thine armpit. It will come forth white without hurt. (That will be) another token.

23. That We may show thee (some) of Our greater portents,

24. Go thou unto pharaoh! Lo! he hath transgressed (the bounds).

25. (Moses) said: My Lord! Relieve my mind

26. And ease my task for me;

27. And loose a knot from my tongue;

28. That they may understand my saying.

29. Appoint for me a henchman from my folk,

30. Aaron, my brother.

31. Confirm my strength with him.

32. And let him share my task,

33. That we may glorify Thee much.

34. And much remember Thee.

35. Lo! Thou art ever seeing us.

36. He said: Thou art granted thy request, O Moses.

37. And indeed, another time, already We have shown thee favour.

38. When We inspired in thy mother that which is inspired.

39. Saying: Throw him into the ark, and throw it into the river, then the river shall throw it on to the bank, and there an enemy to Me and an enemy to him shall take him. And I endued thee with love from Me that thou mightest be trained according to My will,

40. When thy sister went and said: shall I show you one who will nurse him? and We restored thee to thy mother that her eyes might be refreshed and might not sorrow. And thou didst kill a man and We delivered thee from great distress, and tried thee with a heavy trial. And thou didst tarry years among the folk of Midian. Then camest thou (hither) by (My) providence, O Moses,

41. And I have attached thee to Myself.

42. Go, thou and thy brother, with my tokens, and be not faint in remembrance of Me.

43. Go, both of you, unto Pharaoh. Lo! he hath transgressed (the bounds).

44. And speak unto him a gentle word, that peradventure he may heed or fear.

45. They said: Our lord! Lo! we fear that he may be beforehand with us or that he may play the tyrant.

46. He said: Fear not. Lo! I am with you twain, Hearing and Seeing.

47. So go ye unto him and say: Lo! we are two messengers of thy Lord. So let the children of Israel go with us; and torment them not. We bring thee a token from thy Lord. And peace will be for him who followeth right guidance.

48. Lo! it hath been revealed unto us that the doom will be for him who denieth and turneth away.

49. (Pharaoh) said: Who then is the Lord of you twain, O Moses?

50. He said: Our Lord is He Who gave unto everything its nature, then guided it aright.

51. He said: What then is the state of the generations of old?

52. He said: The knowledge thereof is with my Lord in a Record. My Lord neither erreth nor forgetteth.

53. Who hath appointed the earth as a bed and hath threaded roads for you therein and hath sent down water from the sky and thereby We have brought forth divers kinds of vegetation.

54. (Saying): Eat ye and feed your cattle. Lo! herein verily are portents for men of thought.

55. Thereof We created you, and thereunto We return you, and thence We bring you forth a second time.

56. And We verily did show him all Our tokens, but he denied them and refused.

57. He said: Hast come to drive us out from our land by thy magic, O Moses?

58. But we surely can produce magic the like thereof; so appoint a tryst between us and you, which neither we nor thou shall fail to keep, at a place convenient (to us both).

59. (Moses) said: Your tryst shall be the day of the feast, and let the people assemble when the sun hath risen high.

60. Then Pharaoh went and gathered his strength, then came (to the appointed tryst).

61. Moses said unto them: Woe unto you! Invent not a lie against Allah, lest He extirpate you by some punishment. He who lieth faileth miserably.

62. Then they debated one with another what they must do, and they kept their counsel secret.

63. They said: Lo! these are two wizards who would drive you out from your country by their magic, and destroy your best traditions;

64. So arrange your plan, and come in battle line. Whoso is uppermost this day will be indeed successful.

65. They said: O Moses! Either throw first, or let us be the first to throw?

66. He said: Nay, do ye throw! Then lo! their cords and their staves, by their magic, appeared to him as though they ran.

67. And Moses conceived a fear in his mind.

68. We said: Fear not! Lo! thou art the higher.

69. Throw that which is in thy right hand! It will eat up that which they have made. Lo! that which they have made is but a wizard's artifice, and a wizard shall not be successful to whatever point (of skill) he may attain.

70. Then the wizards were (all) flung down prostrate, crying: We believe in the Lord of Aaron and Moses.

71. (Pharaoh) said: ye put faith in him before I give you leave. Lo! he is your chief who taught you magic. Now surely I shall cut off your hands and your feet alternately, and I shall crucify you on the trunks of palm trees and ye shall know for certain which of us hath sterner and more lasting punishment.

72. They said: We choose thee not above the clear proofs that have come unto us, and above Him Who created us. So decree what thou wilt decree. Thou wilt end for us only the life of the world.

73. Lo! we believe in our Lord, that He may forgive us our sins and the magic unto which thou didst force us. Allah is better and more lasting.

74. Lo! whose cometh guilty unto his Lord, verily for him is hell. There he will neither die nor live.

75. But whose cometh unto Him a believer, having done good works; for such are the high stations;

76. Gardens of Eden underneath which rivers flow, wherein they will abide for ever. That is the reward of one who groweth.

77. And verily We inspired Moses, saying: Take away My slaves by night and strike for them a dry path in the sea, fearing not to be overtaken, neither being afraid (of the sea).

78. Then Pharaoh followed with his hosts and there covered them that which did cover them of the sea.

79. And Pharaoh led his folk astray, he did not guide them.

80. O Children of Israel! We delivered you from your enemy, and We made a covenant with you on the holy mountain's side, and sent down on you the manna and quails.

81. (Saying): Eat of the good things wherewith We have provided you, and transgress not in respect thereof lest My wrath come upon you; and he on whom My wrath cometh, he is lost indeed.

82. And lo! verily I am forgiving toward him who repenteth and believeth and doeth good, and afterward walketh aright.

83. And (it was said): What hath made thee hasten from thy folk, O Moses?

84. He said: They are close upon my track. I hastened unto

Thee that Thou mightest be well pleased.

85. He said: Lo! We have tried thy folk in thine absence, and As-Sâmiri hath misled them.

86. Then Moses went back unto his folk, angry and sad. He said: O my people! Hath not your Lord promised you a fair promise? Did the time appointed then appear too long for you or did ye wish that wrath from your Lord should come upon you, that ye broke tryst with me?

87. They said: We broke not tryst with thee of our own will, but we were laden with burdens of ornaments of the folk, then cast them (in the fire), for thus As-Sâmiri proposed.

88. Then he produced for them a calf of saffron hue, which gave forth a lowing sound. And they cried: This is your God and the God of Moses, but he hath forgotten.

89. See they not, then, that it returneth no saying unto them and possesseth for them neither hurt nor use?

90. And Aaron indeed had told them, beforehand: O my people! ye are but being seduced therewith, for lo! your Lord is the beneficent, so follow me and obey my order.

91. They said: We shall by no means cease to be its votaries till Moses return unto us.

92. He (Moses) said: O Aaron! What held thee back when thou didst see them gone astray.

93. That thou followedst me not? Hast thou then disobeyed my order?

94. He said: O son of my mother! Clutch not my beard nor my head! I feared lest thou shouldst say: Thou hast caused division among the Children of Israel, and hast not waited for my word.

95. (Moses) said: And what has thou to say, O Sâmiri?

96. He said: I perceived what they perceive not, so I seized a handful from the footsteps of the messenger, and then threw it in. Thus my soul commended to me.

97. (Moses) said: Then go! and lo! in this life it is for thee to say: Touch me not! and lo! there is for thee a tryst thou canst not break. Now look upon thy god of which thou hast remained a votary. Verily we will burn it and will scatter its dust over the sea.

98. Your God is only Allah, than Whom there is no other God. He embraceth all things in His knowledge.

99. Thus do we relate unto thee (Muhammad) some tidings of that which happened of old, and We have given thee from Our presence a Reminder.

100. Whoso turneth away from it, he verily will bear a burden on the Day of Resurrection.

101. Abiding under it—an evil burden for them on the Day of Resurrection.

102. The day when the Trumpet is blown. On that day we assemble the guilty white-eyed (with terror).

103. Murmuring among themselves: Ye have tarried but ten (days).

104. We are best aware of what they utter when their best in conduct say: Ye have tarried but a day.

105. They will ask thee of the mountains (on that day). Say: My Lord will break them into scattered dust.

106. And leave it as an empty plain.

107. Wherein thou seest neither curve nor ruggedness.

108. On that day they follow the summoner who deceiveth not, and voices are hushed for the Beneficent, and thou hearest but a faint murmur.

109. On that Day no intercession availeth save (that of) him unto whom the Beneficent hath given leave and whose He accepteth.

110. He knoweth (all) that is before them and (all) that is behind them, while they cannot compass it in knowledge.

111. And faces humble themselves before the Living, the Eternal. And he who beareth (a burden of) wrongdoing is indeed a failure (on that Day).

112. And he who hath done some good works, being a believer, he feareth not injustice nor begruding (of his wage).

113. Thus We have revealed it as a Lecture in Arabic, and have displayed therein certain threats, that peradventure they may keep from evil or that it may cause them to take heed.

114. Then exalted be Allah, the True King! And hasten not (O Muhammad) with the Qur'ân ere its revelation hath been perfected unto thee, and say: My Lord! Increase me in knowledge.

115. And verily We made a covenant of old with Adam, but he forgot, and We found no constancy in him.

116. And when We said unto the angels: Fall prostrate before Adam, they fell prostrate (all) save Iblîs; he refused.

117. Therefore We said: O Adam! This is an enemy unto thee and unto thy wife, so let him not drive you both out of the Garden so that thou come to toil.

118. It is (vouchsafed) unto thee that thou hungerest not therein nor art naked.

119. And thou thirstest not therein nor art exposed to the sun's heat.

120. But the Devil whispered to him, saying: O Adam! Shall I show thee the tree of immortality and power that wasteth not

away?

121. Then they twain ate thereof, so that their shame became apparent unto them, and they began to hide by heaping on themselves some of the leaves of the Garden. And Adam disobeyed his Lord, so went astray.

122. Then his Lord chose him; and relented toward him, and guided him.

123. He said: Go down hence, both of you, one of you a foe unto the other. But if there come unto you from Me a guidance, then whoso followeth My guidance, he will not go astray nor come to grief.

124. But he who turneth away from remembrance of Me, his will be a narrow life, and I shall bring him blind to the assembly on the Day of Resurrection.

125. He will say: My Lord! Wherefore hast Thou gathered me (hither) blind, when I was wont to see?

126. He will say: So (it must be). Our revelations came unto thee but thou didst forget them. In like manner thou art forgotten this Day.

127. Thus do We reward him who is prodigal and believeth not the revelations of his Lord; and verily the doom of the Hereafter will be sterner and more lasting.

128. Is it not a guidance for them (to know) how many a generation We destroyed before them, amid whose dwellings they walk? Lo! therein verily are signs for men of thought.

129. And but for a decree that had already gone forth from thy Lord, and a term already fixed, the judgement would (have) been inevitable (in this world).

130. Therefore (O Muhammad), bear with what they say, and celebrate the praises of thy Lord ere the rising of the sun and ere the going down thereof. And glorify Him some hours of the night and at the two ends of the day, that thou mayst find acceptance.

131. And strain not thine eyes toward that which We cause some wedded pairs among them to enjoy, the flower of the life of the world, that We may try them thereby. The provision of thy Lord is better and more lasting.

132. And enjoin upon thy people worship, and be constant therein. We ask not of thee a provision: We provide for thee. And the sequel is for righteousness.

133. And they say: If only he would bring us a miracle from his Lord! Hath there not come unto them the proof of what is in the former Scriptures?

134. And if We had destroyed them with some punishment before it, they would assuredly have said: Our Lord! If only

Thou hadst sent unto us a messenger, so that we might have followed Thy revelations before we were (thus) humbled and disgraced!

135. Say: Each is awaiting; so await ye! Ye will come to know who are the owners of the path of equity, and who is right.

SÛRAH 21

Al-Anbiyâ, "The Prophets", is named from its subject, the history of the former prophets. The speaker in v. 4 and v. 112 is every prophet. There is no historical reference or tradition to enable us to fix the date. It is undoubtedly of Meccan revelation, and lacks the characteristics of the latest and earliest Meccan Sûrahs. It may, therefore, be taken as belonging to the middle group of Meccan Sûrahs.

THE PROPHETS

Revealed at Mecca

In the name of Allah, the Beneficent, the Merciful.

1. Their reckoning draweth nigh for mankind, while they turn away in heedlessness.

2. Never cometh there unto them a new reminder from their Lord but they listen to it while they play.

3. With hearts preoccupied. And they confer in secret. The wrong-doers say: Is this other than a mortal like you? Will ye then succumb to magic when ye see (it)?

4. He saith: My Lord knoweth what is spoken in the heaven and the earth. He is the Hearer, the Knower.

5. Nay, say they, (these are but) muddled dreams; nay, he hath but invented it; nay, he is but a poet. Let him bring us a portent even as those of old (who were God's messengers) were sent (with portents).

6. Not a township believed of those which We destoryed before them (though We sent them portents): would they then believe?

7. And We sent not (as Our messengers) before thee other than men whom We inspired. Ask the followers of the Reminder, if ye know not?

8. We gave them not bodies that would not eat food, nor were they immortals.

9. Then We fulfilled the promise unto them. So We delivered them and whom We would, and We destroyed the prodigals.

10. Now We have revealed unto you a Scripture wherein is your Reminder. Have ye then no sense?

11. How many a community that dealt unjustly have We shattered, and raised up after them another folk!

12. And, when they felt Our might, behold them fleeing from it!

13. (But it was said unto them): Flee not, but return to that (existence) which emasculated you and to your dwellings, that ye may be questioned.

14. They cried: Alas for us! Lo! we were wrongdoers.

15. And this their crying ceased not till We made them as reaped corn, extinct.

16. We created not the heaven and the earth and all that is between them in play.

17. If We had wished to find a pastime, We could have found it in Our presence — if We ever did.

18. Nay, but We hurl the true against the false, and it doth break its head and lo! it vanisheth. And yours will be woe for that which ye ascribe (unto Him).

19. Unto Him belongeth whosoever is in the heavens and the earth. And those who dwell in His presence are not too proud to worship Him, nor do they weary.

20. They glorify (Him) night and day; they flag not.

21. Or have they chosen Gods from the earth who raise the dead?

22. If there were therein Gods beside Allah, then verily both (the heavens and the earth) had been disordered. Glorified be Allah, the Lord of the Throne, from all that they ascribe (unto Him).

23. He will not be questioned as to that which He doeth, but they will be questioned.

24. Or have they chosen other gods beside Him? Say: Bring your proof (of their godhead). This is the Reminder of those with me and those before me, but most of them know not the Truth and so they are averse.

25. And We sent no messenger before thee but We inspired him, (saying): There is no God save Me (Allah), so worship Me.

26. And they say: The Beneficent hath taken unto Himself a son. Be He Glorified! Nay, but (those whom they call sons) are honoured slaves.

27. They speak not until He hath spoken, and they act by His command.

28. He knoweth what is before them and what is behind them, and they cannot intercede except for him whom He accepteth, and they quake for awe of Him.

29. And one of them who should say: Lo! I am a God beside Him, that one We should repay with hell. Thus We repay

wrongdoers.

30. Have not those who disbelieve known that the heavens and the earth were of one piece, then We parted them, and We made every living thing of water? Will they not then believe?

31. And We have placed in the earth firm hills lest it quake with them, and We have placed therein ravines as roads that haply they may find their way.

32. And We have made the sky a roof withheld (from them). Yet they turn away from its portents.

33. And He it is Who created the night and the day, and the sun and the moon. They float, each in an orbit.

34. We appointed immortality for no mortal before thee. What! if thou diest, can they be immortal?

35. Every soul must taste of death, and We try you with evil and with good, for ordeal. And unto Us ye will be returned.

36. And when those who disbelieve behold thee, they but choose thee out for mockery, (saying): Is this he who maketh mention of your gods? And they would deny all mention of the Beneficent.

37. Man is made of haste. I shall show you My portents, but ask Me not to hasten.

38. And they say: When will this promise (be fulfilled), if ye are truthful?

39. If those who disbelieved but knew the time when they will not be able to drive off the fire from their faces and from their backs, and they will not be helped!

40. Nay, but it will come upon them unawares so that it will stupefy them, and they will be unable to repel it, neither will they be reprieved.

41. Messengers before thee, indeed, were mocked, but that whereat they mocked surrounded those who scoffed at them.

42. Say: Who guardeth you in the night or in the day from the Beneficent? Nay, but they turn away from mention of their Lord!

43. Or have they gods who can shield them from Us? They cannot help themselves nor can they be defended from Us.

44. Nay, but We gave these and their fathers ease until life grew long for them. See they not how We visit the land, reducing it of its outlying parts? Can they then be the victors?

45. Say (O Muhammad, unto mankind): I warn you only by the Inspiration. But the deaf hear not the call when they are warned.

46. And if a breath of thy Lord's punishment were to touch them, they assuredly would say: Alas for us! Lo! we were

wrong-doers.

47. And We set a just balance for the Day of Resurrection so that no soul is wronged in aught. Though it be of the weight of a grain of mustard seed. We bring it. And We suffice for reckoners.

48. And We verily gave Moses and Aaron the Criterion (of right and wrong) and a light and a Reminder for those who keep from evil.

49. Those who fear their Lord in secret and who dread the Hour (of doom).

50. This is a blessed Reminder that We have revealed: Will ye then reject it?

51. And We verily gave Abraham of old his proper course, and We were Aware of him.

52. When he said unto his father and his folk: What are these images unto which ye pay devotion?

53. They said: We found our fathers worshippers of them.

54. He said: Verily ye and your fathers were in plain error.

55. They said: Bringest thou unto us the truth, or art thou some jester?

56. He said: Nay, but your Lord is the Lord of the heavens and the earth, Who created them; and I am of those who testify unto that.

57. And, by Allah, I shall circumvent your idols after ye have gone away and turned your backs.

58. Then he reduced them to fragments, all save the chief of them, that haply they might have recourse to it.

59. They said: Who hath done this to our gods? Surely it must be some evil-doer.

60. They said: We heard a youth make mention of them, who is called Abraham.

61. They said: Then bring him (hither) before the people's eyes that they may testify.

62. They said: Is it thou who hast done this to our gods, O Abraham?

63. He said: But this, their chief hath done it. So question them, if they can speak.

64. Then gathered they apart and said: Lo! ye yourselves are the wrongdoers.

65. And they were utterly confounded, and they said: Well thou knowest that these speak not.

66. He said: Worship ye then instead of Allah that which cannot profit you at all, nor harm you?

67. Fie on you and all that ye worship instead of Allah? have ye then no sense?

68. They cried: Burn him and stand by your gods, if ye will be doing.

69. We said: O fire, be coolness and peace for Abraham.

70. And they wished to set a snare for him, but We made them the greater losers.

71. And We rescued him and Lot (and brought them) to the land which We have blessed for (all) peoples.

72. And We bestowed upon him Isaac, and Jacob as a grandson. Each of them We made righteous.

73. And We made them chiefs who guide by Our command, and We inspired in them the doing of good deeds and the right establishment of worship and the giving of alms, and they were worshippers of Us (alone).

74. And unto Lot We gave judgement and knowledge, and We delivered him from the community that did abominations. Lo! they were folk of evil, lewd.

75. And We brought him in unto Our mercy. Lo! he was of the righteous.

76. And Noah, when he cried of old, We heard his prayer and saved him and his household from the great affliction.

77. And delivered him from the people who denied Our revelations. Lo! they were folk of evil, therefore did We drown them all.

78. And David and Solomon, when they gave judgement concerning the field, when people's sheep had strayed and browsed therein by night; and We were witnesses to their judgement.

79. And We made Solomon to understand (the case); and unto each of them. We gave judgement and knowledge. And We subdued the hills and the birds to hymn (His) praise along with David. We were the doers (thereof).

80. And We taught him the art of making garments (of mail) to protect you in your daring. Are ye then thankful?

81. And unto Solomon (We subdued) the wind in its raging. It set by his command toward the land which We had blessed. And of everything We are aware.

82. And of the evil ones (subdued We unto him) some who dived (for pearls) for him and did other work, and We were warders unto them:

83. And Job, when he cried unto his Lord, (saying): Lo! adversity afflicteth me, and Thou art Most Merciful of all who show mercy.

84. Then We heard his prayer and removed that adversity from which he suffered, and We gave him his household (that he had lost) and the like thereof along with them, a mercy from

Our store, and a remembrance for the worshippers;

85. And (mention) Ishmael, and Idrîs, and Dhûl-Kifl. All were of the steadfast.

86. And We brought them in unto Our mercy. Lo! they are among the righteous.

87. And (mention) Dhû'n-Nûn, when he went off in anger and deemed that We had no power over him, but he cried out in the darkness, saying: There is no God save Thee. Be Thou Glorified! Lo! I have been a wrong-doer.

88. Then We heard his prayer and saved him from the anguish. Thus We save believers.

89. And Zachariah, when he cried unto his Lord: My Lord! Leave me not childless, though Thou art the best of inheritors.

90. Then We heard his prayer, and bestowed upon him John, and adjusted his wife (to bear a child) for him. Lo! they used to vie one with the other in good deeds, and they cried unto Us in longing and in fear, and were submissive unto Us.

91. And she who was chaste, therefore We breathed into her (something) of Our spirit and made her and her son a token for (all) peoples.

92. Lo! this, your religion, is one religion, and I am your Lord, so worship Me.

93. And they have broken their religion (into fragments) among them, (yet) all are returning unto Us.

94. Then Whoso doeth good works and is a believer, there will be no rejection of his effort. Lo! We record (it) for him.

95. And there is a ban upon any community which We have destroyed: that they shall not return.

96. Until, when Gog and Magog are let loose, and they hasten out of every mound.

97. And the True Promise draweth nigh; then behold them, staring wide (in terror), the eyes of those who disbelieve! (They say): Alas for us! We (lived) in forgetfulness of this. Ah, but we were wrong-doers!

98. Lo! ye (idolaters) and that which ye worship beside Allah are fuel of hell. Thereunto ye will come.

99. If these had been Gods they would not have come thither, but all will abide therein.

100. Therein wailing is their portion, and therein they hear not.

101. Lo! those unto whom kindness hath gone forth before from Us, they will be far removed from thence.

102. They will not hear the slightest sound thereof, while they abide in that which their souls desire.

103. The supreme Horror will not grieve them, and the

angels will welcome them, (saying): This is your Day which ye were promised;

104. The Day when We shall roll up the heavens as a recorder rolleth up a written scroll. As We began the first creation, We shall repeat it. (It is) a promise (binding) upon Us. Lo! We are to perform it.

105. And verily We have written in the Scripture, after the Reminder: My righteous slaves will inherit the earth:

106. Lo! there is a plain statement for folk who are devout.

107. We sent thee not save as a mercy for the peoples.

108. Say: It is only inspired in me that your God is One God. Will ye then surrender (unto Him)?

109. But if they are averse, then say: I have warned you all alike, although I know not whether nigh or far is that which ye are promised.

110. Lo! He knoweth that which is said openly, and that which ye conceal.

111. And I know not but that this may be a trial for you, and enjoyment for a while.

112. He saith: My Lord! Judge Thou with truth. Our Lord is the Beneficent, Whose help is to be implored against that which ye ascribe (unto Him).

SÛRAH 22

Al-Hajj, "The Pilgrimage", takes its name from vv. 26-38 relating to the pilgrimage to Mecca. This sûrah is ascribed by some authorities to the Meccan, by others to the Madînah period. The copy of the Koran which I have followed throughout has the Madînah ascription, and, as it was copied long before the days of "higher" criticism, and was authorised for use throughout the Ottoman Empire. I retain that ascription. Vv. 11-13, 25-30, 39-41 and 58-60 were, according to all authorities, revealed at Al-Madînah. Nöldeke, greatest of the "higher" critics, says that the ascription is justified on account of the importance of the verses in this sûrah which must, from the nature of their contents, have been revealed at Al-Madînah, while holding that much of the sûrah belongs to the last Meccan period.

THE PILGRIMAGE

Revealed at Al-Madînah

In the name of Allah, the Beneficent, the Merciful.

1. O mankind! Fear your Lord. Lo! the earthquake of the Hour (of Doom) is a tremendous thing.

2. On the day when ye behold it, every nursing mother will forget her nursing and every pregnant one will be delivered of her burden, and thou (Muhammad) wilt see mankind as drunken, yet they will not be drunken, but the Doom of Allah will be strong (upon them).

3. Among mankind is he who disputeth concerning Allah without knowledge, and followeth each forward devil.

4. For him it is decreed that whoso taketh him for friend, he verily will mislead him and will guide him to the punishment of the Flame.

5. O mankind! If ye are in doubt concerning the Resurrection then lo! We have created you from dust, then from a drop of seed, then from a clot, then from a little lump of flesh shapely and shapeless, that We may make (it) clear for you. And We cause what We will to remain in the wombs for an appointed time, and afterward We bring you forth as infants, then (give you growth) that ye attain your full strength. And among you there is he who dieth (young), and among you there is he who is brought back to the most abject time of life, so that, after knowledge, he knoweth naught. And thou (Muhammad) seest the earth barren, but when We send down water thereon, it doth thrill and swell and put forth every lovely kind (of growth).

6. That is because Allah, He is the Truth. Lo! He quickeneth the dead, and lo! He is Able to do all things.

7. And because the Hour will come, there is no doubt thereof; and because Allah will raise those who are in the graves.

8. And among mankind is he who disputeth concerning Allah without knowledge or guidance or a Scripture giving light.

9. Turning away in pride to beguile (men) from the way of Allah. For him in this world is ignominy, and on the Day of Resurrection We make him taste the doom of burning.

10. (And unto him it will be said): This is for that which thy two hands have sent before, and because Allah is no oppressor of His slaves.

11. And among mankind is he who worshippeth Allah upon a narrow marge so that if good befalleth him he is content therewith, but if a trial befalleth him, he falleth away utterly. He loseth both the world and the Hereafter. That is the sheer loss.

12. He calleth, beside Allah, unto that which hurteth him not nor benefiteth him. That is the far error.

13. He calleth unto him whose harm is nearer than his benefit; verily an evil patron and verily and evil friend!

14. Lo! Allah causeth those who believe and do good works to enter the Gardens underneath which rivers flow. Lo! Allah doth what He intendeth.

15. Whoso is wont to think (through envy) that Allah will not give him (Muhammad) victory in the world and the Hereafter (and is enraged at the thought of his victory), let him stretch a rope up to the roof (of his dwelling), and let him hang himself. Then let him see whether his strategy dispelleth that whereat he rageth!

16. Thus We reveal it as plain revelations, and verily Allah guideth whom He will.

17. Lo! those who believe (this Revelation), and those who are Jews, and the Sabaeans and the Christians and the Magians and the idolaters—Lo! Allah will decide between them on the Day of Resurrection. Lo! Allah is Witness over all things.

18. Hast thou not seen that unto Allah payeth adoration whosoever is in the heavens and whosoever is in the earth, and the sun, and the moon, and the stars, and the hills, and the trees, and the beasts, and many of mankind, while there are many unto whom the doom is justly due. He whom Allah scorneth, there is none to give him honour. Lo! Allah doeth what He will.

19. These twain (the believers and the disbelievers) are two opponents who contend concerning their Lord. But as for those who disbelieve, garments of fire will be cut out for them; boiling fluid will be poured down on their heads.

20. Whereby that which is in their bellies, and their skins too, will be melted;

21. And for them are hooked rods of iron.

22. Whenever, in their anguish, they would go forth from thence they are driven back therein and (it is said unto them): Taste the doom of burning.

23. Lo! Allah will cause those who believe and do good works to enter Gardens underneath which rivers flow, wherein they will be allowed armlets of gold, and pearls, and their raiment therein will be silk.

24. They are guided unto gentle speech; they are guided unto the path of the Glorious One.

25. Lo! those who disbelieve and bar (men) from the way of Allah and from the Inviolable Place of Worship, which We have appointed for mankind together, the dweller therein and the nomad; whosoever seeketh wrongful partiality therein, him We shall cause to taste a painful doom.

26. And (remember) when We prepared for Abraham the place of the (holy) House, saying: Ascribe thou no thing as partner unto Me, and purify My House for those who make the round (thereof) and those who stand and those who bow and

make prostration.

27. And proclaim unto mankind the Pilgrimage. They will come unto thee on foot and on every lean camel; they will come from every deep ravine.

28. That they may witness things that are of benefit to them, and mention the name of Allah on appointed days over the beast of cattle that He hath bestowed upon them. Then eat thereof and feed therewith the poor unfortunate.

29. Then let them make an end of their unkemptness and pay their vows and go around the ancient House.

30. That (is the command). And whoso magnifieth the sacred things of Allah, it will be well for him in the sight of his Lord. The cattle are lawful unto you save that which hath been told you. So shun the filth of idols, and shun lying speech.

31. Turning unto Allah (only) not ascribing partners unto Him; for whoso ascribeth partners unto Allah, it is as if he had fallen from the sky and the birds had snatched him or the wind had blown him to a far-off place.

32. That (is the command). And whoso magnifieth the offerings consecrated to Allah, it surely is from devotion of the hearts.

33. Therein are benefits for you for an appointed term; and afterward they are brought for sacrifice unto the ancient House.

34. And for every nation have We appointed a ritual, that they may mention the name of Allah over the beast of cattle that He hath given them for food and your God is One God, therefore surrender unto Him. And give good tidings (O Muhammad) to the humble.

35. Whose hearts fear when Allah is mentioned, and the patient of whatever may befall them, and those who establish worship and who spend of that We have bestowed on them.

36. And the camels! We have appointed them among the ceremonies of Allah. Therein ye have much good. So mention the name of Allah over them when they are drawn up in lines. Then when their flanks fall (dead), eat thereof and feed the beggar and the suppliant. Thus have We made them subject unto you, that haply ye may give thanks.

37. Their flesh and their blood reach not Allah, but the devotion from you reacheth Him. Thus have We made them subject unto you that ye may magnify Allah that He hath guided you. And give good tidings (O Muhammad) to the good.

38. Lo! Allah defendeth those who are true. Lo! Allah loveth not each treacherous ingrate.

39. Sanction is given unto those who fight because they have been wronged; and Allah is indeed Able to give them victory.

40. Those who have been driven from their homes unjustly only because they said: Our Lord is Allah—For had it not been for Allah's repelling some men by means of others, cloisters and churches and oratories and mosques, wherein the name of Allah is oft mentioned, would assuredly have been pulled down. Verily Allah helpeth one who helpeth Him. Lo! Allah is Strong, Almighty—

41. Those who, if We give them power in the land, establish worship and pay the poor-due and enjoin kindness and forbid iniquity. And Allah's is the sequel of events.

42. If they deny thee (Muhammad), even so the folk of Noah, and (the tribes of) Aâd and Thamûd, before thee, denied (Our messengers);

43. And the folk of Abraham and the folk of Lot;

44. (And) the dwellers in Midian, And Moses was denied; but I indulged the disbelievers a long while, then I seized them and how (terrible) was My abhorrence!

45. How many a township have We destroyed while it was sinful, so that it lieth (to this day) in ruins, and (how many) a deserted well and lofty tower!

46. Have they not travelled in the land, and have they hearts wherewith to feel and ears wherewith to hear? For indeed it is not the eyes that grow blind, but it is the hearts, which are within the bosoms, that grow blind.

47. And they will bid thee hasten on the Doom, and Allah faileth not His promise, but lo! a Day with Allah is as a thousand years of what ye reckon.

48. And how many a township did I suffer long though it was sinful! Then I grasped it. Unto Me is the return.

49. Say: O mankind! I am only a plain warner unto you.

50. Those who believe and do good works, for them is pardon and a rich provision;

51. While those who strive to thwart Our revelations, such are rightful owners of the Fire.

52. Never sent We a messenger or a prophet before thee but when He recited (the message) Satan proposed (opposition) in respect of that which he recited thereof. But Allah abolisheth that which Satan proposeth. Then Allah establisheth His revelations. Allah is Knower, Wise;

53. That He may make that which the devil proposeth a temptation for those in whose hearts is a disease, and those whose hearts are hardened—Lo! the evildoers are in open

schism—

54. And that those who have been given knowledge may know that it is the truth from thy Lord, so that they may believe therein and their hearts may submit humbly unto him. Lo! Allah verily is guiding those who believe unto a right path.

55. And those who disbelieve will not cease to be in doubt thereof until the Hour come upon them unawares, or there come unto them the doom of a disastrous day.

56. The Sovereignty on that day will be Allah's. He will judge between them. Then those who believed and did good works will be in gardens of Delight.

57. While those who disbelieved and denied Our revelations, for them will be a shameful doom.

58. Those who fled their homes for the cause of Allah and then were slain or died, Allah verily will provide for them a good provision. Lo! Allah, He verily is Best of all who make provision.

59. Assuredly he will cause them to enter by an entry that they will love. Lo! Allah verily is Knower, Indulgent.

60. That (is so). And whoso hath retaliated with the like of that which he was made to suffer and then hath (again) been wronged, Allah will succour him. Lo! Allah verily is Mild, Forgiving.

61. That is because Allah maketh the night to pass into the day and maketh the day to pass into the night, and because Allah is Hearer, Seer.

62. That is because Allah, He is the True, and that whereon they call instead of Him, it is the False, and because Allah, He is the High, the Great.

63. Seest thou not how Allah sendeth down water from the sky and then the earth becometh green upon the morrow? Lo! Allah is Subtile, Aware.

64. Unto Him belongeth all that is in the heavens and all that is in the earth. Lo! Allah, He verily is the Absolute, the Owner of Praise.

65. Hast thou not seen how Allah hath made all that is in the earth subservient unto you? And the ship runneth upon the sea by His command, and He holdeth back the heaven from falling in the earth unless by His leave. Lo! Allah is, for mankind, Full of Pity, Merciful.

66. And He it is Who gave you life, then He will cause you to die, and then will give you life (again). Lo! man is verily an ingrate.

67. Unto each nation have We given sacred rites which they

are to perform; so let them not dispute with thee of the matter, but summon thou unto thy Lord. Lo! thou indeed followest right guidance.

68. And if they wrangle with thee, say: Allah is best aware of what ye do.

69. Allah will judge between you on the Day of Resurrection concerning that wherein ye used to differ.

70. Hast thou not known that Allah knoweth all that is in the heavens and the earth? Lo! it is in a record. Lo! that is easy for Allah.

71. And they worship instead of Allah that for which no warrant hath been revealed unto them, and that whereof they have no knowledge. For evil-doers there is no helper.

72. And when Our revelations are recited unto them, thou knowest the denial in the faces of those who disbelieve; they all but attack those who recite Our revelations unto them. Say: Shall I proclaim unto you worse than that? The Fire! Allah hath promised it for those who disbelieve. A hapless journey's end!

73. O mankind! a similitude is coined. So pay ye heed to it: Lo! those on whom ye call beside Allah will never create a fly though they combine together for the purpose. And if the fly took something from them: they could not rescue it from him. So weak are (both) the seeker and the sought!

74. They measure not Allah His rightful measure. Lo! Allah is Strong, Almighty.

75. Allah chooseth from the angels messengers and (also) from mankind. Lo! Allah is Hearer, Seer.

76. He knoweth all that is before them and all that is behind them, and unto Allah all things are returned.

77. O, ye who believe! Bow down and prostrate yourselves and worship your Lord, and do good, that haply ye may prosper.

78. And strive for Allah with the endeavour which is His right. He hath chosen you and hath not laid upon you in religion any hardship; the faith of your father Abraham (is yours). He hath named you Muslims of old time and in this (Scripture) that the messenger may be a witness against you, and that ye may be witnesses against mankind. So establish worship, pay the poor-due and hold fast to Allah. He is your Protecting Friend. A blessed Patron and a blessed Helper!

SÛRAH 23

Al Mu'minûn, "The Believers", is so named from a word occurring in the first verse or, it may be said, from its subject, which is the triumph of believers. It is considered to be the last

of the sûrahs revealed at Mecca, immediately before the
Prophet's flight to Yathrib (Al-Madînah).
A late Meccan Sûrah.

THE BELIEVERS

Revealed at Mecca

In the name of Allah, the Beneficent, the Merciful.
1. Successful indeed are the believers
2. Who are humble in their prayers.
3. And who shun vain conversation.
4. And who are payers of the poor-due.
5. And who guard their modesty —
6. Save from their wives or the (slaves) that their right
hands possess, for then they are not blameworthy.
7. But whoso craveth beyond that, such are transgressors —
8. And who are shepherds of their pledge and their
covenant,
9. And who pay heed to their prayers.
10. These are the heirs.
11. Who will inherit Paradise. There they will abide.
12. Verily We created man from a product of wet earth.
13. Then placed him as a drop (of seed) in a safe lodging.
14. Then fashioned We the drop a clot, then fashioned we
the clot a little lump, then fashioned we the little lump bones,
then clothed the bones with flesh and then produced it as
another creation. So blessed be Allah, the Best of Creators!
15. Then lo! after that ye surely die.
16. Then lo! on the Day of Resurrection ye are raised (again).
17. And We have created above you seven paths, and we are
never unmindful of creation.
18. And We send down from the sky water in measure, and
We give it lodging in the earth, and lo! We are able to
withdraw it.
19. Then We produce for you therewith gardens of date-
palms and grapes, wherein is much fruit for you and whereof
ye eat;
20. And a tree that springeth forth from Mount Sinai that
groweth oil and relish for the eaters.
21. And lo! in the cattle there is verily a lesson for you. We
give you to drink of that which is in their bellies and many uses
have ye in them and of them do ye eat;
22. And on them and on the ship ye are carried.
23. And We verily sent Noah unto his folk, and he said: O

my people! Serve Allah. Ye have no other god save Him. Will ye not ward off (evil)?

24. But the chieftains of his folk, who disbelieved, said: This is only a mortal like you who would make himself superior to you. Had Allah willed, He surely could have sent down angels. We heard not of this in the case of our fathers of old.

25. He is only a man in whom is a madness, so watch him for a while.

26. He said: My Lord! Help me because they deny me.

27. Then We inspired in him, saying: Make the ship under Our eyes and Our inspiration. Then when Our command cometh and the oven gusheth water, introduce therein of every (kind) two spouses, and thy household save him thereof against whom the Word hath already gone forth. And plead not with Me on behalf of those who have done wrong. Lo! they will be drowned.

28. And when thou art on board the ship, thou and whoso is with thee, then say: Praise be to Allah who hath saved us from the wrongdoing folk!

29. And say: My Lord! Cause me to land at a blessed landing place, for Thou art best of all who bring to land.

30. Lo! herein verily are portents, for lo! We are ever putting (mankind) to the test.

31. Then, after them. We brought forth another generation;

32. And We sent among them a messenger of their own saying: Serve Allah. Ye have no other god save Him. Will ye not ward off (evil)?

33. And the chieftains of his folk, who disbelieved and denied the meeting of the hereafter and whom We had made soft in the life of the world, said: This is only a mortal like you, who eateth of that whereof ye eat and drinketh of that ye drink.

34. If ye were to obey a mortal like yourselves, ye surely would be losers.

35. Doth he promise you that you, when ye are dead and have become dust and bones, will (again) be brought forth?

36. Begone, begone with that which ye are promised!

37. There is naught but our life of the world; we die and we live, and we shall not be raised (again).

38. He is only a man who hath invented a lie about Allah. We are not going to put faith in him.

39. He said: My Lord! Help me because they deny me.

40. He said: In a little while they surely will become repentant.

41. So the (Awful) Cry overtook them rightfully and We

made them like as wreckage (that a torrent hurleth). A far removal for wrongdoing folk!

42. Then after them We brought forth other generations.

43. No nation can outstrip its term, nor yet postpone it.

44. Then We sent our messengers one after another. Whenever its messenger came unto a nation they denied him; so We caused them to follow one another (to disaster) and We made them bywords. A far removal for folk who believe not!

45. Then We sent Moses and his brother Aaron with our tokens and a clear warrant.

46. Unto Pharaoh and his chiefs, but they scorned (them) and they were despotic folk.

47. And they said: Shall we put faith in two mortals like ourselves and whose folk are servile unto us?

48. So they denied them and became of those who were destroyed.

49. And We verily gave Moses the Scripture, that haply they might go aright.

50. And We made the son of Mary and his mother a portent, and We gave them refuge on a height, a place of flocks and water-springs.

51. O ye messengers! Eat of the good things and do right. Lo! I am Aware of what ye do.

52. And lo! this your religion is one religion and I am your Lord, so keep your duty unto Me.

53. But they (mankind) have broken their religion among them into sects, each sect rejoicing in its tenets.

54. So leave them in their error till a time.

55. Think they that in the wealth and sons wherewith We provide them.

56. We hasten unto them with good things? Nay, but they perceive not.

57. Lo! those who go in awe for fear of their Lord,

58. And those who believe in the revelations of their Lord,

59. And those who ascribe not partners unto their Lord,

60. And those who give that which they give with hearts afraid because they are about to return unto their Lord,

61. These race for the good things and they shall win them in the race.

62. And We task not any soul beyond its scope, and with Us is a Record which speaketh the truth, and they will not be wronged.

63. Nay, but their hearts are in ignorance of this (Qurân) and they have other works, besides which they are doing;

64. Till when We grasp their luxurious ones with the

punishment, behold! they supplicate.

65. Supplicate not this day! Assuredly ye will not be helped by Us.

66. My revelations were recited unto you, but ye used to turn back on your heels.

67. In scorn thereof. Nightly did ye rave together.

68. Have they not pondered the Word, or hath that come unto them which came not unto their fathers of old?

69. Or know they not their messenger and so reject him?

70. Or say they: There is a madness in him? Nay, but he bringeth them the Truth; and most of them are haters of the Truth.

71. And if the Truth had followed their desires, verily the heavens and the earth and whosoever is therein had been corrupted. Nay, We have brought them their Reminder, but from their Reminder they now turn away.

72. Or dost thou ask of them (O Muhammad) any tribute? But the bounty of thy Lord is better, for He is best of all who make provision.

73. And lo! thou summonest them indeed unto a right path.

74. And lo! those who believe not in the Hereafter are indeed astray from the path.

75. Though We had mercy on them and relieved them of the harm afflicting them, they still would wonder blindly on in their contumacy.

76. Already have We grasped them with punishment, but they humble not themselves unto their Lord nor do they pray.

77. Until, when We open for them the gate of extreme punishmment behold! they are aghast thereat.

78. He it is who hath created for you ears and eyes and hearts. Small thanks give ye!

79. And He it is Who hath sown you broadcast in the earth, and unto Him ye will be gathered.

80. And He it is who giveth life and causeth death, and His is the difference of night and day, Have ye then no sense?

81. Nay, but they say the like of that which said the men of old;

82. They say: When we are dead and have become (mere) dust and bones, shall we then forsooth, be raised again?

83. We were already promised this, we and our forefathers. Lo! this is naught but fables of the men of the old.

84. Say: Unto Whom (belongeth) the earth and whosoever is therein, if ye have knowledge?

85. They will say: Unto Allah. Say: Will ye not then remember?

86. Say: Who is Lord of the seven heavens and Lord of the Tremendous Throne?

87. They will say: Unto Allah (all that belongeth). Say: Will ye not then keep duty (unto Him)?

88. Say: In Whose hand is the dominion over all things and He protecteth, while against Him there is no protection if ye have knowledge?

89. They will say: Unto Allah (all that belongeth) Say: How then are ye bewitched?

90. Nay, but We have brought them the Truth and lo! they are liars.

91. Allah hath not chosen any son nor is there any God along with Him; else would each God have assuredly championed that which he created and some of them would assuredly have overcome others. Glorified be Allah above all that they allege.

92. Knower of the Invisible and the Visible! and Exalted be He over all that they ascribe as partners (unto Him)!

93. Say: My Lord! If Thou shouldst show me that which they are promised,

94. My Lord! then set me not among the wrongdoing folk.

95. And verily We are able to show thee that which We have promised them.

96. Repel evil with that which is better. We are best Aware of that which they allege.

97. And say: My Lord! I seek refuge in Thee from suggestions of the evil ones.

98. And I seek refuge in Thee, my Lord, lest they be present with me,

99. Until, when death cometh unto one of them, he saith: My Lord! Send me back.

100. That I may do right in that which I have left behind! But nay! It is but a word that he speaketh; and behind them is a barrier until the day when they are raised.

101. And when the trumpet is blown there will be no kinship among them that day, nor will they ask of one another.

102. Then those whose scales are heavy, they are the successful.

103. And those whose scales are light are those who lose their souls, in hell abiding.

104. The fire burneth their faces, and they are glum therein.

105. (It will be said): Were not My revelations recited unto you, and then ye used to deny them?

106. They will say: Our Lord! our evil fortune conquered us and we were erring folk.

107. Our Lord! Oh bring us forth from hence! If we return (to evil) then indeed we shall be wrong-doers.

108. He saith: Begone therein, and speak not unto Me.

109. Lo! there was a party of My slaves who said: Our Lord! We believe, therefore forgive us and have mercy on us for Thou art best of all who show mercy.

110. But ye chose them from a laughing-stock until they caused you to forget remembrance of Me, while ye laughed at them.

111. Lo! I have rewarded them this day forasmuch as they were steadfast; and they verily are the triumphant.

112. He will say: How long tarried ye in the earth, counting by years?

113. They will say: We tarried but a day or part of a day. Ask of those who kept count!

114. He will say: Ye tarried but a little if ye only knew.

115. Deemed ye then that We had created you for naught, and that ye would not be returned unto Us?

116. Now Allah be Exalted, the True King! There is no God save Him, the Lord of the Throne of Grace.

117. He who crieth unto any other god along with Allah hath no proof thereof. His reckoning is only with his Lord. Lo! disbelievers will not be successful.

118. And (O Muhammad) say: My Lord! Forgive and have mercy, for Thou art best of all who show mercy.

SÛRAH 24

An-Nûr, "Light", takes its name from vv. 35-40, descriptive of the Light of God as it should shine in the homes of believers, the greater part of the sûrah being legislation for the purifying of home life. All its verses were revealed at Al-Madînah. Tradition says that vv. 11-20 relate to the slanderers of Ayeshah in connection with an incident which occurred in the fifth year of the Hijrah when the Prophet was returning from the campaign against the Banî'l-Mustaliq, Ayeshah having been left behind on a march and found and brought back by a young soldier who let her mount his camel and himself led the camel. A weaker tradition places the revelation of vv. 1-10 as late as the ninth year of the Hijrah.

The period of revelation is the fifth and sixth years of the Hijrah.

LIGHT

Revealed at Al-Madînah

In the name of Allah, the Beneficent, the Merciful.

1. (Here is) a Sûrah which We have revealed and enjoined, and wherein We have revealed plain tokens, that haply ye may take heed.

2. The adulterer and the adulteress, scourge ye each one of them (with) a hundred stripes. And let not pity for the twain withhold you from obedience to Allah, if ye believe in Allah and the Last Day. And let a party of believers witness their punishment.

3. The adulterer shall not marry save an adulteress or an idolatress, and the adulteress none shall marry save an adulterer or an idolater. All that is forbidden unto believers.

4. And those who accuse honourable women but bring not our witnesses, scourge them (with) eighty stripes and never (afterward) accept their testimony— They indeed are evil doers—

5. Save those who afterward repent and make amends. (For such) lo! Allah is Forgiving, Merciful.

6. As for those who accuse their wives but have no witnesses except themselves; let the testimony of one of them be four testimonies, (swearing) by Allah that he is of those who speak the truth;

7. And yet a fifth invoking the curse of Allah on him if he is of those who lie.

8. And it shall avert the punishment from her if she bear witness before Allah four times that the thing he saith is indeed false,

9. And a fifth (time) that the wrath of Allah be upon her if he speaketh truth.

10. And had it not been for the grace of Allah and His mercy unto you, and that Allah is Clement, Wise, (ye had been undone).

11. Lo! they who spread the slander are a gang among you. Deem it not a bad thing for you; nay it is good for you. Unto every man of them (will be paid) that which he hath earned of the sin; and as for him among them who had the greater share therein, his will be an awful doom.

12. Why did not the believers men and women, when ye heard it think good of their own folk and say: It is a manifest untruth?

13. Why did they not produce four witnesses? Since they produce not witnesses, they verily are liars in the sight of Allah.

14. Had it not been for the grace of Allah and His mercy unto you in the world and the Hereafter an awful doom had overtaken you for that whereof ye murmured.

15. When ye welcomed it with your tongues, and uttered

with your mouths that whereof ye had no knowledge, ye counted it a trifle, in the sight of Allah it is very great.

16. Wherefore, when ye heard it, said ye not: it is not for us to speak of this. Glory be to thee (O Allah); This is awful calumny.

17. Allah admonisheth you that ye repeat not the like thereof ever, if ye are (in truth) believers.

18. And He expoundeth unto you His revelations. Allah is knower, Wise.

19. Lo! those who love that slander should be spread concerning those who believe, theirs will be   a painful punishment in the world and the Hereafter. Allah knoweth. Ye know not.

20. Had it not been for the grace of Allah and His mercy unto you, and that Allah is Clement, Merciful, (ye had been undone).

21. O ye who believe! Follow not the footsteps of the devil. Unto whomsoever followeth the footsteps of the devil, lo! he commandeth filthiness and wrong. Had it not been for the grace of Allah and His mercy unto you, not one of you would ever have grown pure. But Allah causeth whom He will to grow and Allah is Hearer, Knower.

22. And let not those who possess dignity and ease among you swear not to give to the near of kin and to the needy and to fugitives for the cause of Allah. Let them forgive and show indulgence. Yearn not ye that Allah may forgive you? Allah is Forgiving, Merciful.

23. Lo! as for those who traduce virtuous, believing women (who are) careless, cursed are they in the world and the Hereafter. Theirs will be an awful doom.

24. On the day when their tongues and their hands and their feet testify against them as to what they used to do;

25. On that day Allah will pay them their just due, and they will know that Allah, He is the Manifest Truth.

26. Vile women are for vile men, and vile men for vile women. Good women are for good men, and good men for good women; such are innocent of that which people say: For them is pardon and a bountiful provision.

27. O ye who believe! Enter not houses other than your own without first announcing your presence and invoking peace upon the folk thereof. That is better for you, that ye may be heedful.

28. And if ye find no one therein, still enter not until permission hath been given. And if it be said unto you: Go away again, then go away, for it is purer for you. Allah knoweth what ye do.

236

29. (It is) no sin for you to enter uninhabited houses wherein is comfort for you. Allah knoweth what ye proclaim and what ye hide.

30. Tell the believing men to lower their gaze and be modest. That is purer for them. Lo! Allah is Aware of what they do.

31. And tell the believing women to lower their gaze and be modest, and to display of their adornment only that which is apparent and to draw their veils over their bosoms and not to reveal their adornment save to their own husbands or fathers or husbands' fathers or their sons or their husbands' sons or their brothers or their brothers' sons or sisters' sons or their women, or their slaves, or male attendants who lack vigour, or children who know naught of women's nakedness. And let them not stamp their feet so as to reveal what they hide of their adornment. And turn unto Allah together, O believers, in order that ye may succeed.

32. And marry such of you as are solitary and the pious of your slaves and maid-servants. If they be poor, Allah will enrich them of His bounty. Allah is of ample means, Aware.

33. And let those who cannot find a match keep chaste till Allah give them independence by His grace. And such of your slaves as seek a writing (of emancipation), write it for them if ye are aware of aught of good in them, and bestow upon them of the wealth of Allah which He hath bestowed upon you. Force not your slave-girls to whoredom that ye may seek enjoyment of the life of the world, if they would preserve their chastity. And if one force them, then (unto them), after their compulsion, lo! Allah will be forgiving, Merciful.

34. And verily We have sent down for you revelations that make plain, and the example of those who passed away before you. An admonition unto those who ward off (evil).

35. Allah is the Light of the Heavens and the earth. The similitude of His light is as a niche wherein is a lamp. The lamp is in a glass. The glass is as it were a shining star. (This lamp is) kindled from a blessed tree, an olive neither of the East nor of the West, whose oil would almost glow forth (of itself) though no fire touched it. Light upon light, Allah guideth unto His light whom He will. And Allah speaketh to mankind in allegories, for Allah is Knower of all things.

36. (This lamp is found) in houses which Allah hath allowed to be exalted and that His name shall be remembered therein. Therein do offer praise to Him at morn and evening.

37. Men whom neither merchandise nor sale beguileth from remembrance of Allah and constancy in prayer and

paying to the poor their due; who fear a day when hearts and eyeballs will be overturned;

38. That Allah may reward them with the best of what they did, and increase reward for them of His bounty. Allah giveth blessings without stint to whom He will.

39. As for those who disbelieve, their deeds are as a mirage in a desert. The thirsty one supposeth it to be water till he cometh unto it and findeth it naught, and findeth, in the place thereof, Allah, Who payeth him his due; and Allah is swift at reckoning.

40. Or as darkness on a vast, abysmal sea. There covereth him a wave, above which is a wave, above which is a cloud. Layer upon layer of darkness. When he holdeth out his hand he scarce can see it. And he for whom Allah hath not appointed light, for him there is no light.

41. Hast thou not seen that Allah, He it is Whom all who are in the heavens and the earth praise, and the birds in their flight? Of each He knoweth verily the worship and the praise; and Allah is Aware of what they do.

42. And unto Allah belongeth the sovereignty of the heavens and the earth, and unto Allah is the journeying.

43. Hast thou not seen how Allah wafteth the clouds, then gathereth them, then maketh them layers, and thou seest the rain come forth from between them; He sendeth down from the heaven mountains wherein is hail, and smiteth therewith whom He will, and averteth it from whom He will. The flashing of His lightning all but snatcheth away the sight.

44. Allah causeth the revolution of the day and the night. Lo! herein is indeed a lesson for those who see.

45. Allah hath created every animal of water. Of them is (a kind) that goeth upon its belly and a (a kind) that goeth upon two legs and (a kind) that goeth upon four. Allah createth what He will. Lo! Allah is Able to do all things.

46. Verily We have sent down revelations and explained them. Allah guideth whom He will unto a straight path.

47. And they say: We believe in Allah and the messenger, and we obey; then after that a faction of them turn away. Such are not believers.

48. And when they appeal unto Allah and His messenger to judge between them, lo! a faction of them are averse.

49. But if right had been with them they would have come unto him willingly.

50. Is there in their hearts a disease, or have they doubts, or fear they lest Allah and His messenger should wrong them in judgement? Nay, but such are evil-doers.

51. The saying of (all true) believers when they appeal unto Allah and His messenger to judge between them is only that they say: We hear and we obey. And such are the successful.

52. He who obeyeth Allah and His messenger, and feareth Allah, and keepeth duty (unto Him): such indeed are the victorious.

53. They swear by Allah solemnly that, if thou order them, they will go forth. Say: Swear not; known obedience (is better). Lo! Allah is Informed of what ye do.

54. Say: Obey Allah and obey the messenger. But if ye turn away, then (it is) for him (to do) only that wherewith he hath been charged, and for you (to do) only that wherewith ye have been charged. If ye obey him, ye will go aright. But the messenger hath no other charge than to convey (the message), plainly.

55. Allah hath promised such of you as believe and do good works that He will surely make them to succeed (the present rulers) in the earth even as He caused those who were before them to succeed (others); and that He will surely establish for them their religion which He hath approved for them, and will give them in exchange safety after their fear. They serve Me. They ascribe nothing as partner unto Me. Those who disbelieve henceforth, they are the miscreants.

56. Establish worship and pay the poor-due and obey the messenger, that haply ye may find mercy.

57. Think not that the disbelievers can escape in the land. Fire will be their home—a hapless journey's end!

58. O ye who believe! Let your slaves, and those of you who have not come to puberty, ask leave of you at three times (before they come into your presence): Before the prayer of dawn, and when ye lay aside your raiment for the heat of noon, and after the prayer of night. Three times of privacy for you. It is no sin for them or for you at other times, when some of you go round attendant upon others (if they come into your presence without leave). Thus Allah maketh clear the revelations for you. Allah is Knower, Wise.

59. And when the children among you come to puberty then let them ask leave even as those before them used to ask it. Thus Allah maketh clear His revelations for you. Allah is Knower, Wise.

60. As for women past child-bearing, who have no hope of marriage, it is no sin for them if they discard their (outer) clothing in such a way as not to show adornment. But to refrain is better for them. Allah is Hearer, Knower.

61. No blame is there upon the blind nor any blame upon the lame nor any blame upon the sick nor on yourselves if ye eat from your houses, or the houses of your fathers, or the houses of your mothers, or the houses of your brothers, or the houses of your sisters, or the houses of your fathers' brothers, or the houses of your father's sisters, or the houses of your mothers' brothers, or the houses of your mothers' sisters, or (from that) whereof ye hold the keys, or (from the house) of a friend. No sin shall it be for you whether ye eat together or apart. But when ye enter houses, salute one another with a greeting from Allah, blessed and sweet. Thus Allah maketh clear His revelations for you, that haply ye may understand.

62. They only are the true believers who believe in Allah and His messenger and, when they are with him on some common errand, go not away until they have asked leave of him. Lo! those who ask leave of thee, those are they who believe in Allah and His messenger. So, if they ask thy leave for some affair of theirs, give leave to whom thou wilt of them, and ask for them forgiveness of Allah: Lo! Allah is Forgiving, Merciful.

63. Make not the calling of the messenger among you as your calling one of another. Allah knoweth those of you who steal away, hiding themselves. And let those who conspire to evade orders beware lest grief or painful punishment befall them.

64. Lo! verily unto Allah belongeth whatsoever is in the heavens and the earth. He knoweth your condition. And (He knoweth) the Day when they are returned unto Him so that He may inform them of what they did. Allah is Knower of all things.

SÛRAH 25

Al-Furqân, "The Criterion", takes its name from a word occurring in v. 1. The subject is the folly of superstition and the craving for miraculous events in face of the wonders of God's creation.

It belongs to the middle group of Meccan Sûrahs, except vv. 68-70 which were revealed at Al-Madînah.

THE CRITERION (OF RIGHT AND WRONG)

Revealed at Mecca

In the name of Allah, the Beneficent, the Merciful.

1. Blessed is He Who hath revealed unto His slave the Criterion (of right and wrong), that he may be a warner to the peoples.

2. He unto Whom belongeth the sovereignty of the heavens and the earth, He hath chosen no son nor hath He any partner in the sovereignty. He hath created everything and hath meted out for it a measure.

3. Yet they choose beside Him other gods who create naught but are themselves created, and possess not hurt nor profit for themselves, and possess not death nor life, nor power to raise the dead.

4. Those who disbelieve say: This is naught but a lie that he hath invented, and other folk have helped him with it, so that they have produced a slander and a lie.

5. And they say: Fables of the men of old which he hath had written down so that they are dictated to him morn and evening.

6. Say (unto them, O Muhammad): He Who knoweth the secret of the heavens and the earth hath revealed it. Lo! He ever is Forgiving, Merciful.

7. And they say: What aileth this messenger (of Allah) that he eateth food and walketh in the markets? Why is not an angel sent down unto him, to be a warner with him.

8. Or (why is not) a treasure thrown down unto him, or why hath he not a paradise from whence to eat? And the evil-doers say: Ye are but following a man bewitched.

9. See how they coin similitudes for thee, so that they are all astray and cannot find a road!

10. Blessed is He Who, if He will, will assign thee better than (all) that—Gardens underneath which rivers flow—and will assign thee mansions.

11. Nay, but they deny (the coming of) the Hour, and for those who deny (the coming of) the Hour We have prepared a flame.

12. When it seeth them from afar, they hear the crackling and the roar thereof.

13. And when they are flung into a narow place thereof, chained together, they pray for destruction there.

14. Pray not that day for one destruction, but pray for many destructions!

15. Say: Is that (doom) better or the Garden of Immortality which is promised unto those who ward off (evil)? It will be their reward and journey's end.

16. Therein abiding, they have all that they desire. It is for thy Lord a promise that must be fulfilled.

17. And on the day when He will assemble them and that which they worship instead of Allah and will say: Was it ye

who misled these my slaves or did they (themselves) wander from the way?

18. They will say: Be Thou Glorified! It was not for us to choose any protecting friends beside Thee; but Thou didst give them and their fathers ease till they forgot the warning and became lost folk.

19. Thus they will give you the lie regarding what ye say, then ye can neither avert (the doom) nor obtain help. And whoso among you doeth wrong, We shall make him taste great torment.

20. We never sent before thee any messengers but lo! they ate food and walked in the markets. And We have appointed some of you a test for others: Will ye be steadfast? And thy Lord is ever Seer.

21. And those who look not for a meeting with Us say: Why are angels not sent down unto us and (why) do we not see our Lord? Assuredly they think too highly of themselves and are scornful with great pride.

22. On the day when they behold the angels, on that day there will be no good tidings for the guilty; and they will cry: A forbidding ban!

23. And We shall turn unto the work they did and make it scattered motes.

24. Those who have earned the Garden on that day will be better in their home and happier in their place of noonday rest;

25. A day when the heaven with clouds will be rent asunder and the angels will be sent down, a grand descent.

26. The Sovereignty on that day will be the True (Sovereignty) belonging to the Beneficent One, and it will be a hard day for disbelievers.

27. On the day when the wrongdoer gnaweth his hands, he will say: Ah, would that I had chosen a way together with the messenger (of Allah)!

28. Alas for me! Ah, would that I had never taken such an one for friend!

29. He verily led me astray from the Reminder after it had reached me. Satan was ever man's deserter in the hour of need.

30. And the messenger saith: O my Lord! Lo! mine own folk make this Qur'ân of no account.

31. Even so have We appointed unto every Prophet an opponent from among the guilty; but Allah sufficeth for a Guide and Helper.

32. And those who disbelieve say: Why is the Qur'ân not revealed unto him all at once? (It is revealed) thus that We may

strengthen thy heart therewith; and We arranged it in right order.

33. And they bring thee no similitude but We bring thee the Truth (as against it), and better (than their similitude) as argument.

34. Those who will be gathered on their faces unto Hell: such are worse in plight and further from the right road.

35. We verily gave Moses the Scripture and placed with him his brother Aaron as henchman.

36. Then We said: Go together unto the folk who have denied Our revelations. Then We destroyed them, a complete destruction.

37. And Noah's folk, when they denied the messengers, We drowned them and made of them a portent for mankind. We have prepared a painful doom for evil-doers.

38. And (the tribes of) A'âd and Thamûd, and the dwellers in Ar-Rass, and many generations in between.

39. Each (of them) We warned by examples, and each (of them) We brought to utter ruin.

40. And indeed they have passed by the township whereon was rained the fatal rain. Can it be that they have not seen it? Nay, but they hope for no resurrection.

41. And when they see thee (O Muhammad) they treat thee only as a jest (saying): Is this he whom Allah sendeth as a messenger?

42. He would have led us far away from our gods if we had not been staunch to them. They will know, when they behold the doom, who is more astray as to the road.

43. Hast thou seen him who chooseth for his god his own lust? Wouldst thou then be guardian over him?

44. Or deemest thou that most of them hear or understand? They are but as the cattle—nay, but they are farther astray!

45. Hast thou not seen how thy Lord hath spread the shade—And if He willed he could have made it still—then We have made the sun its pilot;

46. Then We withdraw it unto Us, a gradual withdrawal?

47. And He it is Who maketh night a covering for you, and sleep repose, and maketh day a resurrection.

48. And He it is Who sendeth the winds, glad tidings heralding His mercy, and We send down purifying water from the sky.

49. That We may give life thereby to a dead land, and We give many beasts and men that We have created to drink thereof.

50. And verily We have repeated it among them that they

may remember, but most of mankind begrudge aught save ingratitude.

51. If We willed, We could raise up a warner in every village.

52. So obey not the disbelievers, but strive against them herewith with a great endeavour.

53. And He it is Who hath given independence to the two seas (though they meet); one palatable, sweet, and the other saltish, bitter; and hath set a bar and a forbidding ban between them.

54. And He it is Who hath created man from water, and hath appointed for him kindred by blood and kindred by marriage; for thy Lord is ever Powerful.

55. Yet they worship instead of Allah that which can neither benefit them nor hurt them. The disbeliever was ever a partisan against his Lord.

56. And We have sent thee (O Muhammad) only as a bearer of good tidings and a warner.

57. Say: I ask of you no reward for this, save that whoso will may choose a way unto his Lord.

58. And trust thou in the Living One Who dieth not, and hymn His praise. He sufficeth as the Knower of His bondmen's sins,

59. Who created the heavens and the earth and all that is between them in six Days, then He mounted the Throne. The Beneficent! Ask any one informed concerning Him!

60. And when it is said unto them: Adore the Beneficent! they say: And what is the Beneficent? Are we to adore whatever thou (Muhammad) biddest us? And it increaseth aversion in them.

61. Blessed be He Who hath placed in the heaven mansions of the stars, and hath placed therein a great lamp and a moon giving light!

62. And He it is Who hath appointed night and day in succession, for him who desireth to remember, or desireth thankfulness.

63. The (faithful) slaves of the Beneficent are they who walk upon the earth modestly, and when the foolish ones address them answer: Peace!

64. And who spend the night before their Lord, prostrate and standing.

65. And who say: Our Lord! Avert from us the doom of hell; lo! the doom thereof is anguish;

66. Lo! it is wretched as abode and station;

67. And those who, when they spend, are neither prodigal nor grudging; and there is ever a firm station between the two;

68. And those who cry not unto any other god along with Allah, nor take the life which Allah hath forbidden save in (course of) justice, nor commit adultery—and whoso doeth this shall pay the penalty;

69. The doom will be doubled for him on the Day of Resurrection, and he will abide therein disdained for ever;

70. Save him who repenteth and believeth and doth righteous work; as for such, Allah will change their evil deeds to good deeds. Allah is ever Forgiving, Merciful.

71. And whosoever repenteth and doeth good, he verily repenteth toward Allah with true repentance—

72. And those who will not witness vanity, but when they pass near senseless play, pass by with dignity.

73. And those who, when they are reminded of the revelations of their Lord, fall not deaf and blind thereat.

74. And who say: Our Lord! Vouchsafe us comfort of our wives and of our offspring, and make us patterns for (all) those who ward off (evil).

75. They will be awarded the high place forasmuch as they were steadfast, and they will meet therein with welcome and the word of peace.

76. Abiding there forever. Happy is it as abode and station!

77. Say (O Muhammad, unto the disbelievers): My Lord would not concern himself with you but for your prayer. But now ye have denied (the Truth), therefore there will be judgement.

SÛRAH 26

Ash-Shu'arâ, "The Poets", takes its title from v. 224 ff., where the difference between poets and a Prophet is tersely pointed out; poets being those who say what they do not mean, while a Prophet always practises what he preaches. The pagan Arabs and their poets believed the poetic inspiration to be the work of jinn.

The story of a number of former Prophets is here given to console the believers at a time of persecution, with the assurance that it is no new thing for a messenger of God to be persecuted, but that the persecutors always suffer in the end. It shows also that all the messengers of God came with the same message.

It belongs to the middle group of Meccan Sûrahs, with the exception of vv. 224-227, which were revealed at Al-Madînah.

THE POETS

Revealed at Mecca

In the name of Allah, the Beneficent, the Merciful.

1. Tâ. Sin. Mîm.

2. These are revelations of the Scripture that maketh plain.

3. It may be that thou tormentest thyself (O Muhammad) because they believe not.

4. If We will, We can send down on them from the sky a portent so that their necks would remain bowed before it.

5. Never cometh there unto them a fresh reminder from the Beneficent One, but they turn away from it.

6. Now they have denied (the Truth); but there will come unto them tidings of that whereat they used to scoff.

7. Have they not seen the earth, how much of every fruitful kind We make to grow therein?

8. Lo! herein is indeed a portent; yet most of them are not believers.

9. And lo! thy Lord! He is indeed the Mighty, the Merciful.

10. And when thy Lord called Moses, saying: Go unto the wrongdoing folk.

11. The folk of Pharaoh. Will they not ward off (evil)?

12. He said: My Lord! Lo! I fear that they will deny me,

13. And I shall be embarrassed, and my tongue will not speak plainly, therefore send Aaron (to help me).

14. And they have a crime against me, so I fear that they will kill me.

15. He said: Nay, verily. So go ye twain with Our tokens. Lo! We shall be with you, Hearing.

16. And come together unto Pharaoh and say: Lo! we bear a message of the Lord of the Worlds,

17. (Saying): Let the Children of Israel go with us.

18. (Pharaoh) said (unto Moses): Did we not rear thee among us as a child? And thou didst dwell many years of thy life among us,

19. And thou didst that thy deed which thou didst, and thou wast one of the ingrates,

20. He said: I did it then, when I was of those who are astray.

21. Then I fled from you when I feared you, and my Lord vouchsafed me a command and appointed me (of the number) of those sent (by Him).

22. And this is the past favour wherewith thou reproachest me: that thou hast enslaved the Children of Israel.

23. Pharaoh said: And what is the Lord of the Worlds?

24. (Moses) said: Lord of heavens and the earth and all that is between them, if ye had but sure belief.

25. (Pharaoh) said unto those around him: Hear ye not?

26. He said: Your Lord and the Lord of your fathers.

27. (Pharaoh) said: Lo! your messenger who hath been sent unto you is indeed a madman!

28. He said: Lord of the East and the West and all that is between them, if ye did but understand.

29. (Pharaoh) said: If thou choosest a god other than me, I assuredly shall place thee among the prisoners.

30. He said: Even though I show thee something plain?

31. (Pharaoh) said: Produce it then, if thou art of the truthful!

32. Then he flung down his staff and it became a serpent manifest,

33. And he drew forth his hand and lo! it was white to the beholders.

34. (Pharaoh) said unto the chiefs about him: Lo, this is verily a knowing wizard,

35. Who would drive you out of your land by his magic. Now what counsel ye?

36. They said: Put him off, (him) and his brother, and send them into the cities summoners.

37. Who shall bring unto thee every knowing wizard.

38. So the wizards were gathered together at a set time on a day appointed.

39. And it was said unto the people: Are ye (also) gathering?

40. (They said): Aye, so that we may follow the wizards if they are the winners.

41. And when the wizards came they said unto Pharaoh: Will there surely be a reward for us if we are the winners?

42. He said: Aye, and ye will then surely be of those brought near (to me).

43. Moses said unto them: Throw what ye are going to throw!

44. Then they threw down their cords and their staves and said: By Pharaoh's might, lo! we verily are the winners.

45. Then Moses threw his staff and lo! it swallowed that which they did falsely show.

46. And the wizards were flung prostrate.

47. Crying: We believe in the Lord of the Worlds,

48. The Lord of Moses and Aaron.

49. (Pharaoh) said: Ye put your faith in him before I give you leave. Lo! he doubtless is your chief who taught you magic! But verily he shall come to know. Verily I will cut off your hands and your feet alternately, and verily I will crucify you every

one.

50. They said: It is no hurt, for lo! unto our Lord we shall return.

51. Lo! we ardently hope that our Lord will forgive us our sins because we are the first of the believers.

52. And We inspired Moses, saying: Take away My slaves by night, for ye will be pursued.

53. Then Pharaoh sent into the cities summoners,

54. (Who said): Lo! these indeed are but a little troop,

55. And lo! they are offenders against us.

56. And lo! we are a ready host.

57. Thus did We take them away from gardens and water springs,

58. And treasures and a fair estate.

59. Thus (were those things taken from them) and We caused the Children of Israel to inherit them.

60. And they overtook them at sunrise.

61. And when the two hosts saw each other, those with Moses said: Lo! we are indeed caught.

62. He said: Nay, verily! for lo! my Lord is with me. He will guide me.

63. Then We inspired Moses, saying: Smite the sea with thy staff. And it parted, and each part was a mountain vast.

64. Then brought We near the others to that place.

65. And We saved Moses and those with him, every one;

66. We drowned the others.

67. Lo! herein is indeed a portent, yet most of them are not believers.

68. And lo, thy Lord! He is indeed the Mighty, the Merciful.

69. Recite unto them the story of Abraham:

70. When he said unto his father and his folk: What worship ye?

71. They said: We worship idols, and are ever devoted to them.

72. He said: Do they hear you when ye cry?

73. Or do they benefit or harm you?

74. They said: Nay, but we found our fathers acting on this wise.

75. He said: See now that which ye worship.

76. Ye and your forefathers!

77. Lo! they are (all) an enemy unto me, save the Lord of the Worlds.

78. Who created me, and He doth guide me.

79. And Who feedeth me and watereth me.

80. And when I sicken, then He healeth me,

81. And Who causeth me to die, then giveth me life (again),

82. And Who, I ardently hope, will forgive me my sin on the Day of Judgement.

83. My Lord! Vouchsafe me wisdom and unite me to the righteous.

84. And give unto me a good report in later generations.

85. And place me among the inheritors of the Garden of Delight.

86. And forgive my father. Lo! he is of those who err.

87. And abase me not on the day when they are raised,

88. The day when wealth and sons avail not (any man).

89. Save him who bringeth unto Allah a whole heart.

90. And the Garden will be brought nigh for those who ward off (evil).

91. And hell will appear plainly to the erring.

92. And it will be said unto them: Where is (all) that ye used to worship

93. Instead of Allah? Can they help you or help themselves?

94. Then they will be hurled therein, they and the seducers.

95. And the hosts of Iblîs, together.

96. And they will say, when they are quarrelling therein?

97. By Allah, of a truth we were in error manifest.

98. When we made you equal with the Lord of the Worlds.

99. It was but the guilty who misled us.

100. Now we have no intercessors:

101. Nor any loving friend.

102. Oh, that we had another turn (on earth), that we might be of the believers!

103. Lo! herein is indeed a portent, yet most of them are not believers!

104. And lo, thy Lord! He is indeed the Mighty, the Merciful.

105. Noah's folk denied the messengers (of Allah),

106. When their brother Noah said unto them: Will ye not ward off (evil)?

107. Lo! I am a faithful messenger unto you,

108. So keep your duty to Allah, and obey me.

109. And I ask of you no wage therefor; my wage is the concern only of the Lord of the Worlds.

110. So keep your duty to Allah, and obey me.

111. They said: Shall we put faith in thee, when the lowest (of the people) follow thee?

112. He said: And what knowledge have I of what they may have been doing (in the past)?

113. Lo! their reckoning is my Lord's concern, if ye but knew;

114. And I am not (here) to repulse believers.

115. I am only a plain warner.

116. They said: If thou cease not, O Noah, thou wilt surely be among those stoned (to death).

117. He said: My Lord! Lo! my own folk deny me.

118. Therefore judge Thou between us, a (conclusive) judgement, and save me and those believers who are with me.

119. And We saved him and those with him in the laden ship.

120. Then afterward We drowned the others.

121. Lo! herein is indeed a portent, yet most of them are not believers.

122. And lo, thy Lord, He is indeed the Mighty, the Merciful.

123. (The tribe of) A'âd denied the messengers (of Allah).

124. When their brother Hûd said unto them: Will ye not ward off (evil)?

125. Lo! I am a faithful messenger unto you.

126. So keep your duty to Allah and obey me.

127. And I ask of you no wage therefor; my wage is the concern only of the Lord of the Worlds.

128. Build ye on every high place a monument for vain delight?

129. And seek ye out strongholds, that haply ye may last for ever?

130. And if ye sieze by force, seize ye as tyrants?

131. Rather keep your duty to Allah, and obey me.

132. Keep your duty toward Him Who hath aided you with (the good things) that ye know.

133. Hath aided you with cattle and sons.

134. And gardens and watersprings.

135. Lo! I fear for you the retribution of an awful day.

136. They said: It is all one to us whether thou preachest or art not of those who preach;

137. This is but a fable of the men of old,

138. And we shall not be doomed.

139. And they denied him; therefore We destroyed them. Lo! herein is indeed a portent, yet most of them are not believers.

140. And lo! thy Lord, He is indeed the Mighty, the Merciful.

141. (The tribe of) Thamûd denied the messengers (of Allah).

142. When their brother Sâlih said unto them: Will ye not ward off (evil)?

143. Lo! I am a faithful messenger unto you.

144. So keep your duty to Allah and obey me.

145. And I ask of you no wage therefore; my wage is the concern only of the Lord of the Worlds.

146. Will ye be left secure in that which is here before us,

147. In gardens and watersprings.

148. And tilled fields and heavy-sheathed palm trees,

149. Though ye hew out dwellings in the mountain, being skilful?

150. Therefore keep your duty to Allah and obey me.

151. And obey not the command of the prodigal,

152. Who spread corruption in the earth, and reform not.

153. They said: Thou art but one of the bewitched;

154. Thou art but a mortal like us. So bring some token if thou art of the truthful.

155. He said: (Behold) this she-camel. She hath the right to drink (at the well), and ye have the right to drink, (each) on an appointed day.

156. And touch her not with ill lest there come on you the retribution of an awful day.

157. But they hamstrung her, and then were penitent.

158. So the retribution came on them. Lo! herein is indeed a portent, yet most of them are not believers.

159. And lo! thy Lord! He is indeed the Mighty, the Merciful.

160. The folk of Lot denied the messengers (of Allah).

161. When their brother Lot said unto them: Will ye not ward off (evil)?

162. Lo! I am a faithful messenger unto you.

163. So keep your duty to Allah and obey me.

164. And I ask of you no wage therefore; my wage is the concern only of the Lord of the Worlds.

165. What! Of all creatures do ye come unto the males,

166. And leave the wives your Lord created for you? Nay, but ye are froward folk.

167. They said: If thou cease not, O Lot, thou wilt soon be of the outcast.

168. He said: I am in truth of those who hate your conduct.

169. My Lord! Save me and my household from what they do.

170. So We saved him and his household, every one,

171. Save an old woman among those who stayed behind.

172. Then afterward We destroyed the others.

173. And We rained on them a rain. And dreadful is the rain of those who have been warned.

174. Lo! herein is indeed a portent, yet most of them are not believers.

175. And lo! thy Lord, He is indeed the Mighty, the Merciful

176. The dwellers in the wood (of Midian) denied the messengers (of Allah).

177. When Shu'eyb said unto them: Will ye not ward off (evil)?

178. Lo! I am a faithful messenger unto you,

179. So keep your duty to Allah and obey me.

180. And I ask of you no wage for it; my wage is the concern only of the Lord of the Worlds.

181. Give full measure, and be not of those who give less (than the due).

182. And weigh with the true balance.

183. Wrong not mankind in their goods, and do not evil, making mischief, in the earth.

184. And keep your duty unto Him Who created you and the generations of the men of old.

185. They said: Thou art but one of the bewitched;

186. Thou art but a mortal like us, and lo! we deem thee of the liars.

187. Then make fragments of the heaven fall upon us, if thou art of the truthful.

188. He said: My Lord is best aware of what ye do.

189. But they denied him, so there came on them the retribution of the day of gloom. Lo! it was the retribution of an awful day.

190. Lo! herein is indeed a portent; yet most of them are not believers.

191. And lo! thy Lord! He is indeed the Mighty, the Merciful

192. And lo! it is a revelation of the Lord of the Worlds,

193. Which the True Spirit hath brought down.

194. Upon thy heart, that thou mayest be (one) of the warners,

195. In plain Arabic speech.

196. And lo, it is in the Scriptures of the men of old.

197. Is it not a token for them that the doctors of the Children of Israel know it.

198. And if We had revealed it unto one of any other nation than the Arabs,

199. And he had read it unto them, they would not have believed in it.

200. Thus do We make it traverse the hearts of the guilty.

201. They will not believe in it till they behold the painful doom,

202. So that it will come upon them suddenly, when they perceive not.

203. Then they will say: Are we to be reprieved?

204. Would they (now) hasten on Our doom?

205. Hast thou then seen, if We content them for (long) years,

206. And then cometh that which they were promised,

207. (How) that wherewith they were contented naught availeth them?

208. And We destroyed no township but it had its warners.

209. For reminder; for We never were oppressors.

210. The devils did not bring it down.

211. It is not meet for them, nor is it in their power,

212. Lo! verily they are banished from the hearing.

213. Therefore invoke not with Allah another god, lest thou be one of the doomed.

214. And warn thy tribe of near kindered,

215. And lower thy wing (in kindness) unto those believers who follow thee.

216. And if they (thy kinsfolk) disobey thee, say: Lo! I am innocent of what they do.

217. And put thy trust in the Mighty, the Merciful.

218. Who seeth thee when thou standest up (to pray).

219. And (seeth) thine abasement among those who fall prostrate (in worship).

220. Lo! He, only He, is the Hearer, the Knower.

221. Shall I inform you upon whom the devils descend?

222. They descend on every sinful, false one.

223. They listen eagerly, but most of them are liars.

224. As for poets, the erring follow them.

225. Hast thou not seen how they stray in every valley,

226. And how they say that which they do not?

227. Save those who believe and do good works, and remember Allah much, and vindicate themselves after they have been wronged. Those who do wrong will come to know by what a (great) reverse they will be overturned!

SÛRAH 27

An-Naml, "The Ant", takes its name from the ant mentioned in v. 18. Some commentators, objecting to the miraculous, seek to explain the ants, in the story of Solomon, as an old Arab tribe, the birds as cavalry, Hudhud (the hoopoe) as a man's name, and the jinn as foreign troops. It belongs to the middle group of Meccan Sûrahs.

THE ANT

Revealed at Mecca

In the name of Allah, the Beneficent, the Merciful.

1. Tâ Sîn. These are revelations of the Qur'ân and a
Scripture that maketh plain;

2. A guidance and good tidings for believers.

3. Who establish worship and pay the poor-due and are
sure of the Hereafter.

4. Lo! as for those who believe not in the Hereafter, We
have made their works fair-seeming unto them so that they
are all astray.

5. Those are they for whom is the worst of punishment
and in the Hereafter they will be the greatest losers.

6. Lo! as for thee (Muhammad), thou verily receivest the
Qur'ân from the presence of One Wise, Aware.

7. (Remember) when Moses said unto his household: Lo!
I spy afar off a fire; I will bring you tidings thence, or bring
to you a borrowed flame that ye may warm yourselves.

8. But when he reached it, he was called, saying: Blessed is
Whosoever is in the fire and whosoever is round about it! And
Glorified be Allah, the Lord of the Worlds!

9. O Moses! Lo! it is I, Allah, the Mighty, the Wise.

10. And throw down thy staff! But when he saw it writhing
as it were a demon, he turned to flee headlong; (but it was said
unto him): O Moses! Fear not! Lo! the emissaries fear not in
My presence,

11. Save him who hath done wrong and afterward hath
changed evil for good. And lo! I am Forgiving, Merciful.

12. And put thy hand unto the bosom of thy robe, it will
come forth white but unhurt. (This will be one) among nine
tokens unto Pharaoh and his people. Lo! they were ever evil-
living folk.

13. But when Our tokens came unto them, plain to see, they
said: This is mere magic,

14. And they denied them, though their souls acknowledged
them, for spite and arrogance. Then see the nature of the
consequence for the wrong-doers!

15. And We verily gave knowledge unto David and
Solomon, and they said: Praise be to Allah, Who hath preferred
us above many of His believing slaves!

16. And Solomon was David's heir. And he said: O mankind!
Lo! we have been taught the language of birds, and have been
given (abundance) of all things. This surely is evident favour.

17. And there were gathered together unto Solomon his
armies of the jinn and humankind, and of the birds, and they

were set in battle order;

18. Till, when they reached the Valley of the Ants, an ant exclaimed: O ants! Enter your dwellings lest Solomon and his armies crush you, unperceiving.

19. And (Solomon) smiled, laughing at her speech, and said: My Lord, arouse me to be thankful for Thy favour wherewith Thou hast favoured me and my parents, and to do good that shall be pleasing unto Thee, and include me in (the number of) Thy righteous slaves.

20. And he sought among the birds and said: How is it that I see not the hoopoe, or is he among the absent?

21. I verily will punish him with hard punishment or I verily will slay him, or he verily shall bring me a plain excuse.

22. But he was not long in coming, and he said: I have found out (a thing) that thou apprehendest not, and I come unto thee from Sheba with sure tidings.

23. Lo! I found a woman ruling over them, and she hath been given (abundance) of all things, and hers is a mighty throne.

24. I found her and her people worshipping the sun instead of Allah; and Satan maketh their works fair-seeming unto them, and debarreth them from the way (of Truth), so that they go not aright:

25. So that they worship not Allah, Who bringeth forth the hidden in the heavens and earth, and knoweth what ye hide and what ye proclaim.

26. Allah; there is no God save Him, the Lord of the tremendous Throne.

27. (Solomon) said: We shall see whether thou speakest truth or whether thou art of the liars.

28. Go with this my letter and throw it down unto them; then turn away and see what (answer) they return.

29. (The Queen of Sheba) said (when she received the letter): O chieftains ! Lo! there hath been thrown unto me a noble letter.

30. Lo! it is from Solomon, and lo! it is: In the name of Allah the Beneficent, the Merciful;

31. Exalt not yourselves against me, but come unto me as those who surrender.

32. She said: O chieftains! Pronounce for me in my case. I decide no case till ye are present with me.

33. They said: We are lords of might and lords of great prowess, but it is for thee to command; so consider what thou will command.

34. She said: Lo! kings, when thy enter a township, ruin it

and make the honour of its people shame. Thus will they do.

35. But lo! I am going to send a present unto them, and to see with what (answer) the messeners return.

36. So when (the envoy) came unto Solomon, (the King) said: What! Would ye help me with wealth? But that which Allah hath given me is better than that which He hath given you. Nay it is ye (and not I) who exult in your gift.

37. Return unto them. We verily shall come unto them with hosts that they cannot resist, and we shall drive them out from thence with shame, and they will be abased.

38. He said: O chiefs! Which of you will bring me her throne before they come under me, surrendering?

39. A stalwart of the jinn said: I will bring it thee before thou canst rise from thy place. Lo! I verily am strong and trusty for such work.

40. One with whom was knowledge of the Scripture said: I will bring it thee before thy gaze returneth unto thee. And when he saw it set in his presence, (Solomon) said: This is of the bounty of my Lord, that He may try me whether I give thanks or am ungrateful. Whosoever giveth thanks he only giveth thanks for (the good of) his own soul; and whosoever is ungrateful (is ungrateful only to his own soul's hurt). For lo! my Lord is Absolute in independence, Bountiful.

41. He said: Disguise her throne for her that we may see whether she will go aright or be of those not rightly guided.

42. So, when she came, it was said (unto her): Is thy throne like this? She said: (It is) as though it were the very one. And (Solomon said): We were given the knowledge before her and we had surrendered (to Allah).

43. And (all) that she was wont to worship instead of Allah hindered her, for she came of disbelieving folk.

44. It was said unto her: Enter the hall. And when she saw it she deemed it a pool and bared her legs. (Solomon) said: Lo! it is a hall, made smooth, of glass. She said: My Lord! Lo! I have wronged myself, and I surrender with Solomon unto Allah, the Lord of the Worlds.

45. And We verily sent unto Thamûd their brother Sâlih saying: Worship Allah. And lo! they then became two parties quarrelling.

46. He said: O my people! Why will ye hasten on the evi rather than the good? Why will ye not ask pardon of Allah, that ye may receive mercy.

47. They said: We augur evil of thee and those with thee. He said: Your evil augury is with Allah. Nay, but ye are folk that are being tested.

48. And there were in the city nine persons who made mischief in the land and reformed not.

49. They said: Swear one to another by Allah that we verily will attack him and his household by night, and afterward we will surely say unto his friend: We witnessed not the destruction of his household. And lo! we are truthtellers.

50. So they plotted a plot: and We plotted a plot, while they perceived not.

51. Then see the nature of the consequence of their plotting, for lo! We destroyed them and their people, every one.

52. See, yonder are their dwellings empty and in ruins because they did wrong. Lo! herein is indeed a portent for a people who have knowledge.

53. And we saved those who believed and used to ward off (evil).

54. And Lot! when he said unto his folk: will ye commit abomination knowingly?

55. Must ye needs lust after men instead of women? Nay, but ye are folk who act senselessly.

56. But the answer of his folk was naught save that they said: Expel the household of Lot from your township, for they (forsooth) are folk who would keep clean!

57. Then We saved him and his household save his wife; We destined her to be of those who stayed behind.

58. And We rained a rain upon them. Dreadful is the rain of those who have been warned.

59. Say (O Muhammad): Praise be to Allah, and peace be on His slaves whom He hath chosen! Is Allah best or (all) that ye ascribe as partners (unto Him)?

60. Is not He (best) Who created the heavens and the earth, and sendeth down for you water from the sky wherewith We cause to spring forth joyous orchards, whose trees it never hath been yours to cause to grow. Is there any God beside Allah? Nay, but they are folk who ascribe equals (unto Him)!

61. Is not He (best) Who made the earth a fixed abode, and placed rivers in the folds thereof, and placed firm hills therein, and hath set a barrier between the two seas? Is there any God beside Allah? Nay, but most of them know not!

62. Is not He (best) Who answereth the wronged one when he crieth unto Him and removeth the evil, and hath made you viceroys of the earth? Is there any God beside Allah? Little do they reflect!

63. Is not He (best) Who guideth you in the darkness of the land and the sea, He Who sendeth the winds as heralds of His

mercy? Is there any God beside Allah? High exalted be Allah from all that they ascribe as partner (unto Him)!

64. Is not He (best) Who produceth creation, then reproduceth it, and who provideth for you from the heaven and the earth? Is there any God beside Allah? Say: Bring your proof, if ye are truthful!

65. Say (O Muhammad): None in the heavens and the earth knoweth the Unseen save Allah; and they know not when they will be raised (again).

66. Nay, but doth their knowledge reach to the Hereafter? Nay, for they are in doubt concerning it. Nay, for they cannot see it.

67. Yet those who disbelieve say: When we have become dust like our fathers, shall we verily be brought forth (again)?

68. We were promised this, forsooth, we and our fathers (All) this is naught but fables of the men of old.

69. Say (unto them, O Muhammad): Travel in the land and see the nature of the sequel for the guilty!

70. And grieve thou not for them, nor be in distress because of what they plot (against thee).

71. And they say: When (will) this promise (be fulfilled), if ye are truthful?

72. Say; It may be that a part of that which ye would hasten on is close behind you.

73. Lo! thy Lord is full of bounty for mankind, but most of them do not give thanks.

74. Lo! thy Lord knoweth surely all that their bosoms hide and all that they proclaim.

75. And there is nothing hidden in the heaven or the earth but it is in a clear Record.

76. Lo: this Qur'ân narrateth unto the Children of Israel most of that concerning which they differ.

77. And lo! it is a guidance and a mercy for believers.

78. Lo! thy Lord will judge between them of His wisdom and He is the Mighty, the Wise.

79. Therefore (O Muhammad) put thy trust in Allah, for thou (standest) on the plain Truth.

80. Lo! thou canst not make the dead to hear, nor canst thou make the deaf to hear the call when they have turned to flee

81. Nor canst thou lead the blind out of their error. Thou canst make none to hear, save those who believe Our revelations and who have surrendered.

82. And when the word is fulfilled concerning them, We shall bring forth a beast of the earth to speak unto them because mankind had not faith in our revelations.

83. And (remind them of) the Day when We shall gather out of every nation a host of those who denied Our revelations and they will be set in array.

84. Till, when they come (before their Lord), He will say: Did ye deny My revelations when ye could not compass them in knowledge, or what was it that ye did?

85. And the word will be fulfilled concerning them because they have done wrong and they will not speak.

86. Have they not seen how We have appointed the night that they may rest therein, and the day sight-giving? Lo! therein verily are portents for a people who believe.

87. And (remind them of) the Day when the Trumpet will be blown, and all who are in the heavens and the earth will start in fear, save him whom Allah willeth. And all come unto Him, humbled.

88. And thou seest the hills thou deemest solid flying with the flight of clouds; the doing of Allah Who perfecteth all things. Lo! He is informed of what ye do.

89. Whoso bringeth a good deed will have better than its worth; and such are safe from fear that day.

90. And Whoso bringeth an ill deed, such will be flung down on their faces in the Fire. Are ye rewarded aught save what ye did?

91. (Say): I (Muhammad) am commanded only to serve the Lord of this land which He hath hallowed, and unto Whom all things belong. And I am commanded to be of those who surrender (unto Him),

92. And to recite the Qur'ân. And whoso goeth right, goeth right only for (the good of) his own soul; and as for him, who goeth astray — (Unto him) say: Lo! I am only a warner.

93. And say: Praise be to Allah who will show you His portents so that ye shall know them. And thy Lord is not unaware of what ye (mortals) do.

SÛRAH 28

Al-Qasas, "The Story", takes its name from a word in v. 25. The name is moreover justified by the nature of the sûrah, which consists mostly of the story of Moses, his early struggles and ultimate triumph, revealed at a time when the Prophet's case seemed desperate. It is one of the last Meccan Sûrahs. Some Arabic writers even say that it was revealed during the Hijrah, while others are of opinion that v. 85 only was revealed during the flight.

A late Meccan Sûrah except v. 85 revealed during the Prophet's flight from Mecca to Al-Madînah, and vv. 52-55 revealed at Al-Madînah.

THE STORY

Revealed at Mecca

In the name of Allah, the Beneficent, the Merciful.

1. Tâ. Sîn. Mîm.

2. These are revelations of the Scripture that maketh plain.

3. We narrate unto thee (somewhat) of the story of Moses and Pharaoh with truth, for folk who believe.

4. Lo! Pharaoh exalted himself in the earth and made its people castes. A tribe among them he oppressed, killing their sons and sparing their women. Lo! he was of those who work corruption.

5. And We desired to show favour unto those who were oppressed in the earth, and to make them examples and to make them the inheritors.

6. And to establish them in the earth, and to show Pharaoh and Hâmân and their hosts that which they feared from them

7. And We inspired the mother of Moses saying: Suckle him and when thou fearest for him, then cast him into the river and fear not nor grieve. Lo! We shall bring him back unto thee and shall make him (one) of Our messengers.

8. And the family of Pharaoh took him up, that he might become for them an enemy and a sorrow. Lo! Pharaoh and Hâmân and their hosts were ever sinning.

9. And the wife of Pharaoh said: (He will be) a consolation for me and for thee. Kill him not. Peradventure he may be of use to us, or we may choose him for a son. And they perceived not.

10. And the heart of the mother of Moses became void, and she would have betrayed him if We had not fortified her heart that she might be of the believers.

11. And she said unto his sister: Trace him. So she observed him from afar, and they perceived not.

12. And We had before forbidden fostermothers for him so she said: Shall I show you a household who will rear him for you and take care of him?

13. So We restored him to his mother that she might be comforted and not grieve and that she might know that the promise of Allah is true. But most of them know not.

14. And when he reached his full strength and was ripe, We gave him wisdom and knowledge. Thus do We reward the good.

15. And he entered the city at a time of carelessness of its

folk, and he found therein two men fighting, one of his own caste and the other of his enemies; and he who was of his caste asked him for help against him who was of his enemies. So Moses struck him with his fist and killed him. He said: This is of the devil's doing. Lo! he is an enemy a mere misleader.

16. He said: My Lord! Lo! I have wronged my soul, so forgive me. Then He forgave him. Lo! He is the Forgiving, the Merciful.

17. He said: My Lord! Forasmuch as Thou hast favoured me, I will nevermore be a supporter of the guilty.

18. And morning found him in the city, fearing, vigilant, when behold! he who had appealed to him the day before cried out to him for help. Moses said unto him: Lo! thou art indeed a mere hothead.

19. And when he would have fallen upon the man who was an enemy unto them both, he said: O Moses! Wouldst thou kill me as thou didst kill a person yesterday. Thou wouldst be nothing but a tyrant in the land, thou wouldst not be of the reformers.

20. And a man came from the uttermost part of the city running. He said: O Moses! Lo! the chiefs take council against thee to slay thee; therefore escape. Lo! I am of those who give thee good advice.

21. So he escaped from thence, fearing, vigilant. He said: My Lord! Deliver me from the wrongdoing folk.

22. And when he turned his face toward Midian, He said: Peradventure my Lord will guide me in the right road.

23. And when he came unto the water of Midian he found there a whole tribe of men, watering. And he found apart from them two women keeping back (their flocks), he said: What aileth you? The two said: We cannot give (our flocks) to drink till the shepherds return from the water; and our father is a very old man.

24. So he watered (their flock) for them. Then he turned aside into the shade, and said: My Lord! I am needy of whatever good thou sendest down for me.

25. Then there came unto him one of the two women, walking shyly. She said: Lo! my father biddeth thee that he may reward thee with a payment for that thou didst water (the flock) for us. Then, when he came unto him and told him, the (whole) story, he said: Fear not! Thou hast escaped from the wrongdoing folk.

26. One of the two women said; O my father! Hire him! For the best (man) that thou canst hire is the strong, the trustworthy.

27. He said: Lo! I fain would marry thee to one of these two

daughters of mine on condition that thou hirest thyself to me for (the term of) eight pilgrimages. Then if thou completest ten it will be of thine own accord, for I would not make it hard for thee. Allah willing, thou wilt find me of the righteous.

28. He said: That (is settled) between thee and me. Whichever of the two terms I fulfil, there will be no injustice to me, and Allah is Surety over what we say.

29. Then, when Moses had fulfilled the term, and was travelling with his housefolk, he saw in the distance a fire and said unto his housefolk: Bide ye (here) Lo! I see in the distance a fire; Peradventure I shall bring you tidings thence, or a brand from the fire that ye may warm yourselves.

30. And when he reached it, he was called from the right side of the valley in the blessed field, from the tree: O Moses! Lo! I, even I, am Allah, the Lord of the Worlds;

31. Throw down thy staff. And when he saw it writhing as it had been a demon, he turned to flee headlong, (and it was said unto him): O Moses! Draw nigh and fear not. Lo! thou art of those who are secure.

32. Thrust thy hand into the bosom of thy robe, it will come forth white without hurt. And guard thy heart from fear. Then these shall be two proofs from your Lord unto Pharaoh and his chiefs: Lo! they are evil-living folk.

33. He said: My Lord! Lo! I killed a man among them and I fear that they will kill me.

34. My brother Aaron is more eloquent than me in speech. Therefore send him with me as a helper to confirm me. Lo! I fear that they will give the lie to me.

35. He said: We will strengthen thine arm with thy brother and We will give unto you both power so that they cannot reach you for Our portents. Ye twain, and those who follow you, will be the winners.

36. But when Moses came unto them with Our clear tokens, they said: this is naught but invented magic. We never heard of this among our fathers of old.

37. And Moses said: My Lord is best aware of him who bringeth guidance from His presence, and whose will be the sequel of the Home (of bliss). Lo! wrong-doers will not be successful.

38. And Pharaoh said: O chiefs! I know not that ye have a god other than me, so kindle for me (a fire) O Hâmân to bake the mud; and set for me a lofty tower in order that I may survey the god of Moses; and lo! I deem him of the liars.

39. And he and his hosts were naughty in the land without right, and deemed that they would never be brought back to

Us.

40. Therefore We seized him and his hosts, and abandoned them unto the sea. Behold the nature of the consequence for evil-doers!

41. And We made them patterns that invite unto the fire, and on the day of Resurrection they will not be helped.

42. And we made a curse to follow them in this world and on the Day of Resurrection they will be among the hateful.

43. And We verily gave the Scripture unto Moses after We had destroyed the generations of old; clear testimonies for mankind, and a guidance and a mercy, that haply they might reflect.

44. And thou (Muhammad) wast not on the western side (of the mount) when We expounded unto Moses the commandment, and thou wast not among those present;

45. But We brought forth generations and their lives dragged on for them. And thou wast not a dweller in Midian, reciting unto them our revelations, but we kept sending (messengers to men).

46. And thou wast not beside the Mount when We did call; but (the knowldege of it is) a mercy from thy Lord that thou mayest warn a folk unto whom no warner came before thee that haply they may give heed.

47. Otherwise, if disaster should afflict them because of that which their own hands have sent before (them) they might say: Our Lord! Why sentest Thou no messenger unto us, that we might have followed Thy revelations and been of the believers?

48. But when there came unto them the truth from Our presence, they said: Why is he not given the like of what was given unto Moses? Did they not disbelieve in that which was given unto Moses of old? They say: Two magics that support each other; and they say: Lo! in both we are disbelievers.

49. Say (unto them, O Muhammad): Then bring a Scripture from the presence of Allah that giveth clearer guidance than these two (that) I may follow it, if ye are truthful.

50. And if they answer thee not then know that what they follow is their lusts. And who goeth farther astray than he who followeth his lust without guidance from Allah. Lo! Allah guideth not wrongdoing folk.

51. And now verily We have caused the Word to reach them, that haply they may give heed.

52. Those unto whom We gave the Scripture before it, they believe in it,

53. And when it is recited unto them, they say: We believe

in it. Lo! it is the Truth from our Lord. Lo! even before it we were of those who surrender (unto Him)

54. These will be given their reward twice over because they are steadfast and repel evil with good and spend of that wherewith We have provided them.

55. And when they hear vanity they withdraw from it and say: Unto us our works and unto you your works. Peace be unto you! We desire not the ignorant.

56. Lo! thou (O Muhammad) guidest not whom thou lovest but Allah guideth whom He will. And He is best aware of those who walk aright.

57. And they say: If we were to follow the guidance with thee we should be torn out of our land. Have we not established for them a sure sanctuary, whereunto the produce of all things is brought (in trade), a provision from Our presence? But most of them know not.

58. And how many a community have We destroyed that was thankless for its means of livelihood! And yonder are their dwellings which have not been inhabited after them save a little. And We, even We, were the inheritors.

59. And never did thy Lord destroy the townships, till He had raised up in their mother (-town) a messenger reciting unto them Our revelations. And never did We destroy the townships unless the folk thereof were evil-doers.

60. And whatsoever ye have been given is a comfort of the life of the world and an ornament thereof; and that which Allah hath is better and more lasting. Have ye then no sense?

61. Is he whom We have promised a fair promise which he will find (true) like him whom We suffer to enjoy awhile the comfort of the life of the world, then on the Day of Resurrection he will be of those arraigned?

62. On the Day when He will call unto them and say: Where are My partners whom ye imagined?

63. Those concerning whom the world will have come true will say: Our Lord! These are they whom we led astray. We led them astray even as we ourselves were astray. We declare our innocence before Thee: us they never worshipped.

64. And it will be said: Cry unto your (so-called) partners (of Allah). And they will cry unto them, and they will give no answer unto them, and they will see the Doom. Ah, if they had but been guided!

65. And on the Day when He will call unto them and say: What answer gave ye to the messengers?

66. On that day (all) tidings will be dimmed for them, nor will they ask one of another.

67. But as for him who shall repent and believe and do right, he haply may be one of the successful.

68. Thy Lord bringeth to pass what He willeth and chooseth. They have never any choice. Glorified be Allah and exalted above all that they associate (with Him)!

69. And thy Lord knoweth what their breasts conceal and what they publish.

70. And he is Allah; there is no God save Him. His is all praise in the former and the latter (state) and His is the command, and unto Him ye will be brought back.

71. Say: Have ye thought, if Allah made night everlasting for you till the Day of Resurrection, who is a God beside Allah who could bring you light? Will ye not then hear?

72. Say: Have ye thought, if Allah made day everlasting for you till the Day of Resurrection, who is a God beside Allah who could bring you night wherein ye rest? Will ye not then see?

73. Of His mercy hath He appointed for you night and day, that therein ye may rest and that ye may seek His bounty, and that haply ye may be thankful.

74. And on the Day when He shall call unto them and say: Where are My partners whom ye pretended?

75. And We shall take out from every nation a witness and We shall say: Bring your proof. Then they will know that Allah hath the truth, and all that they invented will have failed them.

76. Now Korah was of Moses', folk, but he oppressed them; and We gave him so much treasure that the stores thereof would verily have been a burden for a troop of mighty men. When his own folk said unto him: Exult not; lo! Allah loveth not the exultant;

77. But seek the abode of the Hereafter in that which Allah hath given thee and neglect not thy portion of the world, and be thou kind even as Allah hath been kind to thee, and seek not corruption in the earth; lo! Allah loveth not corrupters,

78. He said: I have been given it only on account of knowledge I possess. Knew he not that Allah had destroyed already of the generations before him men who were mightier than him in strength and greater in respect of following? The guilty are not questioned of their sins.

79. Then went he forth before his people in his pomp. Those who were desirous of the life of the world said: Ah would that unto us had been given the like of what hath been given unto Korah! Lo! he is lord of rare good fortune.

80. But those who had been given knowledge said: Woe unto you! The reward of Allah for him who believeth and doeth right

is better, and only the steadfast will obtain it.

81. So We caused the earth to swallow him and his dwelling place. Then he had no host to help him against Allah, nor was he of those who can save themselves.

82. And morning found those who had covered his place but yesterday crying: Ah, welladay! Allah enlargeth the provision for whom He will of His slaves and straiteneth it (for whom He will) If Allah had not been gracious unto us. He would have caused it to swallow us (also). Ah welladay! the disbelievers never prosper.

83. As for that Abode of the Hereafter We assign it unto those who seek not oppression in the earth, nor yet corruption. The sequel is for those who ward off (evil).

84. Whoso bringeth a good deed, he will have better than the same; while as for him who bringeth an ill deed, those who do ill deeds will be requited only what they did.

85. Lo! He Who hath given thee the Qur'ân for a law will surely bring thee home again. Say: My Lord is best aware of him who bringeth guidance and him who is in error manifest.

86. Thou hadst no hope that the Scripture would be inspired in thee; but it is a mercy from thy Lord, so never be a helper to the disbelievers.

87. And let them not divert thee from the revelations of Allah after they have been sent down unto thee; but call (mankind) unto thy Lord, and be not of those who ascribe partners (unto Him).

88. And cry not unto any other god along with Allah. There is no God save him. Everything will perish save His countenance. His is the command, and unto Him ye will be brought back.

SÛRAH 29

Al-'Ankabût, "The Spider", takes its name from v. 41 where false beliefs are likened to the spider's web for frailty. Most of this sûrah belongs to the middle or last Meccan period. Some authorities consider vv. 7 and 8, others the whole latter portion of the sûrah, to have been revealed at Al-Madînah. It gives comfort to the Muslims in a time of persecution.

A late Meccan Sûrah.

THE SPIDER

Revealed at Mecca

In the name of Allah, the Beneficent, the Merciful.
1. Alif. Lâm. Mîm.

2. Do men imagine that they will be left (at ease) because they say, We believe, and will not be tested with affliction?

3. Lo! We tested those who were before you. Thus Allah knoweth those who are sincere, and knoweth those who feign.

4. Or do those who do ill deeds imagine that they can outstrip Us? Evil (for them) is that which they decide.

5. Whoso looketh forward to the meeting with Allah (let him know that) Allah's reckoning is surely nigh, and He is the Hearer, the Knower.

6. And whosoever striveth, striveth only for himself, for lo! Allah is altogether Independent of (His) creatures.

7. And as for those who believe and do good works, We shall remit from them their evil deeds and shall repay them the best that they did.

8. We have enjoined on man kindness to parents; but if they strive to make thee join with Me that of which thou hast no knowledge, then obey them not. Unto Me is your return and I shall tell you what ye used to do.

9. And as for those who believe and do good works, We verily shall make them enter in among the righteous.

10. Of mankind is he who saith: We believe in Allah, but, if he be made to suffer for the sake of Allah, he mistaketh the persecution of mankind for Allah's punishment; and then, if victory cometh from thy Lord, will say: Lo! we were with you (all the while). Is not Allah best aware of what is in the bosoms of (His) creatures?

11. Verily Allah knoweth those who believe, and verily He knoweth the hyprocrites.

12. Those who disbelieve say unto those who believe: Follow our way (of religion) and we verily will bear your sins (for you). They cannot bear aught of their sins. Lo! they verily are liars.

13. But they verily will bear their own loads and other loads beside their own, and they verily will be questioned on the Day of Resurrection concerning that which they invented.

14. And verily We sent Noah (as Our messenger) unto his folk, and he continued with them for a thousand years save fifty years; and the flood engulfed them, for they were wrongdoers.

15. And We rescued him and those with him in the ship, and made of it a portent for the peoples.

16. And Abraham! (Remember) when he said unto his folk: Serve Allah, and keep your duty unto Him; that is better for you if ye did but know.

17. Ye serve instead of Allah only idols, and ye only invent a lie. Lo! those whom ye serve instead of Allah own no

provision for you. So seek your provision from Allah, and serve Him, and give thanks unto Him, (for) unto Him ye will be brought back.

18. But if ye deny, then nations have denied before you. The messenger is only to convey (the Message) plainly.

19. See they not how Allah produceth creation, then reproduceth it? Lo! for Allah that is easy.

20. Say (O Muhammad): Travel in the land and see how He originated creation, then Allah bringeth forth the late growth. Lo! Allah is Able to do all things.

21. He punisheth whom He will and showeth mercy unto whom He will, and unto Him ye will be turned.

22. Ye cannot escape (from Him) in the earth or in the sky, and beside Allah there is for you no friend nor helper.

23. Those who disbelieve in the revelations of Allah and in (their) Meeting with Him, such have no hope of My mercy. For such there is a painful doom.

24. But the answer of his folk was only that they said: "Kill him" or "Burn him." Then Allah saved him from the fire. Lo! herein verily are portents for folk who believe.

25. He said: Ye have chosen idols instead of Allah. The love between you is only in the life of the world. Then on the Day of Resurrection ye will deny each other and curse each other, and your abode will be the Fire, and ye will have no helpers.

26. And Lot believed him, and said: Lo! I am a fugitive unto my Lord. Lo! He, only He, is the Mighty, the Wise.

27. And We bestowed on him Isaac and Jacob, and We established the Prophethood and the Scripture among his seed, and We gave him his reward in the world, and lo! in the Hereafter he verily is among the righteous.

28. And Lot! (Remember) when he said unto his folk: Lo! ye commit lewdness such as no creature did before you.

29. For come ye not in unto males, and cut ye not the road (for travellers), and commit ye not abomination in your meetings? But the answer of his folk was only that they said: Bring Allah's doom upon us if thou art a truth-teller!

30. He said: My Lord! Give me victory over folk who work corruption.

31. And when Our messengers brought Abraham the good news, they said: Lo! we are about to destroy the people of that township, for its people are wrong-doers.

32. He said: Lo! Lot is there. They said: We are best aware of who is there. We are to deliver him and his household, all save his wife, who is of those who stay behind.

33. And when Our messengers came unto Lot, he was

troubled upon their account, for he could not protect them; but they said: Fear not, nor grieve! Lo! we are to deliver thee and thy household, (all) save thy wife, who is of those who stay behind.

34. Lo! we are about to bring down upon folk of this township a fury from the sky because they are evil-livers.

35. And verily of that We have left a clear sign for people who have sense.

36. And unto Midian We sent Shu'eyb, their brother. He said: O my people! Serve Allah, and look forward to the Last Day, and do not evil, making mischief, in the earth.

37. But they denied him, and the dreadful earthquake took them, and morning found them prostrate in their dwelling-place.

38. And (the tribes of) A'âd and Thamûd! (Their fate) is manifest unto you from their (ruined and deserted) dwellings. Satan made their deeds seem fair unto them and so debarred them from the Way, though they were keen observers.

39. And Korah, Pharaoh and Hâmân! Moses came unto them with clear proofs (of Allah's Sovereignty), but they were boastful in the land. And they were not winners (in the race).

40. So We took each one in his sin; of them was he on whom We sent a hurricane, and of them was he who was overtaken by the (Awful) Cry, and of them was he whom We caused the earth to swallow, and of them was he whom We drowned. It was not for Allah to wrong them, but they wronged themselves.

41. The likeness of those who choose other patrons than Allah is as the likeness of the spider when she taketh unto herself a house, and lo! the frailest of all houses is the spider's house, if they but knew.

42. Lo! Allah knoweth what thing they invoke instead of Him. He is the Mighty, the Wise.

43. As for these similitudes, We coin them for mankind, but none will grasp their meaning save the wise.

44. Allah created the heavens and the earth with truth. Lo! therein is indeed a portent for believers.

45. Recite that which hath been inspired in thee of the Scripture, and establish worship. Lo! worship preserveth from lewdnes and iniquity, but verily remembrance of Allah is more important. And Allah knoweth what ye do.

46. And argue not with the People of the Scripture unless it be in (a way) that is better, save with such of them as do wrong; and say: We believe in that which hath been revealed unto us and revealed unto you; our God and your God is One, and unto

Him we surrender.

47. In like manner We have revealed unto thee the Scripture, and those unto whom We gave the Scripture aforetime will believe therein; and of these (also) there are some who believe therein. And none deny our revelations save the disbelievers.

48. And thou (O Muhammad) wast not a reader of any Scripture before it, nor didst thou write it with thy right hand, for then might those have doubted, who follow falsehood.

49. But it is clear revelations in the hearts of those who have been given knowledge, and none deny our revelations save wrong-doers.

50. And they say: Why are not portents sent down upon him from his Lord? Say: Portents are with Allah only, and I am but a plain warner.

51. It is not enough for them that We have sent down unto thee the Scripture which is read unto them? Lo! herein verily is mercy, and a reminder for folk who believe.

52. Say (unto them, O Muhammad): Allah sufficeth for witness between me and you. He knoweth whatsoever is in the heavens and the earth. And those who believe in vanity and disbelieve in Allah, they it is who are the losers.

53. They bid thee hasten on the doom (of Allah). And if a term had not been appointed, the doom would assuredly have come unto them (ere now). And verily it will come upon them suddenly when they perceive not.

54. They bid thee hasten on the doom, when lo! hell verily will encompass the disbelievers.

55. On the day when the doom will overwhelm them from above them and from underneath their feet, and He will say: Taste what ye used to do!

56. O my bondmen who believe! Lo! My earth is spacious. Therefore serve Me only.

57. Every soul will taste of death. Then unto Us ye will be returned.

58. Those who believe and do good works, them verily We shall house in lofty dwellings of the Garden underneath which rivers flow. There they will dwell secure. How sweet the guerdon of the toilers,

59. Who persevere, and put their trust in their Lord!

60. And how many an animal there is that beareth not its own provision! Allah provideth for it and for you. He is the Hearer, the Knower.

61. And if thou wert to ask them: Who created the heavens and the earth, and constrained the sun and the moon (to their appointed work)? they would say: Allah, How then are they

turned away?

62. Allah maketh the provision wide for whom He will of His bondmen, and straiteneth it for whom (He will). Lo! Allah is Aware of all things.

63. And if thou wert to ask them: Who causeth water to come down from the sky, and therewith reviveth the earth after its death? they verily would say: Allah. Say: Praise be to Allah! But most of them have no sense.

64. This life of the world is but a pastime and a game. Lo! the home of the Hereafter—that is Life, if they but knew.

65. And when they mount upon the ships they pray to Allah, making their faith pure for Him only, but when He bringeth them safe to land, behold! they ascribe partners (unto Him),

66. That they may disbelieve in that which We have given them, and that they may take their ease. But they will come to know.

67. Have they not seen that We have appointed a sanctuary immune (from violence), while mankind are ravaged all around them? Do they then believe in falsehood and disbelieve in the bounty of Allah?

68. Who doeth greater wrong than he who inventeth a lie concerning Allah, or denieth the truth when it cometh unto him? Is not there a home in hell for disbelievers?

69. As for those who strive in Us, We surely guide them to Our paths, and lo! Allah is with the good.

SÛRAH 30

Ar-Rûm, "The Romans", takes its name from a word in the first verse.

The armies of the Eastern Roman Empire had been defeated by the Persians in all the territories near Arabia. In the year A.D. 613 Jerusalem and Damascus fell, and in the following year Egypt. A Persian army invaded Anatolia and was threatening Constantinople itself in the year A.D. 615 or 616 (the sixth or seventh year before the Hijrah) when, according to the best authorities, this Sûrah was revealed at Mecca. The pagan Arabs triumphed in the news of Persian victories over the Prophet and his little band of followers, because the Christian Romans were believers in the One God, whereas the Persians were not. They argued that the power of Allah could not be supreme and absolute, as the Prophet kept proclaiming it to be, since the forces of a pagan empire had been able to defeat His worshippers.

The Prophet's answer was provided for him in this grand assertion of Theocracy, which shows the folly of all those who

think of Allah as a partisan. It opens with two prophecies: that
the Romans would be victorious over the Persians, and that the
little persecuted company of Muslims in Arabia would have
reason to rejoice, "within ten years." In fact, in A.D. 624 the
Roman armies entered purely Persian territory, and in the same
year a little army of Muslims, led by the Prophet, overthrew
the flower of Arab chivalry upon the field of Badr.

But the prophecies are only the prelude to a proclamation
of God's universal kingdom, which is shown to be an actual
Sovereignty. The laws of nature are expounded as the laws of
Allah in the physical sphere, and in the moral and political
spheres mankind is informed that there are similar laws of
life and death, of good and evil, action and inaction, and their
consequences — laws which no one can escape by wisdom or by
cunning. His mercy, like His law, surrounds all things, and the
standard of His judgement is the same for all. He is not remote
or indifferent, partial or capricious. Those who do good earn
His favour, and those who do ill earn His wrath, no matter
what may be their creed or race; and no one, by the lip
profession of a creed, is able to escape His law of consequences.

It belongs to the middle group of Meccan Sûrahs.

THE ROMANS

Revealed at Mecca

In the name of Allah, the Merciful, the Beneficent.

1. Alif. Lâm. Mîm.
2. The Romans have been defeated.
3. In the nearer land, and they, after their defeat will be
victorious.
4. Within ten years — Allah's is the command in the
former case and in the latter — and in that day believers will
rejoice.
5. In Allah's help to victory. He helpeth to victory whom
He will. He is the Mighty, the Merciful.
6. It is a promise of Allah. Allah faileth not His promise,
but most of mankind know not.
7. They know only some appearance of the life of the
world, and are heedless of the Hereafter.
8. Have they not pondered upon themselves? Allah
created not the heavens and the earth, and that which is
between them, save with truth and for a destined end. But
truly many of mankind are disbelievers in the meeting with
their Lord.
9. Have they not travelled in the land and seen the nature

of the consequence for those who were before them? They were stronger than these in power, and they dug the earth and built upon it more than these have built. Messengers of their own came unto them with clear proofs (of Allah's Sovereignty). Surely Allah wronged them not, but they did wrong themselves.

10. Then evil was the consequence to those who dealt in evil, because they denied the revelations of Allah and made a mock of them.

11. Allah produceth creation, then He reproduceth it, then unto Him ye will be returned.

12. And in the day when the Hour riseth the unrighteous will despair.

13. There will be none to intercede for them of those whom they made equal with Allah. And they will reject their partners (whom they ascribed unto Him).

14. In the day when the Hour cometh, in that day they will be sundered.

15. As for those who believed and did good works, they will be made happy in a Garden.

16. But as for those who disbelieved and denied Our revelations, and denied the meeting of the Hereafter, such will be brought to doom.

17. So glory be to Allah when ye enter the night and when ye enter the morning—

18. Unto Him be praise in the heavens and the earth!—and at the sun's decline and in the noonday.

19. He bringeth forth the living from the dead, and He bringeth forth the dead from the living, and He reviveth the earth after her death. And even so will ye be brought forth.

20. And of His signs is this: He created you of dust, and behold you human beings, ranging widely!

21. And of His signs is this: He created for you helpmates from yourselves that ye might find rest in them, and He ordained between you love and mercy. Lo, herein indeed are portents for folk who reflect.

22. And of His signs is the creation of the heavens and the earth, and the difference of your languages and colours. Lo! herein indeed are portents for men of knowledge.

23. And of His signs is your slumber by night and by day, and your seeking of His bounty. Lo! herein indeed are portents for folk who heed.

24. And of His signs is this: He showeth you the lightning for a fear and for a hope, and sendeth down water from the sky, and thereby quickeneth the earth after her death. Lo! herein indeed are portents for folk who understand.

25. And of His signs is this: The heavens and the earth stand fast by His command, and afterward, when He calleth you, lo! from the earth ye will emerge.

26. Unto Him belongeth whosoever is in the heavens and in the earth. All are obedient unto Him.

27. He it is who produceth creation, then reproduceth it, and it is easier for Him. His is the Sublime Similitude in the heavens and in the earth. He is the Mighty, the Wise.

28. He coineth for you a similitude of yourselves. Have ye, from among those whom your right hands possess, partners in the wealth We have bestowed upon you, equal with you in respect thereof, so that ye fear them as ye fear each other (that ye ascribe unto Us partners out of that which We created)? Thus We display the revelations for people who have sense.

29. Nay, but those who do wrong follow their own lusts without knowledge. Who is able to guide him whom Allah hath sent astray? For such there are no helpers.

30. So set thy purpose (O Muhammad) for religion as a man by nature upright—the nature (framed) of Allah, in which He hath created man. There is no altering (the laws of) Allah's creation. That is the right religion, but most men know not—

31. Turning unto Him (only); and be careful of your duty unto Him, and establish worship, and be not of those who ascribe partners (unto Him);

32. Of those who split up their religion and became schismatics, each sect exulting in its tenets.

33. And when harm toucheth men they cry unto their Lord, turning to Him in repentance; then, when they have tasted of His mercy, behold! some of them attribute partners to their Lord.

34. So as to disbelieve in that which We have given them. (Unto such it is said): Enjoy yourselves awhile, but ye will come to know.

35. Or have We revealed unto them any warrant which speaketh of that which they associate with Him?

36. And when We cause mankind to taste of mercy they rejoice therein; but if an evil thing befall them as the consequence of their own deeds, lo! they are in despair!

37. See they not that Allah enlargeth the provision for whom He will, and straiteneth (it for whom He will). Lo! herein indeed are portents for folk who believe.

38. So give to the kinsman his due, and to the needy, and to the wayfarer. That is best for those who seek Allah's countenance. And such are they who are successful.

39. That which ye give in usury in order that it may increase

on (other) people's property hath no increase with Allah; but that which ye give in charity, seeking Allah's countenance, hath increase manifold.

40. Allah is He Who created you and then sustained you, then causeth you to die, then giveth life to you again. Is there any of your (so called) partners (of Allah) that doeth aught of that? Praised and Exalted be He above what they associate (with Him)!

41. Corruption doth appear on land and sea because of (the evil) which men's hands have done, that He may make them taste a part of that which they have done, in order that they may return.

42. Say (O Muhammad, to the disbelievers): Travel in the land and see the nature of the consequence for those who were before you! Most of them were idolaters.

43. So set thy purpose resolutely for the right religion, before the inevitable day cometh from Allah. On that day mankind will be sundered —

44. Whoso disbelieveth must (then) bear the consequences of his disbelief, while those who do right make provision for themselves —

45. That He may reward out of His bounty those who believe and do good works. Lo! He loveth not the disbelievers (in His guidance)

46. And of His signs is this: He sendeth herald winds to make you taste His Mercy, and that the ships may sail at His command, and that ye may seek His favour, and that haply ye may be thankful.

47. Verily We sent before thee (Muhammad) messengers to their own folk. They brought them clear proofs (of Allah's Sovereignty). Then We took vengeance upon those who were guilty (in regard to them). To help believers is incumbent upon Us.

48. Allah is He Who sendeth the winds so that they raise clouds, and spreadeth them along the sky as pleaseth Him, and causeth them to break and thou seest the rain downpouring from within them. And when He maketh it to fall on whom He will of His bondmen, lo! they rejoice;

49. Though before that, even before it was sent down upon them, they were in despair.

50. Look therefore, at the points of Allah's mercy (in creation): how He quickeneth the earth after her death. Lo! He verily is the Quickener of the Dead, and He is able to do all things.

51. And if We sent a wind and they beheld it yellow, they

verily would still continue in their disbelief.

52. For verily thou (Muhammad) canst not make the dead to hear, nor canst thou make the deaf to hear the call when they have turned to flee.

53. Nor canst thou guide the blind out of their error. Thou canst make none to hear save those who believe in Our revelations so that they surrender (unto Him).

54. Allah is He who shaped you out of weakness, then, appointed after weakness strength, then, after strength, appointed weakness and grey hair. He createth what He will. He is the Knower, the Mighty.

55. And on the day when the Hour riseth the guilty will vow that they did tarry but an hour—thus were they ever deceived.

56. But those to whom knowledge and faith are given will say: The truth is, ye have tarried, by Allah's decree, Until the Day of Resurrection. This is the Day of Resurrection, but ye used not to know.

57. In that day their excuses will not profit those who did injustice, nor will they be allowed to make amends.

58. Verily We have coined for mankind in the Qur'ân all kinds of similitude; and indeed if thou camest unto them with a miracle, those who disbelieve would verily exclaim: Ye are but tricksters!

59. Thus doth Allah seal the hearts of those who know not.

60. So have patience (O Muhammad)! Allah's promise is the very truth, and let not those who have no certainty make thee impatient.

SÛRAH 31

Luqmân takes its name from v. 12 ff., which contain mention of the wisdom of Luqmân, a sage whose memory the Arabs reverenced, but who is unknown to Jewish Scripture. He is said to have been a negro slave and the fables associated with his name are so like those of Aesop that the usual identification seems justified. The sûrah conveys assurance of success to the Muslims at a time of persecution.

It belongs to the middle or last group of Meccan Sûrahs; except vv. 27 and 28 which were revealed at Al-Madînah.

LUQMÂN

Revealed at Mecca

In the name of Allah, the Beneficent, the Merciful.
1. Alif. Lâm. Mîm.

2. These are revelations of the wise Scripture,

3. A guidance and a mercy for the good,

4. Those who establish worship and pay the poor-due and have sure faith in the Hereafter.

5. Such have guidance from their Lord. Such are the successful.

6. And of mankind is he who payeth for mere pastime of discourse, that he may mislead from Allah's way without knowledge, and maketh it the butt of mockery. For such there is a shameful doom.

7. And when Our revelations are recited unto him he turneth away in his pride as if he heard them not, as if there were a deafness in his ears. So give him tidings of a painful doom.

8. Lo! those who believe and do good works, for them are gardens of delight.

9. Wherein they will abide. It is a promise of Allah in truth. He is the Mighty, the Wise.

10. He hath created the heavens without supports that ye can see, and hath cast into the earth firm hills, so that it quake not with you; and He hath dispersed therein all kinds of beasts. And We send down water from the sky and We cause (plants) of every goodly kind to grow therein.

11. This is the Creation of Allah. Now show me that which those (ye worship) beside Him have created. Nay, but the wrongdoers are in error manifest.

12. And verily We gave Luqmân wisdom, saying: Give thanks unto Allah; and whosoever giveth thanks, he giveth thanks for (the good of) his soul. And whosoever refuseth — Lo! Allah is Absolute, Owner of Praise.

13. And (remember) when Luqmân said unto his son, when he was exhorting him: O my dear son! Ascribe no partners unto Allah. Lo! to ascribe partners (unto Him) is a tremendous wrong —

14. And We have enjoined upon man concerning his parents — His mother beareth him in weakness upon weakness, and his weaning is in two years — Give thanks unto Me and unto thy parents. Unto Me is the Journeying.

15. But if they strive with thee to make thee ascribe unto Me as partner that of which thou hast no knowledge, then obey them not. Consort with them in the world kindly, and follow the path of him who repenteth unto Me. Then unto Me will be your return, and I shall tell you what ye used to do —

16. O my dear son! Lo! though it be but the weight of a grain of mustard-seed, and though it be in a rock, or in the heavens,

or in the earth, Allah will bring it forth. Lo! Allah is Subtile, Aware.

17. O my dear son! Establish worship and enjoin kindness and forbid iniquity, and persevere whatever may befall thee. Lo! that is of the steadfast heart of things.

18. Turn not thy cheek in scorn toward folk, nor walk with pertness in the land, Lo! Allah loveth not each braggart boaster.

19. Be modest in thy bearing and subdue thy voice. Lo! the harshest of all voices is the voice of the ass.

20. See ye not how Allah hath made serviceable unto you whatsoever is in the skies and whatsoever is in the earth and hath loaded you with His favours both without and within? Yet of mankind is he who disputeth concerning Allah, without knowledge or guidance or a Scripture giving light.

21. And if it be said unto them: Follow that which Allah hath revealed, they say: Nay, but we follow that wherein we found our fathers. What! Even though the devil were inviting them unto the doom of flame?

22. Whosoever surrendereth his purpose to Allah while doing good, he verily hath grasped the firm hand-hold. Unto Allah belongeth the sequel of all things.

23. And whosoever disbelieveth, let not his disbelief afflict thee (O Muhammad). Unto Us is their return, and We shall tell them what they did. Lo! Allah is Aware of what is in the breasts (of men).

24. We give them comfort for a little, and then We drive them to a heavy doom.

25. If thou shouldst ask them: Who created the heavens and the earth? they would answer: Allah. Say: Praise be to Allah! But most of them know not.

26. Unto Allah belongeth whatsoever is in the heavens and the earth. Lo! Allah, He is the Absolute, the Owner of Praise.

27. And if all the trees in the earth were pens, and the sea, with seven more seas to help it, (were ink), the words of Allah could not be exhausted. Lo! Allah is Mighty, Wise.

28. Your creation and your raising (from the dead) are only as (the creation and the raising of) a single soul. Lo! Allah is Hearer, Knower.

29. Hast thou not seen how Allah causeth the night to pass into the day and causeth the day to pass into the night, and hath subdued the sun and the moon (to do their work) each running unto an appointed term; and that Allah is Informed of what ye do?

30. That (is so) because Allah, He is the True, and that which

they invoke beside Him is the False, and because Allah, He is the Sublime, the Great.

31. Hast thou not seen how the ships glide on the sea by Allah's grace, that He may show you of His wonders? Lo! therein indeed are portents for very steadfast, grateful (heart).

32. And if a wave enshroudeth them like awnings, they cry unto Allah, making their faith pure for Him only. But when He bringeth them safe to land, some of them compromise. None denieth Our signs save every traitor ingrate.

33. O mankind! Keep your duty to your Lord and fear a Day when the parent will not be able to avail the child in aught, nor the child to avail the parent. Lo! Allah's promise is the very truth. Let not the life of the world beguile you, nor let the deceiver beguile you in regard to Allah.

34. Lo! Allah! With Him is knowledge of the Hour. He sendeth down the rain, and knoweth that which is in the wombs. No soul knoweth what it will earn tomorrow, and no soul knoweth in what land it will die. Lo! Allah is Knower, Aware.

SÛRAH 32

As-Sajdah "The Prostration", takes its name from a word in v. 15.

It belongs in the middle group of Meccan Sûrahs.

THE PROSTRATION

Revealed at Mecca

In the name of Allah, the Beneficent, the Merciful.

1. Alif. Lâm. Mîm.

2. The revelation of the Scripture whereof there is no doubt is from the Lord of the Worlds.

3. Or say that: He hath invented it? Nay, but it is the Truth from thy Lord, that thou mayst warn a folk to whom no warner came before thee, that haply they may walk aright.

4. Allah it is Who created the heavens and the earth, and that which is between them, in six Days. Then He mounted the throne. Ye have not, beside Him, a protecting friend or mediator. Will ye not then remember?

5. He directeth the ordinance from the heaven unto the earth then it ascendeth unto Him in a Day, whereof the measure is a thousand years of that ye reckon.

6. Such is the Knower of the Invisible and the Visible, the Mighty, the Merciful.

7. Who made all things good which He created, and He

began the creation of man from clay;

8. Then He made his seed from a draught of despised fluid;

9. Then He fashioned him and breathed into him of His spirit; and appointed for you hearing and sight and hearts. Small thanks give ye!

10. And they say: When we are lost in the earth, how can we then be re-created? Nay but they are disbelievers in the meeting with their Lord.

11. Say: The angel of death, who hath charge concerning you, will gather you, and afterward unto your Lord ye will be returned.

12. Couldst thou but see when the guilty hang their heads before their Lord, (and say): Our Lord! We have now seen and heard, so send us back; we will do right now we are sure.

13. And if We had so willed, We could have given every soul its guidance, but the word from Me concerning evil-doers took effect: that I will fill hell with the jinn and mankind together.

14. So taste (the evil of your deeds). Forasmuch as ye forgot the meeting of this your day; lo! We forget you. Taste the doom of immortality because of what ye used to do.

15. Only those believe in our revelations who, when they are reminded of them, fall down prostrate and hymn the praise of their Lord, and they are not scornful,

16. Who forsake their beds to cry unto their Lord in fear and hope and spend of what We have bestowed on them.

17. No soul knoweth what is kept hid for them of joy, as a reward for what they used to do.

18. Is he who is a believer like unto him who is an evil-liver? They are not alike.

19. But as for those who believe and do good works, for them are the Gardens of Retreat—a welcome (in reward) for what they used to do.

20. And as for those who do evil, their retreat is the Fire. Whenever they desire to issue forth from thence, they are brought back thither. Unto them it is said: Taste the torment of the Fire which ye used to deny.

21. And verily We make them taste the lower punishment before the greater, that haply they may return.

22. And who doth greater wrong than he who is reminded of the revelations of his Lord, then turneth from them. Lo! We shall requite the guilty.

23. We verily gave Moses the Scripture; so be not ye in doubt of his receiving it; and We appointed it a guidance for the Children of Israel.

24. And when they became steadfast and believed firmly in our revelations, We appointed from among them leaders who guided by our command.

25. Lo! thy Lord will judge between them on the Day of Resurrection concerning that wherein they used to differ.

26. Is it not a guidance for them (to observe) how many generations We destroyed before them, amid whose dwelling-places they do walk? Lo, therein verily are the portents! Will they not then heed?

27. Have they not seen how We lead the water to the barren land and therewith bring forth crops whereof their cattle eat, and they themselves? Will they not then see?

28. And they say: When cometh this victory (of yours) if ye are truthful?

29. Say (unto them): On the day of the victory the faith of those who disbelieve (and who then will believe) will not avail them, neither will they be reprieved.

30. So withdraw from them (O Muhammad), and await (the event). Lo! they (also) are awaiting (it).

SÛRAH 33

Al-Ahzâb, "The Clans", takes its name from the army of the allied clans which came against Yathrib (Al-Madînah) in the fifth year of the Hijrah (vv. 9-25). Certain of the Banî Nadîr a Jewish tribe whom the Prophet had expelled from Yathrib on the ground of treason (see Sûrah 59), went first to the leaders of Qureysh in Mecca and then to the chiefs of the great desert tribe of Ghatafân, urging them to extirpate the Muslims and promising them help from the Jewish population of Yathrib. As a result of their efforts, Qureysh with all their clans, and Ghatafân with all their clans marched to destroy Yathrib.

When the Prophet had news of their designs, he ordered a trench to be dug before the city and himself led the work of digging it. The trench was finished when the clans arrived 10,000 strong. The Prophet went out against them with his army of 3000, the trench being between the two armies. For nearly a month the Muslims were exposed to showers of arrows, in constant expectation of attack by much superior forces; and to make matters worse, news came that the Jewish tribe of Banî Qureyzah in their rear had broken their alliance with the Muslims and made common cause with Qureysh.

The women and children had been put in strongholds–towers like the peel-towers of Northern England, of which every family of note had one for refuge in time of raids. These were practically unguarded and some of the Muslims asked permission of the Prophet to leave the battle front and go to guard them, though they were not then in danger because the Banî Qureyzah were not likely to show their treachery until the victory of the clans was certain.

The case of the Muslims seemed, humanly, speaking hopeless. But a secret sympathiser in the enemy camp managed to sow distrust between the Banî Qureyzah and the chiefs of the clans, making both feel uneasy. The obstacle of the trench was unexpected and seemed formidable; and when a fierce bitter wind from the sea blew for three days and nights so furiously that they could not keep a shelter up, or light a fire, or boil a pot, Abû Sufyân, the leader of Qureysh, raised the siege in disgust. And when Ghatafân one morning found Qureysh had gone, they too departed for their homes.

On the very day when the Muslims returned from the trench began the seige of the traitorous Banî Qureyzah in their towers of refuge. It lasted for twenty-five days. When they at length surrendered some of the tribe of Aûs, whose adherents they were, asked the Prophet to show them the same grace that he had shown to the tribe of Khazraj, in the case of Banî Nadîr in allowing them to intercede for their dependents.

The Prophet said: "Would you like that one of you should decide concerning them? "They said: "Yes,"and he appointed Sa'd ibn Mu'âdh, a great chief of Aûs, who had been wounded and was being cared for in the Mosque. Sa'd was sent for and he ordered their men to be put to death, their women and children to be made captive, and their property to be divided among the Muslims at the Prophet's will.

I have taken this account from the narrative of Ibn Khaldûn, which is concise, rather than from that in Ibn Hishâm, which is exceedingly diffuse, the two accounts being in absolute agreement. Vv. 26 and 27 refer to the punishment of Banî Qureyzah.

In v. 37 the reference is to the unhappy marriage of Zeyd, the Prophet's freedman and adopted son, with Zeynab, the Prophet's cousin, a proud lady of Qureysh. The Prophet had arranged the marriage with the idea of breaking down the old barrier of pride of caste, and had shown but little consideration for Zeynab's feelings. Tradition says that both she and her brother were averse to the match, and that she had always wished to marry the Prophet. For Zeyd, the marriage was nothing but a cause of embarrassment and humiliation. When the Prophet's attention was first called to their unhappiness, he urged Zeyd to keep his wife and not divorce her, being apprehensive of the talk that would arise if it became known that a marriage arranged by him had proved unhappy. At last, Zeyd did actually divorce Zeynab, and the Prophet was commanded to marry her in order, by his example, to disown the superstitious customs of the pagan Arabs, in such matters, of treating their adopted sons as their real sons, which was against the laws of God (i.e. the laws of nature); whereas in arranging a marriage, the woman's inclinations ought to be considered. Unhappy marriage was no part of Allah's ordinance, and was not to be held sacred in Islâm.

The Sûrah contains further reference to the wives of the Prophet in connection with which it may be mentioned that from the age of twenty-five till the age of fifty he had only one wife, Khadîjah, fifteen years his senior, to whom he was devotedly attached and whose memory he cherished till his dying day. With the exception of 'Ayeshah, the daughter of his closest friend, Abû Bakr whom he married at her father's request when she was still a child, all his later marriages were with widows whose state was pitiable for one reason or another. Some of them were widows of men killed in war. One was a captive, when he made the marriage the excuse for emancipating all the conquered tribe and restoring their property. Two were the daughters of his enemies, and his alliance with them was a cause of peace. It is noteworthy that the period of these marriages was also the period of his greatest activitiy, when he had little rest from campaigning, and was always busy with the problems of a growing empire.

The period of revelation is between the end of the fifth and the end of the seventh years of the Hijrah.

THE CLANS

Revealed at Al-Madînah

In the name of Allah, the Beneficent, the Merciful.

1. O Prophet! Keep thy duty to Allah and obey not the disbelievers and the hypocrites. Lo! Allah is Knower, Wise.

2. And follow that which is inspired in thee from thy Lord. Lo! Allah is Aware of what ye do.

3. And put thy trust in Allah, for Allah is sufficient as Trustee.

4. Allah hath not assigned unto any man two hearts within his body, nor hath He made your wives whom ye declare (to be your mothers) your mothers, nor hath He made those whom ye claim (to be your sons) your sons. This is but a saying of your mouths. But Allah sayeth the truth and He showeth the way.

5. Proclaim their real parentage. That will be more equitable in the sight of Allah. And if you know not their

fathers, then (they are) your brethren in the faith, and your
clients. And there is no sin for you in the mistakes that ye
make unintentionally, but what your hearts purpose (that
will be a sin for you). Allah is Forgiving, Merciful.

6. The Prophet is closer to the believers than their selves,
and his wives are (as) their mothers. And the owners of
kinship are closer one to another in the ordinance of Allah than
(other) believers and the fugitives (who fled from Mecca)
except that ye should do kindness to your friends. This is
written in the Book (of nature).

7. And when We exacted a covenant from the Prophets,
and from thee (O Muhammad) and from Noah and Abraham
and Moses and Jesus son of Mary. We took from them a
solemn covenant;

8. That He may ask of the loyal of their loyalty. And He
hath prepared a painful doom for the unfaithful.

9. O ye who believe! Remember Allah's favour unto you
when there came against you hosts, and We sent against them
a great wind and hosts ye could not see. And Allah is ever Seer
of what ye do.

10. When they came upon you from above you and from
below you, and when eyes grew wild and hearts reached to
the throats, and ye were imagining vain thoughts concerning
Allah.

11. There were the believers sorely tried, and shaken with
a mighty shock.

12. And when the hypocrites, and those in whose hearts is
a disease, were saying: Allah and His messenger promised us
naught but delusion.

13. And when a party of them said : O folk of Yathrib! There
is no stand (possible) for you, therefore turn back. And certain
of them (even) sought permission of the Prophet, saying : Our
homes lie open (to the enemy). And they lay not open. They
but wished to flee.

14. If the enemy had entered from all sides and they had
been exhorted to treachery, they would have committed it,
and would have hesitated thereupon but little.

15. And verily they had already sworn unto Allah that they
would not turn their backs (to the foe). An oath to Allah must
be answered for.

16. Say: Flight will not avail you if ye flee from death or
killing, and then ye dwell in comfort but a little while.

17. Say: Who is he who can preserve you from Allah if He
intendeth harm for you, or intendeth mercy for you. They will
not find that they have any friend or helper other than Allah.

18. Allah already knoweth those of you who hinder, and

those who say unto their brethren : "Come ye hither unto us!" and they come not to the stress of battle save a little.

19. Being sparing of their help to you (believers). But when the fear cometh, then thou (Muhammad) seest them regarding thee with rolling eyes like one who fainteth unto death. Then, when the fear departeth, they scald you with sharp tongues in their greed for wealth (from the spoil). Such have not believed. Therefore Allah maketh their deeds fruitless. And that is easy for Allah.

20. They hold that the clans have not retired (for good); and if the clans should advance (again), they would fain be in the desert with the wandering Arabs, asking for the news of you; and if they were among you, they would not give battle, save a little.

21. Verily in the messenger of Allah you have a good example for him who looketh unto Allah and the Last Day, and remembereth Allah much.

22. And when the true believers saw the clans, they said: This is that which Allah and His messenger promised us. Allah and His messenger are true. It did but confirm them in their faith and resignation.

23. Of the believers are men who are true to that which they covenanted with Allah. Some of them have paid their vow by death (in battle), and some of them still are waiting; and they have not altered in the least;

24. That Allah may reward the true men for their truth, and punish the hypocrites if He will, or relent toward them (if He will). Lo! Allah is Forgiving, Merciful.

25. And Allah repulsed the disbelievers in their wrath; they gained no good. Allah averted their attack from the believers. Allah is Strong, Mighty.

26. And He brought those of the People of the Scripture who supported them down from their strongholds, and cast panic into their hearts. Some ye slew, and ye made captive some.

27. And He caused you to inherit their land and their houses and their wealth, and land ye have not trodden. Allah is Able to do all things.

28. O Prophet! Say unto thy wives : If ye desire the world's life and its adornment, come! I will content you and will release you with a fair release.

29. But if ye desire Allah and His messenger and the abode of the hereafter, then Lo! Allah hath prepared for the good among you an immense reward.

30. O ye wives of the Prophet! Whosoever of you committeth manifest lewdness, the punishment for her will be doubled, and that is easy for Allah.

31. And whosoever of you is submissive unto Allah and His messenger and doeth right, We shall give her reward twice over, and We have prepared for her a rich provision.

32. O ye wives of the Prophet! Ye are not like any other women. If ye keep your duty (to Allah), then be not soft of speech, lest he in whose heart is a disease aspire (to you), but utter customary speech.

33. And stay in your houses. Bedizen not yourselves with the bedizenment of the Time of Ignorance. Be regular in prayer, and pay the poor-due, and obey Allah and His messenger. Allah's wish is but to remove uncleanness far from you, O Folk of the Household and cleanse you with a thorough cleansing.

34. And bear in mind that which is recited in your houses of the revelations of Allah and wisdom. Lo! Allah is Subtile, Aware.

35. Lo! men who surrender unto Allah, and women who surrender, and men who believe and women who believe, and men who obey and women who obey, and men who speak the truth and women who speak the truth, and men who persevere (in righteousness) and women who persevere, and men who are humble and women who are humble, and men who give alms and women who give alms, and men who fast and women who fast, and men who guard their modesty and women who guard (their modesty), and men who remember Allah much and women who remember - Allah hath prepared for them forgiveness and a vast reward.

36. And it becometh not a believing man or a believing woman, when Allah and His messenger have decided an affair (for them), that they should (after that) claim any say in their affair; and whoso is rebellious to Allah and His messenger, he verily goeth astray in error manifest.

37. And when thou saidst unto him on whom Allah hath conferred favour and thou hast conferred favour: Keep thy wife to thyself, and fear Allah. And thou didst hide in thy mind that which Allah was to bring to light, and thou didst fear mankind whereas Allah had a better right that thou shouldst fear Him. So when Zeyd had performed the necessary formality (of divorce) from her, We gave her unto thee in marriage, so that (henceforth) there may be no sin for believers in respect of wives of their adopted sons, when the latter have performed the necessary formality (of release) from them. The commandment of Allah must be fulfilled.

38. There is no reproach for the Prophet in that which

Allah maketh his due. That was Allah's way with those who passed away of old - and the commandment of Allah is certain destiny —

39. Who delivered the messages of Allah and feared Him, and feared none save Allah. Allah keepeth good account.

40. Muhammad is not the father of any man among you, but he is the messenger of Allah and the Seal of the Prophets; and Allah is Aware of all things.

41. O ye who believe! Remember Allah with much remembrance.

42. And glorify Him early and late.

43. He it is Who blesseth you, and His angels (bless you), that He may bring you forth from darkness unto light; and He is ever Merciful to the believers.

44. Their salutation on the day when they shall meet Him will believers: Peace. And He hath prepared for them a goodly recompense.

45. O Prophet! Lo! We have sent thee as a witness and a bringer of good tidings and a warner.

46. And as a summoner unto Allah by His permission, and as a lamp that giveth light.

47. And announce unto the believers the good tidings that they will have great bounty from Allah.

48. And incline not to the disbelievers and the hypocrites. Disregard their noxious talk, and put thy trust in Allah. Allah is sufficient as Trustee.

49. O ye who believe! If ye wed believing women and divorce them before you have touched them, then there is no period that ye should reckon. But content them and release them handsomely.

50. O Prophet! Lo! We have made lawful unto thee thy wives unto whom thou hast paid their dowries, and those whom thy right hand possesseth of those whom Allah hath given thee as spoils of war, and the daughters of thine uncle on the father's side and the daughters of thine aunts on the father's side, and the daughters of thine uncles on the mother's side and the daughters of thine aunts on the mother's side who emigrated with thee, and a believing woman if she give herself unto the Prophet and the Prophet desire to ask her in marriage - a privilege for thee only, not for the (rest of) believers - We are aware of that which We enjoined upon them concerning their wives and those whom their right hands possess - that thou mayst be free from blame, for Allah is Forgiving, Merciful.

51. Thou canst defer whom you wilt of them and receive unto thee whom thou wilt, and whomsoever thou desirest of those whom thou hast set aside (temporarily), it is no sin for thee (to receive her again); that is better; that they may be comforted and not grieve, and may all be pleased with what thou givest them. Allah knoweth what is in your hearts (O men) and Allah is Forgiving, Clement.

52. It is not allowed thee to take (other) women henceforth, nor that thou shouldst change them for other wives even though their beauty please thee, save those whom thy right hand possesseth. And Allah is Watcher over all things.

53. O ye who believe! Enter nor the dwellings of the Prophet for a meal without waiting for the proper time, unless permission be granted you. But if ye are invited, enter, and, when your meal is ended, then disperse. Linger not for conversation. Lo! that would cause annoyance to the Prophet, and he would be shy of (asking) you (to go); but Allah is not shy of the truth. And when ye ask of them (the wives of the Prophet) anything, ask it of them from behind a curtain. That is purer for your hearts and for their hearts. And it is not for you to cause annoyance to the messenger of Allah, nor that ye should ever marry his wives after him. Lo! that in Allah's sight would be an enormity.

54. Whether ye divulge a thing or keep it hidden, lo! Allah is ever Knower of all things.

55. It is no sin for them (thy wives) (to converse freely) with their fathers, or their sons, or their brothers, or their brother's sons, or the sons of their sisters or of their own women, or their slaves. O women! Keep your duty to Allah. Lo! Allah is Witness over all things.

56. Lo! Allah and His angels shower blessings on the Prophet. O Ye who believe! Ask blessings on him and salute him with a worthy salutation.

57. Lo! Those who malign Allah and His messenger, Allah hath cursed them in the world and the Hereafter, and hath prepared for them the doom of the disdained.

58. And those who malign believing men and believing women undeservedly, they bear the guilt of slander and manifest sin.

59. O Prophet! Tell thy wives and thy daughters and the women of the believers to draw their cloaks close round them (when they go abroad). That will be better, that so they may be recognized and not annoyed. Allah is ever Forgiving, Merciful.

60. If the hypocrites, and those in whose hearts is a disease,

and the alarmists in the city do not cease, We verily shall urge thee on against them, then they will be your neighbours in it but a little while.

61. Accursed, they will be seized wherever found and slain with a (fierce) slaughter.

62. That was the way of Allah in the case of those who passed away of old; thou wilt not find for the way of Allah aught of power to change.

63. Men ask you of the Hour. Say: The knowledge of it is with Allah only. What can convey (the knowledge) unto thee? It may be that the Hour is nigh.

64. Lo! Allah hath cursed the disbelievers, and hath prepared for them a flaming fire.

65. Wherein they will abide for ever. They will find (then) no protecting friend nor helper.

66. On the day when their faces are turned over in the fire, they say: Oh, would that we had obeyed Allah and had obeyed His Messenger!

67. And they say: Our Lord! Lo! we obeyed our princes and great men, and they misled us from the Way.

68. Our Lord! Oh, give them double torment and curse them with a mighty curse.

69. O ye who believe! Be not as those who slandered Moses, but Allah proved his innocence of that which they alleged, and he was well esteemed in Allah's sight.

70. O ye who believe! Guard you duty to Allah, and speak words straight to the point;

71. He will adjust your works for you and will forgive you your sins. Whosoever obeyeth Allah and His messenger, he verily hath gained a signal victory.

72. Lo! We offered the trust unto the heavens and the earth and the hills, but they shrank from bearing it and were afraid of it. And man assumed it. Lo! he hath proved a tyrant and a fool.

73. So Allah punisheth hypocritical men and hypocritical women, and idolatrous men and idolatrous women. But Allah pardoneth believing men and believing women, and Allah is Forgiving, Merciful.

SÛRAH 34

Saba, "Sheba", takes its name from v. 15 ff., where Sheba (*Saba*), a region in the Yaman, is mentioned as having been devastated by a flood. It warns of the effects of luxury. An early Meccan Sûrah.

SABA

Revealed at Mecca

In the name of Allah, the Beneficent, the Merciful.

1. Praise be to Allah, unto Whom belongeth whatsoever is in the heavens and whatsoever is in the earth. His is the praise in the Hereafter, and He is the Wise, the Aware.

2. He knoweth that which goeth down into the earth and that which cometh forth from it, and that which descendeth from the heaven and that which ascendeth into it. He is the Merciful, the Forgiving.

3. Those who disbelieve say: The Hour will never come unto us. Say: Nay, by my Lord, but it is coming unto you surely. (He is) the Knower of the Unseen. Not an atom's weight, or less than that or greater, escapeth Him in the heavens or in the earth, but it is in a clear Record.

4. That He may reward those who believe and do good works. For them is pardon and a rich provision.

5. But those who strive against Our revelations, challenging (Us), theirs will be a painful doom of wrath.

6. Those who have been given knowledge see that what is revealed unto thee from thy Lord is the truth and leadeth unto the path of the Mighty, the Owner of Praise.

7. Those who disbelieve say: Shall we show you a man who will tell you (that) when ye have become dispersed in dust with most complete dispersal, still, even then, ye will be created anew?

8. Hath he invented a lie concerning Allah, or is there in him a madness? Nay, but those who disbelieve in the Hereafter are in torment and far error.

9. Have they not observed what is before them and what is behind them of the sky and the earth? If We will, We can make the earth swallow them, or cause obliteration from the sky to fall on them. Lo! herein surely is a portent for every slave who turneth (to Allah) repentant.

10. And assuredly We gave David grace from Us, (saying): O ye hills and birds, echo his psalms of praise! And We made the iron supple unto him,

11. Saying: Make thou long coats of mail and measure the links (thereof). And do ye right. Lo! I am Seer of what ye do.

12. And unto Solomon (We gave) the wind, whereof the morning course was a month's journey and the evening course a month's journey, and We caused the fount of copper to gush forth for him, and (we gave him) certain of the jinn who worked

before him by permission of his Lord. And such of them as deviated from Our command, them We caused to taste the punishment of flaming fire.

13. They made for him what he willed: synagogues and statues, basins like wells and boilers built into the ground. Give thanks, O House of David! Few of My bondmen are thankful.

14. And when We decreed death for him, nothing showed his death to them save a creeping creature of the earth which gnawed away his staff. And when he fell the jinn saw clearly how, if they had known the unseen, they would not have continued in despised toil.

15. There was indeed a sign for Sheba in their dwelling - place : Two gardens on the right hand and the left (as who should say): Eat of the provision of your Lord and render thanks to Him. A fair land and an indulgent Lord!

16. But they were forward, so We sent on them the flood of 'Iram, and in exchange for their two gardens gave them two gardens bearing bitter fruit, the tamarisk and here and there a lote-tree.

17. This We awarded them because of their ingratitude. Punish We ever any save the ingrates?

18. And We set, between them and the towns which We had blessed, towns easy to be seen, and We made the stage between them easy, (saying): Travel in them safely both by night and day.

19. But they said: Our Lord! Make the stage between our journeys longer. And they wronged themselves, therefore We made them bywords (in the land) and scattered them abroad, a total scattering. Lo! herein verily are portents for each steadfast, grateful (heart)!

20. And Satan indeed found his calculation true concerning them, We would know him who believeth in the Hereafter from him who is in doubt thereof; and thy Lord (O Muhammad) taketh note of all things.

22. Say (O Muhammad): Call upon those whom ye set up beside Allah! They possess not an atom's weight either in the heavens or the earth, nor have they any share in either, nor hath He an auxiliary among them.

23. No intercession availeth with Him save for him whom He permitteth. Yet, when fear is banished from their hearts, they say: What was it that your Lord said? They say: The Truth. And He is the Sublime, the Great.

24. Say: Who giveth you provision from the sky and the earth? Say: Allah. Lo! we or you assuredly are rightly guided or in error manifest.

25. Say: Ye will not be asked of what we committed, nor shall we be asked of what ye do.

26. Say: Our Lord will bring us all together, then He will judge between us with truth. He is the All-knowing Judge.

27. Say: Show me those whom ye have joined unto Him as partners. Nay (ye dare not)! For He is Allah, the Mighty, the Wise.

28. And We have not sent thee (O Muhammad) save as a bringer of good tidings and a warner to all mankind; but most of mankind know not.

29. And they say: When is this promise (to be fulfilled) if ye are truthful?

30. Say (O Muhammad): Yours is the promise of a Day which ye cannot postpone nor hasten by an hour.

31. And those who disbelieve say: We believe not in this Qur'ân nor in that which was before it; but oh, if thou couldst see, when the wrong-doers are brought up before their Lord, how they cast the blame one to another; how those who were despised (in the earth) say unto those who were proud: But for you, we should have been believers.

32. And those who were proud say unto those who were despised: Did we drive you away from the guidance after it had come unto you? Nay, but ye were guilty.

33. Those who were despised say unto those who were proud: Nay but (it was your) scheming night and day, when ye commanded us to disbelieve in Allah and set up rivals unto Him. And they are filled with remorse when they behold the doom; and We place carcans on the necks of those who disbelieved. Are they requited aught save what they did?

34. And We sent not unto any township a warner, but its pampered ones declared: Lo! we are disbelievers in that which ye bring unto us.

35. And they say: We are more (than you) in wealth and children. We are not the punished.

36. Say (O Muhammad): Lo! my Lord enlargeth the provision for whom He will and narroweth it (for whom He will). But most of mankind know not.

37. And it is not your wealth nor your children that will bring you near unto Us, but he who believeth and doeth good (he draweth near). As for such, theirs will be twofold reward for what they did, and they will dwell secure in lofty halls.

38. And as for those who strive against Our revelations, challenging, they will be brought to the doom.

39. Say: Lo! my Lord enlargeth the provision for whom he will of His bondmen, and narroweth (it) for him. And

whatsoever ye spend (for good) He replaceth it. And He is the Best of Providers.

40. And on the day when He will gather them all together, He will say unto the angels: Did these worship you?

41. They will say: Be Thou glorified. Thou art our Protector from them! Nay, but they worshipped the jinn; most of them were believers in them.

42. That day ye will possess no use nor hurt one for another. And We shall say unto those who did wrong. Taste the doom of the Fire which ye used to deny.

43. And if Our revelations are recited unto them in plain terms, they say: This is naught else than a man who would turn you away from what your fathers used to worship; and they say: This is naught else than an invented lie. Those who disbelieve say of the truth when it reacheth them: This is naught else than mere magic.

44. And We have given them no Scriptures which they study, nor sent We unto them, before thee, any warner.

45. Those before them denied, and these have not attained a tithe of that which We bestowed on them (of old); yet they denied My messengers. How intense then was My abhorrence (of them)!

46. Say (unto them, O Muhammad): I exhort you unto one thing only: That ye awake, for Allah's sake, by twos and singly, and then reflect: There is no madness in your comrade. He is naught else than a warner unto you in face of a terrific doom.

47. Say: Whatever reward I might have asked of you is yours. My reward is the affair of Allah only. He is Witness over all things.

48. Say: Lo! my Lord hurleth the truth. (He is) the Knower of Things Hidden.

49. Say: The Truth hath come, and falsehood showeth not its face and will not return.

50. Say: If I err, I err only to my own loss, and if I am rightly guided it is because of that which my Lord hath revealed unto me. Lo! He is Hearer, Nigh.

51. Couldst thou but see when they are terrified with no escape, and are seized from near at hand;

52. And say: We (now) believe therein. But how can they reach (faith) from afar off,

53. When they disbelieved in it of yore. They aim at the unseen from afar off.

54. And a gulf is set between them and that which they desire, as was done for people of their kind of old. Lo! They

were in hopeless doubt.

SÛRAH 35

Al-malâ'ikah, "The Angels", also called Al-Fâtir, "The Creator", takes its name in either case from a word in an early Meccan Sûrah.

THE ANGELS

Revealed at Mecca

In the name of Allah, the Beneficent, the Merciful.

1. Praise be to Allah, the Creator of the heavens and the earth, who appointeth the angels messengers having wings two, three and four. He multiplieth in creation what he will. Lo: Allah is Able to do all things.

2. That which Allah openeth unto mankind of mercy none can withold it; and that which He withholdeth none can release thereafter. He is the Mighty, the Wise.

3. O mankind! Remember Allah's grace toward you! Is there any creator other than Allah who provideth for you from the sky and the earth? There is no God save Him. Whither then are ye turned?

4. And if they deny thee, (O Muhammad), messengers (of Allah) were denied before thee. Unto Allah all things are brought back.

5. O mankind! Lo! the promise of Allah is true. So let not the life of the world beguile you, and let not the (avowed) beguiler beguile you with regard to Allah.

6. Lo! the devil is an enemy for you, so treat him as an enemy. He only summoneth his faction to be owners of the flaming Fire.

7. Those who disbelieve, theirs will be an awful doom; and those who believe and do good works, theirs will be forgiveness and a great reward.

8. Is he, the evil of whose deeds is made fair-seeming unto him so that he deemeth it good, (other than Satan's dupe)? Allah verily sendeth whom He will astray, and guideth whom He will; so let not thy soul expire in sighings for them. Lo: Allah is Aware of what they do!

9. And Allah it is who sendeth the winds and they raise a cloud; then We lead it unto a dead land and revive therewith the earth after its death. Such is the Resurrection.

10. Whoso desireth power (should know that) all power belongeth to Allah. Unto Him good words ascend, and the pious deed doth He exalt; but those who plot iniquities, theirs

will be an awful doom; and the plotting of such (folk) will come to naught.

11. Allah created you from dust, then from a little fluid, then He made you pairs (the male and female). No female beareth or bringeth forth save with His knowledge. And no one groweth old who groweth old, nor is aught lessened of his life, but it is recorded in a Book. Lo! that is easy for Allah.

12. And two seas are not alike: this, fresh, sweet, good to drink, this (other) bitter, salt. And from them both ye eat fresh meat and derive the ornament that ye wear. And thou seest the ship cleaving them with its prow that ye may seek of His bounty, and that haply ye may give thanks.

13. He maketh the night to pass into the day and He maketh the day to pass into the night. He hath subdued the sun and moon to service. Each runneth unto an appointed term. Such is Allah, your Lord; His is the Sovereignty; and those unto whom ye pray instead of Him own not so much as the white spot on a date-stone.

14. If ye pray unto them they hear not your prayer, and if they heard they could not grant it you. On the Day of Resurrection they will disown association with you. None can inform you like Him Who is Aware.

15. O mankind! Ye are the poor in your relation to Allah. And Allah! He is the Absolute, the Owner of Praise.

16. If He will, He can be rid of you and bring (instead of you) some new creation.

17. That is not a hard thing for Allah.

18. And no burdened soul can bear another's burden, and if one heavy laden crieth for (help with) his load, naught of it will be lifted even though he (unto whom he crieth) be of kin. Thou warnest only those who fear their Lord in secret, and have established worship. He who groweth (in goodness), groweth only for himself, (he cannot by his merit redeem others). Unto Allah is the journeying.

19. The blind man is not equal with the seer;

20. Nor is darkness (tantamount to) light;

21. Nor is the shadow equal with the sun's full heat;

22. Nor are the living equal with the dead. Lo! Allah maketh whom He will to hear. Thou canst not reach those who are in the graves.

23. Thou art but a warner.

24. Lo: We have sent thee with the Truth, a bearer of glad

tidings and a warner; and there is not a nation but a warner hath passed among them.

25. And if they deny thee, those before them also denied. Their messengers came unto them with clear proofs (of Allah's sovereignty), and with the Psalms and the Scripture giving light.

26. Then seized I those who disbelieved, and how intense was My abhorrence!

27. Hast thou not seen that Allah causeth water to fall from the sky, and We produce therewith fruit of divers hues; and among the hills are streaks white and red, of divers hues, and (others) raven-black;

28. And of men and beasts and cattle, in like manner, divers hues? The erudite among His bondsmen fear Allah alone Lo! Allah is Mighty, Forgiving.

29. Lo! Those who read the Scripture of Allah, and establish worship, and spend of that which We have bestowed on them secretly and openly, they look forward to imperishable gain.

30. That He will pay them their wages and increase them of His grace. Lo! He is Forgiving, Responsive.

31. As for that which We inspire in thee of the Scripture, it is the Truth confirming that which was (revealed) before it. Lo! Allah is indeed Observer, Seer of His slaves.

32. Then We have the Scripture as inheritance unto those whom We elected of Our bondmen. But of them are some who wrong themselves and of them are some who are lukewarm, and of them are some who outstrip (others) through good deeds, by Allah's leave. That is the great favour!

33. Gardens of Eden! They enter them wearing armlets of gold and pearl and their raiment therein is silk.

34. And they say: Praise be to Allah who hath put grief away from us. Lo! Our Lord is Forgiving, Bountiful.

35. Who, of His grace, hath installed us in the mansion of eternity, where toil toucheth us not nor can weariness affect us.

36. But as for those who disbelieve, for them is fire of hell; it taketh not complete effect upon them so that they can die, nor is its torment lightened for them. Thus We punish every ingrate.

37. And they cry for help there, (saying): Our Lord! Release us; we will do right, not (the wrong) that we used to do. Did not We grant you a life long enough for him who reflected to reflect therein? And the warner came unto you. Now taste (the flavour of your deeds), for evil-doers have no helper.

38. Lo! Allah is the Knower of the Unseen of the heavens and the earth. Lo! He is Aware of the secret of (men's) breasts.

39. He is it who hath made you regents in the earth; so he who disbelieveth, his disbelief be on his own head. Their disbelief increaseth for the disbelievers, in their Lord's sight, naught save abhorrence. Their disbelief increaseth for the disbelievers naught save loss.

40. Say: Have ye seen your partner-gods to whom ye pray beside Allah? Show me what they created of the earth! Or have they any portion in the heavens? Or have We given them a Scripture so that they act on clear proof therefrom? Nay, the evil-doers promise one another only to deceive.

41. Lo! Allah graspeth the heavens and the earth that they deviate not, and if they were to deviate there is not one that could grasp them after Him. Lo! He is ever Clement, Forgiving.

42. And they swore by Allah, their most binding oath, that if a warner came unto them they would be more tractable than any of the nations; yet, when a warner came unto them it aroused in them naught save repugnance.

43. (Shown in their) behaving arrogantly in the land and plotting evil; and the evil plot encloseth but the men who make it. Then, can they expect aught save the treatment of the folk of old? Thou wilt not find for Allah's way of treatment and substitute, nor wilt thou find for Allah's way of treatment aught of power to change.

44. Have they not travelled in the land and seen the nature of the consequence for those who were before them, and they were mightier than these in power? Allah is not such that aught in the heavens or in the earth escapeth Him. Lo! He is the Wise, the Mighty.

45. If Allah took mankind to task by that which they deserve, He would not leave a living creature on the surface of the earth; but He reprieveth them unto an appointed term, and when their term cometh - then verily (they will know that) Allah is ever Seer of His slaves.

SÛRAH 36

Yâ Sîn takes its name from the two letters of the Arabic alphabet which stand as the first verse and are generally held to signify Yâ Insân ("O Man"). This sûrah is regarded with special reverence, and is recited in times of adversity, illness, fasting and on the approach of death.

It belongs to the middle group of Meccan Sûrahs.

YÂ SÎN

Revealed at Mecca

In the name of Allah, the Beneficent, the Merciful.

1. Yâ Sîn

2. By the wise Qur'ân,

3. Lo! thou art of those sent

4. On a straight path,

5. A revelation of the Mighty, the Merciful.

6. That thou mayst warn a folk whose fathers were not warned, so they are heedless.

7. Already hath the word proved true of most of them., for they believe not.

8. Lo! we have put on their necks carcans reaching unto the chins, so that they are made stiff-necked.

9. And We have set a bar before them and a bar behind them, and (thus) have covered them so that they see not.

10. Whether thou warn them or thou warn them not, it is alike for them, for they believe not.

11. Thou warnest only him who followeth the Reminder and feareth the Beneficent in secret. To him bear tidings of forgiveness and a rich reward.

12. Lo! We it is Who bring the dead to life. We record that which they send before (them), and their footprints. And all things We have kept in a clear register.

13. Coin for them a similitude: The people of the city when those sent (from Allah) came unto them;

14. When We sent unto them twain, and they denied them both, so We reinforced them with a third, and they said: Lo! we have been sent unto you.

15. They said: Ye are but mortals like unto us. The Beneficent hath naught revealed. Ye do but lie!

16. They answered: Our Lord knoweth that we are indeed sent unto you,

17. And our duty is but plain conveyance (of the message).

18. (The people of the city) said: We augur ill of you. If ye desist not, we shall surely stone you, and grievous torture will befall you at our hands.

19. They said: Your evil augury be with you! Is it because ye are reminded (of the truth)? Nay, but ye are forward folk?

20. And there came from the uttermost part of the city a man running. He cried: O my people! Follow those who have been sent!

21. Follow those who ask of you no fee, and who are rightly guided.

22. For what cause should I not serve Him Who hath created me, and unto Whom ye will be brought back?

23. Shall I take (other) gods in place of Him when, if the

Beneficent should wish me any harm, their intercession will avail me naught, nor can they save?

24. Then truly I should be in error manifest.

25. Lo! I have believed in your Lord, so hear me!

26. It was said (unto him): Enter Paradise. He said: Would that my people knew

27. With what (munificence) my Lord hath pardoned me and made me of the honoured ones!

28. We sent not down against his people after him a host from heaven, nor do We ever send.

29. It was but one Shout, and lo! they were extinct.

30. Ah, the anguish for the bondmen! Never came there unto them a messenger but they did mock him!

31. Have they not seen how many generations We destroyed before them, which indeed return not unto them;

32. But all, without exception, will be brought before Us.

33. A token unto them is the dead earth. We revive it, and We bring forth from it grain so that they eat thereof;

34. And We have placed therein gardens of the date-palm and grapes, and We have caused springs of water to gush forth therein,

35. That they may eat of the fruit thereof, and their hands made it not. Will they not, then, give thanks?

36. Glory be to Him Who created all the sexual pairs, of that which the earth groweth, and of themselves, and of that which they know not!

37. A token to them is night. We strip it of the day, and lo! they are in darkness.

38. And the sun runneth on unto a resting-place for him. That is the measuring of the Mighty, the Wise.

39. And for the moon We have appointed mansions till she return like an old shrivelled palm-leaf.

40. It is not for the sun to overtake the moon, nor doth the night outstrip the day. They float each in an orbit.

41. And a token unto them is that We bear their offspring in the laden ship,

42. And have created for them of the like thereof whereon they ride.

43. And if We will, We drown them, and there is no help for them, neither can they be saved;

44. Unless by mercy from Us and as comfort for a while.

45. When it is said unto them: Beware of that which is before you and that which is behind you, that haply ye may find mercy (they are heedless).

46. Never came a token of the tokens of their Lord to them,

but they did turn away from it!

47. And when it is said unto them: Spend of that wherewith Allah hath provided you, those who disbelieve say unto those who believe: Shall we feed those whom Allah, if He willed, would feed? Ye are in naught else than error manifest.

48. And they say: When will this promise be fulfilled, if you are truthful?

49. They await but one Shout, which will surprise them while they are disputing.

50. Then they cannot make bequest, nor can they return to their own folk.

51. And the trumpet is blown and lo! from the graves they hie unto their Lord,

52. Crying: Woe upon us! Who hath raised us from our place of sleep! This is that which the Beneficent did promise, and the messengers spoke truth,

53. It is but one Shout, and behold them brought together before Us!

54. This day no soul is wronged in aught; nor are ye requited aught save what ye used to do.

55. Lo! those who merit paradise this day are happily employed,

56. They and their wives, in pleasant shade, on thrones reclining;

57. Theirs the fruit (of their good deeds) and theirs (all) that they ask;

58. The word from a Merciful Lord (for them) is: Peace!

59. But avaunt ye, O ye guilty, this day!

60. Did I not charge you, O ye sons of Adam, that ye worship not the devil - Lo! he is your open foe! -

61. But that ye worship Me? That was the right path.

62. Yet he hath led astray of you a great multitude. Had ye then no sense?

63. This is hell which ye were promised (if ye followed him).

64. Burn therein this day for that ye disbelieved.

65. This day We seal up mouths, and hands speak out and feet bear witness as to what they used to earn.

66. And had We willed, We verily could have quenched their eyesight so that they should struggle for the way. Then how could they have seen?

67. And had We willed, We verily could have fixed them in their place, making them powerless to go forward or turn back.

68. He whom We bring unto old age, We reverse him in creation (making him go back to weakness after strength).

Have ye then no sense?

69. And We have not taught him (Muhammad) poetry, nor is it meet for him. This is naught else than a Reminder and a Lecture making plain.

70. To warn whosoever liveth, and that the word may be fulfilled against the disbelievers.

71. Have they not seen how We have created for them of Our handiwork the cattle, so that they are their owners.

72. And have subdued them unto them, so that some of them they have for riding, some for food?

73. Benefits and (divers) drinks have they from them. Will they not then give thanks?

74. And they have taken (other) gods beside Allah, in order that they may be helped.

75. It is not in their power to help them; but they (the worshippers) are unto them a host in arms.

76. So let not their speech grieve thee (O Muhammad), Lo! We know what they conceal and what they proclaim.

77. Hath not man seen that We have created him from a drop of seed. Yet lo! he is an open opponent.

78. And he hath coined for Us a similitude, and hath forgotton the fact of his creation, saying: Who will revive these bones when they have rotted away?

79. Say: He will revive them who produced them at the first, for He is Knower of every creation.

80. Who hath appointed for you fire from the green tree, and behold! ye kindle from it.

81. Is not He Who created the heavens and the earth Able to create the like of them? Aye, that He is! for He is the All-wise Creator.

82. But His command, when He intendeth a thing, is only that he saith unto it: Be! and it is.

83. Therefore glory be to Him in Whose hand is the dominion over all things! Unto Him ye will be brought back.

SÛRAH 37

As-Sâffât takes its name from a word in the first verse. The reference in the first three verses is to the angels, as is made clear by vv. 164-166, where the revealing angel speaks in person. Tradition says that soothsayers and astrologers throughout the East were bewildered at the time of the Prophet's coming by the appearance in the heavens of a comet and many meteors which baffled all their science and made them afraid to sit at nights on high peaks to watch the stars, as was their general custom. They told enquirers that their familiars could no longer guide them, being themselves completely at a loss and terrified. This is the explanation usually given of vv. 7-9, and of a passage of similar import in Sûrah 72, vv. 8-10.

It stands early in the middle group of Meccan Sûrahs.

THOSE WHO SET THE RANKS

Revealed at Mecca

In the name of Allah, the Beneficent, the Merciful.

1. By those who set the ranks in battle order.

2. And those who drive away (the wicked) with reproof.

3. And those who read (the Word) for a reminder.

4. Lo! thy Lord is surely One;

5. Lord of the heavens and of the earth and all that is between them, and Lord of the sun's risings.

6. Lo! We have adorned the lowest heaven with an ornament, the planets.

7. With security from every forward devil.

8. They cannot listen to the Highest Chiefs for they are pelted from every side.

9. Outcast, and theirs is a perpetual torment;

10. Save him who snatcheth a fragment, and there pursueth him a piercing flame.

11. Then ask them (O Muhammad): Are they stronger as a creation, or those (others) whom We have created? Lo! We created them of plastic clay.

12. Nay, but thou dost marvel when they mock.

13. And heed not when they are reminded.

14. And seek to scoff when they behold a portent.

15. And they say: Lo! this is mere magic.

16. When we are dead and have become dust and bones, shall we then, forsooth, be raised (again)?

17. And our forefathers?

18. Say (O Muhammad): Yea, in truth; and ye will be brought low.

19. There is but one Shout, and lo: they behold.

20. And say: Ah, woe for us! This is the Day of Judgement.

21. This is the Day of Separation, which ye used to deny.

22. (And it is said unto the angels): Assemble those who did wrong, together with their wives and what they used to worship

23. Instead of Allah, and lead them to the path to hell;

24. And stop them, for they must be questioned.

25. What aileth you that ye help not one another?

26. Nay, but this day they make full submission.

27. And some of them draw near unto others, mutually questioning.

28. They say: Lo! ye used to come unto us, imposing, (swearing that ye spoke the truth).

29. They answer: Nay, but ye (yourselves) were not believers.

30. We had no power over you, but ye were wayward folk.

31. Now the Word of our Lord hath been fulfilled concerning us. Lo! we are about to taste (the doom).

32. Thus we misled you. Lo! we were (ourselves) astray.

33. Then lo! this day they (both) are sharers in the doom.

34. Lo! thus deal We with the guilty.

35. For when it was said unto them, There is no god save Allah, they were scornful.

36. And said: Shall we forsake our gods for a mad poet?

37. Nay, but he brought the Truth, and he confirmed those sent (before him).

38. Lo! (now) verily ye taste the painful doom -

39. Ye are requited naught save what ye did -

40. Save single-minded slaves of Allah;

41. For them there is a known provision

42. Fruits. And they will be honoured.

43. In the Gardens of delight,

44. On couches facing one another;

45. A cup from a gushing spring is brought round for them,

46. White, delicious to the drinkers.

47. Wherein there is no headache nor are they made mad thereby.

48. And with them are those of modest gaze, with lovely eyes,

49. (Pure) as they were hidden eggs (of the ostrich).

50. And some of them draw near unto others, mutually questionning.

51. A speaker of them saith: Lo! I had a comrade.

52. Who used to say: Art thou in truth of those who put faith (in his words)?

53. Can we, when we are dead and have become mere dust and bones - can we (then) verily be brought to book?

54. He saith: Will ye look?

55. Then looketh he and seeth him in the depth of hell.

56. He saith: By Allah, thou verily didst all but cause my ruin,

57. And had it not been for the favour of my Lord, I too had been of those haled forth (to doom).

58. Are we then not to die

59. Saving our former death, and are we not to be punished?

60. Lo! this is the supreme triumph.

61. For the like of this, then, let the workers work.

62. Is this better as a welcome, or the tree of Zaqqûm?

63. Lo! We have appointed it a torment for wrong-doers.

64. Lo! it is tree that springeth in the heart of hell.

65. Its crop is as it were the heads of devils.

66. And lo! they verily must eat thereof, and fill (their) bellies therewith.

67. And afterward, lo! thereupon they have a drink of boiling water.

68. And afterward, lo! their return is surely unto hell.

69. They indeed found their fathers astray,

70. But they make haste (to follow) in their footsteps.

71. And verily most of the men of old went astray before them,

72. And verily We sent among them warners.

73. Then see the nature of the consequence for those warned,

74. Save single-minded slaves of Allah.

75. And Noah verily prayed unto Us, and gracious was the Hearer of his prayer.

76. And We saved him and his household from the great distress,

77. And made his seed the survivors,

78. And left for him among the later folk (the salutation):

79. Peace be unto Noah among the peoples!

80. Lo! thus do We reward the good.

81. Lo! he is one of Our believing slaves.

82. Then We did drown the others.

83. And lo! of his persuasion verily was Abraham.

84. When he came unto his Lord with a whole heart;

85. When he said unto his father and his folk: What is it that ye worship?

86. Is it a falsehood - gods beside Allah - that ye desire?

87. What then is your opinion of the Lord of the Worlds?

88. And he glanced a glance at the stars

89. Then said: Lo! I feel sick!

90. And they turned their backs and went away from him.

91. Then turned he to their gods and said: Will ye not eat?

92. What aileth you that ye speak not?

93. Then he attacked them, striking with his right hand.

94. And (his people) came toward him, hastening.

95. He said: Worship ye that which ye yourselves do carve

96. When Allah hath created you and what ye make?

97. They said: Build for him a building and fling him in the red-hot fire.

98. And they designed a snare for him, but We made them the undermost.

99. And he said: Lo! I am going unto my Lord Who will guide me.

100. My Lord! vouchsafe me of the righteous.

101. So We gave him tidings of a gentle son.

102. And when (his son) was old enough to walk with him, (Abraham) said; O my dear son, I have seen in a dream that I must sacrifice thee. So look, what thinkest thou? He said: O my father! Do that which thou art commanded. Allah willing, thou shalt find me of the steadfast.

103. Then, when they had both surrendered (to Allah), and he had flung him down upon his face.

104. We called unto him: O Abraham!

105. Thou hast already fulfilled the vision. Lo! thus do We reward the good.

106. Lo! that verily was a clear test.

107. Then We ransomed him with a tremendous victim.

108. And We left for him among the later folk (the salutation):

109. Peace be unto Abraham!

110. Thus do We reward the good.

111. Lo! he is one of Our believing slaves.

112. And We gave him tidings of the birth of Isaac, a prophet of the righteous.

113. And We blessed him and Isaac. And of their seed are some who do good, and some who plainly wrong themselves.

114. And We verily gave grace unto Moses and Aaron,

115. And saved them and their people from the great distress,

116. And helped them so that they became the victors.

117. And We gave them the clear Scripture.

118. And showed them the right path.

119. And We left for them among the later folk (the salutation).

120. Peace be unto Moses and Aaron!

121. Lo! thus do We reward the good.

122. Lo! they are two of our believing slaves.

123. And lo! Elias was of those sent (to warn).

124. When he said unto his folk: Will ye not ward off (evil)?

125. Will ye cry unto Baal and forsake the Best of Creators,

126. Allah, your Lord and Lord of your forefathers?

127. But they denied him, so they surely will be haled forth (to the doom)

128. Save single-minded slaves of Allah.

129. And We left for him among the later folk (the salutation);

130. Peace be unto Elias!

131. Lo! thus do We reward the good.

132. Lo! he is one of our believing slaves.

133. And lo! Lot verily was of those sent (to warn).

134. When We saved him and his household, every one,

135. Save an old woman among those who stayed behind;

136. Then We destroyed the others.

137. And lo! ye verily pass by (the ruin of) them in the morning

138. And at night-time; have ye then no sense?

139. And lo! Jonah verily was of those sent (to warn)

140. When he fled unto the laden ship,

141. And then drew lots and was of those rejected;

142. And the fish swallowed him while he was blameworthy;

143. And had he not been one of those who glorify (Allah)

144. He would have tarried in its belly till the day when they are raised;

145. Then We cast him on a desert shore while he was sick;

146. And We caused a tree of gourd to grow above him;

147. And We sent him to a hundred thousand (folk) or more

148. And they believed, therefore We gave them comfort for a while.

149. Now ask them (O Muhammad): Hath thy Lord daughters whereas they have sons?

150. Or created We the angels females while they were present?

151. Lo! it is of their falsehood that they say.

152. Allah hath begotten. And lo! verily they tell a lie.

153. (And again of their falsehood): He hath preferred daughters to sons.

154. What aileth you? How judge ye?

155. Will ye not then reflect?

156. Or have ye a clear warrant?

157. Then produce your writ, if ye are truthful.

158. And they imagine kinship between him and the jinn, whereas the jinn know well that they will be brought before (Him).

159. Glorified be Allah from that which they attribute (unto

Him),

160. Save single-minded slaves of Allah.

161. Lo! verily, ye and that which ye worship.

162. Ye cannot excite (anyone) against Him.

163. Save him who is to burn in hell.

164. There is not one of Us but hath his known position.

165. Lo! We, even We are they who set the ranks.

166. Lo! We, even We are they who hymn His praise.

167. And indeed they used to say:

168. If we had but a reminder from the men of old.

169. We would be single-minded slaves of Allah.

170. Yet (now that it is come) they disbelieve therein; but they will come to know.

171. And verily Our word went forth of old unto Our bondmen sent (to warn).

172. That they verily would be helped,

173. And that Our host, they verily would be the victors.

174. So withdraw from them (O Muhammad) awhile,

175. And watch, for they will (soon) see.

176. Would they hasten on Our doom?

177. But when it cometh home to them, then it will be a hapless morn for those who have been warned.

178. Withdraw from them awhile.

179. And watch, for they will (soon) see.

180. Glorified be thy Lord, the Lord of Majesty, from that which they attribute (unto Him).

181. And peace be unto those sent (to warn).

182. And praise be to Allah, Lord of the Worlds!

SÛRAH 38

Sad. This sûrah takes its name from the letter of the Arabic Alphabet which stands alone as the first verse. Tradition says that the first ten verses were revealed when the leaders of Qureysh tried to persuade Abû Tâlib to withdraw his protection from the Prophet, or when Abû Tâlib died. The former is the more probable.

Its place is in the middle group of Meccan Sûrahs.

SÂD

Revealed at Mecca

In the name of Allah, the Beneficent, the Merciful.

1. Sâd. By the renowned Qur'ân,

2. Nay, but those who disbelieve are in false pride and schism.

3. How many a generation We destroyed before them, and they cried out when it was no longer the time for escape!

4. And they marvel that a warner from among themselves hath come unto them, and the disbelievers say: This is a wizard, a charlatan.

5. Maketh he the gods One God? Lo! that is an astounding thing.

6. The chiefs among them go about, exhorting: Go and be staunch to your gods! Lo! this is a thing designed.

7. We have not heard of this in later religion. This is naught but an invention.

8. Hath the reminder been revealed unto him (alone) among us? Nay, but they are in doubt concerning My reminder; nay but they have not yet tasted My doom.

9. Or are theirs the treasures of the mercy of thy Lord, the Mighty, the Bestower?

10. Or is the kingdom of the heavens and the earth and all that is between them theirs? Then let them ascend by ropes!

11. A defeated host are (all) the factions that are there.

12. The folk of Noah before them denied (their messenger) and (so did the tribe of) A'âd, and Pharaoh firmly planted,

13. And (the tribe of) Thamûd, and the folk of Lot, and the dwellers in the wood: these were the factions.

14. Not one of them but did deny the messengers, therefore My doom was justified.

15. These wait for but one Shout, there will be no second thereto.

16. They say: Our Lord! Hasten on for us our fate before the Day of Reckoning.

17. Bear with what they say, and remember our bondman David, lord of might. Lo! he was ever turning in repentance (toward Allah).

18. Lo! We subdued the hills to hymn the praises (of their Lord) with him at nightfall and sunrise,

19. And the birds assembled; all were turning unto Him.

20. We made his kingdom strong and gave him wisdom and decisive speech.

21. And hath the story of the litigants come unto thee? How they climbed the wall into the royal chamber;

22. How they burst in upon David; and he was afraid of them. They said: Be not afraid! (We are) two litigants, one of whom hath wronged the other, therefore judge aright between us; be not unjust; and show us the fair way.

23. Lo! this my brother hath ninety and nine ewes while I had one ewe; and he said: Entrust it to me, and he conquered

me in speech.

24. (David) said: He hath wronged thee in demanding thine ewe in addition to his ewes, and lo! many partners oppress one another, save such as believe and do good works, and they are few. And David guessed that We had tried him, and he sought forgiveness of his Lord, and he bowed himself and fell down prostrate and repented.

25. So We forgave him that; and lo! he had access to Our presence and a happy journey's end.

26. (And it was said unto him): O David! Lo! We have set thee as a viceroy in the earth; therefore judge aright between mankind, and follow not desire that it beguile thee from the way of Allah. Lo! those who wander from the way of Allah have an awful doom, forasmuch as they forgot the Day of Reckoning.

27. And We created not the heaven and the earth and all that is between them in vain. That is the opinion of those who disbelieve. And woe unto those who disbelieve, from the Fire!

28. Shall We treat those who believe and do good works as those who spread corruption in the earth; or shall We treat the pious as the wicked?

29. (This is) a Scripture that We have revealed unto thee, full of blessing, that they may ponder its revelations, and that men of understanding may reflect.

30. And We bestowed on David, Solomon. How excellent a slave! Lo! he was ever turning in repentance (toward Allah).

31. When there were shown to him at eventide light-footed coursers.

32. And he said: Lo! I have preferred the good things (of the world) to the remembrance of my Lord; till they were taken out of sight behind the curtain.

33. (Then he said): Bring them back to me, and fell to slashing (with his sword their) legs and necks.

34. And verily We tried Solomon, and set upon his throne a (mere) body. Then did he repent.

35. He said: My Lord! Forgive me and bestow on me sovereignty such as shall not belong to any after me. Lo! Thou art the Bestower.

36. So We made the wind subservient unto him, setting fair by his command whithersoever he intended.

37. And the unruly, every builder and diver (made We subservient),

38. And others linked together in chains,

39. (Saying): This is Our gift, so bestow thou, or withhold, without reckoning.

40. And lo! he hath favour with Us, and a happy journey's end.

41. And make mention (O Muhammad) of Our bondman Job, when he cried to his Lord (saying): Lo! the devil doth afflict me with distress and torment.

42. (And it was said unto him): Strike the ground with thy foot. This (spring) is a cool bath and a refreshing drink.

43. And We bestowed on him (again) his household and therewith the like thereof, a mercy from Us, and a memorial for men of understanding.

44. And (it was said unto him): Take in thine hand a branch and smite therewith, and break not thine oath. Lo! We found him steadfast, how excellent a slave! Lo! he was ever turning in repentance (to his Lord).

45. And make mention of Our bondmen, Abraham, Isaac and Jacob, men of parts and vision.

46. Lo! We purified them with a pure thought, remembrance of the Home (of the Hereafter).

47. Lo! in our sight they are verily of the elect, the excellent.

48. And make mention of Ishmael and Elisha and Dhû'I-Kifl. All are of the chosen.

49. This is a reminder. And lo! for those who ward off (evil) is a happy journey's end,

50. Gardens of Eden, whereof the gates are opened for them,

51. Wherein, reclining, they call for plenteous fruit and cool drink (that is) therein.

52. And with them are those of modest gaze, companions.

53. This it is that ye are promised for the Day of Reckoning.

54. Lo! this in truth is Our provision, which will never waste away.

55. This (is for the righteous). And lo! for the transgressors there will be an evil journey's end,

56. Hell, where they will burn, an evil resting place.

57. Here is a boiling and an ice-cold draught, so let them taste it,

58. And other (torment) of the kind in pairs (the two extremes)!

59. Here is an army rushing blindly with you. (Those who are already in the fire say): No word of welcome for them. Lo! they will roast at the Fire.

60. They say: Nay, but you (misleaders), for you there is no word of welcome. Ye prepared this for us (by your misleading). Now hapless is the plight.

61. They say: Our Lord! Whoever did prepare this for us, oh, give him double portion of the Fire!

62. And they say: What aileth us that we behold not men whom we were wont to count among the wicked?

63. Did we take them (wrongly) for a laughing-stock, or have our eyes missed them?

64. Lo! that is very truth: the wrangling of the dwellers in the Fire.

65. Say (unto them, O Muhammad): I am only a warner, and there is no God save Allah, the One, the Absolute,

66. Lord of the heavens and the earth and all that is between them, the Mighty, the Pardoning.

67. Say: It is tremendous tidings.

68. Whence ye turn away!

69. I had no knowledge of the Highest Chiefs when they disputed.

70. It is revealed unto me only that I may be a plain warner.

71. When thy Lord said unto the angels: lo! I am about to create a mortal out of mire,

72. And when I have fashioned him and breathed into him of My spirit, then fall down before him prostrate,

73. The angels fell down prostrate, every one.

74. Saving Iblîs; he was scornful and became one of the disbelivers.

75. He said: O Iblîs! What hindereth thee from falling prostrate before that which I have created with both my hands? Art thou too proud or art thou of the high exalted?

76. He said: I am better than him. Thou createdst me of fire, whilst him Thou didst create of clay.

77. He said: Go forth from hence, for lo! thou art outcast,

78. And lo! My curse is on thee till the Day of Judgement.

79. He said: My Lord! Reprieve me till the day when they are raised.

80. He said: Lo! thou art of those reprieved.

81. Until the day of the time appointed.

82. He said: Then, by Thy might, I surely will beguile them every one,

83. Save Thy single-minded slaves among them.

84. He said: The Truth is, and the Truth I speak,

85. That I shall fill hell with thee and with such of them as follow thee, together.

86. Say (O Muhammad, unto mankind): I ask of you no fee for this, and I am no impostor.

87. Lo! it is naught else than a reminder for all peoples

88. And ye will come in time to know the truth thereof.

SÛRAH 39

Az-Zumar, "The Troops", takes its name from a peculiar word, meaning troops or companies, which occurs in v. 71, and again in v. 73. Some authorities think that vv. 53 and 54 were revealed at Al-Madînah.

It seems manifestly to belong to the middle group of Meccan Sûrahs, though Nöldeke places it in his last group.

THE TROOPS

Revealed at Mecca

In the name of Allah, the Beneficent, the Merciful.

1. The revelation of the Scripture is from Allah, the Mighty, the Wise.

2. Lo! We have revealed the Scripture unto thee (Muhammad) with truth; so worship Allah, making religion pure for Him (only).

3. Surely pure religion is for Allah only. And those who choose protecting friends beside Him (say): We worship them only that they may bring us near unto Allah. Lo! Allah will judge between them concerning that wherein they differ. Lo! Allah guideth not him who is a liar, an ingrate.

4. If Allah had willed to choose a son, he could have chosen what he would of that which He hath created. Be He glorified! He is Allah, the One, the Absolute.

5. He hath created the heavens and the earth with truth. He maketh night to succeed day, and He maketh day to succeed night, and he constraineth the sun and the moon to give service, each running on for an appointed term. Is not He the Mighty, the Forgiver?

6. He created you from one being, then from that (being) He made its mate; and He hath provided for you of cattle eight kinds. He created you in the wombs of your mothers, creation after creation, in a threefold gloom. Such is Allah, your Lord. His is the Sovereignty. There is no God save Him. How then are ye turned away?

7. If ye are thankless, yet Allah is Independent of you, though He is not pleased with thanklessness for His bondmen; and if ye are thankful He is pleased therewith for you. No laden soul will bear another's load. Then unto your Lord is your return; and he will tell you what ye used to do. Lo! He knoweth what is in the breasts (of men).

8. And when some hurt toucheth man, he crieth unto his

312

Lord, turning unto Him (repentant). Then, when He granteth him a boon from Him he forgetteth that for which he cried unto Him before, and setteth up rivals to Allah that he may beguile (men) from His way. Say (O Muhammad, unto such an one): Take pleasure in thy disbelief a while. Lo! thou art of the owners of the Fire.

9. Is he who payeth adoration in the watches of the night, prostrate and standing, bewaring of the Hereafter and hoping for the mercy of his Lord, (to be accounted equal with a disbeliever)? Say (unto them, O Muhammad): Are those who know equal with those who know not? But only men of understanding will pay heed.

10. Say: O My Bondmen who believe! Observe your duty to your Lord. For those who do good in this world there is good, and Allah's earth is spacious. Verily the steadfast will be paid their wages without stint.

11. Say (O Muhammad): Lo! I am commanded to worship Allah, making religion pure for Him (only).

12. And I am commanded to be the first of those who surrender (unto Him).

13. Say: Lo! if I should disobey my Lord, I fear the doom of a tremendous Day.

14. Say: Allah I worship, making my religion pure for him (only).

15. Then worship what ye will beside Him. Say: The losers will be those who lose themselves and their housefolk on the Day of Resurrection. Ah, that will be the manifest loss!

16. They have an awning of fire above them and beneath them a dais (of fire). With this doth Allah appal His bondmen. O My bondmen, therefore fear Me!

17. And those who put away false gods lest they should worship them and turn to Allah in repentance, for them there are glad tidings. Therefore give good tidings (O Muhammad) to My bondmen.

18. Who hear advice and follow the best thereof. Such are those whom Allah guideth, and such are men of understanding.

19. Is he on whom the word of doom is fulfilled (to be helped), and canst thou (O Muhammad) rescue him who is in the Fire?

20. But those who keep their duty to their Lord, for them are lofty halls with lofty halls above them, built (for them), beneath which rivers flow. (It is) a promise of Allah. Allah faileth not His promise.

21. Hast thou not seen how Allah hath sent down water from the sky and hath caused it to penetrate the earth as water-

springs, and afterward thereby produceth crops of divers hues; and afterward they wither and thou seest them turn yellow; then He maketh them chaff. Lo! herein verily is a reminder for men of understanding.

22. Is he whose bosom Allah hath expanded for the Surrender (unto Him), so that he followeth a light from His Lord, (as he who disbelieved)? Then woe unto those whose hearts are hardened against remembrance of Allah. Such are in plain error.

23. Allah hath (now) revealed the fairest of statements, a Scripture consistent, (wherein promises of reward are) paired (with threats of punishment), whereat doth creep the flesh of those who fear their Lord, so that their flesh and their hearts soften to Allah's reminder. Such is Allah's guidance, wherewith he guideth whom He will. And him whom Allah sendeth astray, for him there is no guide.

24. Is he then, who will strike his face against the awful doom upon the Day of Resurrection (as he who doeth right)? And it will be said unto the wrong-doers: Taste what ye used to earn.

25. Those before them denied, and so the doom came on them whence they knew not.

26. Thus Allah made them taste humiliation in the life of the world, and verily the doom of the Hereafter will be greater if they did but know.

27. And verily We have coined for mankind in this Qur'ân all kinds of similitudes, that haply they may reflect;

28. A Lecture in Arabic, containing no crookedness, that haply they may ward off (evil).

29. Allah coineth a similitude: A man in relation to whom are several part-owners, quarrelling, and a man belonging wholly to one man. Are the two equal in similitude? Praise be to Allah! But most of them know not.

30. Lo! thou wilt die, and lo! they will die;

31. Then lo! on the Day of Resurrection, before your Lord ye will dispute.

32. And who doth greater wrong than he who telleth a lie against Allah, and denieth the truth when it reacheth him? Will not the home of disbelievers be in hell?

33. And whoso bringeth the truth and believeth therein- Such are the dutiful.

34. They shall have what they will of their Lord's bounty. That is the reward of the good:

35. That Allah will remit from them the worst of what they did, and will pay them for reward the best they used to do.

36. Will not Allah defend His slave? Yet they would frighten thee with those beside Him. He whom Allah sendeth astray, for him there is no guide.

37. And he whom Allah guideth, for him there can be no misleader. Is not Allah Mighty, Able to Requite (the wrong)?

38. And verily, if thou shouldst ask them: Who created the heavens and the earth? they will say: Allah. Say: Bethink you then of those ye worship beside Allah, if Allah willed some hurt for me, could they remove from me His hurt; or if He willed some mercy for me, could they restrain His mercy? Say: Allah is my all. In Him do (all) the trusting put their trust.

39. Say: O my people! Act in your manner. I too am acting. Thus ye will come to know

40. Who it is unto whom cometh a doom that will abase him, and on whom there falleth everlasting doom.

41. Lo! We have revealed unto thee (Muhammad) the Scripture for mankind with truth. Then whosoever goeth right it is for his soul, and whosoever strayeth, strayeth only to its hurt. And thou art not a warder over them.

42. Allah receiveth (men's) souls at the time of their death, and that (soul) which dieth not (yet) in its sleep. He keepeth that (soul) for which He hath ordained death and dismisseth the rest till an appointed term. Lo! herein verily are portents for people who take thought.

43. Or choose they intercessors other than Allah? Say: What! Even though they have power over nothing and have no intelligence?

44. Say: Unto Allah belongeth all intercession. His is the Sovereignty of the heavens and the earth. And afterward unto Him ye will be brought back.

45. And when Allah alone is mentioned, the hearts of those who believe not in the Hereafter are repelled, and when those (whom they worship) beside Him are mentioned, behold! they are glad.

46. Say: O Allah! Creator of the heavens and the earth! Knower of the Invisible and the Visible! Thou wilt judge between Thy slaves concerning that wherein they used to differ.

47. And though those who do wrong possess all that is in the earth, and therewith as much again, they verily will seek to ransom themselves therewith on the Day of Resurrection from the awful doom; and there will appear unto them, from their Lord, that wherewith they never reckoned.

48. And the evils that they earned will appear unto them, and that whereat they used to scoff will surround them.

49. Now when hurt toucheth a man he crieth unto Us, and

315

afterward when We have granted him a boon from Us, he saith; Only by force of knowledge I obtained it. Nay, but it is a test. But most of them know not.

50. Those before them said it, yet (all) that they had earned availed them not;

51. But the evils that they earned smote them; and such of these as do wrong, the evils that they earn will smite them; they cannot escape.

52. Know they not that Allah enlargeth providence for whom He will, and Straiteneth it (for whom He will). Lo! herein verily are portents for people who believe.

53. Say: O My slaves who have been prodigal to their own hurt! Despair not of the mercy of Allah, Who forgiveth all sins. Lo! He is the Forgiving, the Merciful.

54. Turn unto Him repentant, and surrender unto Him, before there come unto you the doom, when ye cannot be helped.

55. And follow the better (guidance) of that which is revealed unto you from Your Lord, before the doom cometh on you suddenly when ye know not,

56. Lest any soul should say: Alas, my grief that I was unmindful of Allah, and I was indeed among the scoffers!

57. Or should say: if Allah had but guided me I should have been among the dutiful!

58. Or should say, when it seeth the doom: Oh, that I had but a second chance that I might be among the righteous!

59. (But now the answer will be): Nay, for My revelations came unto thee, but thou didst deny them and wast scornful and wast among the disbelievers.

60. And on the Day of Resurrection thou (Muhammad) seest those who lied concerning Allah with their faces blackened. Is not the home of the scorners in hell?

61. And Allah delivereth those who ward off (evil) because of their deserts. Evil toucheth them not, nor do they grieve.

62. Allah is Creator of all things, and He is Guardian over all things.

63. His are the keys of the heavens and the earth, and they who disbelieve the revelations of Allah - such are they who are the losers.

64. Say (O Muhammad, to the disbelievers): Do ye bid me serve other than Allah? O ye fools!

65. And verily it hath been revealed unto thee as unto those before thee (saying): If thou ascribe a partner to Allah thy work will fail and thou indeed wilt be among the losers.

66. Nay, but Allah must thou serve, and be among the

thankful!

67. And they esteem not Allah as He hath the right to be esteemed, when the whole earth is His handful on the Day of Resurrection, and the heavens are rolled in His right hand. Glorified is He and High Exalted from all that they ascribe as partner (unto Him).

68. And the trumpet is blown, and all who are in the heavens and the earth swoon away, save him whom Allah willeth. Then it is blown a second time, and behold them standing waiting!

69. And the earth shineth with the light of her Lord, and the Book is set up, and the prophets and the witnesses are brought, and it is judged between them with truth, and they are not wronged.

70. And each soul is paid in full for what it did. And He is best aware of what they do.

71. And those who disbelieve are driven unto hell in troops till, when they reach it and the gates thereof are opened, and the warders thereof say unto them: Came there not unto you messengers of your own, reciting unto you the revelations of your Lord and warning you of the meeting of this your Day? They say: Yea, verily. But the word of doom for disbelievers is fulfilled.

72. It is said (unto them): Enter ye the gates of hell to dwell therein. Thus hapless is the journey's end of the scorners.

73. And those who keep their duty to their Lord are driven unto the Garden in troops till, when they reach it, and the gates thereof are opened, and the warders thereof say unto them: Peace be unto you! Ye are good, so enter ye (the Garden of delight), to dwell therein;

74. They say: Praise be to Allah, Who hath fulfilled His promise unto us and hath made us inherit the land, sojourning in the Garden where we will! So bounteous is the wage of workers.

75. And thou (O Muhammad) seest the angels thronging round the Throne, hymning the praises of their Lord. And they are judged aright. And it is said: Praise be to Allah, the Lord of the Worlds!

SÛRAH 40

Al-Mû'min, "The Believer", takes its name from vv. 24-45, which describe the attempt of a believer, in the house of Pharaoh, to dissuade his people from opposing Moses and Aaron. It is the first of seven sûrahs beginning with the Arabic letters Hâ, Mîm, all of which are sometimes referred to as Hâ, Mîm.

It belongs to the middle group of Meccan Sûrahs. Some authorities hold vv. 56 and 57 to have been revealed at Al-Madînah.

THE BELIEVER

Revealed at Mecca

In the name of Allah, the Beneficent, the Merciful.

1. Hâ. Mîm.

2. The revelation of the Scripture is from Allah, the Mighty, the Knower.

3. The Forgiver of sin, the Accepter of repentance, the Stern in punishment, the Bountiful. There is no God save Him. Unto Him is the journeying.

4. None argue concerning the revelations of Allah save those who disbelieve, so let not their turn of fortune in the land deceive thee (O Muhammad).

5. The folk of Noah and the factions after them denied (their messengers) before these, and every nation purposed to seize their messenger and argued falsely, (thinking) thereby to refute the Truth. Then I seized them, and how (awful) was My punishment.

6. Thus was the word of thy Lord concerning those who disbelieve fulfilled: that they are owners of the fire.

7. Those who bear the Throne, and all who are round above it, hymn the praises of their Lord and believe in Him and ask forgiveness for those who believe (saying): Our Lord! Thou comprehendest all things in mercy and knowledge, therefore forgive those who repent and follow Thy way. Ward off from them the punishment of hell.

8. Our Lord! And make them enter the Gardens of Eden which thou hast promised them, with such of their fathers and their wives and descendants as do right. Lo! Thou, only Thou, art the Mighty, the Wise.

9. And ward off from them ill deeds; and he from whom thou wardest off ill deeds that day, him verily hast Thou taken into mercy. That is the supreme triumph.

10. Lo! (On that day) those who disbelieve are informed by proclamation: Verily Allah's abhorrence is more terrible than your abhorrence one of another, when ye were called unto the faith but did refuse.

11. They say: Our Lord! Twice hast Thou made us die, and twice hast Thou made us live. Now we confess our sins is there any way to go out?

12. (It is said unto them): This is (your plight) because,

when Allah only was invoked, ye disbelieved, but when some partner was ascribed to Him ye were believing. But the command belongeth only to Allah, the Sublime, the Majestic.

13. He it is Who showeth you His portents, and sendeth down for you provision from the sky. None payeth heed save him who turneth (unto Him) repentant.

14. Therefore (O believers) pray unto Allah, making religion pure for Him (only), however much the disbelievers be averse.

15. The Exalter of ranks, the Lord of the Throne. He casteth the Spirit of His command upon whom He will of His slaves, that He may warn of the Day of Meeting;

16. The day when they come forth, nothing of them being hidden from Allah. Whose is the sovereignty this day? It is Allah's, the One, the Almighty.

17. This day is each soul requited that which it hath earned; no wrong (is done) this day. Lo! Allah, is swift at reckoning.

18. Warn them (O Muhammad) of the Day of the approaching (doom), when the hearts will be choking the throats, (when) there will be no friend for the wrong-doers, nor any intercessor who will be heard.

19. He knoweth the traitor of the eyes, and that which the bosoms hide.

20. Allah judgeth with truth, while those to whom they cry instead of Him judge not at all. Lo! Allah, He is the Hearer, the Seer.

21. Have they not travelled in the land to see the nature of the consequence for those who disbelieved before them? They were mightier than these in power and (in the) traces (which they left behind them) in the earth. Yet Allah seized them for their sins, and they had no protector from Allah.

22. That was because their messengers kept bringing them clear proofs (of Allah's Sovereignty) but they disbelieved; so Allah seized them. Lo! He is Strong, Severe in punishment.

23. And verily We sent Moses with Our revelations and a clear warrant

24. Unto Pharaoh and Hâmân and Korah, but they said: A lying sorcerer!

25. And when he brought them the Truth from Our presence, they said: Slay the sons of those who believe with him, and spare their women. But the plot of disbelievers is in naught but error.

26. And Pharaoh said: Suffer me to kill Moses, and let him cry unto his Lord. Lo! I fear that he will alter your religion or that he will cause confusion in the land.

27. Moses said: Lo! I seek refuge in my Lord and your Lord from every scorner who believeth not in a Day of Reckoning.

28. And a believing man of Pharaoh's family, who hid his faith, said: Would ye kill a man because he saith: My Lord is Allah, and hath brought you clear proofs from your Lord? If he is lying, then his lie is upon him; and if he is truthful, then some of that wherewith he threateneth you will strike you. Lo! Allah guideth not one who is a prodigal, a liar.

29. O my people! Yours is the kingdom to-day, ye being upper-most in the land. But who would save us from the wrath of Allah should it reach us? Pharaoh said: I do but show you what I think, and I do but guide you to wise policy.

30. And he who believed said: O my people! Lo! I fear for you a fate like that of the factions (of old);

31. A plight like that of Noah's folk, and A'âd and Thamûd, and those after them, and Allah willeth no injustice for (His) slaves.

32. And, O my people! Lo! I fear for a Day of Summoning.

33. A day when ye will turn to flee, having no preserver from Allah: and he whom Allah sendeth astray, for him there is no guide.

34. And verily Joseph brought you of old clear proofs, yet ye ceased not to be in doubt concerning what he brought you till, when he died, he said: Allah will not send any messenger after him. Thus Allah deceiveth him who is a prodigal, a doubter.

35. Those who wrangle concerning the revelations of Allah without any warrant that hath come unto them, it is greatly hateful in the sight of Allah and in the sight of those who believe. Thus doth Allah print on every arrogant, disdainful heart.

36. And Pharaoh said: O Hâmân! Build for me a tower that haply I may reach the roads.

37. The roads of the heavens, and may look upon the God of Moses, though verily I think him a liar. Thus was the evil that he did made fair-seeming unto Pharaoh, and he was debarred from the (right) way. The plot of Pharaoh ended but in ruin.

38. And he who believed said: O my people! Follow me. I will show you the way of right conduct.

39. O my people! Lo! this life of the world is but a passing comfort, and lo! the Hereafter, that is the enduring home.

40. Whoso doeth in ill-deed, he will be repaid the like thereof, while whoso doeth right, whether male of female, and is a believer, (all) such will enter the Garden, where they

will be nourished without stint.

41. And, O my people! What aileth me that I call you unto deliverance when ye call me unto the Fire?

42. Ye call me to disbelieve in Allah and ascribe unto him as partners that whereof I have no knowledge, while I call you unto the Mighty, the Forgiver.

43. Assuredly that whereunto ye call me hath no claim in the world or in the Hereafter, and our return will be unto Allah, and the prodigals will be owners of the fire.

44. And Ye will remember what I say unto you. I confide my cause unto Allah. Lo! Allah is Seer of (His) slaves.

45. So Allah warded off from him the evils which they plotted, while a dreadful doom encompassed Pharaoh's folk.

46. The Fire; they are exposed to it morning and evening; and on the day when the hour upriseth (it is said): Cause Pharaoh's folk to enter the most awful doom.

47. And when they wrangle in the fire, the weak say unto those who were proud: Lo! we were a following unto you: will ye therefore rid us of a portion of the Fire?

48. Those who were proud say: Lo! we are all (together) herein. Lo! Allah hath judged between (His) slaves.

49. And those in the Fire say unto the guards of hell: Entreat your Lord that He relieve us of a day of the torment.

50. They say: Came not your messengers unto you with clear proofs? They say: Yea, verily. They say: Then do ye pray, although the prayer of disbelievers is in vain.

51. Lo! We verily do help Our messengers, and those who believe, in the life of the world and on the day when the witnesses arise,

52. The day when their excuse availeth not the evil-doers, and theirs is the curse, and theirs the ill abode.

53. And We verily gave Moses the guidance, and We caused the Children of Israel to inherit the Scripture,

54. A guide and a reminder for men of understanding.

55. Then have patience (O Muhammad). Lo! the promise of Allah is true. And ask forgiveness of thy sin, and hymn the praise of the Lord at fall of night and in the early hours.

56. Lo! those who wrangle concerning the revelations of Allah without a warrant having come unto them, there is naught else in their breasts save pride which they will never attain. So take thou refuge in Allah. Lo! He, only He, is the Hearer, the Seer.

57. Assuredly the creation of the heavens and the earth is

greater than the creation of mankind; but most of mankind know not.

58. And the blind man and the seer are not equal, neither are those who believe and do good works (equal with) the evil-doer. Little do ye reflect!

59. Lo! the Hour is surely coming, there is no doubt thereof; yet most of mankind believe not.

60. And your Lord hath said: Pray unto me and I will hear your prayer. Lo! those who scorn My service, they will enter hell, disgraced.

61. Allah it is Who hath appointed for you night that ye may rest therein, and day for seeing. Lo! Allah is a Lord of bounty for mankind, yet most of mankind give not thanks.

62. Such is Allah, your Lord, the Creator of all things. There is no God save Him. How then are ye perverted?

63. Thus are they preverted who deny the revelations of Allah.

64. Allah it is Who appointed for you the earth for a dwelling place and the sky for a canopy, and fashioned you and perfected your shapes, and hath provided you with good things. Such is Allah, your Lord. Then blessed be Allah, the Lord of the Worlds!

65. He is the Living One. There is no God save Him. So pray unto him, making religion pure for Him (only). Praise be to Allah, the Lord of the Worlds!

66. Say (O Muhammad): I am forbidden to worship those unto whom ye cry beside Allah since there have come unto me clear proofs from my Lord, and I am commanded to surrender to the Lord of the Worlds.

67. He it is Who created you from dust, then from a drop (of seed) then from a clot, then bringeth you forth as a child, then (ordaineth) that ye attain full strength and afterward that ye become old men - though some among you die before - and that ye reach an appointed term, that haply ye may understand.

68. He it is Who quickeneth and giveth death. When He ordaineth a thing, he saith unto it only: Be! and it is.

69. Hast thou not seen those who wrangle concerning the revelations of Allah, how they are turned away?

70. Those who deny the Scripture and that wherewith We send Our messengers. But they will come to know.

71. When carcans are about their necks and chains. They are dragged.

72. Through boiling waters; then they are thrust into the Fire.

73. Then it is said unto them: Where are (all) that ye used to make partners (in the Sovereignty)

74. Beside Allah? They say: They have failed us; but we used not to pray to anything before. Thus doth Allah send astray the disbelievers (in His guidance).

75. (And it is said unto them): This is because ye exulted in the earth without right, and because ye were petulant.

76. Enter ye the gates of hell to dwell therein. Evil is the habitation of the scornful.

77. Then have patience (O Muhammad). Lo! the promise of Allah is true. And whether We left thee see a part of that which We promise them, or (whether) We cause thee to die, still unto us they will be brought back;

78. Verily We sent messengers before thee, among them those of whom We have told thee, and some of whom We have not told thee; and it was not given to any messenger that he should bring a portent save by Allah's leave, but when Allah's commandment cometh (the cause) is judged aright, and the followers of vanity will then be lost.

79. Allah it is Who hath appointed for you cattle, they ye may ride on some of them, and eat of some -

80. (Many) benefits ye have from them - and that ye may satisfy by their means a need that is in your breasts, and may be borne upon them as upon the ship.

81. And He showeth you His tokens. Which, then, of the tokens of Allah do ye deny?

82. Have they not travelled in the land to see the nature of the consequence for those before them? They were more numerous than these, and mightier in power and (in the) traces (which they left behind them) in the earth. But all that they used to earn availed them not.

83. And when their messengers brought them clear proofs (of Allah's Sovereignty) they exulted in the knowledge they (themselves) possessed. And that which they were wont to mock befell them.

84. Then, when they saw Our doom, they said: We believe in Allah only and reject (all) that we used to associate (with Him).

85. But their faith could not avail them when they saw Our doom. This is Allah's law which hath ever taken course for his Bondsmen. And then the disbelievers will be ruined.

SÛRAH 41

Fusilat, "They Are Expounded", derives its title from a word in v. 2. It is also often called Hâ, Mîm, As-Sajdah, from a word in v. 37, Hâ Mîm being added to distinguish it from Sûrah 32, which is called As-Sajdah.

It belongs to the middle group of Meccan Sûrahs.

FUSILAT ("THEY ARE EXPOUNDED")

Revealed at Mecca

In the name of Allah, the Beneficent, the Merciful.

1. Hâ. Mîm.

2. A revelation from the Beneficent, the Merciful.

3. A Scripture whereof the verses are expounded, a Lecture in Arabic for people who have knowledge.

4. Good tidings and a warning. But most of them turn away so that they hear not.

5. And they say: Our hearts are protected from that unto which thou (O Muhammad) callest us, and in our ears there is a deafness, and between us and thee there is a veil. Act, then. Lo! we also shall be acting.

6. Say (unto them O Muhammad): I am only a mortal like you. It is inspired in me that your God is One God, therefore take the straight path unto Him and seek forgiveness of Him. And woe unto the idolaters.

7. Who give not the poor-due, and who are disbelievers in the Hereafter.

8. Lo! as for those who believe and do good works, for them is a reward enduring.

9. Say (O Muhammad, unto the idolaters): Disbelieve ye verily in Him Who created the earth in two Days, and ascribe ye unto Him rivals? He (and none else) is the Lord of the Worlds.

10. He placed therein firm hills rising above it, and blessed it and measured therein its sustenance in four Days, alike for (all) who asks;

11. Then turned He to the heaven when it was smoke, and said unto it and unto the earth: Come both of you, willingly or loth. They said: We come, obedient.

12. Then He ordained them seven heavens in two Days and inspired in each heaven its mandate; and we decked the nether heaven with lamps, and rendered it inviolable. That is the measuring of the Mighty, the Knower.

13. But if they turn away, then say: I warn you of a thunderbolt like the thunderbolt (which fell of old upon the tribes) of A'âd and Thamûd;

14. When their messengers came unto them from before them and behind them, saying: Worship none but Allah! they said: If our Lord had willed, He surely would have sent down angels (unto us), so lo! we are disbelievers in that wherewith

ye have been sent.

15. As for A'âd, they were arrogant in the land without right, and they said: Who is mightier than us in power? Could they not see that Allah Who created them, He was mightier than them in power? And they denied Our revelations.

16. Therefore We let loose on them a raging wind in evil days, that We might make them taste the torment of disgrace in the life of the world. And verily the doom of the Hereafter will be more shameful, and they will not be helped.

17. And as for Thamûd, We gave them guidance, but they preferred blindness to the guidance, so the bolt of the doom of humiliation overtook them because of what they used to earn.

18. And We delivered those who believed and used to keep their duty to Allah.

19. And (make mention of) the day when the enemies of Allah are gathered unto the Fire, they are driven on.

20. Till, when they reach it, their ears and their eyes and their skins testify against them as to what they used to do.

21. And they say unto their skins: Why testify ye against us? They say: Allah hath given us speech Who giveth speech to all things, and Who created you at the first, and unto Whom ye are returned.

22. Ye did not hide yourselves lest your ears and your eyes and your skins should testify against you, but ye demand that Allah knew not much of what ye did.

23. That, your thought which ye did think about your Lord, hath ruined you; and ye find yourselves (this day) among the lost.

24. And though they are resigned, yet the Fire is still their home; and if they ask for favour, yet they are not of those unto whom favour can be shown.

25. And We assigned them comrades (in the world), who made their present and their past fair-seeming unto them. And the Word concerning nations of the jinn and humankind who passed away before them hath effect for them. Verily they are the losers.

26. Those who disbelieve say: Heed not this Qur'ân, and drown the hearing of it; haply ye may conquer.

27. But verily We shall cause those who disbelieve to taste an awful doom, and verily We shall requite them the worst of what they used to do.

28. That is the reward of Allah's enemies: the Fire. Therein

is their immortal home, payment for asmuch as they denied Our revelations.

29. And those who disbelieve will say: Our Lord! Show us those who beguiled us of the jinn and humankind. We will place them underneath our feet that they may be among the nethermost.

30. Lo! those who say: Our Lord is Allah, and afterward are upright, the angels descent upon them, saying: Fear not nor grieve, but hear good tidings of the paradise which ye are promised.

31. We are your protecting friends in the life of the world and in the Hereafter. There ye will have (all) that your souls desire, and there ye will have (all) for which ye pray.

32. A gift of welcome from the Forgiving, the Merciful.

33. And who is better in speech than him who prayeth unto his Lord and doeth right, and saith: Lo! I am of those who surrender (unto Him).

34. The good deed and the evil deed are not alike. Repel the evil deed with one which is better, then lo! he, between whom and thee there was enmity (will become) as though he was a bosom friend.

35. But none is granted it save those who are steadfast, and none is granted it save the owner of great happiness.

36. And if a whisper from the devil reach thee (O Muhammad) then seek refuge in Allah. Lo! He is the Hearer, the Knower.

37. And of His portents are the night and the day and the sun and the moon. Adore not the sun nor the moon; but adore Allah who created them, if it is in truth Him whom ye worship.

38. But if they are too proud - still those who are with thy Lord glorify Him night and day, and tire not.

39. And of His portents (is this): that thou seest the earth lowly, but when We send down water thereon it thrilleth and groweth. Lo! He Who quickeneth it is verily the Quickener of the dead. Lo! He is Able to do all things.

40. Lo! Those who distort Our revelations are not hid from Us. Is he who is hurled into the Fire better, or he who cometh secure on the Day of Resurrection? Do what ye will. Lo! He is Seer of what ye do.

41. Lo! those who disbelieve in the Reminder when it cometh unto them (are guilty), for lo! it is an unassailable Scripture.

42. Falsehood cannot come at it from before it or behind it. (It is) a revelation from the Wise, the Owner of Praise.

43. Naught is said unto thee (Muhammad) save what was said unto the messengers before thee. Lo! thy Lord is owner

of forgiveness, and owner (also) of dire punishment.

44. And if We had appointed it a Lecture in a foreign tongue they would assuredly have said: If only its verses were expounded (so that we might understand)? What! A foreign tongue and an Arab? - Say unto them (O Muhammad): For those who believe it is a guidance and a healing; and as for those who disbelieve, there is a deafness in their ears, and it is blindness for them. Such are called to from afar.

45. And We verily gave Moses the Scripture, but there hath been dispute concerning it; and but for a Word that had already gone forth from thy Lord, it would ere now have been judged between them; but lo! they are in hopeless doubt concerning it.

46. Whoso doeth right it is for his soul, and who doeth wrong it is against it. And thy Lord is not at all a tyrant to His slaves.

47. Unto Him is referred (all) knowledge of the Hour. And no fruits burst forth from their sheaths, and no female carrieth or bringeth forth but with His knowledge. And on the day when he calleth unto them: Where are now My partners? they will say: We confess unto Thee, not one of us is a witness (for them).

48. And those to whom they used to cry of old have failed them, and they perceive they have no place of refuge.

49. Man tireth not of praying for good, and if ill toucheth him, then he is disheartened, desperate.

50. And verily, if We cause him to taste mercy after some hurt that hath touched him, he will say: This is my own; and I deem not that the Hour will ever rise, and if I am brought back to my Lord, I surely shall be better off with Him - But We verily shall tell those who disbelieve (all) that they did, and We verily shall make them taste hard punishment.

51. When We show favour unto man, he withdraweth and turneth aside, but when ill toucheth him then he aboundeth in prayer.

52. Bethink you: if it is from Allah and ye reject it - Who is further astray than one who is at open feud (with Allah)?

53. We shall show them Our portents on the horizons and within themselves until it will be manifest unto them that it is the Truth. Doth not thy Lord suffice, since He is Witness over all things?

54. How! Are they still in doubt about the meeting with their Lord? Lo! Is not He surrounding all things?

SÛRAH 42

Ash-Shûrâ "Counsel", takes its name from a word in v. 38.

It belongs to the middle group of Meccan Sûrahs.

COUNSEL

Revealed at Mecca

In the name of Allah, the Beneficent, the Merciful.

1. Hâ. Mîm.

2. A'în. Sîn. Qâf.

3. Thus Allah the Mighty, the Knower inspireth thee (Muhammad) as (He inspired) those before thee.

4. Unto Him belongeth all that is in the heavens and all that is in the earth, and He is the Sublime, the Tremendous.

5. Almost might the heavens above be rent asunder while the angels hymn the praise of their Lord and ask forgiveness for those on the earth. Lo! Allah is the Forgiver, the Merciful.

6. And as for those who choose protecting friends beside Him, Allah is Warden over them, and thou art in no wise a guardian over them.

7. And thus We have inspired in thee a Lecture in Arabic, that thou mayest warn the mother-town and those around it, and mayest warn of a day of assembling whereof there is no doubt. A host will be in the Garden, and a host of them in the Flame.

8. Had Allah willed, He could have made them one community, but Allah bringeth whom He will into His mercy. And the wrong-doers have no friend nor helper.

9. Or have they chosen protecting friends besides Him? But Allah, He (alone) is the Protecting Friend. He quickeneth the dead, and He is Able to do all things.

10. And in whatsoever ye differ, the verdict therein belongeth to Allah. Such is my Lord, in Whom I put my trust, and unto Whom I turn.

11. The Creator of the heavens and the earth. He hath made you pairs of yourselves, and of the cattle also pairs, whereby He multiplieth you. Naught is as His likeness; and He is the Hearer, the Seer.

12. His are the keys of the heavens and the earth. He enlargeth providence for whom He will and straiteneth (it for whom He will). Lo! He is Knower of all things.

13. He hath ordained for you that religion which He commended unto Noah, and that which We inspire in thee (Muhammad), and that which We commended unto Abraham and Moses and Jesus, saying: Establish the religion, and be not divided therein. Dreadful for the idolaters is that unto which thou callest them. Allah chooseth for Himself whom He will,

and guideth unto himself him who turneth (toward Him).

14. And they were not divided until after the knowledge came unto them, through rivalry among themselves; and had it not been for a Word that had already gone forth from thy Lord for an appointed term, it surely had been judged between them. And those who were made to inherit the Scripture after them are verily in hopeless doubt concerning it.

15. Unto this, then, summon (O Muhammad). And be thou upright as thou art commanded, and follow not their lusts, but say: I believe in whatever Scripture Allah hath sent down, and I am commanded to be just among you. Allah is our Lord and your Lord. Unto us our works and unto you your works; no argument between us and you. Allah will bring us together, and unto Him is the journeying.

16. And those who argue concerning Allah after He hath been acknowledged, their argument hath no weight with their Lord, and wrath is upon them and theirs will be an awful doom.

17. Allah it is Who hath revealed the Scripture with truth, and the Balance. How canst thou know? It may be that the Hour is nigh.

18. Those who believe not therein seek to hasten it; while those who believe are fearful of it and know that it is the Truth. Are not they who dispute, in doubt concerning the Hour, far astray?

19. Allah is gracious unto His slaves. He provideth for whom He will. And He is the Strong, the Mighty.

20. Whoso desireth the harvest of the Hereafter, We give him increase in its harvest. And Whoso desireth the harvest of the world, We give him thereof, and he hath no portion in the Hereafter.

21. Or have they partners (of Allah) who have made lawful for them in religion that which Allah allowed not? And but for a decisive word (gone forth already), it would have been judged between them. Lo! for wrong-doers is a painful doom.

22. Thou seest the wrong-doers fearful of that which they have earned, and it will surely befall them; while those who believe and do good works (will be) in flowering meadows of the Gardens, having what they wish from their Lord. This is the great preferment.

23. This it is which Allah announceth unto His bondmen who believe and do good works. Say (O Muhammad, unto mankind): I ask of you no fee therefore, save loving kindness among kinsfolk. And whoso scoreth a good deed We add unto its good for him. Lo! Allah is forgiving, Responsive.

24. Or say they: He hath invented a lie concerning Allah? If Allah willed, he could have sealed thy heart (against them). And Allah will wipe out the lie and will vindicate the truth by His words. Lo! He is aware of what is hidden in the breasts (of men).

25. And He it is Who accepteth repentance from his bondmen, and pardoneth the evil deeds, and knoweth what ye do.

26. And accepteth those who do good works, and giveth increase unto them of His bounty. And as for disbelivers, theirs will be an awful doom.

27. And if Allah were to enlarge the provision for His slaves they would surely rebel in the earth, but He sendeth down by measure as he willeth. Lo! He is Informed, a Seer of His bondmen.

28. And He it is Who sendeth down the saving rain after they have despaired, and spreadeth out His mercy. He is the Protecting Friend, the Praiseworthy.

29. And of His portents is the creation of the heaven and the earth, and of whatever beasts He hath dispersed therein. And He is Able to gather them when He will.

30. Whatever of misfortune striketh you, it is what your right hands have earned. And He forgiveth much.

31. Ye cannot escape in the earth, for beside Allah ye have no protecting friend nor any helper.

32. And of his portents are the ships, like banners on the sea;

33. If He will He calmeth the wind so that they keep still upon its surface - Lo! herein verily are signs for every steadfast grateful (heart) -

34. Or he causeth them to perish on account of that which they have earned - And He forgiveth much -

35. And that those who argue concerning Our revelations may know they have no refuge.

36. Now whatever ye have been given is but a passing comfort for the life of the world, and that which Allah hath is better and more lasting for those who believe and put their trust in their Lord.

37. And those who shun the worst of sins and indecencies and, when they are wroth, forgive.

38. And those who answer the call of their Lord and establish worship, and whose affairs are a matter of counsel, and who spend of what We have bestowed on them.

39. And those who, when great wrong is done to them, defend themselves.

40. The guerdon of an ill-deed is an ill the like thereof. But

whosoever pardoneth and amendeth, his wage is the affair of Allah. Lo! He loveth no wrong-doers.

41. And whoso defendeth himself after he hath suffered wrong - for such, there is no way (of blame) against them.

42. The way (of blame) is only against those who oppress mankind, and wrongfully rebel in the earth. For such there is a painful doom.

43. And verily whoso is patient and forgiveth - lo! that, verily, is (of) the steadfast heart of things.

44. He whom Allah sendeth astray, for him there is no protecting friend after Him. And thou (Muhammad) wilt see the evil-doers when they see the doom, (how) they say: Is there any way of return?

45. And thou wilt see them exposed to (the Fire), made humble by disgrace, and looking with veiled eyes. And those who believe will say: Lo! the (eternal) losers are they who lose themselves and their housefolk on the Day of Resurrection. Lo! are not the wrong-doers in perpetual torment?

46. And they will have no protecting friends to help them instead of Allah. He whom Allah sendeth astray, for him there is no road.

47. Answer the call of your Lord before there cometh unto you from Allah a Day which there is no averting. Ye have no refuge on that Day, nor have ye any (power of) refusal.

48. But if they are averse, We have not sent thee as a warder over them. Thine is only to convey (the message). And lo! when We cause man to taste of mercy from us he exulteth therefore. And if some evil striketh them because of that which their own hands have sent before, then lo! man is an ingrate.

49. Unto Allah belongeth the sovereignty of the heavens and the earth. He createth what He will. He bestoweth female (offspring) upon whom He will, and bestoweth male (offspring) upon whom He will;

50. Or He mingleth them, males and females, and He maketh barren whom He will. Lo! He is Knower, Powerful.

51. And it was not (vouchsafed) to any mortal that Allah should speak to him unless (it be) by revelation or from behind a veil, or (that) He sendeth a messenger to reveal what He will by His leave. Lo! He is Exalted, Wise.

52. And thus have We inspired in thee (Muhammad) a Spirit of Our command. Thou knewest not what the Scripture was, nor what the Faith. But We have made it a light whereby We guide whom We will of Our bondmen. And lo! thou verily dost guide unto a right path.

53. The path of Allah, unto Whom belongeth whatsoever is

in the heavens and whatsoever is in the earth. Do not all things reach Allah at last?

SÛRAH 43

Az-Zukhruf, "Ornaments of Gold", is the fourth of the Hâ Mîm Sûrahs. It takes its name from a word meaning golden ornaments which occurs in v. 35.

It belongs to the middle group of Meccan Sûrahs.

ORNAMENTS OF GOLD

Revealed at Mecca

In the name of Allah, the Beneficent, the Merciful.

1. Hâ Mîm.

2. By the Scripture which maketh plain.

3. Lo! We have appointed it a Lecture in Arabic that haply ye may understand.

4. And Lo! in the Source of Decrees, which We possess, it is indeed sublime, decisive,

5. Shall We utterly ignore you because ye are a wanton folk?

6. How many a prophet did We send among the men of old!

7. And never came there unto them a prophet but they used to mock him.

8. Then we destroyed men mightier than these in prowess; and the example of the men of old hath gone (before them).

9. And if thou (Muhammad) ask them: Who created the heavens and the earth, they will surely answer: The Mighty, the Knower created them;

10. Who made the earth a resting-place for you, and placed roads for you therein, that haply ye may find your way;

11. And who sendeth down water from the sky in (due) measure, and We revive a dead land therewith. Even so will ye be brought forth;

12. He Who created all the pairs, and appointed for you ships and cattle whereupon ye ride.

13. That ye may mount upon their backs, and may remember your Lord's favour when ye mount thereon, and may say: Glorified be He Who hath subdued these unto us, and we were not capable (of subduing them);

14. And lo! unto our Lord we are returning.

15. And they allot to Him a portion of His bondmen! Lo! man is verily a mere ingrate.

16. Or chooseth He daughters of all that He hath created, and honoureth He you with sons?

17. And if one of them hath tidings of that which he likeneth to the Beneficent One, his countenance becometh black and he is full of inward rage.

18. (Liken they then to Allah) that which is bred up in outward show, and in dispute cannot make itself plain?

19. And they make the angels, who are the slaves of the Beneficent, females. Did they witness their creation? Their testimony will be recorded and they will be questioned.

20. And they say: If the Beneficent One had (so) willed, we should not have worshipped them. They have no knowledge whatsoever of that. They do but guess.

21. Or have We given them any Scripture before (this Qur'ân) so that they are holding fast thereto?

22. Nay, for they say only: Lo! we found our fathers following a religion, and we are guided by their footprints.

23. And even so We sent not a warner before thee (Muhammad) into any township but its luxurious ones said: Lo! we found our fathers following a religion, and we are following their footprints.

24. (And the warner) said: What! Even though I bring you better guidance than that ye found your fathers following? They answered: Lo! in what ye bring we are disbelievers.

25. So We requited them. Then see the nature of the consequence for the rejecters!

26. And when Abraham said unto his father and his folk: Lo! I am innocent of what ye worship

27. Save Him Who did create me, for He will surely guide me.

28. And he made it a word enduring among his seed, that haply they might return.

29. Nay, but I let these and their fathers enjoy life (only) till there should come unto them the Truth and a messenger making plain.

30. And now that the Truth hath come unto them they say: This is mere magic, and lo! we are disbelievers therein.

31. And they say: If only this Qur'ân had been revealed to some great man of the two towns?

32. Is it they who apportion their Lord's mercy? We have apportioned among them their livelihood in the life of the world, and raised some of them above others in rank that some of them may take labour from others; and the mercy of thy Lord is better than (the wealth) that they amass.

33. And were is not that mankind would have become one community, We might well have appointed, for those who

disbelieve in the Beneficent, roofs of silver for their houses and stairs (of silver) whereby to mount.

34. And for their houses doors (of silver) and couches of silver whereon to recline,

35. And ornaments of gold. Yet all that would have been but a provision of the life of the world. And the Hereafter with your Lord would have been for those who keep from evil.

36. And he whose sight is dim to the remembrance of the Beneficent, We assign unto him a devil who becometh his comrade;

37. And lo! they surely turn them from the way of Allah, and yet they deem that they are rightly guided;

38. Till, when he cometh unto Us, he saith (unto his comrade): Ah, would that between me and thee there were the distance of the two horizons - an evil comrade!

39. And it profiteth you not this day, because ye did wrong, that ye will be sharers in the doom.

40. Canst thou (Muhammad) make the deaf to hear, or canst thou guide the blind or him who is in error manifest?

41. And if We take thee away, We surely shall take vengeance on them.

42. Or (if) We show thee that wherewith We threaten them; for lo! We have complete command of them.

43. So hold thou fast to that which is inspired in thee. Lo! thou art on a right path.

44. And lo! it is in truth a Reminder for thee and for thy folk; and ye will be questioned.

45. And ask those of Our messengers whom We sent before thee: Did We ever appoint gods to be worshipped beside the Beneficent?

46. And verily We sent Moses with Our revelations unto Pharaoh and his chiefs, and he said: I am a messenger of the Lord of the Worlds.

47. But when he brought them Our tokens, behold! they laughed at them.

48. And every token that We showed them was greater than its sister (token), and We grasped them with the torment, that haply they might turn again.

49. And they said: O wizard! Entreat thy Lord for us by the pact that He hath made with thee. Lo! we verily will walk aright.

50. But when We eased them of the torment, behold! they broke their word.

51. And Pharaoh caused a proclamation to be made among his people saying: O my people! Is not mine the sovereignty of Egypt and these rivers flowing under me? Can ye not then discern?

52. I am surely better than this fellow, who is despicable, and can hardly make (his meaning) plain!

53. Why, then, have armlets of gold not been set upon him, or angels sent along with him?

54. Thus he persuaded his people to make light (of Moses) and they obeyed him. Lo! they were a wanton folk.

55. So, when they angered Us, We punished them and drowned them every one.

56. And We made them a thing past, and an example for those after (them).

57. And when the son of Mary is quoted as an example, behold! the folk laugh out,

58. And say: Are our gods better, or is He? They raise not the objection save for argument. Nay! but they are contentious folk.

59. He is nothing but a slave on whom We bestowed favour, and We made him a pattern for the Children of Israel.

60. And had We willed We could have set among you angels to be viceroys in the earth.

61. And lo! verily there is knowledge of the Hour. So doubt ye not concerning it, but follow Me. This is the right path.

62. And let not Satan turn you aside. Lo! he is an open enemy for you.

63. When Jesus came with clear proofs (of Allah's sovereignty), he said: I have come unto you with wisdom, and to make plain some of that concerning which ye differ. So keep your duty to Allah, and obey me.

64. Lo! Allah, He is my Lord and your Lord. So worship Him. This is a right path.

65. But the factions among them differed. Then woe unto those who do wrong from the doom of a painful day.

66. Await they aught save the Hour, that it shall come upon them suddenly, when they know not?

67. Friends on that day will be foes one to another, save those who kept their duty (to Allah).

68. O My slaves! For you there is no fear this day, nor is it ye who grieve;

69. (Ye) who believed Our revelations and were self-surrendered,

70. Enter the Garden, ye and your wives, to be made glad.

71. Therein are brought round for them trays of gold and

goblets, and therein is all that souls desire and eyes find
sweet. And ye are immortal therein.

72. This is the Garden which ye are made to inherit because
of what ye used to do.

73. Therein for you is fruit in plenty whence to eat.

74. Lo! the guilty are immortal in hell's torment.

75. It is not relaxed for them, and they despair therein.

76. We wronged them not, but they it was who did the
wrong.

77. And they cry: O master! Let thy Lord make an end of
us. He saith: Lo! here ye must remain.

78. We verily brought the Truth unto you, but ye were, most
of you, averse to the Truth.

79. Or do they determine any thing (against the Prophet)?
Lo! We (also) are determining.

80. Or deem they that We cannot hear their secret thoughts
and private confidences? Nay, but Our envoys, present with
them, do record.

81. Say (O Muhammad): The Beneficent One hath no son.
I am first among the worshippers.

82. Glorified by the Lord of the heavens and the earth, the
Lord of the Throne, from that which they ascribe (unto Him)!

83. So let them flounder (in their talk) and play until they
meet the Day which they are promised.

84. And He it is Who in the heavens is God, and in the earth
God. He is the Wise, the Knower.

85. And blessed be He unto Whom belongeth the Sovereignty
of the heavens and the earth and all that is between them, and
with Whom is knowledge of the Hour, and unto Whom ye will
be returned.

86. And those unto whom they cry instead of Him possess
no power of intercession, saving him who beareth witness unto
the Truth knowingly.

87. And if thou ask them who created them, they will surely
say: Allah. How then are they turned away?

88. And he saith: O my Lord! Lo! those are a folk who believe
not.

89. Then bear with them (O Muhammad) and say: Peace. But
they will come to know.

SÛRAH 44

Ad-Dukhân, "The Smoke", takes its name from a word in v.
10. Tradition says that smoke here refers prophetically to the
haze of dust which surrounded Mecca at the time of the great
drought and famine which preceded the Muslim conquest of

Mecca and facilitated it.

It belongs to the middle group of Meccan Sûrahs.

SMOKE

Revealed at Mecca

In the name of Allah, the Beneficent, the Merciful.

1. Hâ, Mîm.

2. By the Scripture that maketh plain.

3. Lo! We revealed it on a blessed night—Lo! We are ever warning—

4. Whereupon every wise command is made clear.

5. As a command from Our presence—Lo! We are ever sending—

6. A mercy from thy Lord. Lo! He is the Hearer, the Knower,

7. Lord of the heavens and the earth and all that is between them, if ye would be sure.

8. There is no God save Him. He quickeneth and giveth death, your Lord and Lord of your forefathers.

9. Nay, but they play in doubt.

10. But watch thou (Muhammad) for the day when the sky will produce visible smoke.

11. That will envelop the people. This will be a painful torment.

12. (Then they will say): Our Lord relieve us of the torment. Lo! we are believers.

13. How can there be remembrance for them, when a messenger making plain (the truth) had already come unto them,

14. And they had turned away from him and said: One taught (by others), a mad man?

15. Lo! We withdraw the torment a little. Lo! ye return (to disbelief).

16. On the day when We shall seize them with the greater seizure (then), in truth We shall punish.

17. And verily We tried before them Pharaoh's folk, when there came unto them a noble messenger.

18. Saying: Give up to me the slaves of Allah. Lo! I am a faithful messenger unto you.

19. And saying: Be not proud against Allah. Lo! I bring you a clear warrant.

20. And lo! I have sought refuge in my Lord and your Lord lest ye stone me to death.

21. And if ye put no faith in me, then let me go.

22. And he cried unto his Lord (saying): These are guilty

folk.

23. Then (his Lord commanded): Take away my slaves by night. Lo! ye will be followed,

24. And leave the sea behind at rest, for lo! they are a drowned host.

25. How many were the gardens and the water-springs that they left behind.

26. And the cornlands and the goodly sites.

27. And pleasant things wherein they took delight!

28. Even so (it was), and We made it an inheritance for other folk;

29. And the heaven and the earth wept not for them, nor were they reprieved.

30. And We delivered the Children of Israel from the shameful doom;

31. (We delivered them) from Pharaoh. Lo! he was a tyrant of the wanton ones.

32. And We chose them purposely, above (all) creatures.

33. And We gave them portents wherein was a clear trial.

34. Lo! these, forsooth, are saying:

35. There is naught but our first death, and we shall not be raised again.

36. Bring back our fathers, if ye speak the truth!

37. Are they better, or the folk of Tubb'a and those before them? We destroyed them, for surely they were guilty.

38. And We created not the heavens and the earth, and all that is between them, in play.

39. We created them not save with truth; but most of them know not.

40. Assuredly the Day of Decision is the term of all of them.

41. A day when friend can in naught avail friend, nor can they be helped.

42. Save him on whom Allah hath mercy. Lo! He is the Mighty, the Merciful.

43. Lo! the tree of Zaqqûm.

44. The food of the sinner!

45. Like molten brass, it seetheth in their bellies.

46. As the seething of boiling water.

47. (And it will be said): Take him and drag him to the midst of hell.

48. Then pour upon his head the torment of boiling water.

49. (Saying): Taste! Lo! thou wast forsooth the mighty, the noble!

50. Lo! This is what whereof ye used to doubt.

51. Lo! those who kept their duty will be in a place secure.

52. Amid gardens and water-springs.

53. Attired in silk and silk embroidery, facing one another.

54. Even so (it will be). And We shall wed them unto fair ones with wide, lovely eyes.

55. They call therein for every fruit in safety.

56. They taste not death therein, save the first death. And He hath saved them from the doom of hell.

57. A bounty from thy Lord. That is the supreme triumph.

58. And We have made (this Scriputre) easy in thy language only that they may heed.

59. Wait then (O Muhammad). Lo! they (too) are waiting.

SÛRAH 45

Al-Jâthîyah, "Crouching", takes its name from a word in v. 28. It belongs to the middle group of Meccan Sûrahs.

CROUCHING

Revealed at Mecca

In the name of Allah, the Beneficent, the Merciful.

1. Hâ. Mîm.

2. The revelation of the Scripture is from Allah, the Mighty, the Wise.

3. Lo! in the heavens and the earth are portents for believers.

4. And in your creation, and all the beasts that He scattereth in the earth, are portents for a folk whose faith is sure.

5. And the difference of night and day and the provision that Allah sendeth down from the sky and thereby quickeneth the earth after her death, and the ordering of the winds, are portents for a people who have sense.

6. These are the portents of Allah which We recite unto thee (Muhammad) with truth. Then in what fact, after Allah and His portents, will they believe?

7. Woe unto each sinful liar.

8. Who heareth the revelations of Allah receive unto him, and then continueth in pride as though he heard them not. Give him tidings of a painful doom.

9. And when he knoweth aught of Our revelations he maketh it a jest. For such there is a shameful doom.

10. Beyond them there is hell, and that which they have earned will naught avail them, nor those whom they have chosen for protecting friends beside Allah. Theirs will be an awful doom.

11. This is guidance. And those who disbelieve the revelations of their Lord, for them there is a painful doom of wrath.

12. Allah it is Who hath made the sea of service unto you that the ships may run thereon by His command, and that ye may seek of His bounty, and that haply ye may be thankful;

13. And hath made of service unto you whatsoever is in the heavens and whatsoever is in the earth; it is all from Him. Lo! herein verily are portents for people who reflect.

14. Tell those who believe to forgive those who hope not for the days of Allah; in order that He may requite folk what they used to earn.

15. Whoso doeth right, it is for his soul, and whoso doeth wrong, it is against it. And afterward unto your Lord ye will be brought back.

16. And verily We gave the Children of Israel the Scripture and the Command and the Prophethood, and provided them with good things and favoured them above (all) peoples;

17. And gave them plain commandments. And they differed not until after the knowledge came unto them, through rivalry among themselves. Lo! thy Lord will judge between them on the Day of Resurrection concerning that wherein they used to differ.

18. And now have We set thee (O Muhammad) on a clear road of (Our) commandment; so follow it, and follow not the whims of those who know not.

19. Lo! they can avail thee naught against Allah. And lo! as for the wrongdoers, some of them are friends of others; and Allah is the Friend of those who ward off (evil).

20. This is a clear indication for mankind, and a guidance and a mercy for a folk whose faith is sure.

21. Or do those who commit ill deeds suppose that We shall make them as those who believe and do good works, the same in life and death? Bad is their judgement!

22. And Allah hath created the heavens and the earth with truth, and that every soul may be repaid what it hath earned. And they will not be wronged.

23. Hast thou seen him who maketh his desire his god, and Allah sendeth him astray purposely, and sealeth up his hearing and his heart, and setteth on his sight a covering? Then who will lead him after Allah (hath condemned him)? Will ye not then heed?

24. And they say: There is naught but our life of the world; we die and we live, and naught destroyeth us save time; when they have no knowledge whatsoever of (all) that; they do but

guess.

25. And when Our clear revelations are recited unto them their only argument is that they say: Bring (back) our fathers, then, if ye are truthful.

26. Say (unto them, O Muhammad): Allah giveth life to you, then causeth you to die, then gathereth you unto the Day of Resurrection whereof there is no doubt. But most of mankind know not.

27. And unto Allah belongeth the Sovereignty of the heavens and the earth; and on the day when the Hour riseth; on that day those who follow falsehood will be lost.

28. And thou wilt see each nation crouching, each nation summoned to its record. (And it will be said unto them): This day ye are requited what ye used to do.

29. This Our Book pronounceth against you with truth Lo! We have caused (all) that ye did to be recorded.

30. Then, as for those who believed and did good works, their Lord will bring them in unto His mercy. That is the evident triumph.

31. And as for those who disbelieved (it will be said unto them): Were not Our revelations recited unto you? But ye were scornful and became a guilty folk.

32. And when it was said: Lo! Allah's promise is the truth, and there is no doubt of the Hour's coming, ye said: We know not what the hour is. We deem it naught but a conjecture, and we are by no means convinced.

33. And the evils of what they did will appear unto them, and that which they used to deride will befall them.

34. And it will be said: This day We forget you, even as ye forgot the meeting of this your day; and your habitation is the Fire, and there is none to help you.

35. This, forasmuch as ye made the revelations of Allah a jest, and the life of the world beguiled you. Therefore this day they come not forth from thence, nor can they make amends.

36. Then praise be to Allah; Lord of the heavens and Lord of the earth, the Lord of the Worlds.

37. And unto Him (alone) belongeth majesty in the heavens and the earth, and He is the Mighty, the Wise.

SÛRAH 46

Al-Ahqâf, "The Wind-Curved Sandhills" (a formation which will be familiar to all desert travellers, and which especially characterised the region in which the tribe of A'âd were said originally to have lived), takes its name from a word in v. 21

341

and is the last of the *Hâ Mîm* group.

It belongs to the middle group of Meccan Sûrahs, with the exception of v. 10, vv.15-18, and v.35, which were revealed at Al-Madînah.

THE WIND-CURVED SANDHILLS

Revealed at Mecca

In the name of Allah, the Beneficent, the Merciful.

1. Hâ. Mîm.

2. The revelation of the Scripture is from Allah the Mighty, the Wise.

3. We created not the heavens and the earth and all that is between them save with truth, and for a term appointed. But those who disbelieve turn away from that whereof they are warned.

4. Say (unto them, O Muhammad): Have ye thought on all that ye invoke beside Allah? Show me what they have created of the earth. Or have they any portion in the heavens? Bring me a scripture before this (Scripture), or some vestige of knowledge (in support of what ye say), if ye are truthful.

5. And who is further astray than those who, instead of Allah, pray unto such as hear not their prayer until the Day of Resurrection, and are unconscious of their prayer.

6. And when mankind are gathered (to the Judgement) will become enemies for them, and will become deniers of having been worshipped.

7. And when Our clear revelations are recited unto them, those who disbelieve say of the Truth when it reacheth them: this is mere magic.

8. Or say they: He hath invented it? Say (O Muhammad): If I have invented it, still ye have no power to support me against Allah. He is best aware of what ye say among yourselves concerning it. He sufficeth for a witness between me and you. And He is the Forgiving, the Merciful.

9. Say: I am no new thing among the messengers (of Allah), nor know I what will be done with me or with you. I do but follow that which is inspired in me, and I am but a plain warner.

10. Bethink you: If it is from Allah and ye disbelieve therein, and a witness of the Children of Israel hath already testified to the like thereof and hath believed, and ye are too proud (what plight is yours)? Lo! Allah guideth not wrong-doing folk.

11. And those who disbelieve say of those who believe: If it had been (any) good, they would not have been before us

in attaining it: And since they will not be guid
say: This is an ancient lie;

12. When before it there was the Scripture of
example and a mercy; and this is a confirming Script.
Arabic language, that it may warn those who do wro and
bring good tidings for the righteous.

13. Lo! those who say: Our Lord is Allah, and thereafter
walk aright, there shall no fear come upon them neither shall
they grieve.

14. Such are rightful owners of the Garden, immortal
therein, as a reward for what they used to do.

15. And We have commended unto man kindness toward
parents. His mother beareth him with reluctance, and bringeth
him forth with reluctance, and the bearing of him and the
weaning of him is thirty months, till, when he attaineth full
strength and reacheth forty years, he saith: My Lord! Arouse
me that I may give thanks for the favour wherewith Thou hast
favoured me and my parents, and that I may do right acceptable
unto Thee. And be gracious unto me in the matter of my seed.
Lo! I have turned unto Thee repentant, and lo! I am of those
who surrender (unto Thee).

16. Those are they from whom We accept the best of what
they do, and overlook their evil deeds. (They are) among the
owners of the Garden. This is the true promise which they were
promised (in the world).

17. And whoso saith unto his parents: Fie upon you both!
Do ye threaten me that I shall be brought forth (again) when
generations before me have passed away? And they twain cry
unto Allah for help (and say): Woe unto thee! Believe! Lo! the
promise of Allah is true. But he saith: This is naught save fables
of the men of old.

18. Such are those on whom the Word concerning nations
of the jinn and mankind which have passed away before them
hath effect. Lo! they are the losers.

19. And for all there will be ranks from what they do, that
He may pay them for their deeds! And they will not be
wronged.

20. And on the day when those who disbelieve are exposed
to the Fire (it will be said): Ye squandered your good things
in the life of the world and sought comfort herein. Now this
day ye are rewarded with the doom of ignominy because ye
were disdainful in the land without a right, and because ye used
to transgress.

21. And make mention (O Muhammad) of the brother of
A'âd when he warned his folk among the wind-curved

..dhills—and verily warners came and went before and after him—saying: Serve none but Allah. Lo! I fear for you the doom of a tremendous Day.

22. They said: Thou hast come to turn us away from our gods? Then bring upon us that wherewith thou threatenest us, if thou art of the truthful.

23. He said: The knowledge is with Allah only. I convey unto you that wherewith I have been sent, but I see you are a folk that know not.

24. Then, when they beheld it as a dense cloud coming toward their valleys, they said; Here is a cloud bringing us rain. Nay, but it is that which ye did seek to hasten, a wind wherein is painful torment.

25. Destroying all things by commandment of its Lord. And morning found them so that naught could be seen save their dwellings. Thus do We reward the guilty folk.

26. And verily We had empowered them with that wherewith We have not empowered you, and had assigned them ears and eyes and hearts; but their ears and eyes and hearts availed them naught since they denied the revelations of Allah; and what they used to mock befell them.

27. And verily We have destroyed townships round about you, and displayed (for them) Our revelation, that haply they might return.

28. Then why did those whom they had chosen for gods as a way of approach (unto Allah) not help them? Nay, but they did fail them utterly. And (all) that was their lie, and what they used to invent.

29. And when We inclined toward thee (Muhammad) certain of the jinn, who wished to hear the Qur'ân and, when they were in its presence, said: Give ear! and, when it was finished, turned back to their people, warning.

30. They said: O our people! Lo! we have heard a Scripture which hath been revealed after Moses, confirming that which was before it, guiding unto the truth and a right road.

31. O our people! respond to Allah's summoner and believe in Him. He will forgive you some of your sins and guard you from a painful doom.

32. And whoso respondeth not to Allah's summoner he can nowise escape in the earth, and ye (can find) no protecting friends instead of Him. Such are in error manifest.

33. Have they not seen that Allah, Who created the heavens and the earth and was not wearied by their creation, is Able to give life to the death? Aye, He verily is Able to do all things.

34. And on the day when those who disbelieve are exposed

to the Fire (they will be asked): Is not this real? They will say: Yea, by our Lord. He will say: Then taste the doom for that ye disbelieved.

35. Then have patience (O Muhammad) even as the stout of heart among the messengers (of old) had patience, and seek not to hasten on the doom for them. On the day when they see that which they are promised (it will seem to them) as though they had tarried but an hour of daylight. A clear message. Shall any be destroyed save evil-living folk?

SÛRAH 47

Muhammad. This sûrah takes its name from the mention of the Prophet by name in v. 2. Most commentators agree that v. 18 was revealed when the Prophet, forced to flee from Mecca, looked back, weeping, for a last sight of his native city. Some have considered the whole sûrah to be a Meccan revelation, but with no good reason.

It belongs to the first and second years after the Hijrah, with the exception of v. 18, which was revealed during the Hijrah.

MUHAMMAD

Revealed at Al-Madînah

In the name of Allah, the Beneficent, the Merciful.

1. Those who disbelieve and turn (men) from the way of Allah, he rendereth their actions vain.

2. And those who believe and do good works and believe in that which is revealed unto Muhammad—and it is the truth from their Lord—He riddeth them of their ill deeds and improveth their state.

3. That is because those who disbelieve follow falsehood and because those who believe follow the truth from their Lord. Thus Allah coineth their similitudes for mankind.

4. Now when ye meet in battle those who disbelieve, then it is smiting of the necks until, when ye have routed them, then making fast of bonds; and afterward either grace or ransom till the war lay down its burdens. That (is the ordinance). And if Allah willed He could have punished them (without you) but (thus it is ordained) that He may try some of you by means of others. And those who are slain in the way of Allah, He rendereth not their actions vain.

5. He will guide them and improve their state.

6. And bring them in unto the Garden which he hath made known to them.

7. O ye who believe! If ye help Allah, He will help you and will make your foothold firm.

8. And those who disbelieve, perdition is for them, and He will make their actions vain.

9. That is because they are averse to that which Allah hath revealed, therefore maketh He their actions fruitless.

10. Have they not travelled in the land to see the nature of the consequence for those who were before them? Allah wiped them out. And for the disbelievers there will be the like thereof.

11. That is because Allah is patron of those who believe, and because the disbelievers have no patron.

12. Lo! Allah will cause those who believe and do good works to enter Gardens underneath which rivers flow; while those who disbelieve take their comfort in this life and eat even as the cattle eat, and the Fire is their habitation.

13. And how many a township stronger than thy township (O Muhammad) which hath cast thee out, have We destroyed, and they had no helper!

14. Is he who relieth on a clear proof from his Lord like those for whom the evil that they do is beautified while they follow their own lusts?

15. A similitude of the Garden which those who keep their duty (to Allah) are promised: Therein are rivers of water unpolluted, and rivers of milk whereof the flavour changeth not, and rivers of wine delicious to the drinkers, and rivers of clear-run honey; therein for them is every kind of fruit, with pardon from their Lord. (Are those who enjoy all this) like those who are immortal in the Fire and are given boiling water to drink so that it teareth their bowels?

16. Among them are some who give ear unto thee (Muhammad) till, when they go forth from thy presence, they say unto those who have been given knowledge: What was that he said just now? Those are they whose hearts Allah hath sealed, and they follow their own lusts.

17. While as for those who walk aright, He addeth to their guidance, and giveth them their protection (against evil).

18. Await they aught save the Hour, that it should come upon them unawares? And the beginning thereof have already come. But now, when it hath come upon them, can they take their warning?

19. So know (O Muhammad) that there is no God save Allah, and ask forgiveness for thy sin and for believing men and believing women. Allah knoweth (both) your place of turmoil and your place of rest.

20. And those who believe say: If only a Sûrah were revealed! But when a decisive Sûrah is revealed and war is mentioned therein, thou seest those in whose hearts is a disease looking at thee with the look of men fainting unto death. Therefore woe unto them!

21. Obedience and a civil word. Then, when the matter is determined, if they are loyal to Allah it will be well for them.

22. Would ye then, if ye were given the command, work corruption in the land and sever your ties of kinship?

23. Such are they whom Allah crusheth so that he deafeneth them and maketh blind their eyes.

24. Will they then not meditate on the Qur'ân, or are there locks on the hearts?

25. Lo! those who turn back after the guidance hath been manifested unto them, Satan hath seduced them, and he giveth them the rein.

26. That is because they say unto those who hate what Allah hath revealed: We will obey you in some matters; and Allah knoweth their secret talk.

27. Then how (will it be with them) when the angels gather them, smiting their faces and their backs!

28. That will be because they followed that which angereth Allah, and hated that which pleaseth Him. Therefore He hath made their actions vain.

29. Or do those in whose hearts is a disease deem that Allah will not bring to light their (secret) hates?

30. And if We would, We could show them unto thee (Muhammad) so that thou shouldst know them surely by their marks. And thou shalt know them by the burden of their talk. And Allah knoweth your deeds.

31. And verily We shall try you till We know those of you who strive hard (for the cause of Allah) and the steadfast, and till We test your record.

32. Lo! those who disbelieve and turn from the way of Allah and oppose the messenger after the guidance hath been manifested unto them, they hurt Allah not a jot, and He will make their actions fruitless.

33. O ye who believe! Obey Allah and obey the messenger, and render not your actions vain.

34. Lo! those who disbelieve and turn from the way of Allah and then die disbelievers, Allah surely will not pardon them.

35. So do not falter and cry out for peace when ye (will be) the uppermost, and Allah is with you, and He will not grudge (the reward of) your actions.

36. The life of the world is but a sport and a pastime. And

if ye believe and ward off (evil), He will give you your wages, and will not ask of you your worldly wealth.

37. If He should ask it of you and importune you, ye would hoard it, and He would bring to light your (secret) hates.

38. Lo! ye are those who are called to spend in the way of Allah, yet among you there are some who hoard. And as for him who hoardeth, he hoardeth only from his soul. And Allah is the Rich, and ye are the poor. And if ye turn away He will exchange you for some other folk, and they will not be the likes of you.

SÛRAH 48

Al-Fath, takes its name from the word *Fath* meaning "Victory" which occurs several times, and refers, not to the conquest of Mecca, but to the truce of Al-Hudeybîyeh, which, though at the time it seemed a set-back to the Muslims, proved in fact the greatest victory for Al-Islâm.

In the sixth year of the Hijrah, the Prophet set out with some 1400 Muslims from Al-Madînah and the country round, in the garb of pilgrims, not for war but to visit the Ka'bah. When they drew near Mecca, they were warned that Qureysh had gathered their allies against them, and that their cavalry under Khâlid ibn Al-Walîd was on the road before them. Making a detour through gullies of the hills, they escaped the cavalry and, coming into the valley of Mecca, encamped at Al-Hudeybîyeh below the city. The Prophet resolutely refused to give battle and persisted in attempts to parley with Qureysh who had sworn not to let him reach the Ka'bah. The Muslims were all the while in a position of some danger. Finally Othmân ibn 'Affân was sent into the city, as the man most likely to be well received on account of his relationships. Othmân was detained by the Meccans, and news that he had been murdered reached the Muslims in their camp.

It was then that the Prophet, sitting under a tree, took from his comrades the oath (referred to in v. 18) that they would hold together and fight to the death. Then it became known that the rumour of Othmân's death was false, and Qureysh at length agreed to a truce of which the terms were favourable to them. The Prophet and his multitude were to give up the project of visiting the sanctuary for that year, but were to make the pilgrimage the following year when the idolaters undertook to evacuate Mecca for three days to allow them to do so. Fugitives from Qureysh to the Muslims were to be returned, but not fugitives from the Muslims to Qureysh; and there was to be no hostility between the parties for ten years.

"And there was never a victory", says Ibn Khaldûn, "greater than this victory; for, as Az-Zuhrî says, when it was war the people did not meet, but when the truce came and war laid down its burdens and people felt safe one with another, then they met and indulged in conversation and discussion. And no man spoke of Al-Islâm to another but the latter espoused it, so that there entered Al-Islâm in those two years (i.e. between Al-Hudeybîyeh and the breaking of the truce by Qureysh) as many as all those who had entered it before, or more.".

The date of revelation is the sixth year of the Hijrah.

VICTORY

Revealed at Al-Madînah

In the name of Allah, the Beneficent, the Merciful.

1. Lo! We have given thee (O Muhammad) a signal victory,

2. That Allah may forgive thee of thy sin that which is past and that which is to come, and may perfect His favour unto thee, and may guide thee on a right path,

3. And that Allah may help thee with strong help—

4. He it is Who sent down peace of reassurance into the hearts of the believers that they might add faith unto their faith. Allah's are the hosts of the heavens and the earth, and Allah is ever Knower, Wise—

5. That He may bring the believing men and the believing women into Gardens underneath which rivers flow, wherein they will abide, and may remit from them their evil deeds—That, in the sight of Allah, is the supreme triumph—

6. And may punish the hypocritical men and the hypocritical women, and the idolatrous men and the idolatrous women, who think an evil thought concerning Allah. For them is the evil turn of fortune, and Allah is wroth against them and hath cursed them, and hath made ready for them hell, a hapless journey's end.

7. Allah's are the hosts of the heavens and the earth, and Allah is ever Mighty, Wise.

8. Lo! We have sent thee (O Muhammad) as a witness and a bearer of good tidings and a warner.

9. That ye (mankind) may believe in Allah and His messenger, and may honour Him, and may revere Him, and may glorify Him at early dawn and at the close of day.

10. Lo! those who swear allegiance unto thee (Muhammad), swear allegiance only unto Allah. The Hand of Allah is above their hands. So whosoever breaketh his oath, breaketh it only

to his soul's hurt; while whosoever keepeth his covenant with Allah, on him will He bestow immense reward.

11. Those of the wandering Arabs who were left behind will tell thee: Our possessions and our households occupied us, so ask forgiveness for us! They speak with their tongues that which is not in their hearts. Say: Who can avail you aught against Allah, if He intend you hurt or intend you profit? Nay, but Allah is ever Aware of what ye do.

12. Nay, but ye deemed that the messenger and the believers would never return to their own folk, and that was made fair-seeming in your hearts, and ye did think an evil thought, and ye were worthless folk.

13. And as for him who believeth not in Allah and His messenger— Lo! We have prepared a flame for disbelievers.

14. And Allah's is the Sovereignty of the heavens and the earth. He forgiveth whom He will , and punisheth whom He will. And Allah is every Forgiving, Merciful.

15. Those who were left behind will say, when ye set forth to capture booty: Let us go with you. They fain would change the verdict of Allah. Say (unto them, Muhammad): Ye shall not go with us. Thus hath Allah said beforehand. Then they will say: Ye are envious of us. Nay, but they understand not, save a little.

16. Say unto those of the wandering Arabs who were left behind: Ye will be called against a folk of mighty prowess, to fight them untill they surrender; and if ye obey, Allah will give you a fair reward; but if ye turn away as ye did turn away before, He will punish you with a painful doom.

17. There is no blame for the blind, nor is there blame for the lame, nor is there blame for the sick (that they go not forth to war). And whoso obeyeth Allah and His messenger, He will make him enter Gardens underneath which river flow; and whoso turneth back, him will He punish with a painful doom.

18. Allah was well pleased with the believers when they swore allegiance unto thee beneath the tree, and He knew what was in their hearts, and He sent down peace of reassurance on them, and hath rewarded them with a near victory;

19. And much booty that they will capture. Allah is ever Mighty, Wise.

20. Allah promiseth you much booty that ye will capture, and hath given you this in advance, and hath withheld men's hand from you, that it may be a token for the believers, and that He may guide you on a right path.

21. And other (gain), which ye have not been able to achieve,

Allah will compass it. Allah is Able to do all things.

22. And if those who disbelieve join battle with you they will take to flight, and afterward they will find no protecting friend nor helper.

23. It is the law of Allah which hath taken course aforetime. Thou wilt not find for the law of Allah aught of power to change.

24. And He it is Who hath withheld men's hands from you, and hath withheld your hands from them, in the valley of Mecca, after he had made you victors over them. Allah is Seer of what ye do.

25. These it was who disbelieved and debarred you from the Inviolable Place of Worship, and debarred the offering from reaching its goal. And if it had not been for believing men and believing women, whom ye know not—lest ye should tread them under foot and thus incur guilt for them unknowingly; that Allah might bring into His mercy whom He will—If (the believers and the disbelievers) had been clearly separated We verily had punished those of them who disbelieved with painful punishment.

26. When those who disbelieved had set up in their hearts zealotry, the zealotry of the Age of Ignorance, then Allah sent down His peace of reassurance upon His messenger and upon the believers and imposed on them the word of self-restraint, for they were worthy of it and meet for it. And Allah is Aware of all things.

27. Allah hath fulfilled the vision for His messenger in very truth. Ye shall indeed enter the Inviolable Place or Worship, if Allah will, secure, (having your hair) shaven and cut, not fearing. But He knoweth that which ye know not, and hath given you a near victory beforehand.

28. He it is Who hath sent His messenger with the guidance and the religion of truth, that He may cause it to prevail over all religion. And Allah sufficeth as a witness.

29. Muhammad is the messenger of Allah. And those with him are hard against the disbelievers and merciful among themselves. Thou (O Muhammad) seest them bowing and falling prostrate (in worship), seeking bounty from Allah and (His) acceptance. The mark of them is on their foreheads from the traces of prostration. Such is their likeness in the Torah and their likeness in the Gospel—likes as sown corn that sendeth forth its shoot and strengtheneth it and riseth firm upon its stalk, delighting the sowers—that He may enrage the disbelievers with (the sight of) them. Allah hath promised, unto such of them as believe and do good works, forgiveness and immense

reward.

SÛRAH 49

Al-Hujurât takes its name from v. 4, which, with the following verse, is said to refer to the behaviour of a deputation at a time when deputations from all parts of Arabia were coming to Al-Madînah to profess allegiance to the Prophet. The whole sûrah, dealing as it does with manners, and particularly with behaviour toward the Prophet, evidently belongs to a period when there were many seeking audience, among them many who were quite uncivilised.

The data of revelation is the ninth year of the Hijrah, "the year of deputations", as it is called.

THE PRIVATE APARTMENTS

Revealed at Al-Madînah

In the name of Allah, the Beneficent, the Merciful.

1. O ye who believe! Be not forward in the presence of Allah and His messenger, and keep your duty to Allah. Lo! Allah is Hearer, Knower.

2. O ye who believe! Lift not up your voices above the voice of the Prophet, nor shout when speaking to him as ye shout to one another, lest your works be rendered vain while ye perceive not.

3. Lo! they who subdue their voices in the presence of the messenger of Allah, those are they whose hearts Allah hath proven unto righteousness. Theirs will be forgiveness and immense reward.

4. Lo! those who call thee from behind the private apartments, most of them have no sense.

5. And if they had had patience till thou camest forth unto them, it had been better for them. And Allah is Forgiving, Merciful.

6. O ye who believe! If an evil-liver bring you tidings, verify it, lest ye smite some folk in ignorance and afterward repent of what ye did.

7. And know that the messenger of Allah is among you. If he were to obey you in much of the government, ye would surely be in trouble; but Allah hath endeared the faith to you and hath beautified it in your hearts, and hath made disbelief and lewdness and rebellion hateful unto you. Such are they who are rightly guided.

8. (It is) a bounty and a grace from Allah; and Allah is Knower, Wise.

9. And if two parties of believers fall to fighting, then make peace between them. And if one party of them doeth wrong to the other, fight ye that which doeth wrong till it return unto the ordinance of Allah; then, if it return, make peace between them justly, and act equitably. Lo! Allah loveth the equitable.

10. The believers are naught else than brothers. Therefore make peace between your brethren and observe your duty to Allah that haply ye may obtain mercy.

11. O ye who believe! Let not a folk deride a folk who may be better than they (are), nor let women (deride) women who may be better than they are, neither defame one another, nor insult one another by nicknames. Bad is the name of lewdness after faith. And whoso turneth not in repentance, such are evil-doers.

12. O ye who believe! Shun much suspicion; for lo! some suspicion is a crime. And spy not, neither backbite one another. Would one of you love to eat the flesh of his dead brother? Ye abhor that (so abhor the other)! And keep your duty (to Allah). Lo! Allah is Relenting, Merciful.

13. O Mankind! Lo! We have created you male and female, and have made you nations and tribes that ye may know one another. Lo! the noblest of you, in the sight of Allah, is the best in conduct. Lo! Allah is Knower, Aware.

14. The wandering Arabs say: We believe. Say (unto them, O Muhammad): Ye believe not, but rather say "We submit," for the faith hath not yet entered into your hearts. Yet, if ye obey Allah and His messenger, He will not withhold from you aught of (the reward of) your deeds. Lo! Allah is Forgiving, Merciful.

15. The (true) believers are those only who believe in Allah and His messenger and afterward doubt not, but strive with their wealth and their lives for the cause of Allah. Such are the sincere.

16. Say (unto them, O Muhammad): Would ye teach Allah your religion, when Allah knoweth all that is in the heavens and all that is in the earth, and Allah is Aware of all things?

17. They make it a favour unto thee (Muhammad) that they have surrendered (unto Him). Say: Deem not your Surrender a favour unto me; nay, but Allah doth confer a favour on you, inasmuch as He hath led you to the Faith, if ye are earnest.

18. Lo! Allah knoweth the Unseen of the heavens and the earth. And Allah is Seer of what ye do.

SÛRAH 50

Takes its name from the letter of the Arabic alphabet

which stands alone at the beginning of the first verse.

It belongs to the middle group of Meccan Sûrahs.

QÂF

Revealed at Mecca

In the name of Allah, the Beneficent, the Merciful.

1. Qâf. By the glorious Qur'ân,

2. Nay, but they marvel that a warner of their own hath come unto them; and the disbelievers say: This is a strange thing:

3. When we are dead and have become dust (shall we be brought back again)? That would be a far return!

4. We know that which the earth taketh of them, and with Us is a recording Book.

5. Nay, but they have denied the truth when it came unto them, therefore they are now in troubled case.

6. Have they not then observed the sky above them, how We have constructed it and beautified it, and how there are no rifts therein?

7. And the earth have We spread out, and have flung firm hills therein, and have caused of every lovely kind to grow thereon.

8. A vision and a reminder for every penitent slave.

9. And We send down from the sky blessed water whereby We give growth unto gardens and the grain of crops,

10. And lofty date-palms with ranged clusters,

11. Provision (made) for men; and therewith We quicken a dead land. Even so will be the resurrection of the dead.

12. The folk of Noah denied (the truth) before them, and (so did) the dwellers at Ar-Rass and (the tribe of) Thamûd,

13. And (the tribe of) A'âd, and Pharaoh, and the brethren of Lot,

14. And the dwellers in the wood, and the folk of Tubb'a: every one denied their messengers, therefore My threat took effect.

15. Were We then worn out by the first creation? Yet they are in doubt about a new creation.

16. We verily created man and We know what his soul whispereth to him, and We are nearer to him than his jugular vein.

17. When the two Receivers receive (him), seated on the right hand and on the left.

18. He uttereth no word but there is with him an observer

ready.

19. And the agony of death cometh in truth. (And it is said unto him): This is that which thou wast wont to shun.

20. And the trumpet is blown. This is the threatened Day.

21. And every soul cometh, along with it a driver and a witness.

22. (And unto the evil-doer it is said): Thou wast in heedlessness of this. Now We have removed from thee thy covering, and piercing is thy sight this day.

23. And (unto the evil-doers) his comrade saith: This is that which I have ready (as testimony).

24. (And it is said): Do ye twain hurl to hell each rebel ingrate,

25. Hinderer of good, transgressor, doubter,

26. Who setteth up another god along with Allah. Do ye twain hurl him to the dreadful doom.

27. His comrade saith: Our Lord! I did not cause him to rebel, but he was (himself) far gone in error.

28. He saith: contend not in My presence, when I had already proffered unto you the warning.

29. The sentence that cometh from Me cannot be changed, and I am in no wise a tyrant unto the slaves.

30. On the day when We say unto hell. Art thou filled, and it saith: Can there be more to come?

31. And the Garden is brought nigh for those who keep from evil, no longer distant.

32. (And it is said): That is that which ye were promised. (It is) for every penitent and heedful one,

33. Who feareth the Beneficent in secret and cometh with a contrite heart.

34. Enter it in peace. This is the day of immortality.

35. There they have all that they desire, and there is more with us.

36. And how many a generation We destroyed before them, who were mightier than these in prowess so that they overran the lands! Had they any place of refuge (when the judgement came)?

37. Lo! therein verily is a reminder for him who hath a heart, or giveth ear with full intelligence.

38. And verily We created the heavens and the earth, and all that is between them, in six Days, and naught of weariness touched Us.

39. Therefore (O Muhammad) bear with what they say, and hymn the praise of thy Lord before the rising and before the setting of the sun;

40. And in the night-time hymn His praise, and after the (prescribed) prostrations.

41. And listen on the day when the crier crieth from a near place,

42. The day when they will hear the (Awful) Cry in truth. That is the day of coming forth (from the graves).

43. Lo! We it is Who quicken and give death, and unto us is the journeying.

44. On the day when the earth splitteth asunder from them, hastening forth (they come). That is a gathering easy for us (to make).

45. We are best aware of what they say, and thou (O Muhammad) are in no wise a compeller over them. But warn by the Qur'ân him who feareth My threat.

SÛRAH 51

Adh-Dhâriyât, "The Winnowing Winds", takes its name from a word in v. 1. I have followed the usual interpretation of the first four verses, but they may also be taken as all referring to winds or to angels.

THE WINNOWING WINDS

Revealed at Mecca

In the name of Allah, the Beneficent, the Merciful.

1. By those that winnow with a winnowing.

2. And those that bear the burden (of the rain)

3. And those that glide with ease (upon the sea)

4. And those who distribute (blessings) by command

5. Lo! that wherewith ye are threatened is indeed true,

6. And lo! the judgement will indeed befall.

7. By the heaven full of paths,

8. Lo! ye, forsooth, are of various opinion (concerning the truth).

9. He is made to turn away from it who is (himself) averse.

10. Accursed by the conjecturers

11. Who are careless in an abyss!

12. They ask: When is the Day of Judgement?

13. (It is) the day when they will be tormented at the Fire,

14. (And it will be said unto them): Taste your torment (which ye inflicted). This is what ye sought to hasten.

15. Lo! those who keep from evil will dwell amid gardens and watersprings,

16. Taking that which their Lord giveth them; for lo! aforetime they were doers of good;

17. They used to sleep but little of the night,

18. And ere the dawning of each day would seek forgiveness,

19. And in their wealth the beggar and the outcast had due share.

20. And in the earth are portents for those whose faith is sure,

21. And (also) in yourselves. Can ye then not see?

22. And in the heaven is your providence and that which ye are promised;

23. And by the Lord of the heavens and the earth, it is the truth, even as (it is true) that ye speak.

24. Hath the story of Abraham's honoured guests reached thee (O Muhammad)?

25. When they came in unto him and said: Peace! he answered, Peace! (and thought): Folk unknown (to me).

26. Then he went apart unto this housefolk so that they brought a fatted calf.

27. And he set it before them, saying: Will ye not eat?

28. Then he conceived a fear of them. They said: Fear not! and gave him tidings of (the birth of) a wise son.

29. Then his wife came forward, making moan, and smote her face, and cried: A barren old woman!

30. They said: Even so saith thy Lord. Lo! He is the Wise, the Knower.

31. (Abraham) said: And (afterward) what is your errand, O ye sent (from Allah)?

32. They said: Lo! we are sent unto a guilty folk,

33. That we may send upon them stones of clay,

34. Marked by thy Lord for (the destruction of) the wanton.

35. Then we brought forth such believers as were there.

36. But We found there but one house of those surrendered (to Allah)

37. And We left behind therein a portent for those who fear a painful doom.

38. And in Moses (too, there is a portent) when We sent him unto Pharaoh with clear warrant.

39. But he withdrew (confiding) in his might, and said: A wizard or a mad man.

40. So We seized him and his hosts and flung them in the sea, for he was reprobate.

41. And in (the tribe of) A'âd (there is a portent) when We sent the fatal wind against them.

42. It spared naught that it reached, but made it (all) as dust.

43. And in (the tribe of) Thamûd (there is a portent) when it was told them: Take your ease awhile.

44. But they rebelled against their Lord's decree, and so the thunderbolt overtook them even while they gazed;

45. And they were unable to rise up, nor could they help themselves.

46. And the folk of Noah aforetime. Lo! they were licentious folk.

47. We have built the heaven with might, and We it is who make the vast extent (thereof).

48. And the earth have We laid out, how gracious is the Spreader (thereof)!

49. And all things We have created by pairs, that haply ye may reflect.

50. Therefore flee unto Allah; lo! I am a plain warner unto you from Him.

51. And set not any other god along with Allah; lo! I am a plain warner unto you from Him.

52. Even so there came no messenger unto those before them but they said: A wizard or a madman!

53. Have they handed down (the saying) as an heirloom one unto another? Nay, but they are forward folk.

54. So withdraw from them (O Muhammad), for thou art in no wise blameworthy,

55. And warn, for warning profiteth believers.

56. I created the jinn and humankind only that they might worship Me.

57. I seek no livelihood from them, nor do I ask that they should feed Me.

58. Lo! Allah! He it is that giveth livelihood, the Lord of unbreakable might.

59. And lo! for those who (now) do wrong there is an evil day like unto the evil day (which came for) their likes (of old); so let them not ask Me to hasten on (that day).

60. And woe unto those who disbelieve, from (that) their day which they are promised.

SÛRAH 52

At-Tûr, "The Mount", takes name from the opening verse. An early Meccan Sûrah.

THE MOUNT

Revealed at Mecca

In the name of Allah, the Beneficent, the Merciful.

1. By the Mount,

2. And a Scripture inscribed.

3. On fine parchment unrolled,

4. And the House frequented,

5. And the roof exalted,

6. And the sea kept filled,

7. Lo! the doom of thy Lord will surely come to pass;

8. There is none that can ward it off.

9. On the day when the heaven will heave with (awful) heaving,

10. And the mountains move away with (awful) movement,

11. Then woe that day unto the deniers,

12. Who play in talk of grave matters;

13. The day when they are thrust with a (disdainful) thrust, into the fire of hell.

14. (And it is said unto them): This is the Fire which ye were wont to deny.

15. Is this magic, or do ye not see?

16. Endure the heat thereof, and whether ye are patient of it or impatient of it is all one for you. Ye are only being paid for what ye used to do.

17. Lo! those who kept their duty dwell in gardens and delight,

18. Happy because of what their Lord hath given them, and (because) their Lord hath warded off from them the torment of hell-fire.

19. (And it is said unto them): Eat and drink in health (as reward) for what ye used to do,

20. Reclining on ranged couches. And We wed them unto fair ones with wide, lovely eyes.

21. And they who believed and whose seed follow them in faith, We cause their seed to join them (there) and, We deprive them of naught of their (life's) work. Every man is a pledge for that which he hath earned.

22. And We provide them with fruit and meat such as they desire.

23. There they pass from hand to hand a cup wherein is neither vanity nor cause of sin.

24. And there go round, waiting on them menservants of their own, as they were hidden pearls.

25. And some of them draw near unto others, questioning,

26. Saying: Lo! of old, when we were with our families, we were ever anxious;

27. But Allah hath been gracious unto us and hath preserved us from the torment of the breath of Fire.

28. Lo! We used to pray unto Him of old. Lo! He is the

Benign, the Merciful.

29. Therefore warn (men, O Muhammad). By the grace of Allah thou art neither soothsayer nor madman.

30. Or say they: (he is) a poet, (one) for whom we may expect the accident of time?

31. Say (unto them): Expect (your fill)! Lo! I am with you among the expectant.

32. Do their minds command them to do this, or are they an outrageous folk?

33. Or say they: He hath invented it? Nay, but they will not believe!

34. Then let them produce speech the like thereof, if they are truthful.

35. Or were they created out of naught? Or are they the creators ?

36. Or did they create the heavens and the earth? Nay, but they are sure of nothing!

37. Or do they own the treasures of thy Lord? Or have they been given charge (thereof)?

38. Or have they any stairway (unto heaven) by means of which they overhear (decrees). Then let their listener produce some warrant manifest!

39. Or hath He daughters whereas ye have sons?

40. Or askest thou (Muhammad) a fee from them so that they are plunged in debt?

41. Or possess they the Unseen so that they can write (it) down?

42. Or seek they to ensnare (the messenger)? But those who disbelieve, they are the ensnared!

43. Or have they any god beside Allah? Glorified be Allah from all that they ascribe as partner (unto Him)!

44. And if they were to see a fragment of the heaven falling, they would say: A heap of clouds.

45. Then let them be (O Muhammad), till they meet their day, in which they will be thunder-stricken.

46. A day in which their guile will naught avail them, nor will they be helped.

47. And verily, for those who do wrong, there is a punishment beyond that, But most of them know not.

48. So wait patiently (O Muhammad) for thy Lord's decree, for surely thou art in Our sight; and hymn the praise of thy Lord when thou uprisest,

49. And in the night-time also hymn His praise, and at the setting of the stars.

SÛRAH 53

An-Najm, "The Star", takes its name from a word in the first verse.

An early Meccan Sûrah.

THE STAR

Revealed at Mecca

In the name of Allah, the Beneficent, the Merciful.

1. By the Star when it setteth,
2. Your comrade erreth not, nor is deceived;
3. Nor doth he speak of (his own) desire.
4. It is naught save an inspiration that is inspired,
5. Which One of mighty powers hath taught him,
6. One vigorous; and he grew clear to view
7. When he was on the uppermost horizon.
8. Then he drew nigh and came down
9. Till he was (distant) two bows' length or even nearer,
10. And He revealed unto His slave that which He revealed.
11. The heart lied not (in seeing) what it saw.
12. Will ye then dispute with him concerning what he seeth?
13. And verily he saw him yet another time
14. By the lote-tree of the utmost boundary,
15. Nigh unto which is the Garden of Abode.
16. When that which shroudeth did enshroud the lote-tree,
17. The eye turned not aside nor yet was overbold.
18. Verily he saw one of the greater revelations of his Lord.
19. Have ye thought upon Al-Lât and Al-'Uzzâ.
20. And Manât, the third, the other?
21. Are yours the males and His the females?
22. That indeed were an unfair division!
23. They are but names which ye have named, ye and your father, for which Allah hath revealed no warrant. They follow but a guess and that which (they) themselves desire. And now the guidance from their Lord hath come unto them.
24. Or shall man have what he coveteth?
25. But unto Allah belongeth the after (life), and the former.
26. And how many angels are in the heavens whose intercession availeth naught save after Allah giveth leave to whom He chooseth and accepteth!
27. Lo! it is those who disbelieve in the Hereafter who name the angels with the names of females.
28. And they have no knowledge thereof. They follow but a guess, and lo! a guess can never take the place of the truth.
29. Then withdraw (O Muhammad) from him who fleeth

from Our remembrance and desireth but the life of the world.

30. Such is their sum of knowledge; Lo! thy Lord is best aware of him who strayeth, and He is best aware of him who goeth right.

31. And unto Allah belongeth whatsoever is in the heavens and whatsoever is in the earth, that He may reward those who do evil with that which they have done, and reward those who do good with goodness.

32. Those who avoid enormities of sin and abominations, save the unwilled offences — (for them) lo! thy Lord is of vast mercy. He is best aware of you (from the time) when He created you from the earth, and when ye were hidden in the bellies of your mothers. Therefore ascribe not purity unto yourselves. He is best aware of him who wardeth off (evil).

33. Didst thou (O Muhammad) observe him who turned away,

34. And gave a little, then was grudging?

35. Hath he knowledge of the Unseen so that he seeth?

36. Or hath he not had news of what is in the books of Moses.

37. And Abraham who paid his debt:

38. That no laden one shall bear another's load,

39. And that man hath only that for which he maketh effort,

40. And that his effort will be seen,

41. And afterward he will be repaid for it with fullest payment;

42. And that thy Lord, He is the goal;

43. And that He it is Who maketh laugh, and maketh weep,

44. And that He it is Who giveth death and giveth life;

45. And that He createth the two spouses, the male and the female,

46. From a drop (of seed) when it is poured forth;

47. And that He hath ordained the second bringing forth;

48. And that He it is Who enricheth and contenteth:

49. And that He it is Who is the Lord of Sirius:

50. And that He destroyed the former (tribe of) A'âd,

51. And (the tribe of) Thamûd He spared not;

52. And the folk of Noah aforetime, Lo! they were more unjust and more rebellious;

53. And Al-Mu'tafikah He destroyed.

54. So that there covered them which did cover.

55. Concerning which then, of the bounties of thy Lord, canst thou dispute?

56. This is a warner of the warner of old.

57. The threatened Hour is nigh.

58. None beside Allah can disclose it.

59. Marvel ye then at this statement.

60. And laugh and not weep,

61. While ye amuse yourselves?

62. Rather prostrate yourselves before Allah and serve Him.

SÛRAH 54

Al-Qamar, "The Moon", takes its name from the first verse: "The hour drew nigh and the moon was rent in twain". A strange appearance of the moon in the sky, as if it had been torn asunder, is recorded in the traditions of several Companions of the Prophet as having astonished the people of Mecca about the time when the idolaters were beginning to persecute the Muslims.

An early Meccan Sûrah.

THE MOON

Revealed at Mecca

In the name of Allah, the Beneficent, the Merciful.

1. The hour drew nigh and the moon was rent in twain.

2. And if they behold a portent they turn away and say: Prolonged illusion.

3. They denied (the Truth) and followed their own lusts. Yet everything will come to a decision.

4. And surely there hath come unto them news whereof the purport should deter,

5. Effective wisdom; but warnings avail not.

6. So withdraw from them (O Muhammad) on the day when the Summoner summoneth unto a painful thing.

7. With downcast eyes, they come forth from the graves as they were locusts spread abroad,

8. Hastening toward the Summoner; the disbelievers say: This is a hard day.

9. The folk of Noah denied before them, yea, they denied Our slave and said: A madman; and he was repulsed.

10. So he cried unto his Lord, saying: I am vanquished, so give help.

11. Then opened We the gates of heaven with pouring water.

12. And caused the earth to gush forth springs, so that the waters met for a predestined purpose.

13. And We carried him upon a thing of planks and nails,

14. That ran (upon the waters) in Our sight, as a reward for

him who was rejected.

15. And verily We left it as a token; but is there any that remembereth?

16. Then see how (dreadful) was My punishment after My warnings!

17. And in truth We have made the Qur'ân easy to remember; but is there any that remembereth?

18. (The tribe of) A'âd rejected warnings. Then how (dreadful) was My punishment after My warnings.

19. Lo! We let loose on them a raging wind on the day of constant calamity,

20. Sweeping men away as though they were uprooted trunks of palm-trees.

21. Then see how (dreadful) was My punishment after My warnings!

22. And in truth We have made the Qur'ân easy to remember; but is there any that remembereth?

23. (The tribe of) Thamûd rejected warnings.

24. For they said: Is it a mortal man, alone among us, that we are to follow? Then indeed we should fall into error and madness.

25. Hath the remembrance been given unto him alone among us? Nay, but he is a rash liar.

26. (Unto their warner it was said): To-morrow they will know who is the rash liar.

27. Lo! We are sending the she-camel as a test for them; so watch them and have patience;

28. And inform them that the water is to be shared between (her and) them. Every drinking will be witnessed.

29. But they called their comrade and he took and hamstrung (her).

30. Then see how (dreadful) was My punishment after My warnings!

31. Lo! We sent upon them one Shout, and they became as the dry twigs (rejected by) the builder of a cattle-fold.

32. And in truth We have made the Qur'ân easy to remember; but is there any that remembereth?

33. The folk of Lot rejected warnings.

34. Lo! We sent a storm of stones upon them (all) save the family of Lot, whom We rescued in the last watch of the night,

35. As grace from Us. Thus We reward him who giveth thanks.

36. And he indeed had warned them of Our blow, but they did doubt the warnings.

37. They even asked of him his guests for an ill purpose.

Then We blinded their eyes (and said): Taste now My punishment after My warnings!

38. And in truth the punishment decreed befell them early in the morning.

39. Now taste My punishment after My warnings!

40. And in truth We have made the Qur'ân easy to remember; but is there any that remembereth?

41. And warnings came in truth unto the house of Pharaoh.

42. Who denied Our revelations, every one. Therefore We grasped them with the grasp of the Mighty, the Powerful.

43. Are your disbelievers better than those, or have ye some immunity in the Scriptures?

44. Or say they: We are a host victorious?

45. The hosts will all be routed and will turn and flee.

46. Nay, but the Hour (of doom) is their appointed tryst, and the Hour will be more wretched and more bitter (than their earthly failure).

47. Lo! The guilty are in error and madness.

48. On the day when they are dragged into the Fire upon their faces (it is said unto them): Feel the touch of hell.

49. Lo! We have created every thing by measure.

50. And Our commandment is but one (commandment), as the twinkling of an eye.

51. And verily We have destroyed your fellows; but is there any that remembereth?

52. And every thing they did is in the Scriptures,

53. And every small and great thing is recorded.

54. Lo! The righteous will dwell among gardens and rivers,

55. Firmly established in the favour of a Mighty King.

SÛRAH 55

Ar-Rahmân takes its name from the first verse. In the refrain: "Which is it, of the favours of your Lord, that ye deny?" *ye* and the verb are in the dual form, and the question is generally believed to be addressed to mankind and the jinn. Some have held that vv. 46-79 refer, not to the paradise hereafter, but to the later conquests of the Muslims, the four gardens being Egypt, Syria, Mesopotamia and Persia. There may well be a double meanings.

An early Meccan Sûrah.

THE BENEFICENT

Revealed at Mecca

In the name of Allah, the Beneficent, the Merciful.

1. The Beneficent
2. Hath made known the Qur'ân.
3. He hath created man.
4. He hath taught him utterance.
5. The sun and the moon are made punctual.
6. The stars and the trees adore.
7. And the sky He hath uplifted; and He hath set the measure,
8. That ye exceed not the measure,
9. But observe the measure strictly, nor fall short thereof.
10. And the earth hath He appointed for (His) creatures,
11. Wherein are fruit and sheathed palm-trees.
12. Husked grain and scented herb.
13. Which is it, of the favours of your Lord, that ye deny?
14. He created man of clay like the potter's.
15. And the Jinn did He create of smokeless fire.
16. Which is it, of the favours of your Lord, that ye deny?
17. Lord of the two Easts, and Lord of the two Wests.
18. Which is it, of the favours of your Lord, that ye deny?
19. He hath loosed the two seas. They meet.
20. There is a barrier between them. They encroach not (one upon the other).
21. Which is it, of the favours of your Lord, that ye deny?
22. There cometh forth from both of them the pearl and coral-stone.
23. Which is it, of the favours of your Lord, that ye deny?
24. His are the ships displayed upon the sea, like banners?
25. Which is it, of the favours of your Lord, that ye deny?
26. Everyone that is thereon will pass away;
27. There remaineth but the countenance of thy Lord of Might and Glory.
28. Which is it, of the favours of your Lord, that ye deny?
29. All that are in the heavens and the earth entreat Him. Every day He exerciseth (universal) power.
30. Which is it, of the favours of your Lord, that ye deny?
31. We shall dispose of you, O ye two dependents (man and jinni).
32. Which is it, of the favours of your Lord, that ye deny?
33. O company of jinn and men, if ye have power to penetrate (all) regions of the heavens and the earth, then penetrate (them)! Ye will never penetrate them save with (Our) sanction.
34. Which is it, of the favours of your Lord, that ye deny?
35. There will be sent, against you both, heat of fire and flash of brass, and ye will not escape.

36. Which is it, of the favours of your Lord, that ye deny?

37. And when the heaven splitteth asunder and becometh rosy like red hide—

38. Which is it, of the favours of your Lord, that ye deny?—

39. On that day neither man nor jinni will be questioned of his sin.

40. Which is it, of the favours of your Lord, that ye deny?

41. The guilty will be known by their marks, and will be taken by the forelocks and the feet.

42. Which is it, of the favours of your Lord, that ye deny?

43. This is hell which the guilty deny.

44. They go circling round between it and fierce, boiling water.

45. Which is it, of the favours of your Lord, that ye deny?

46. But for him who feareth the standing before his Lord there are two gardens.

47. Which is it, of the favours of your Lord, that ye deny?

48. Of spreading branches.

49. Which is it, of the favours of your Lord, that ye deny?

50. Wherein are two fountains flowing.

51. Which is it, of the favours of your Lord, that ye deny?

52. Wherein is every kind of fruit in pairs.

53. Which is it, of the favours of your Lord, that ye deny?

54. Reclining upon couches lined with silk brocade, the fruit of both gardens near to hand.

55. Which is it, of the favours of your Lord, that ye deny?

56. Therein are those of modest gaze, whom neither man nor jinni will have touched before them,

57. Which is it, of the favours of your Lord, that ye deny?

58. (In beauty) like the jacynth and the coral-stone.

59. Which is it, of the favours of your Lord, that ye deny?

60. Is the reward of goodness, aught save goodness?

61. Which is it, of the favours of your Lord, that ye deny?

62. And beside them are two other gardens.

63. Which is it, of the favours of your Lord, that ye deny?

64. Dark green with foliage.

65. Which is it, of the favours of your Lord, that ye deny?

66. Wherein are two abundant springs.

67. Which is it, of the favours of your Lord, that ye deny?

68. Wherein is fruit, the date-palm and pomegranate.

69. Which is it, of the favours of your Lord, that ye deny?

70. Wherein (are found) the good and beautiful—

71. Which is it, of the favours of your Lord, that ye deny?—

72. Fair ones, close-guarded in pavilions—

73. Which is it, of the favours of your Lord, that ye deny?—

74. Whom neither man nor jinni will have touched before them—

75. Which is it, of the favours of your Lord, that ye deny?—

76. Reclining on green cushions and fair carpets.

77. Which is it, of the favours of your Lord, that ye deny?

78. Blessed be the name of thy Lord, Mighty and Glorious!

SÛRAH 56

Al-Wâqi'âh, "The Event", takes its name from a word in the first verse of the sûrah.

An early Meccan Sûrah.

THE EVENT

Revealed at Mecca

In the name of Allah, the Beneficent, the Merciful.

1. When the event befalleth—

2. There is no denying that it will befall—

3. Abasing (some), exalting (others);

4. When the earth is shaken with a shock

5. And the hills are ground to powder.

6. So that they become a scattered dust.

7. And ye will be three kinds:

8. (First) those on the right hand; what of those on the right hand?

9. And (then) those on the left hand; what of those on the left hand?

10. And the foremost in the race, the foremost in the race:

11. Those are they who will be brought nigh

12. In gardens of delight;

13. A multitude of those old

14. And a few of those of later time,

15. On lined couches,

16. Reclining therein face to face.

17. There wait on them immortal youths

18. With bowls and ewers and a cup from a pure spring

19. Wherefrom they get no aching of the head nor any madness.

20. And fruit that they prefer

21. And flesh of fowls that they desire.

22. And (there are) fair ones with wide, lovely eyes,

23. Like unto hidden pearls,

24. Reward for what they used to do.

25. There hear they no vain speaking nor recrimination

26. (Naught) but the saying: Peace, (and again) Peace.

27. And those on the right hand; what of those on the right hand?

28. Among thornless lote-trees

29. And clustered plantains,

30. And spreading shade,

31. And water gushing,

32. And fruit in plenty

33. Neither out of reach nor yet forbidden,

34. And raised couches;

35. Lo! We have created them a (new) creation.

36. And made them virgins,

37. Lovers, friends,

38. For those on the right hand;

39. A multitude of those of old.

40. And a multitude of those of later time.

41. And those on the left hand: What of those on the left hand?

42. In scorching wind and scalding water.

43. And shadow of black smoke,

44. Neither cool nor refreshing.

45. Lo! heretofore they were effete with luxury

46. And used to persist in the awful sin.

47. And they used to say; When we are dead and have become dust and bones, shall we then, forsooth, be raised again,

48. And also our forefathers?

49. Say (unto them, O Muhammad): Lo! those of old and those of later time.

50. Will all be brought together to the tryst of an appointed day,

51. Then lo! ye, the erring, the deniers,

52. Ye verily will eat of a tree called Zaqqûm

53. And will fill your bellies therewith;

54. And thereon ye will drink of boiling water,

55. Drinking even as the camel drinketh.

56. This will be their welcome on the Day of Judgement.

57. We created you. Will ye then admit the truth?

58. Have ye seen that which ye emit?

59. Do ye create it or are We the Creator?

60. We mete out death among you, and We are not to be outrun,

61. That We may transfigure you and make you what ye know not.

62. And verily ye know the first creation. Why, then, do ye not reflect.

63. Have ye seen that which ye cultivate?

64. Is it ye who foster it, or are We the Fosterer?

65. If We willed, We verily could make it chaff, then would ye cease not to exclaim:

66. Lo! we are laden with debt!

67. Nay, but we are deprived!

68. Have ye observed the water which ye drink?

69. Is it ye who shed it from the raincloud, or are We the shedder?

70. If We willed We verily could make it bitter. Why, then, give ye not thanks?

71. Have ye observed the fire which ye strike out;

72. Was it ye who made the tree thereof to grow, or were We the grower?

73. We, even, We, appointed it a memorial and a comfort for the dwellers in the wilderness.

74. Therefore (O Muhammad), praise the name of thy Lord, the Tremendous.

75. Nay, I swear by the places of the stars—

76. And lo! that verily is a tremendous oath, if ye but knew—

77. That (this) is indeed a noble Qur'ân

78. In a Book kept hidden

79. Which none toucheth save the purified,

80. A revelation from the Lord of the Worlds.

81. Is it this Statement that ye scorn,

82. And make denial thereof your livelihood?

83. Why, then, when (the soul) cometh up to the throat (of the dying)

84. And ye are at that moment looking

85. —And We are nearer unto him than ye are, but ye see not—

86. Why then, if ye are not in bondage (unto Us),

87. Do ye not force it back, if ye are truthful?

88. Thus if he is of those brought nigh,

89. Then breath of life, and plenty, and a Garden of delight.

90. And if he is of those on the right hand,

91. Then (the greeting) "Peace be unto thee" from those on the right hand.

92. But if he is of the rejecters, the erring,

93. Then the welcome will be boiling water

94. And roasting at hell fire.

95. Lo! this is certain truth.

96. Therefore (O Muhammad) praise the name of thy Lord, the Tremendous.

SÛRAH 57

Al-Hadid, "Iron", takes its name from a word in v. 25.

The reference in the 'word' "victory" in v. 10, is undoubtedly to the conquest of Mecca, though Nôldeke takes it to refer to the battle of Badr, and so would place the sûrah in the fourth or fifth year of the Hijrah. The words of the verse are against such an assumption since no Muslims "spent and fought" before the battle at Badr, which was the beginning of their fighting.

The date of revelation must be the eighth or ninth year of the Hijrah.

IRON

Revealed at Al-Madinah

In the name of Allah, the Beneficent, the Merciful.

1. All that is in the heavens and the earth glorifieth Allah; and He is the Mighty, the Wise.

2. His is the Sovereignty of the heavens and the earth; He quickeneth and He giveth death; and He is Able to do all things.

3. He is the First and the Last, and the Outward and the Inward; and He is Knower of all things.

4. He it is Who created the heavens and the earth in six Days; then He mounted the Throne. He knoweth all that entereth the earth and all that emergeth therefrom and all that cometh down from the sky and all that ascendeth therein; and He is with you wheresoever ye may be. And Allah is Seer of what ye do.

5. His is the Sovereignty of the heavens and the earth, and unto Allah (all) things are brought back.

6. He causeth the night to pass into the day, and He causeth the day to pass into the night, and He is Knower of all that is in the breasts.

7. Believe in Allah and His messenger, and spend of that whereof He hath made you trustees; and such of you as believe and spend (aright) theirs will be a great reward.

8. What aileth you that ye believe not in Allah, when the messenger calleth you to believe in your Lord, and He had already made a covenant with you, if ye are believers?

9. He it is Who sendeth down clear revelations unto His slave, that He may bring you forth from darkness unto light; and lo! for you Allah is Full of Pity, Merciful.

10. And what aileth you that ye spend not in the way of Allah, when unto Allah belongeth the inheritance of the

heavens and the earth? Those who spent and fought before the victory are not upon a level (with the rest of you). Such are greater in rank than those who spent and fought afterwards. Unto each hath Allah promised good. And Allah is Informed of what ye do.

11. Who is he that will lend unto Allah a goodly loan, that He may double it for him and his may be a rich reward?

12. On the day when thou (Muhammad) wilt see the believers, men and women, their light shining forth before them and on their right hands, (and wilt hear it said unto them): Glad news for you this day: Gardens underneath which rivers flow, wherein ye are immortal. That is the supreme triumph.

13. On the day when the hypocritical men and the hypocritical women will say unto those who believe: Look on us that we may borrow from your light! it will be said: Go back and seek for light! Then there will separate them a wall wherein is a gate, the inner side whereof containeth mercy, while the outer side thereof is toward the doom.

14. They will cry unto them (saying): Were we not with you? They will say: Yea, verily; but ye tempted one another, and hesitated, and doubted, and vain desires beguiled you till the ordinance of Allah came to pass; and the deceiver deceived you concerning Allah;

15. So this day no ransom can be taken from you nor from those who disbelieved. Your home is the Fire; that is your patron, and a hapless journey's end.

16. Is not the time ripe for the hearts of those who believe to submit to Allah's reminder and to the truth which is revealed, that they become not as those who received the Scripture of old but the term was prolonged for them and so their hearts were hardened, and many of them are evil-livers.

17. Know that Allah quickeneth the earth after its death. We have made clear Our revelations for you, that haply ye may understand.

18. Lo! those who give alms, both men and women, and lend unto Allah a goodly loan, it will be doubled for them, and theirs will be a rich reward.

19. And those who believe in Allah and His messengers, they are the loyal; and the martyrs are with their Lord; they have their reward and their light; while as for those who disbelieve and deny Our revelations, they are owners of hell-fire.

20. Know that the life of this world is only play, and idle talk, and pageantry, and boasting among you, and rivalry in respect of wealth and children; as the likeness of vegetation after rain, whereof the growth is pleasing to the husbandman, but afterward it drieth up and thou seest it turning yellow, then

it becometh straw. And in the Hereafter there is grievous punishment, and (also) forgiveness from Allah and His good pleasure, whereas the life of the world is but matter of illusion.

21. Race one with another for forgiveness from your Lord and a Garden whereof the breadth is as the breadth of the heavens and the earth, which is in store for those who believe in Allah and His messengers. Such is the bounty of Allah, which He bestoweth upon whom He will, and Allah is of infinite bounty.

22. Naught of disaster befalleth in the earth or in yourselves but it is in a Book before We bring it into being—Lo! that is easy for Allah—

23. That ye grieve not for the sake of that which hath escaped you, nor yet exult because of that which hath been given. Allah loveth not all prideful boasters,

24. Who hoard and who enjoin upon the people avarice. And whosoever turneth away, still Allah is the Absolute, the Owner of Praise.

25. We verily sent Our messengers with clear proofs, and revealed with them the Scripture and the Balance, that mankind may observe right measure, and He revealed iron, wherein is mighty power and (many) uses for mankind, and that Allah may know him who helpeth Him and His messengers, though unseen. Lo! Allah is Strong, Almighty.

26. And We verily sent Noah and Abraham and placed the Prophethood and the Scripture among their seed, and among them there is he who goeth right, but many of them are evil-livers.

27. Then We caused Our messengers to follow in their footsteps; and We caused Jesus, son of Mary, to follow, and gave him the Gospel, and placed compassion and mercy in the hearts of those who followed him. But monasticism they invented—We ordained it not of them —only seeking Allah's pleasure, and they observed it not with right observance. So We give those of them who believe their reward, but many of them are evil-livers.

28. O ye who believe! Be mindful of your duty to Allah and put faith in His messenger. He will give you twofold of His mercy and will appoint for you a light wherein ye shall walk, and will forgive you. Allah is Forgiving, Merciful;

29. That the People of the Scripture may know that they control naught of the bounty of Allah, but that the bounty is in Allah's hand to give to whom He will. And Allah is of infinite bounty.

SÛRAH 58

Al-Mujâdilah, "She That Disputeth", takes its name from a word in verse 1.

A woman had complained to the Prophet that her husband had put her away for no good reason by employing an old formula of the pagan Arabs, saying that her back was for him as the back of his mother, and she "disputed" with the Prophet because he would take no action against the man before this revelation came to him. There is a brief reference to the same method of getting rid of wives in Sûrah 33, v. 4. This Sûrah must therefore have been revealed before Sûrah 33.

The date of revelation is the fourth or fifth year of the Hijrah.

SHE THAT DISPUTETH

Revealed at Al-Madinah

In the name of Allah, the Beneficent, the Merciful.

1. Allah hath heard the saying of her that disputeth with thee (Muhammad) concerning her husband, and complaineth unto Allah. And Allah heareth your colloquy. Lo! Allah is Hearer, Knower

2. Such of you as put away your wives (by saying they are as their mothers)—They are not their mothers; none are their mothers except those who have them birth—they indeed utter an ill word and a lie. And lo! Allah is Forgiving, Merciful.

3. Those who put away their wives (by saying they are as their mothers) and afterward would go back on that which they have said, (the penalty) in that case (is) the freeing of a slave before they touch one another. Unto this ye are exhorted; and Allah is informed of what ye do.

4. And he who findeth not (the wherewithal), let him fast for two successive months before they touch one another; and for him who is unable to do so (the penance is) the feeding of sixty needy ones. This, that ye may put trust in Allah and His messenger. Such are the limits (imposed by Allah); and for disbelievers is a painful doom.

5. Those who oppose Allah and His messengers will be abased even as those before them were abased; and We have sent down clear tokens, and for disbelievers is a shameful doom.

6. On the day when Allah will raise them all together and inform them of what they did. Allah hath kept account of it while they forgot it. And Allah is Witness over all things.

7. Hast thou not seen that Allah knoweth all that is in the

heavens and all that is in the earth? There is no secret conference of three but He is their fourth, nor of five but He is their sixth, nor of less than that or more that He is with them wheresoever they may be; and afterward, on the Day of Resurrection, He will inform them of what they did. Lo! Allah is Knower of all things.

8. Hast thou not observed those who were forbidden conspiracy, and afterward returned to that which they had been forbidden, and (now) conspire together for crime and wrong-doing and disobedience toward the messenger? And when they come unto thee they greet thee with a greeting wherewith Allah greeteth thee not, and say within themselves. Why should Allah punish us for what we say? Hell will suffice them; they will feel the heat thereof—a hapless journey's end!

9. O ye who believe! When ye conspire together, conspire not together for crime and wrongdoing and disobedience toward the messenger, but conspire together for righteousness and piety, and keep your duty toward Allah, unto whom ye will be gathered.

10. Lo! Conspiracy is only of the devil, that he may vex those who believe, but he can harm them not at all unless by Allah's leave. In Allah let believers put their trust.

11. O ye who believe! When it is said, Make room! in assemblies, then make room; Allah will make way for you (hereafter). And when it is said, Come up higher! go up higher; Allah will exalt those who believe among you, and those who have knowledge, to high ranks. Allah is informed of what ye do.

12. O ye who believe! When ye hold conference with the messenger, offer an alms before your conference. That is better and purer for you. But if ye cannot find (the wherewithal) then lo! Allah is Forgiving, Merciful.

13. Fear ye to offer alms before your conference? Then, when ye do it not and Allah hath forgiven you, establish worship and pay the poor-due and obey Allah and His messenger. And Allah is Aware of what ye do.

14. Hast thou not seen those who take for friends a folk with whom Allah is wroth? They are neither of you nor of them, and they swear a false oath knowingly.

15. Allah hath prepared for them a dreadful doom. Evil indeed is that which they are wont to do.

16. They make a shelter of their oaths and turn (men) from the way of Allah; so theirs will be a shameful doom.

17. Their wealth and their children will avail them naught

against Allah. Such are rightful owners of the Fire; they will abide therein.

18. On the day when Allah will raise them all together, then will they swear unto Him as they (now) swear unto you, and they will fancy that they have some standing. Lo! is it not they who are the liars?

19. The devil hath engrossed them and so hath caused them to forget remembrance of Allah. They are the devil's party. Lo! is it not the devil's party who will be the losers?

20. Lo! those who oppose Allah and His messenger, they will be among the lowest.

21. Allah hath decreed: Lo! I verily shall conquer, I and My messengers. Lo! Allah is Strong, Almighty.

22. Thou wilt not find folk who believe in Allah and the Last Day loving those who oppose Allah and His messenger, even though they be their fathers or their sons or their brethren or their clan. As for such, He hath written faith upon their hearts and hath strengthened them with a Spirit from Him, and He will bring them into Gardens underneath which rivers flow, wherein they will abide. Allah is well pleased with them, and they are well pleased with Him. They are Allah's party, Lo! is it not Allah's party who are the successful?

SÛRAH 59

Al-Hashr, "Exile", takes its name from vv. 2-17, which refer to the exile of the Bani Nadir, a Jewish tribe of Al-Madinah (for treason and projected murder of the Prophet) and the confiscation of their property. The "Hypocrites", as the lukewarm Muslims were called, had secretly sympathised with these Jews, whose opposition had grown strong since the Muslim reverse at Mt. Uhud, and had promised to side with them if it came to a collision with the Muslims; and to emigrate with them if they were forced to emigrate. But when the Muslims marched against the Bani Nadir, and the latter took refuge in their strong towers, the Hypocrites did nothing. And when at length they were reduced and exiled, the Hypocrites did not go with them into exile.

The date of revelation is the fourth year of the Hijrah.

EXILE

Revealed at Al-Madinah

In the name of Allah, the Beneficent, the Merciful.

1. All that is in the heavens and all that is in the earth glorifieth Allah, and He is the Mighty, the Wise.

2. He it is Who hath caused those of the people of the Scripture who disbelieved to go forth from their homes unto the first exile. Ye deemed not that they would go forth, while they deemed that their strongholds would protect them from Allah. But Allah reached them from a place whereof they recked not, and cast terror in their hearts so that they ruined their houses with their own hands and the hands of the believers. So learn a lesson, O ye who have eyes!

3. And if Allah had not decreed migration for them, He verily would have punished them in this world, and theirs in the Hereafter is the punishment of the Fire.

4. That is because they were opposed to Allah and His messengers; and whoso is opposed to Allah, (for him) verily Allah is stern in reprisal.

5. Whatsoever palm-trees ye cut down or left standing on their roots, it was by Allah's leave, in order that He might confound the evil-livers.

6. And that which Allah gave as spoil unto His messenger from them, ye urged not any horse or riding-camel for the sake thereof, but Allah giveth His messenger lordship over whom He will. Allah is Able to do all things.

7. That which Allah giveth as spoil unto His messenger from the people of the townships, it is for Allah and His messenger and for the near of kin and the orphans and the needy and the wayfarer, that it become not a commodity between the rich among you. And whatsoever the messenger giveth you, take it. And whatsoever he forbiddeth, abstain (from it). And keep your duty to Allah. Lo! Allah is stern in reprisal.

8. And (it is) for the poor fugitives who have been driven out from their homes and their belongings, who seek bounty from Allah and help Allah and His messenger. They are the loyal.

9. Those who entered the city and the faith before them love those who flee unto them for refuge, and find in their breasts no need for that which hath been given them, but prefer (the fugitives) above themselves though poverty become their lot. And whoso is saved from his own avarice— such are they who are successful.

10. And those who came (into the faith) after them say: Our Lord! Forgive us and our brethren who were before us in the faith, and place not in our hearts any rancour toward those who believe. Our Lord! Thou art Full of Pity, Merciful.

11. Hast thou not observed those who are hypocrites, (how) they tell their brethren who disbelieve among the People of the Scripture: If ye are driven out, we surely will go out with you,

and we will never obey anyone against you, and if ye are attacked we verily will help you. And Allah beareth witness that they verily are liars.

12. (For) indeed if they are driven out they go not out with them, and indeed if they are attacked they help them not, and indeed if they had helped them they would have turned and fled, and then they would not have been victorious.

13. Ye are more awful as a fear in their bosoms than Allah. That is because they are a folk who understand not.

14. They will not fight against you in a body save in fortified villages or from behind walls. Their adversity among themselves is very great. Ye think of them as a whole whereas their hearts are divers. That is because they are a folk who have no sense.

15. On the likeness of those (who suffered) a short time before them, they taste the ill-effects of their conduct, and theirs is painful punishment.

16. (And the hypocrites are) on the likeness of the devil when he telleth man to disbelieve, then, when he disbelieveth saith Lo! I am quit of thee. Lo! I fear Allah, the Lord of the Worlds.

17. And the consequence for both will be that they are in the Fire, therein abiding. Such is the reward of evildoers.

18. O ye who believe! Observe your duty to Allah. And let every soul look to that which it sendeth on before for the morrow. And observe your duty to Allah! Lo! Allah is Informed of what ye do.

19. And be not yet as those who forgot Allah, therefore He caused them to forget their souls. Such are the evildoers.

20. Not equal are the owners of the Fire and the owners of the Garden. The owners of the Garden, they are the victorious.

21. If We had caused this Qur'ân to descend upon a mountain, thou (O Muhammad) verily hadst seen it humbled, rent asunder by the fear of Allah. Such similitudes coin We for mankind that haply they may reflect.

22. He is Allah, than whom there is not other God, the Knower of the Invisible and the Visible. He is the Beneficent the Merciful.

23. He is Allah, than whom there is no other God, the Sovereign Lord, the holy One, Peace, the Keeper of Faith, the Guardian, the Majestic, the Compeller, the Superb. Glorified be Allah from all that they ascribe as partner (unto Him).

24. He is Allah, the Creator, the Shaper out of naught, the Fashioner. His are the most beautiful names. All that is in the heavens and the earth glorifieth Him, and He is the Mighty, the Wise.

SÛRAH 60

Al-Mumtahanah, "She who is to be Examined", takes its name from v. 10, where the believers are told to examine women who come to them as fugitives from the idolaters and, if they find them sincere converts to Al-Islam, not to return them to the idolaters. This marked a modification in the terms of the Truce of Hudeybîyah, by which the Prophet had engaged to return all fugitives, male and female, while the idolaters were not obliged to give up renegades from Al-Islam. The more terrible persecution which women had to undergo, if extradited, and their helpless social condition were the causes of the change. Instead of giving up women refugees who were sincere, and not fugitives on account of crime or some family quarrel, the Muslims were to pay an indemnity for them; while as for Muslim husbands whose wives might flee to Qureysh, no indemnity was to be paid by the latter but, when some turn of fortune brought wealth to the Islâmic State, they were to be repaid by the State what their wives had taken of their property. In v. 12 is the pledge which was to be taken from the women refugees after their examination.

The date of revelation is the eighth year of the Hijrah.

SHE THAT IS TO BE EXAMINED

Revealed at Al-Madînah

In the name of Allah, the Beneficent, the Merciful.

1. O ye, who believe! Choose not My enemy and your enemy for friends. Do ye give them friendship when they disbelieve in that truth which hath come unto you, driving out the messenger and you because ye believe in Allah, your Lord? If ye have come forth to strive in My way and seeking My good pleasure, (show them not friendship). Do ye show friendship unto them in secret, when I am Best Aware of what ye hide and what ye proclaim? And whosoever doeth it among you, he verily hath strayed from the right way.

2. If they have the upper hand of you, they will be your foes, and will stretch out their hands and their tongues toward you with evil (intent), and they long for you to disbelieve.

3. Your ties of kindred and your children will avail you naught upon the Day of Resurrection. He will part you. Allah is Seer of what ye do.

4. There is goodly pattern for you in Abraham and those

with him, when they told their folk: Lo! we are guiltless of you and all that ye worship beside Allah. We have done with you. And there hath arisen between us and you hostility and hate for ever until ye believe in Allah only — save that which Abraham promised his father (when he said): I will ask forgiveness for thee, though I own nothing for thee from Allah — Our Lord! In Thee we put our trust, and unto Thee we turn repentant, and unto Thee is the journeying.

5. Our Lord! Make us not a prey for those who disbelieve, and forgive us, our Lord! Lo! Thou, only Thou, art the Mighty, the Wise.

6. Verily ye have in them a goodly pattern for everyone who looketh to Allah and the Last Day. And whosoever may turn away, lo! still Allah, He is the Absolute, the Owner of Praise.

7. It may be that Allah will ordain love between you and those of them with whom ye are at enmity. Allah is Mighty, and Allah is Forgiving, Merciful.

8. Allah forbidden you not those who warred not against you on account of religion and drove you not out from your homes, that ye should show them kindness and deal justly with them. Lo! Allah loveth the just dealers.

9. Allah forbiddeth you only those who warred against you on account of religion and have driven you out from your homes and helped to drive you out, that ye make friends of them. Whosoever maketh friends of them — (All) such are wrongdoers.

10. O ye who believe! When believing women come unto you as fugitives, examine them. Allah is best aware of their faith. Then, if ye know them for true believers send them not back unto the disbelievers. They are not lawful for the disbelievers, nor are the disbelievers lawful for them. And give the disbelievers that which they have spent (upon them). And it is no sin for you to marry such women when ye have given them their dues. And hold not to the ties of disbelieving women; and ask for (the return of) that which ye have spent; and let the disbelievers ask for that which they have spent. That is the judgement of Allah. He judgeth between you. Allah is Knower, Wise.

11. And if any of your wives have gone from you unto the disbelievers and afterward ye have your turn (of triumph), then give unto whose wives have gone the like of that which they have spent, and keep your duty to Allah in whom ye are believers.

12. O Prophet! If believing women come unto thee, taking oath of allegiance unto thee that they will ascribe nothing as

partner unto Allah, and will neither steal nor commit adultery nor kill their children, nor produce any lie that they have devised between their hands and feet, nor disobey thee in what is right, then accept their allegiance and ask Allah to forgive them. Lo! Allah is forgiving, Merciful.

13. O ye who believe! Be not friendly with a folk with whom Allah is wroth, (a folk) who have despaired of the Hereafter as the disbelievers despair of those who are in the graves.

SÛRAH 61

As-Saff, "The Ranks", takes its name from a word in v. 4. In the copy of the Koran which I have followed, it is stated to have been revealed at Mecca, though its contents evidently refer to the Madînah period. It may have been revealed while the Prophet and his companions were encamped in the valley of Mecca during the negotiations of the Truce of Hudeybîyah, with which some of its verses are associated by tradition.

In that case the date of revelation would be the sixth year of the Hijrah.

THE RANKS

Revealed at Al-Madînah

In the name of Allah, the Beneficent, the Merciful.

1. All that is in the heavens and all that is in the earth glorifieth Allah, and He is the Mighty, the Wise.

2. O ye who believe! Why say ye that which ye do not?

3. It is most hateful in the sight of Allah that ye say that which ye do not.

4. Lo! Allah loveth those who battle for His cause in ranks, as if they were a solid structure.

5. And (remember) when Moses said unto his people: O my people! Why persecute ye me, when ye well know that I am Allah's messenger unto you? So when they went astray Allah sent their hearts astray. And Allah guideth not the evil-living folk.

6. And when Jesus son of Mary said: O Children of Israel! Lo! I am the messenger of Allah unto you, confirming that which was (revealed) before me in the Torah, and bringing good tidings of a messenger who cometh after me, whose name is the Praised One. Yet when he hath come unto them with clear proofs, they say: This is mere magic.

7. And who doth greater wrong than he who inventeth a lie against Allah when he is summoned unto Al-Islâm? And

Allah guideth not wrongdoing folk.

8. Fain would they put out the light of Allah with their mouths, but Allah will perfect His light however much the disbelievers are averse.

9. He it is who hath sent His messenger with the guidance and the religion of truth, that He may make it conqueror of all religion however much idolaters may be averse.

10. O ye who believe! Shall I show you a commerce that will save you from a painful doom?

11. Ye should believe in Allah and His messenger, and should strive for the cause of Allah with your wealth and your lives. That is better for you, if ye did but know.

12. He will forgive you your sins and bring you into Gardens underneath which rivers flow, and pleasant dwellings in Gardens of Eden. That is the supreme triumph.

13. And (He will give you) another blessing which ye love: help from Allah and present victory. Give good tidings (O Muhammad) to believers.

14. O ye who believe! Be Allah's helpers, even as Jesus son of Mary said unto the disciples: Who are my helpers for Allah? They said: We are Allah's helpers. And a party of the Children of Israel believed, while a party disbelieved. Then We strengthened those who believed against their foe, and they became the uppermost.

SÛRAH 62

Al-Jum'ah, "The Congregation", takes its name from a word in v. 9, where obedience to the call to congregational prayer is enjoined. Tradition says that vv. 9-11 refer to an occasion when a caravan entered Al-Madînah with beating of drums at the time when the Prophet was preaching in the mosque, and that the congregation broke away to look at it except twelve men. If, as one version of the tradition says, the caravan was that of Dahyah al-Kalbi, the incident must have occurred before the fifth year of the Hijrah, because Dahyah was a Muslim in the fifth year. A.H. The date of revelation is between the years 2 and 4 A.H.

THE CONGREGATION

Revealed at Al-Madînah

In the name of Allah, the Beneficent, the Merciful.

1. All that is in the heavens and all that is in the earth glorifieth Allah, the Sovereign Lord, the Holy One, the Mighty, the Wise.

2. He it is Who hath sent among the unlettered ones a messenger of their own, to recite unto them His revelations and to make them grow, and to teach them the Scripture and wisdom, though heretofore they were indeed in error manifest.

3. Along with others of them who have not yet joined them. He is the Mighty, the Wise.

4. That is the bounty of Allah; which He giveth unto whom He will. Allah is of infinite bounty.

5. The likeness of those who are entrusted with the Law of Moses, yet apply it not, is as the likeness of the ass carrying books. Wretched is the likeness of folk who deny the revelations of Allah. And Allah guideth not wrongdoing folk.

6. Say (O Muhammad): O ye who are Jews! If ye claim that ye are favoured of Allah apart from (all) mankind, then long for death if ye are truthful.

7. But they will never long for it because of all that their own hands have sent before, and Allah is Aware of evil-doers.

8. Say (unto them, O Muhammad): Lo! the death from which ye shrink will surely meet you, and afterward ye will be returned unto the Knower of the Invisible and the Visible, and He will tell you what ye used to do.

9. O ye who believe! When the call is heard for the prayer of the day of congregation, haste unto remembrance of Allah and leave your trading. That is better for you if ye did but know.

10. And when the prayer is ended, then disperse in the land and seek of Allah's bounty, and remember Allah much, that ye may be successful.

11. But when they spy merchandise or pastime they break away to it and leave thee standing. Say: That which Allah hath is better than pastime and than merchandise, and Allah is the best of providers.

SÛRAH 63

Al-Munâfiqûn, "The Hypocrites" takes its name from a word occurring in the first verse. v. 8 refers to a remark of Abdullah ibn Ubeyy, the "Hypocrite" leader, expressing the desire that the old aristocracy of Yathrib, of which he had been the acknowledged chief, might regain the ascendancy and turn out the refugees from Mecca, whom he regarded as intruders.

The date of the revelation is the fourth year of the Hijrah.

THE HYPOCRITES

Revealed at Al-Madînah

In the name of Allah, the Beneficent, the Merciful.

1. When the hypocrites come unto thee (O Muhammad), they say: We bear witness that thou art indeed Allah's messenger. And Allah knoweth that thou art indeed His messenger, and Allah beareth witness that the hypocrites are speaking falsely.

2. They make their faith a pretext so that they may turn (men) from the way of Allah. Verily evil is that which they are wont to do.

3. That is because they believed, then disbelieved, therefore their hearts are sealed so that they understand not.

4. And when thou seest them their figures please thee; and if they speak thou givest ear unto their speech. (They are) as though they were blocks of wood in striped cloaks. They deem every shout to be against them. They are the enemy, so beware of them. Allah confound them! How they are perverted!

5. And when it is said unto them: Come! The messenger of Allah will ask forgiveness for you! they avert their faces and thou seest them turning away, disdainful.

6. Whether thou ask forgiveness for them or ask not forgiveness for them, Allah will not forgive them. Lo! Allah guideth not the evil-living folk.

7. They it is who say: Spend not on behalf of those (who dwell) with Allah's messenger that they may disperse (and go away from you); when Allah's are the treasures of the heavens and the earth; but the hypocrites comprehend not.

8. They say: Surely, if we return to Al-Madînah the mightier will soon drive out the weaker; when might belongeth to Allah and to His messenger and the believers; but the hypocrites know not.

9. O ye who believe! Let not your wealth nor your children distract you from remembrance of Allah. Those who do so, they are the losers.

10. And spend of that wherewith We have provided you before death cometh unto one of you and he saith: My Lord! If only thou wouldst reprieve me for a little while, then I would give alms and be among the righteous.

11. But Allah reprieveth no soul when its term cometh, and Allah is Aware of what ye do.

SÛRAH 64

At-Taghâbun, "Mutual Disillusion", takes its name from a word in v. 9.

The date of revelation is possibly the year 1 A.H., though it is generally regarded as a late Meccan Sûrah, vv. 14 ff. being taken as referring to the pressure brought to bear by wives and families to prevent Muslims leaving Mecca at the time of the Hijrah.

MUTUAL DISILLUSION

Revealed at Mecca

In the name of Allah, the Beneficent, the Merciful.

1. All that is in the heavens and all that is in the earth glorifieth Allah; unto Him belongeth sovereignty and unto Him belongeth praise, and He is Able to do all things.

2. He it is Who created you, but one of you is a disbeliever and one of you is a believer, and Allah is Seer of what ye do.

3. He created the heavens and the earth with truth, and He shaped you and made good your shapes, and unto Him is the journeying.

4. He knoweth all that is in the heavens and all that is in the earth, and He knoweth what ye conceal and what ye publish: And Allah is Aware of what is in the breasts (of men).

5. Hath not the story reached you of those who disbelieved of old and so did taste the ill-effects of their conduct, and theirs will be a painful doom.

6. That was because their messengers (from Allah) kept coming unto them with clear proofs (of Allah's sovereignty), but they said: Shall mere mortals guide us? So they disbelieved and turned away, and Allah was independent (of them). Allah is Absolute, Owner of Praise.

7. Those who disbelieve assert that they will not be raised again. Say (unto them, O Muhammad): Yea, verily, by my Lord! ye will be raised again and then ye will be informed of what ye did; and that is easy for Allah.

8. So believe in Allah and His messenger and the light which We have revealed. And Allah is Aware of what ye do.

9. The day when He shall gather you unto the Day of Assembling, that will be a day of mutual disillusion. And whoso believeth in Allah and doeth right, He will remit from his evil deeds and will bring him into Gardens underneath which rivers flow, therein to abide for ever. That is the supreme triumph.

10. But those who disbelieve and deny Our revelations, such are owners of the Fire; they will abide therein—a hapless journey's end!

11. No calamity befalleth save by Allah's leave. And whosoever believeth in Allah, He guideth his heart. And Allah is Knower of all things.

12. Obey Allah and obey His messenger; but if ye turn away, then the duty of Our messenger is only to convey (the message) plainly.

13. Allah! There is no God save Him. In Allah, therefore, let believers put their trust.

14. O ye who believe! Lo! Among your wives and your children there are enemies for you, therefore beware of them. And if ye efface and overlook and forgive, then lo! Allah is Forgiving, Merciful.

15. Your wealth and your children are only a temptation, whereas Allah! with Him is an immense reward.

16. So keep your duty to Allah as best ye can, and listen, and obey, and spend; that is better for your souls. And whoso is saved from his own greed, such are the successful.

17. If ye lend unto Allah a goodly loan, He will double it for you and will forgive you, for Allah is Responsive, Clement,

18. Knower of the Invisible and the Visible, the Mighty, the Wise.

SÛRAH 65

At-Talâq, "Divorce", is so called from vv. 1-7, which contain an amendment to the laws of divorce which are set forth in Sûrah 2. This is generally referred-traditionally to a mistake made by Ibn 'Umar in divorcing his wife, which is said to have happened in the 6th year of the Hijrah. But others relate that the Prophet on that occasion only quoted this verse which had already been revealed.

The date of revelation is the sixth year of the Hijrah or a little earlier.

DIVORCE

Revealed at Al-Madînah

In the name of Allah, the Beneficent, the Merciful.

1. O Prophet! When ye (men) put away women, put them away for their (legal) period and reckon the period, and keep your duty to Allah, your Lord. Expel them not from their houses nor let them go forth unless they commit open immorality. Such are the limits (imposed by) Allah; and whoso transgresseth Allah's limits, he verily wrongeth his erward bring some new thing to pass.

2. Then, when they have reached their term, take them

back in kindness or part from them in kindness, and call to witness two just men among you, and keep your testimony upright for Allah. Whoso believeth in Allah and the Last Day is exhorted to act thus. And whosoever keepeth his duty to Allah, Allah will appoint a way out for him,

3. And will provide for him from (a quarter) whence he hath no expectation. And whosoever putteth his trust in Allah, He will suffice him. Lo! Allah bringeth His command to pass. Allah hath set a measure for all things.

4. And for such of your women as despair of menstruation, if ye doubt, their period (of waiting) shall be three months, along with those who have it not. And for those with child, their period shall be till they bring forth their burden. And whosoever keepeth his duty to Allah, He maketh his course easy for him.

5. That is the commandment of Allah which He revealeth unto you. And whoso keepeth his duty to Allah, He will remit from him his evil deeds and magnify reward for him.

6. Lodge them where ye dwell, according to your wealth, and harass them not so as to straiten life for them. And if they are with child, then spend for them till they bring forth their burden. Then, if they give suck for you, give them their due payment and consult together in kindness; but if ye make difficulties for one another, then let some other woman give suck for him (the father of the child).

7. Let him who hath abundance spend of his abundance, and he whose provision is measured, let him spend of that which Allah hath given him. Allah asketh naught of any soul save that which He hath given it. Allah will vouchsafe, after hardship, ease.

8. And how many of community revolted against the ordinance of its Lord and His messengers, and we called it to a stern account and punished it with dire punishment,

9. So that it tasted the ill-effects of its conduct, and the consequence of its conduct was loss.

10. Allah hath prepared for them stern punishment; so keep your duty to Allah, O men of understanding! O ye who believe! Now Allah hath sent down unto you a reminder.

11. A messenger reciting unto you the revelations of Allah made plain, that He may bring forth those who believe and do good works from darkness unto light. And whosoever believeth in Allah and doeth right, He will bring him into Gardens underneath which rivers flow, therein to abide for

ever. Allah hath made good provision for him.

12: Allah it is who hath created seven heavens, and of the
earth the like thereof. The commandment cometh down
among them slowly, that ye may know that Allah is Able to
do all things, and that Allah surroundeth all things in
knowledge.

SÛRAH 66

At-Tahrîm, "Banning", takes its name from a word in v. 1.
There are three traditions as to the occasion of vv. 1-4:

(1) The Prophet was very fond of honey. One of his wives
received a present of honey from a relative and by its means
inveigled the Prophet into staying with her longer than was
customary. The others felt aggrieved, and Ayeshah devised a
little plot. Knowing the Prophet's horror of unpleasant
smells, she arranged with two other wives that they should
hold their noses when he came to them after eating the
honey, and accuse him of having eaten the produce of a very
rank-smelling tree. When they accused him of having eaten
Maghâfir the Prophet said that he had eaten only honey. They
said: "The bees had fed on *Maghâfir?*" The Prophet was
dismayed and vowed to eat no more honey.

(2) Hafsah found the Prophet in her room with Mârya—the
Coptic girl, presented to him by the ruler of Egypt, who
became the mother of his only male child, Ibrâhîm—on a day
which custom had assigned to Ayeshah. Moved by Hafsah's
distress, the Prophet vowed that he would have no more to
do with Mârya, and asked her not to tell Ayeshah. But
Hafsah's distress had been largely feigned. No sooner had the
Prophet gone than she told Ayeshah with glee how easily she
had got rid of Mârya.

(3) Before Al-Islám women had no standing in Arabia. The
Koran gave them legal rights and an assured position, which
some of them were inclined to exaggerate. The Prophet was
extremely kind to his wives. One day Omar had to rebuke his
wife for replying to him in a tone which he considered
disrespectful. She assured him it was the tone in which his
own daughter Hafsah, Ayeshah and others of the Prophet's
wives answered the Prophet. Omar went at once and
remonstrated with Hafsah and with another of the Prophet's
wives to whom he was related. He was told to mind his own
business, which increased his horror and dismay. Soon
afterwards the Prophet separated from his wives for a time,

and it was thought that he was going to divorce them. Then Omar ventured to tell the story of his own vain effort to reform them, at which the Prophet laughed heartily.

Traditions (1) and (3) are the better authenticated and are alone adduced by the great traditionists. But the commentators generally prefer (2) as more explanatory of the text. All allude to a tendency on the part of some of the wives of the Prophet to presume on their new status and the Prophet's well-known kindness—a tendency so marked that, if allowed to continue, it would have been of bad example to the whole community. The Koran first rebukes the Prophet for yielding to their desires to the extent of undertaking to forgo a thing which Allah had made lawful for him—in the case of (2), fulfilment of his vow involved a wrong to Mârya—and then reproves the women for their double-dealing and intrigue.

The above traditions have been made by some non-Muslim writers the text for strictures which appear irrelevant because their ideology is altogether un-Islamic. The Prophet has never been regarded by Muslims as other than a human messenger of God; sanctity has never been identified with celibacy. For Christendom the strictest religious ideal has been celibacy, monogamy is already a concession to human nature. For Muslims, monogamy is the ideal, polygamy the concession to human nature. Polygamy is of the nature of some men in all countries, and of all men in some countries. Having set a great example of monogamic marriage, the Prophet was to set a great example of polygamic marriage, by following which men of that temperament could live righteous lives. He encountered all the difficulties inherent in the situation, and when he made mistakes the Koran helped him to retrieve them. Al-Islâm did not institute polygamy. It restricted an existing institution by limiting the number of a man's legal wives, by giving to every woman a legal personality and legal rights which had to be respected, and making every man legally responsible for his conduct towards every woman. Whether monogamy or polygamy should prevail in a particular country or period is a matter of social and economic convenience. The Prophet himself was permitted to have more wives than were allowed to others because, as head of the State, he was responsible for the support of women who had no other protector. With the one exception of Ayeshah, all his wives had been widows.

BANNING

Reavealed at Mecca

In the name of Allah, the Beneficent, the Merciful.

1. O Prophet! Why bannest thou that which Allah hath made lawful for thee, seeking to please thy wives? And Allah is Forgiving, Merciful.

2. Allah hath made lawful for you (Muslims) absolution from your oaths (of such a kind), And Allah is your Protector. He is the Knower, the Wise.

3. When the Prophet confided a fact unto one of his wives and when she afterward divulged it and Allah apprised him thereof, he made known (to her) part thereof and passed over part. And when he told it her she said : Who hath told thee? He said: The Knower, the Aware hath told me.

4. If ye twain turn unto Allah repentant, (ye have cause to do so) for your hearts desired (the ban); and if ye aid one another against him (Muhammad) then lo! Allah, even He, is his protecting Friend, and Gabriel and the righteous among the believers; and furthermore the angels are his helpers.

5. It may happen that his Lord, if he divorce you, will give him in your stead wives better than you, submissive (to Allah), believing, pious, penitent, inclined to fasting, widows and maids.

6. O ye who believe! Ward off from yourselves and your families a Fire whereof the fuel is men and stones, over which are set angels strong, severe, who resist not Allah in that which He commandeth them, but do that which they are commanded.

7. (Then it will be said): O ye who disbelieve! Make no excuses for yourselves this day. Ye are only being paid for what ye used to do.

8. O ye who believe! Turn unto Allah in sincere repentance! It may be that your Lord will remit from you your evil deeds and bring you into Gardens underneath which rivers flow, on the day when Allah will not abase the Prophet and those who believe with him. Their light will run before them and on their right hands: they will say: Our Lord! Perfect our light for us, and forgive us! Lo! Thou art Able to do all things.

9. O Prophet! Strive against the disbelievers and the hypocrites, and be stern with them. Hell will be their home, a hapless journey's end.

10. Allah citeth an example for those who disbelieve: the wife of Noah and the wife of Lot, who were under two of our

righteous slaves yet betrayed them so that they (the husbands) availed them naught against Allah and it was said (unto them): Enter the Fire along with those who enter.

11. And Allah citeth an axample for those who believe: the wife of Pharaoh when she said: My Lord! Build for me a home with thee in the Garden, and deliver me from Pharaoh and his work, and deliver me from evildoing folk;

12. And Mary, daughter of 'Imrân, whose body was chaste, therefore We breathed therein something of Our Spirit. And she put faith in the words of her Lord and His Scriptures, and was of the obedient.

SÛRAH 67

Al-Mulk takes its name from a world in the first verse. It belongs to the middle group of Meccan Sûrahs.

THE SOVEREIGNTY

Revealed at Mecca

In the name of Allah, the Beneficent, the Merciful.

1. Blessed is He in Whose hand is the Sovereignty, and He is Able to do all things.

2. Who hath created life and death that He may try you, which of you is best to conduct; and He is the Mighty, the Forgiving.

3. Who hath created seven heavens in harmony. Thou (Muhammad) canst see no fault in the Beneficent One's creation; then look again: Canst thou see any rifts?

4. Then look again and yet again, thy sight will return unto thee weakened and made dim.

5. And verily We have beautified the world's heaven with lamps, and We have made them missiles for the devils, and for them We have prepared the doom of flame.

6. And for those who disbelieve in their Lord there is the doom of hell, a hapless journey's end!

7. When they are flung therein they hear its roaring as it boileth up,

8. As it would burst with rage. Whenever a (fresh) host is flung therein the wardens thereof ask them: Came there unto you no warner?

9. They say: Yea, verily, a warner came unto us; but we denied and said: Allah hath naught revealed; ye are in naught but a great error.

10. And they say: Had we been wont to listen or have sense, we had not been among the dwellers in the flames.

11. So they acknowledge their sins; but far removed (from mercy) are the dwellers in the flames.

12. Lo! those who fear their Lord in secret, theirs will be forgiveness and a great reward.

13. And keep your opinion secret or proclaim it, lo! He is knower of all that is in the breasts (of men).

14. Should He not know what He created? And He is the Subtile, the Aware.

15. He it is Who hath made the earth subservient unto you, so walk in the paths thereof and eat of His providence. And unto Him will be the resurrection (of the dead).

16. Have ye taken security from Him Who is in the heaven that He will not cause the earth to swallow you when lo! it is convulsed?

17. Or have ye taken security from Him Who is in the heaven that He will not let loose on you a hurricane? But ye shall know the manner of My warning.

18. And verily those before them denied, then (see) the manner of My wrath (with them)!

19. Have they not seen the birds above them spreading out their wings and closing them? Naught upholdeth them save the Beneficent. Lo! He is Seer of all things.

20. Or who is he that will be an army unto you to help you instead of the Beneficent? The disbelievers are in naught but illusion.

21. Or who is he that will provide for you if He should withhold His providence? Nay, but they are set in pride and forwardness.

22. Is he who goeth groping on his face more rightly guided, or he who walketh upright on a beaten road?

23. Say (unto them, O Muhammand): He it is Who gave you being, and hath assigned unto you ears and eyes and hearts. Small thanks give ye!

24. Say : He it is Who multiplieth you in the earth, and unto Whom ye will be gathered.

25. And they say: When (will) this promise (be fulfilled), if ye are truthful?

26. Say : The knowledge is with Allah only, and I am but a plain warner;

27. But when they see it nigh, the faces of those who disbelieve will be awry, and it will be said (unto them): This is that for which ye used to call.

28. Say (O Muhammad): Have ye thought: Whether Allah causeth me (Muhammad) and those with me to perish or hath mercy on us, still, who will protect the disbelievers from a

painful doom?

29. Say: He is the Beneficent. In Him we believe and in Him we put our trust. And ye will soon know who it is that is in error manifest.

30. Say: have ye thought: If (all) your water were to disappear into the earth, who then could bring you gushing water?

SÛRAH 68

Al-Qalam, "The Pen", takes its name from a word in the first verse. A very early Meccan Sûrah.

THE PEN

Revealed at Mecca

In the name of Allah, the Beneficent, the Merciful.

1. Nûn. By the pen and that which they write (therewith),

2. Thou art not, for thy Lord's favour unto thee, a madman.

3. And lo! thine verily will be a reward unfailing.

4. And lo! thou art of a tremendous nature.

5. And thou wilt see and they will see

6. Which of you is the demented.

7. Lo! thy Lord is best aware of him who strayeth from his way, and He is best aware of those who walk aright.

8. Therefore obey not thou the rejecters.

9. Who would have had thee compromise, that they may compromise.

10. Neither obey thou each feeble oath-monger,

11. Detracter, spreader abroad of slanders,

12. Hinderer of the good, transgressor, malefactor

13. Greedy therewithal, intrusive.

14. It is because he is possessed of wealth and children

15. That, when Our revelations are recited unto him, he saith: Mere fables of the men of old.

16. We shall brand him on the nose.

17. Lo! we have tried them as We tried the owners of the garden when they vowed they would pluck its fruit next morning,

18. And made no exception (for the will of Allah);

19. Then a visitation came upon it while they slept.

20. And in the morning it was as if plucked,

21. And they cried out one unto another in the morning,

22. Saying: Run unto your field if ye would pluck (the fruit).

23. So they went off, saying one unto another in low tones:

24. No needy man shall enter it today against you.

25. They went betimes, strong in (this) purpose.

26. But when they saw it, they said: Lo! we are in error!

27. Nay, but we are desolate!

28. The best among them said: Said I not unto you: Why glorify ye not (Allah)?

29. They said: Glorified be our Lord! Lo! we have been wrong-doers.

30. Then some of them drew near unto others, self-reproaching.

31. They said: Alas for us! In truth we were outrageous.

32. It may be that our Lord will give us better than this in place thereof. Lo! we beseech our Lord.

33. Such was the punishment. And verily the punishment of the Hereafter is greater if they did but know.

34. Lo! for those who keep from evil are gardens of bliss with their Lord.

35. Shall We then treat those who have surrendered as We treat the guilty?

36. What aileth you? How foolishly ye judge!

37. Or have ye a Scripture wherein ye learn

38. That ye shall indeed have all that ye choose?

39. Or have ye a covenant on oath from Us that reacheth to the Day of Judgement, that yours shall be all that ye ordain?

40. Ask them (O Muhammad) which of them will vouch for that!

41. Or have they other gods? Then let them bring their other gods if they are truthful.

42. On the day when it befalleth in earnest, and they are ordered to prostrate themselves but are not able.

43. With eyes downcast, abasement stupefying them. And they had been summoned to prostrate themselves while they were yet unhurt.

44. Leave Me (to deal) with those who give the lie to this pronouncement. We shall lead them on by steps from whence they know not.

45. Yet I bear with them, for lo! My scheme is firm.

46. Or dost thou (Muhammad) ask a fee from them so that they are heavily taxed?

47. Or is the Unseen theirs that they can write (thereof)?

48. But wait thou for thy Lord's decree, and be not like him of the fish, who cried out in despair.

49. Had it not been that favour from his Lord had reached

him he surely had been cast into the wilderness while he was reprobate.

50. But his Lord chose him and placed him among the righteous.

51. And Lo! Those who disbelieve would fain disconcert thee with their eyes when they hear the Reminder, and they say: Lo! he is indeed mad.

52. When it is naught else than a Reminder to creation.

SÛRAH 69

Al-Hâqqah takes its name from a word recurring in the first three verses.

It belongs to the middle group of Meccan Sûrahs.

THE REALITY

Revealed at Mecca

In the name of Allah, the Beneficent, the Merciful.

1. The Reality!

2. What is the Reality?

3. Ah, what will convey unto thee what the reality is!

4. (The tribes of) Thamûd and Aâd disbelieved in the judgement to come.

5. As for Thamûd, they were destroyed by the lightning.

6. And as for A'âd, they were destroyed by a fierce roaring wind,

7. Which He imposed on them for seven long nights and eight long days so that thou mightest have seen men lying overthrown, as they were hollow trunks of palm-trees.

8. Canst thou (O Muhammad) see any remnant of them?

9. And Pharaoh and those before him, and the communities that were destroyed, brought error,

10. And they disobeyed the messenger of their Lord, therefore did He grip them with a tightening grip.

11. Lo! when the waters rose, We carried you upon the ship

12. That We might make it a memorial for you, and that remembering ears (that heard the story) might remember.

13. And when the trumpet shall sound one blast

14. And the earth with the mountains shall be lifted up and crused with one crash.

15. Then, on that day will the Event befall.

16. And the heaven will split asunder, for that day it will be frail.

17. And the angels will be on the sides thereof, and eight will uphold the Throne of their Lord that day, above them.

18. On that day ye will be exposed; not a secret of you will be hidden.

19. Then, as for him who is given his record in his right hand, he will say: Take, read my book!

20. Surely I knew that I should have to meet my reckoning.

21. Then he will be in blissful state

22. In a high Garden

23. Whereof the clusters are in easy reach.

24. (And it will be said unto those therein): Eat and drink at ease for that which ye sent on before you in past days.

25. But as for him who is given his record in his left hand, he will say: Oh, would that I had not been given my book

26. And knew not what my reckoning!

27. Oh, would that it had been death!

28. My wealth hath not availed me,

29. My power hath gone from me.

30. (It will be said): Take him and fetter him

31. And then expose him to hell-fire

32. And then insert him in a chain whereof the length is seventy cubits.

33. Lo! he used not to believe in Allah the Tremendous,

34. And urged not on the feeding of the wretched,

35. Therefore hath he no lover here this day,

36. Nor any food save filth

37. Which none but sinners eat.

38. But nay! I swear by all that ye see

39. And all that ye see not

40. That it is indeed the speech of an illustrious messenger.

41. It is not poet's speech—little is it that ye believe!

42. Nor diviner's speech—little is it that ye remember!

43. It is a revelation from the Lord of the Worlds.

44. And if he had invented false sayings concerning Us,

45. We assuredly had taken him by the right hand

46. And then severed his life-artery,

47. And not one of you could have held Us off from him.

48. And lo! it is a warrant unto those who ward off (evil).

49. And lo! We know that some among you will deny (it).

50. And lo! it is indeed an anguish for the disbelievers.

51. And lo! it is absolute truth.

52. So glorify the name of thy Tremendous Lord.

SÛRAH 70

Al-Ma'ârij takes its name from a word in verse 3. An early Meccan Sûrah.

THE ASCENDING STAIRWAYS

Revealed at Mecca

In the name of Allah the Beneficent, the Merciful.

1. A questioner questioned concerning the doom about to fall

2. Upon the disbelievers, which none can repel,

3. From Allah, Lord of the Ascending Stairways

4. (Whereby) the angels and the Spirit ascend unto Him in a Day whereof the span is fifty thousand years.

5. But be patient (O Muhammad) with a patience fair to see.

6. Lo! they behold it afar off

7. While We behold it nigh:

8. The day when the sky will become as molten copper,

9. And the hills become as flakes of wool,

10. And no familiar friend will ask a question of his friend

11. Though they will be given sight of them. The guilty man will long be able to ransom himself from the punishment of that day at the price of his children

12. And his spouse and his brother

13. And his kin that harboured him

14. And all that are in the earth, if then it might deliver him.

15. But nay! for lo! it is the fire of hell

16. Eager to roast;

17. It calleth him who turned and fled (from trught),

18. And hoarded (wealth) and withheld it.

19. Lo! man was created anxious,

20. Fretful when evil befalleth him

21. And, when good befalleth him, grudging;

22. Save worshippers

23. Who are constant at their worship

24. And in whose wealth there is a right acknowledged

25. For the beggar and the destitute

26. And those who believe in the Day of Judgement,

27. And those who are fearful of their Lord's doom—

28. Lo! the doom of their Lord is that before which none can feel secure—

29. And those who preserve their chastity.

30. Save with their wives and those whom their right hands possess, for thus they are not blameworthy;

31. But whoso seeketh more than that, those are they who are transgressors;

32. And those who keep their pledges and their covenant.

33. And those who stand by their testimony.

34. And those who are attentive at their worship.

35. These will dwell in Gardens, honoured.

36. What aileth those who disbelieve, that they keep staring toward thee (O Muhammad) open-eyed,

37. On the right and on the left, in groups?

38. Doth every man among them hope to enter the Garden of Delight?

39. Nay, verily. Lo! We created them from what they know.

40. But nay! I swear by the Lord of the rising-places and the setting-places of the planets that We verily are Able.

41. To replace them by others better than them. And We are not to be outrun.

42. So let them chat and play until they meet their Day which they are promised.

43. The day when they come forth from the graves in haste, as racing to a goal,

44. With eyes aghast, abasement stupefying them: Such is the Day which they are promised.

SÛRAH 71

Takes its name from its subject, which is the preaching of the prophet Noah. An early Meccan Sûrah.

NOAH

Revealed at Mecca

In the name of Allah, the Beneficent, the Merciful

1. Lo! We sent Noah unto his people (saying): Warn thy people ere the painful doom come unto them.

2. He said: O my people! Lo! I am a plain warner unto you

3. (Bidding you): Serve Allah and keep your duty unto Him and obey me,

4. That He may forgive you somewhat of your sins and respite you to an appointed term. Lo! the term of Allah, when it cometh, cannot be delayed, if ye but knew.

5. He said: My Lord! Lo! I have called unto my people night and day

6. But all my calling doth but add to their repugnance;

7. And lo! whenever I call unto them that Thou mayest pardon them they thrust their fingers in their ears and cover themselves with their garments and persist (in their refusal) and magnify themselves in pride.

8. And lo! I have called unto them aloud,

9. And lo! I have made public proclamation unto them, and I have appealed to them in private.

10. And I have said: Seek pardon of your Lord. Lo! He was ever Forgiving.

11. He will let loose the sky for you in plenteous rain

12. And will help you with wealth and sons, and will assign unto you Gardens and will assign unto you rivers.

13. What aileth you that ye hope not toward Allah for dignity

14. When He created you by (divers) stages?

15. See ye not how Allah hath created seven heavens in harmony,

16. And hath made the moon a light therein, and made the sun a lamp?

17. And Allah hath caused you to grow as a growth from the earth,

18. And afterward He maketh you return thereto, and He will bring you forth again, a (new) forthbringing.

19. And Allah hath made the earth a wide expanse for you

20. That ye may thread the valley-ways thereof.

21. Noah said: My Lord! Lo! they have disobeyed me and followed one whose wealth and children increase him in naught save ruin;

22. And they have plotted a mighty plot,

23. And they have said: Forsake not your gods. Forsake not Wadd, nor Suwâ, nor Yaghûth and Ya'ûq and Nasr.

24. And they have led many astray, and Thou increasest the wrong-doers in naught save error.

25. Because of their sins they were drowned, then made to enter a Fire. And they found they had no helpers in place of Allah.

26. And Noah said: My Lord! Leave not one of the disbelievers in the land.

27. If thou shouldst leave them, they will mislead Thy slaves and will beget none save lewd ingrates.

28. My Lord! Forgive me and my parents and him who entereth my house believing, and believing men and believing women, and increase not the wrongdoers in aught save ruin.

SÛRAH 72

Al-Jinn takes it name from a word in the first verse, and also from the subject of verses 1-18. The meaning of the word jinn in the Koran has exercised the minds of Muslim commentators, ancient and modern. Mr. Ya'qûb Hasan of Madras, in the first volume of a remarkable work in Urdu, *Kitâbu`l-Hudâ,* shows that it has at least three meanings in the Koran and that one of those meanings is something akin to "clever foreigners" as in the case of the Jinn who worked for Solomon. But undoubtedly the first and obvious meaning is "elemental spirits," to whom, as to mankind, the Koran came as a guidance. The incident is said to have occurred during the Prophet's return from his unsuccessful missionary journey to Tâ'îf.

A late Meccan Sûrah.

THE JINN

Revealed at Mecca

In the name of Allah, the Beneficent, the Merciful.

1. Say (O Muhammad): It is revealed unto me that a company of the Jinn gave ear, and they said: Lo! it is marvellous Qur'ân,

2. Which guideth unto righteousness, so we believe in it and we ascribe unto our Lord.

3. And (we believe) that He—exalted be the glory of our Lord!—hath taken neither wife nor son,

4. And that the foolish one among us used to speak concerning Allah an atrocious lie.

5. And lo! we had supposed that humankind and Jinn would not speak a lie concerning Allah—

6. And indeed (O Muhammad) individuals of humankind used to invoke the protection of individuals of the Jinn, so that they increased them in revolt (against Allah);

7. And indeed they supposed, even as ye suppose, that Allah would not raise anyone (from the dead)—

8. And (the Jinn who had listened to the Qur'ân said): We had sought the heaven but had found it filled with strong warders and meteors.

9. And we used to sit on places (high) therein to listen. But he who listeneth now findeth a flame in wait for him;

10. And we know not whether harm is boded unto all who are in the earth, or whether their Lord intendeth guidance for them.

11. And among us there are righteous folk and among us there are far from that. We are sects having different rules.

12. And we know that we cannot escape from Allah in the earth, nor can we escape by flight.

13. And when we heard the guidance, we believed therein,

and whoso believeth in his Lord, he feareth neither loss nor oppression.

14. And there are among us some who have surrendered (to Allah) and there are among us some who are unjust. And whoso hath surrendered to Allah, such have taken the right path purposefully.

15. And as for those who are unjust, they are firewood for hell.

16. If they (the idolaters) tread the right path, We shall give them to drink of water in abundance.

17. That We may test them thereby, and whoso turneth away from the remembrance of his Lord; He will thrust him into ever-growing torment.

18. And the places of worship are only for Allah, so pray not unto anyone along with Allah.

19. And when the slave of Allah stood up in prayer to Him, they crowded on him, almost stifling.

20. Say (unto them, O Muhammad): I pray unto Allah only, and ascribe unto Him no partner.

21. Say: Lo! I control not hurt nor benefit for you.

22. Say: Lo! none can protect me from Allah, nor can I find any refuge beside Him.

23. (Mine is) but conveyance (of the truth) from Allah, and His messages; and whoso disobeyeth Allah and His messenger, lo! his is fire of hell, wherein such dwell for ever.

24. Till (the day) when they shall behold that which they are promised (they may doubt); but then they will know (for certain) who is weaker in allies and less in multitude.

25. Say (O Muhammad, unto the disbelievers): I know not whether that which ye are promised is nigh, or if my Lord hath set a distant term for it.

26. (He is) the Knower of the Unseen, and He revealeth unto none His secret,

27. Save unto every messenger whom He hath chosen, and then He maketh a guard to go before him and a guard behind him

28. That He may know that they have indeed conveyed the messages of their Lord. He surroundeth all their doing, and He keepeth count of all things.

SÛRAH 73

Al-Muzammil takes its title from a word in verse 1. After his first trance and vision, the Prophet went to his wife Khadîjah and told her to wrap him up in cloaks, and that was afterwards his habit on such occasions, at any rate, in the early days at Mecca.

A very early Meccan revelation with the exception of the last verse, which all authorities assign to Al-Madînah.

THE ENSHROUDED ONE

Revealed at Mecca

In the name of Allah, the Beneficent, the Merciful.

1. O thou wrapped up in thy raiment!

2. Keep vigil the night long, save a little —

3. A half thereof, or abate a little thereof

4. Or add (a little thereto — and chant the Qur'ân in measure,

5. For We shall charge thee with a word of weight.

6. Lo! the vigil of the night is (a time) when impression is more keen and speech more certain.

7. Lo! thou hast by day a chain of business;

8. So remember the name of thy Lord and devote thyself with a complete devotion —

9. Lord of the East and the West; there is no God save Him; so choose thou Him alone for thy defender —

10. And bear with patience what they utter, and part from them with a fair leave-taking.

11. Leave Me to deal with the deniers, lords of ease and comfort (in this life); and do thou respite them awhile.

12. Lo! with Us are heavy fetters and a raging fire,

13. And food which choketh (the partaker), and a painful doom

14. On the day when the earth and the hills rock, and the hills become a heap of running sand.

15. Lo! We have sent unto you a messenger as witness against you, even as We sent unto Pharaoh a messenger.

16. But Pharaoh rebelled against the messenger, whereupon We seized him with no gentle grip.

17. Then how, if ye disbelieve, will ye protect yourselves upon the day which will turn children grey.

18. The very heaven being then rent asunder. His promise is to be fulfilled.

19. Lo! This is a Reminder. Let him who will, then, choose a way unto his Lord.

20. Lo! thy Lord knoweth how thou keepest vigil sometimes nearly two-thirds of the night, or (sometimes) half or a third thereof, as do a party of those with thee. Allah measureth the night and the day. He knoweth that ye count it not, and turneth unto you in mercy. Recite, then of the

Qur'ân that which is easy for you. He knoweth that there are sick folk among you, while others travel in the land in search of Allah's bounty, and others (still) are fighting for the cause of Allah. So recite of it that which is easy (for you), and establish worship and pay the poor-due, and (so) lend unto Allah a goodly loan. Whatsoever good ye send before you for your souls, ye will surely find it with Allah, better and greater in the recompense. And seek forgiveness of Allah. Lo! Allah is forgiving, Merciful.

SÛRAH 74

Al-Mudath-thir takes its name from a word in verse 1: The Prophet was accustomed to wrap himself in his cloak at the time of his trances. A tradition says that some time—about six months—elapsed between the first revelation (Sûrah 96, vv. 1-5) and the second revelation in this sûrah. Then the Prophet suddenly again beheld the angel who had appeared to him on Mt. Hirâ, and wrapped himself in his cloak, whereupon this sûrah was revealed to him. Another opinion is that by this sûrah the Prophet was ordered to begin the public preaching of Al-Islâm, his preaching having until then been done privately among his family and intimates. He is said to have begun his public preaching three years after his call.

In either case this is a very early Meccan Sûrah.

THE CLOAKED ONE

Revealed at Mecca

In the name of Allah, the Beneficent, the Merciful.

1. O thou enveloped in the cloak,
2. Arise and warn!
3. Thy Lord magnify,
4. Thy raiment purify,
5. Pollution shun!
6. And show not favour, seeking worldly gain!
7. For the sake of thy Lord, be patient!
8. For when the trumpet shall sound,
9. Surely that day will be a day of anguish,
10. Not of ease, for disbelievers.
11. Leave me (to deal) with him whom I created lonely,
12. And then bestowed upon him ample means,
13. And sons abiding in his presence
14. And made (life) smooth for him.
15. Yet he desireth that I should give more.
16. Nay! For lo! he hath been stubborn to Our revelations.

17. On him I shall impose a fearful doom.
18. For lo! he did consider; then he planned—
19. (Self-) destroyed is he, how he planned!
20. Again (self-) destroyed is he, how he planned!
21. Then looked he,
22. Then frowned he and showed displeasure.
23. Then turned he away in pride.
24. And said: This is naught else than magic from of old;
25. This is naught else than speech of mortal man.
26. Him shall I fling unto the burning.
27. — Ah.what will convey unto thee what that burning is!—
28. It leaveth naught; it spareth naught
29. It shrivelleth the man.
30. Above it are nineteen.
31. We have appointed only angels to be wardens of the fire, and their number have We made to be a stumbling-block for those who disbelieve; that those to whom the Scripture hath been given may have certainty, and that believers may increase in faith; and that those to whom the Scripture hath been given and believers may not doubt; and that those in whose hearts there is disease, and disbelievers, may say What meaneth Allah by this similitude? Thus Allah sendeth astray whom He will, and whom He will He guideth. None knoweth the hosts of thy Lord save Him. This is naught else than a Reminder unto mortals.
32. Nay, by the Moon
33. And the night when it withdraweth
34. And the dawn when it shineth forth,
35. Lo! this is one of the greatest (portents)
36. As a warning unto men,
37. Unto him of you who will advance or hang back.
38. Every soul is a pledge for its own deeds;
39. Save those who will stand on the right hand.
40. In gardens they will ask one another
41. Concerning the guilty:
42. What hath brought you to this burning?
43. They will answer: We were not of those who prayed
44. Nor did we feed the wretched.
45. We used to wade (in vain dispute) with (all) waders
46. And we used to deny the Day of Judgement,
47. Till the inevitable came unto us.
48. The mediation of no mediators will avail them then
49. Why now turn they away from the Admonishment,
50. As they were frightened asses.

51. Fleeing from a lion?

52. Nay, but everyone of them desireth that he should be given open pages (from Allah).

53. Nay, verily. They fear not the Hereafter.

54. Nay, verily. Lo! this is an Admonishment.

55. So whosoever will may heed.

56. And they will not heed unless Allah willeth (it). He is the fount of fear. He is the fount of Mercy.

SÛRAH 75

Al-Qiyâmah takes its name from a word in the first verse. An early Meccan Sûrah.

THE RISING OF THE DEAD

Revealed at Mecca

In the name of Allah, the Beneficent, the Merciful.

1. Nay, I swear by the Day of Resurrection;

2. Nay, I swear by the accusing soul (that this Scripture is true).

3. Thinketh man that We shall not assemble his bones?

4. Yea, verily. Yea, We are able to restore his very fingers!

5. But man would fain deny what is before him.

6. He asketh: When will be this Day of Resurrection?

7. But when sight is confounded

8. And the moon is eclipsed

9. And sun and moon are united,

10. On that day man will cry: Whither to flee!

11. Alas! No refuge!

12. Unto thy Lord is the recourse that day.

13. On that day man is told the tale of that which he hath sent before and left behind.

14. Oh, but man is a telling witness against himself,

15. Although he tender his excuses.

16. Stir not thy tongue herewith to hasten it.

17. Lo! upon Us (resteth) the putting together thereof and the reading thereof.

18. And when We read it, follow thou the reading;

19. Then lo! upon Us (resteth) the explanation thereof.

20. Nay, but ye do love the fleeting Now

21. And neglect the Hereafter.

22. That day will faces be resplendent,

23. Looking toward their Lord;

24. And that day will other faces be despondent,

25. Thou wilt know that some great disaster is about to fall

- - -

on them.

26. Nay, but when the life cometh up to the throat

27. And men say: Where is the wizard (who can save him now)?

28. And he knoweth that it is the parting;

29. And agony is heaped on agony;

30. Unto thy Lord that day will be the driving.

31. For he neither trusted, nor prayed.

32. But he denied and flouted.

33. Then went he to his folk with glee.

34. Nearer unto thee and nearer,

35. Again nearer unto thee and nearer (is the doom).

36. Thinketh man that he is to be left aimless?

37. Was he not a drop of fluid which gushed forth?

38. Then he became a clot; then (Allah) shaped and fashioned

39. And made of him a pair, the male and female.

40. Is not He (who doeth so) able to bring the dead to life?

SÛRAH 76

Al-Insân or *Ad-Dahr* is, in either case, so called from a word in the first verse. An early Meccan Sûrah.

"TIME" OR "MAN"

Revealed at Mecca

In the name of Allah, the Beneficent, the Merciful.

1. Hath thee come upon man (ever) any period of time in which he was a thing unremembered?

2. Lo! We create man from a drop of thickened fluid to test him; so We make him hearing, knowing.

3. Lo! We have shown him the way, whether he be grateful or disbelieving.

4. Lo! We have prepared for disbelievers manacles and carcans and a raging fire.

5. Lo! the righteous shall drink of a cup whereof the mixture is of water of Kâfûr.

6. A spring wherefrom the slaves of Allah drink, making it gush forth abundantly,

7. (Because) they perform the vow and fear a day whereof the evil is wide-spreading,

8. And feed with food the needy wretch, the orphan and the prisoner, for love of Him,

9. (Saying:) We feed you, for the sake of Allah only. We wish for no reward nor thanks from you;

10. Lo! we fear from our Lord a day of frowning and of fate.

11. Therefore Allah hath warded off from them the evil of that day, and hath made them find brightness and joy;

12. And hath awarded them for all that they endured, a Garden and silk attire;

13. Reclining therein upon couches, they will find there neither (heat of) a sun nor bitter cold.

14. The shade thereof is close upon them and the clustered fruits thereof bow down.

15. Goblets of silver are brought round for them, and beakers (as) of glass

16. (Bright as) glass but (made) of silver, which they (themselves) have measured to the measure (of their deeds).

17. There are they watered with a cup whereof the mixture is of Zanjabîl,

18. The water of a spring therein, named Salsabîl.

19. There serve them youths of everlasting youth, whom, when thou seest, thou wouldst take for scattered pearls.

20. When thou seest, thou wilt see there bliss and high estate.

21. Their raiment will be fine green silk and gold embroidery. Bracelets of silver will they wear. Their Lord will slake their thirst with a pure drink.

22. (And it will be said unto them): Lo! this is a reward for you, your endeavour (upon earth) hath found acceptance.

23. Lo! We, even We, have revealed unto thee the Qur'ân, a revelation;

24. So submit patiently to thy Lord's command, and obey not of them any guilty one or disbeliever.

25. Remember the name of thy Lord at morn and evening.

26. And worship Him (a portion) of the night. And glorify Him through the livelong night.

27. Lo! these love fleeting life, and put behind them (the remembrance of) a grievous day.

28. We, even We, created them, and strengthened their frame. And when We will, We can replace them, bringing others like them in their stead.

29. Lo! this is an Admonishment, that whosoever will may choose a way unto his Lord.

30. Yet ye will not, unless Allah willeth. Lo! Allah is Knower, Wise.

31. He maketh whom He will enter His mercy, and for evildoers hath prepared a painful doom.

SÛRAH 77

Al-Mursalât takes its name from a word in the first verse. Verses 1, 2 and 3 taken to refer to winds, verses 4 and 5 to angels. An early Meccan Sûrah.

THE EMISSARIES

Revealed at Mecca

In the name of Allah, the Beneficent, the Merciful.

1. By the emissary winds, (sent) one after another.
2. By the raging hurricanes,
3. By those which cause earth's vegetation to revive;
4. By those who winnow with a winnowing.
5. By those who bring down the Reminder,
6. To excuse or to warn,
7. Surely that which ye are promised will befall.
8. So when the stars are put out,
9. And when the sky is riven asunder,
10. And when the mountains are blown away,
11. And when the messengers are brought unto their time appointed —
12. For what day is the time appointed?
13. For the Day of Decision.
14. And what will convey unto thee what the Day of Decision is!
15. Woe unto the repudiators on that day!
16. Destroyed We not the former folk,
17. Then caused the latter folk to follow after?
18. Thus deal We ever with the guilty.
19. Woe unto the repudiators on that day!
20. Did We not create you from a base fluid
21. Which We laid up in a safe abode
22. For a known term?
23. Thus We arranged. How excellent is our arranging!
24. Woe unto the repudiators on that day!
25. Have We not made the earth a receptacle
26. Both for the living and the dead,
27. And placed therein high mountains and given you to drink sweet water therein?
28. Woe unto the repudiators on that day!
29. (It will be said unto them:) Depart unto that (doom) which ye used to deny;
30. Depart unto the shadow falling threefold.
31. (Which yet is) no relief nor shelter from the flame.

32. Lo! it throweth up sparks like the castles,
33. (Or) as it might be camels of bright yellow hue.
34. Woe unto the repudiator on that day!
35. This is a day wherein they speak not,
36. Nor are they suffered to put forth excuses.
37. Woe unto the repudiators on that day!
38. This is the Day of Decision, We have brought you and the men of old together.
39. If now ye have any wit, outwit Me.
40. Woe unto the repudiators on the day!
41. Lo! those who kept their duty are amid shade and fountains.
42. And fruits such as they desire.
43. (Unto them it is said:) Eat, drink and welcome, O ye blessed, in return for what ye did
44. Thus do We reward the good.
45. Woe unto the repudiators on that day!
46. Eat and take your ease (on earth) a little. Lo! Ye are guilty.
47. Woe unto the repudiators on that day!
48. When it is said unto them: Bow down, they bow not down!
49. Woe unto the repudiators on that day!
50. In what statement, after this, will they believe?

SÛRAH 78

An-Nabâ' takes its name from a word in the second verse. An early Meccan Sûrah.

THE TIDINGS

Revealed at Mecca

In the name of Allah, the Beneficent, the Merciful.
1. Whereof do they question one another?
2. (It is) of the awful tidings,
3. Concerning which they are in disagreement.
4. Nay, but they will come to know!
5. Nay, again but they will come to know!
6. Have We not made the earth an expanse,
7. And the high hills bulwarks?
8. And We have created you in pairs,
9. And have appointed your sleep for repose,
10. And have appointed the night as a cloak,
11. And have appointed the day for livelihood.
12. And We have built above you seven strong (heavens),

13. And have appointed a dazzling lamp,

14. And have sent down from the rainy clouds abundant water,

15. Thereby to produce grain and plant,

16. And gardens of thick foliage.

17. Lo! the Day of Decision is a fixed time,

18. A day when the trumpet is blown, and ye come in multitudes,

19. And the heaven is opened and becometh as gates,

20. And the hills are set in motion and become as a mirage.

21. Lo! Hell lurketh in ambush,

22. A home for the rebellious.

23. They will abide therein for ages.

24. Therein taste they neither coolness nor (any) drink

25. Save boiling water and a paralysing cold.

26. Reward proportioned (to their evil deeds).

27. For lo! They looked not for a reckoning;

28. They called Our revelations false with strong denial.

29. Everything have We recorded in a Book.

30. So taste (of that which ye have earned). No increase do We give you save of torment.

31. Lo! for the duteous is achievement—

32. Gardens enclosed and vineyards,

33. And maidens for companions,

34. And a full cup.

35. There hear they never vain discourses, nor lying—

36. Requital for thy Lord—a gift in payment—

37. Lord of the heavens and the earth, and (all) that is between them, the Beneficent; with Whom none can converse.

38. On the day when the angels and the Spirit stand arrayed, they speak not, saving him whom the Beneficent alloweth and who speaketh right.

39. That is the True Day. So whoso will should seek recourse unto his Lord.

40. Lo! We warn you of a doom at hand, a day whereon a man will look on that which his own hands have sent before, and the disbeliever will cry: "Would that I were dust!"

SÛRAH 79

An-Nâzi'ât takes its name from a word in the first verse. An early Meccan Sûrah.

THOSE WHO DRAG FORTH

Revealed at Mecca

In the name of Allah, the Beneficent, the Merciful.

1. By those who drag forth to destruction,

2. By the meteors rushing,

3. By the lone stars floating,

4. By the angels hastening,

5. And those who govern the event,

6. On the day when the first trumpet resoundeth

7. And the second followeth it,

8. On that day hearts beat painfully

9. While eyes are downcast

10. (Now) they are saying: Shall we really be restored to our first state.

11. Even after we are crumbled bones?

12. They say: Then that would be a vain proceeding.

13. Surely it will need but one shout,

14. And lo! they will be awakened.

15. Hath there come unto thee the history of Moses?

16. How his Lord called him in the holy vale of Tuwa,

17. (Saying:) Go thou unto Pharaoh—Lo! he hath rebelled—

18. And say (unto him): Hast thou (will) to grow (in grace)?

19. Then I will guide thee to thy Lord and thou shalt fear (Him).

20. And he showed him the tremendous token.

21. But he denied and disobeyed,

22. Then turned he away in haste,

23. Then gathered he and summoned

24. And proclaimed: "I (Pharaoh) am your Lord the Highest."

25. So Allah seized him (and made him) an example for the after (life) and for the former.

26. Lo! herein is indeed a lesson for him who feareth.

27. Are ye the harder to create, or is the heaven that He built?

28. He raised the height thereof and ordered it;

29. And He made dark the night thereof, and He brought forth the morn thereof.

30. And after that He spread the earth.

31. And produced therefrom the water thereof and the pasture thereof.

32. And He made fast the hills,

33. A provision for you and for your cattle.

34. But when the great disaster cometh,

35. The day when man will call to mind his (whole) endeavour,

36. And hell will stand forth visible to him who seeth,

37. Then, as for him who rebelled

38. And chose the life of the world,

39. Lo! hell will be his home.

40. But as for him who feared to stand before his Lord and restrained his soul from lust,

41. Lo! the Garden will be his home

42. They ask thee of the Hour: when will it come to port?

43. Why (ask they)? What hast thou to tell thereof?

44. Unto thy Lord belongeth (knowledge of) the term thereof.

45. Thou art but a warner unto him who feareth it.

46. On the day when they behold it, it will be as if they had but tarried for an evening or the morn thereof.

SÛRAH 80

'*Abasa*, "He Frowned", takes its name from the first word. One day when the Prophet was in conversation with one of the great men of Qureysh (his own tribe), seeking to persuade him of the truth of Al-Islâm, a blind man came and asked a question concerning the faith. The Prophet was annoyed at the interruption, frowned and turned away from the blind man. In this sûrah he is told that a man's importance is not to be judged from his appearance or worldly station.

An early Meccan Sûrah.

HE FROWNED

Revealed at Mecca

In the name of Allah, the Beneficent, the Merciful.

1. He frowned and turned away.

2. Because the blind man came unto him.

3. What could inform thee but that he might grow (in grace)

4. Or take heed and so the reminder might avail him?

5. As for him who thinketh himself independent,

6. Unto him thou payest regard.

7. Yet it is not thy concern if he grow not (in grace).

8. But as for him who cometh unto thee with earnest purpose

9. And hath fear,

10. From him thou art distracted.

11. Nay, but verily it is an Admonishment,

12. So let whosoever will pay heed to it,

13. On honoured leaves

14. Exalted, purified,
15. (Set down) by scribes
16. Noble and righteous,
17. Man is (self-) destroyed: how ungrateful!
18. From what thing doth he create him?
19. From a drop of seed. He createth him and proportioneth him.
20. Then maketh the way easy for him,
21. Then causeth him to die, and burieth him,
22. Then, when He will, He bringeth him again to life.
23. Nay, but (man) hath not done what He commanded him.
24. Let man consider his food:
25. How We pour water in showers
26. Then split the earth in clefts.
27. And cause the grain to grow therein
28. And grapes and green fodder
29. And olive-trees and palm-trees
30. And garden-closes of thick foliage
31. And fruits and grasses:
32. Provision for you and your cattle.
33. But when the Shout cometh
34. On the day when a man fleeth from his brother
35. And his mother and his father
36. And his wife and his children,
37. Every man that day will have concern enough to make him heedless (of others).
38. On that day faces will be bright as dawn,
39. Laughing, rejoicing at good news;
40. And other faces, on that day, with dust upon them,
41. Veiled in darkness,
42. Those are the disbelievers, the wicked.

SÛRAH 81

At-Takwîr takes its name from a word in verse 1. Verses 8 and 9 contain an allusion to the practice of the pagan Arabs of burying alive girl-children whom they deemed superfluous. An early Meccan Sûrah.

THE OVERTHROWING

Revealed at Mecca

In the name of Allah, the Beneficent, the Merciful.
1. When the sun is overthrown,
2. And when the stars fall,

3. And when the hills are moved,

4. And when the camels big with young are abandoned,

5. And when the wild beasts are herded together,

6. And when the seas rise,

7. And when souls are reunited,

8. And when the girl-child that was buried alive is asked

9. For what sin she was slain,

10. And when the pages are laid open,

11. And when the sky is torn away,

12. And when hell is lighted,

13. And when the garden is brought nigh,

14. (Then) every soul will know what it hath made ready.

15. Oh, but I call to witness the planets,

16. The stars which rise and set,

17. And the close of night,

18. And the breath of morning.

19. That this is in truth the word of an honoured messenger,

20. Mighty, established in the presence of the Lord of the Throne,

21. (One) to be obeyed, and trustworthy;

22. And your comrade is not mad.

23. Surely he beheld him on the clear horizon.

24. And he is not avid of the Unseen.

25. Nor is this the utterance of a devil worthy to be stoned.

26. Whither then go ye?

27. This is naught else than a reminder unto creation.

28. Unto whomsoever of you willeth to walk straight.

29. And ye will not, unless (it be) that Allah willeth, the Lord of Creation.

SÛRAH 82

Al-Infitâr takes its name from a word in verse 1. An early Meccan Sûrah.

THE CLEAVING

Revealed at Mecca

In the name of Allah, the Beneficent, the Merciful

1. When the heaven is cleft asunder,

2. When the planets are dispersed,

3. When the seas are poured forth,

4. And the sepulchres are overturned,

5. A soul will know what it hath sent before (it) and what left behind.

6. O man! What hath made thee careless concerning thy Lord, the Bountiful,

7. Who created thee, then fashioned, then proportioned thee?

8. Into whatsoever form He will, He casteth thee.

9. Nay, but they deny the Judgement.

10. Lo! There are above you guardians,

11. Generous and recording,

12. Who know (all) that ye do.

13. Lo! the righteous verily will be in delight.

14. And lo! The wicked verily will be in hell;

15. They will burn therein on the Day of Judgement,

16. And will not be absent thence.

17. Ah, what will convey unto thee what the Day of Judgement is!

18. Again, what will convey unto thee what the Day of Judgement is!

19. A day on which no soul hath power at all for any (other) soul. The (absolute) command on that day is Allah's.

SÛRAH 83

At-Tatfîf, "Defrauding", takes its name from a word in verse 1. An early Meccan Sûrah.

DEFRAUDING

Revealed at Mecca

In the name of Allah, the Beneficent, the Merciful

1. Woe unto the defrauders:

2. Those who when they take the measure from mankind demand it full.

3. But if they measure unto them or weigh for them, they cause them loss.

4. Do such (men) not consider that they will be raised again

5. Unto an awful day,

6. The day when (all) mankind stand before the Lord of the Worlds?

7. Nay, but the record of the vile is in Sijjîn-

8. Ah! What will convey unto thee what Sijjîn is!-

9. A written record.

10. Woe unto the repudiators on that day!

11. Those who deny the Day of Judgement

12. Which none denieth save each criminal transgressor,

13. Who, when thou readest unto him Our revelations,

saith: (Mere) fables of the men of old.

14. Nay, but that which they have earned is rust upon their hearts.

15. Nay, but surely on that day they will be covered from (the mercy of) their Lord.

16. Then lo! they verily will burn in hell,

17. And it will be said (unto them): This is that which ye used to deny.

18. Nay, but the record of the righteous is in 'Iliyîn-

19. Ah, what will convey unto thee what 'Iliyîn is!-

20. A written record,

21. Attested by those who are brought near (unto their Lord).

22. Lo! the righteous verily are in delight,

23. On couches, gazing,

24. Thou wilt know in their faces the radiance of delight.

25. They are given to drink of a pure wine, sealed,

26. Whose seal is musk-For this let (all) those strive who strive for bliss-

27. And mixed with water of Tasnîm,

28. A spring whence those brought near to Allah drink.

29. Lo! the guilty used to laugh at those who believed,

30. And wink one to another when they passed them;

31. And when they returned to their own folk, they returned jesting;

32. And when they saw them they said: Lo! these have gone astray.

33. Yet they were not sent as guardians over them.

34. This day it is those who believe who have the laugh of disbelievers,

35. On high couches, gazing.

36. Are not the disbelievers paid for what they used to do?

SÛRAH 84

Al-Inshiqâq, "The Sundering", takes its name from a word in verse 1. An early Meccan Sûrah.

THE SUNDERING

Revealed at Mecca

In the name of Allah, the Beneficent, the Merciful.

1. When the heaven is split asunder

2. And attentive to her Lord in fear,

3. And when the earth is spread out.

4. And hath cast out all that was in her, and is empty

5. And attentive to her Lord in fear!

6. Thou, verily, O man, art working toward thy Lord a work which thou wilt meet (in His presence).

7. Then whoso is given his account in his right hand

8. He truely will receive an easy reckoning

9. And will return unto his folk in joy.

10. But whoso is given his account behind his back,

11. He surely will invoke destruction

12. And be thrown to scorching fire.

13. He verily lived joyous with his folk,

14. He verily deemed that he would never return (unto Allah).

15. Nay, but lo! his Lord is ever looking on him!

16. Oh, I swear by the afterglow of sunset,

17. And by the night and all that it enshroudeth,

18. And by the moon when she is at the full,

19. That ye shall journey on from plane to plane.

20. What aileth them, then, that they believe not

21. And, when the Qur'ân is recited unto them, worship not (Allah)?

22. Nay, but those who disbelieve will deny;

23. And Allah knoweth best what they are hiding.

24. So give them tidings of painful doom,

25. Save those who believe and do good works, for theirs is a reward unfailing.

SÛRAH 85

Al-Buruj takes its name from a word in verse 1 which I have translated "mansions of the stars." The word has the meaning of towers or mansions and applied to the signs of the Zodiac. Verses 4 to 7 are generally taken to refer to the massacre of the Christians of Najrân in Al-Yaman by a Jewish king Dhû Nawâs, an event of great historical importance since it caused the intervention of the Negus and led to the Abyssinian supremacy in the Yaman which lasted until the War of the Elephant (Sûrah 105) in the Prophet's year of birth. Professor Horowitz thinks that the words "owners of the ditch, of the fuel-fed fire" refer not to any historical event but to the condition of all persecutors in the hereafter.

An early Meccan Sûrah.

THE MANSIONS OF THE STARS

Revealed at Mecca

In the name of Allah, the Beneficent, the Merciful.

1. By the heaven, holding mansions of the stars,
2. And by the promised Day.
3. And by the witness and that whereunto he beareth testimony,
4. (Self-) destroyed were the owners of the ditch
5. Of the fuel-fed fire,
6. When they sat by it,
7. And were themselves the witnesses of what they did to the believers.
8. They had naught against them save that they believed in Allah, the Mighty, the Owner of praise,
9. Him unto Whom belongeth the Sovereignty of the heavens and the earth; and Allah is of all things the witness.
10. Lo! they who persecute believing men and believing women and repent not, theirs verily will be the doom of hell, and theirs the doom of burning.
11. Lo! those who believe and do good works, theirs will be Gardens underneath which rivers flow. That is the Great Success.
12. Lo! the punishment of thy Lord is stern.
13. Lo! He it is who produceth, then reproduceth,
14. And He is the Forgiving, the Loving,
15. Lord of the Throne of Glory,
16. Doer of what He will.
17. Hath there come unto thee the story of the hosts.
18. Of Pharaoh and (the tribe of) Thamûd?
19. Nay, but those who disbelieve live in denial
20. And Allah, all unseen, surroundeth them.
21. Nay, but it is a glorious Qur'ân.
22. On a guarded tablet.

SÛRAH 86

At-Târiq takes its name from a word in verse 1. There are other meanings to the word Târiq, but I have chosen that which must have occurred to every hearer of this Sûrah, especially as in verse 3 it is stated that a star is meant. The Morning Star has here a mystic sense, and is taken to refer to the Prophet himself. Some have thought that it refers to a comet which alarmed the East about the time of the Prophet's call. Others believe that this and other introductory verses, hard to elucidate, hide scientific facts unimagined at the period of revelation, and are related to the verses following them. Ghamrâwi Bey, my collaborator in the revision of this work, informed me that the late Dr. Sidqi among others considered that the reference here is to the fertilising germ

penetrating the ovary, the subject being the same as vv. 5-7.
An early Meccan Sûrah.

THE MORNING STAR

Revealed at Mecca

In the name of Allah, the Beneficent, the Merciful
1. By the heaven and the morning Star
2. —Ah, what will tell thee what the Morning Star is!
3. —The piercing Star!
4. No human soul but hath a guardian over it.
5. So let man consider from what he is created
6. He is created from a gushing fluid
7. That issued from between the loins and ribs
8. Lo! He verily is able to return him (unto life)
9. On the day when hidden thoughts shall be searched out.
10. Then will he have no might nor any helper.
11. By the heaven which giveth the returning rain,
12. And the earth which splitteth (with the growth of trees and plants).
13. Lo! this (Qur'ân) is a conclusive word,
14. It is no pleasantry.
15. Lo! they plot a plot (against thee, O Muhammad)
16. And I plot a plot (against them).
17. So give a respite to the disbelievers. Deal thou gently with them for a while.

SÛRAH 87

Al-A'ala takes its name from a word in verse 1. An early Meccan Sûrah.

THE MOST HIGH

Revealed at Mecca

In the name of Allah, the Beneficent, the Merciful
1. Praise the name of thy Lord the Most high,
2. Who createth, then disposeth;
3. Who measureth, then guideth;
4. Who bringeth forth the pasturage,
5. Then turneth it to russet stubble.
6. We shall make thee read (O Muhammad) so that thou shalt not forget.
7. Save that which Allah willeth. Lo! He knoweth the disclosed and that which still is hidden;
8. And we shall ease thy way unto the state of ease.

9. Therefore remind (men), for of use is the reminder.
10. He will heed who feareth,
11. But the most hapless will flout it,
12. He who will be flung to the great fire
13. Wherein he will neither die nor live.
14. He is successful who groweth,
15. And remembereth the name of his Lord, so prayeth.
16. But ye prefer the life of the world.
17. Although the Hereafter is better and more lasting.
18. Lo! this is in the former scrolls,
19. The Books of Abraham and Moses.

SÛRAH 88

*Al-Ghâshiyah takes its name from a word in verse 1.
An early Meccan Sûrah.*

THE OVERWHELMING

Revealed at Mecca

In the name of Allah, the Beneficent, the Merciful

1. Hath there come unto thee tidings of the Overwhelming?
2. On that day (many) faces will be downcast,
3. Toiling, weary,
4. Scorched by burning fire,
5. Drinking from a boiling spring,
6. No food for them save bitter thorn-fruit
7. Which doth not nourish nor release from hunger.
8. On that day other faces will be calm,
9. Glad for their effort past,
10. In a high garden
11. Where they hear no idle speech
12. Wherein is a gushing spring,
13. Wherein are couches raised
14. And goblets set at hand
15. And cushions ranged
16. And silken carpets spread.
17. Will they not regard the camels, how they are created?
18. And the heaven, how it is raised.
19. And the hills, how they are set up?
20. And the earth, how it is spread?
21. Remind them, for thou art but a remembrancer,
22. Thou art not at all a warder over them.
23. But whoso is averse and disbelieveth,
24. Allah will punish him with direst punishment.

25. Lo! unto Us is their return
26. And Ours their reckoning.

SÛRAH 89

Al-Fajr takes its name from verse 1. A very early Meccan Sûrah.

THE DAWN

Revealed at Mecca

In the name of Allah, the Beneficent, the Merciful
1. By the Dawn
2. And ten nights,
3. And the Even and the Odd,
4. And the night when it departeth,
5. There surely is an oath for thinking man.
6. Dost thou not consider how thy Lord dealt with (the tribe of) A'âd,
7. With many-columned Iram,
8. The like of which was not created in the lands;
9. And with (the tribe of) Thamûd, who clove the rocks in the valley;
10. And with Pharaoh, firm of might,
11. Who (all) were rebellious (to Allah) in these lands,
12. And multiplied iniquity therein?
13. Therefore thy Lord poured on them the disaster of His punishment.
14. Lo! thy Lord is ever watchful.
15. As for man, whenever his Lord trieth him by honouring him, and is gracious unto him, he saith: My Lord honoureth me.
16. But whenever He trieth him by straitening his means of life, he saith: My Lord despiseth me.
17. Nay, but ye (for your part) honour not the orphan
18. And urge not on the feeding of the poor,
19. And ye devour heritages with devouring greed
20. And love wealth with abounding love
21. Nay, but when the earth is ground to atoms, grinding, grinding,
22. And thy Lord shall come with angels, rank on rank,
23. And hell is brought near that day; on that day man will remember, but how will the remembrance (then avail him)?

24. He will say: Ah, would that I had sent before me (some provision) for my life!

25. None punisheth as He will punish on that day!

26. None bindeth as He then will bind.

27. But ah! Thou soul at peace!

28. Return unto thy Lord, content in His good pleasure!

29. Enter thou among My bondmen!

30. Enter thou My Garden!

SÛRAH 90

Al-Balad takes its name from a word in verse 1. A very early Meccan Sûrah

THE CITY

Revealed at Mecca

In the name of Allah, the Beneficent, the Merciful

1. Nay, I swear by this city-

2. And thou art an indweller of this city-

3. And the begetter and that which he begat,

4. We verily have created man in an atmosphere:

5. Thinketh he that none hath power over him?

6. And he saith: I have destroyed vast wealth:

7. Thinketh he that none beholdeth him?

8. Did We not assign unto him two eyes

9. And a tongue and two lips.

10. And guide him to the parting of the mountain ways?

11. But he hath not attempted the Ascent-

12. Ah, what will convey unto thee what the Ascent is!-

13. (It is) to free a slave,

14. And to feed in the day of hunger

15. An orphan near of kin,

16. Or some poor wretch in misery,

17. And to be of those who believe and exhort one another to perseverance and exhort one another to pity.

18. Their place will be on the right hand.

19. But those who disbelieve Our revelations, their place will be on the left hand.

20. Fire will be an awning over them.

SÛRAH 91

Ash-Shams takes its name from a word in verse 1. A very early Meccan Sûrah

THE SUN

Revealed at Mecca

In the name of Allah, the Beneficent, the Merciful
1. By the sun and his brightness,
2. And the moon when she followeth him,
3. And the day when it revealteth him,
4. And the night, when it enshroudeth him,
5. And the heaven and Him who built it,
6. And the earth and Him who spread it,
7. And a soul and Him who perfected it
8. And inspired it (with conscience of) what is wrong for it and (what is) right for it.
9. He is indeed successful who causeth it to grow,
10. And he is indeed a failure who stunteth it.
11. (The tribe of) Thamûd denied (The truth) in their rebellious pride.
12. When the basest of them broke forth
13. And the messenger of Allah said; It is the she camel of Allah, so let her drink!
14. But they denied him, and they hamstrung her, so Allah doomed them for their sin and raised (their dwellings).
15. He dreadeth not the sequel (of events).

SÛRAH 92

Al-Leyl takes its name from a word in verse 1. A very early Meccan Sûrah

THE NIGHT

Revealed at Mecca

In the name of Allah, the Beneficent, the Merciful
1. By the night enshrouding
2. And the day resplendent
3. And Him who hath created male and female,
4. Lo! your effort is dispersed (towards divers ends).
5. As for him who giveth and is dutiful (toward Allah)
6. And believeth in goodness;
7. Surely we will ease his way unto the state of ease.
8. But as for him who hoardeth and deemeth himself independent,
9. And disbelieveth in goodness;
10. Surely We will ease his way unto adversity.
11. His riches will not save him when he perisheth.
12. Lo! Ours it is (to give) the guidance
13. And lo! unto Us belong the latter portion and the

former.

14. Therefore have I warned you of the flaming Fire
15. Which only the most wretched must endure,
16. He who denieth and turneth away.
17. Far removed from it will be the rigteous
18. Who giveth his wealth that he may grow (in goodness),
19. And none hath with him any favour for reward,
20. Except as seeking (to fulfil) the purpose of his Lord Most High.
21. He verily will be content.

SÛRAH 93

Ad-Duhâ, "The Morning Hours", takes its name from the first verse. There was an interval during which the Prophet received no revelation and the idolaters mocked him, saying: "Allah, of Whom we used to hear so much, has forsaken poor Muhammad and now hates him." Then came this revelation. The Prophet had been a leading citizen of Mecca until he received his call. Now he was regarded as a madman. He was a man near fifty, and the prophecy in this Sûrah that "the latter portion would be better for him than the former" Must have seemed absurd to those who heard it. Yet the latter portion of the Prophet's life, the last ten years, is the most wonderful record of success in human history.

An early Meccan Sûrah

THE MORNING HOURS

Revealed at Mecca

In the name of Allah, the Beneficent, the Merciful

1. By the morning hours
2. And by the night when it is stillest,
3. Thy Lord hath not forsaken thee nor doth He hate thee,
4. And verily the latter portion will be better for thee than the former,
5. And verily thy Lord will give unto thee so that thou wilt be content.
6. Did He not find thee an orphan and protect (thee)?
7. Did He not find thee wandering and direct (thee)?
8. Did He not find thee destitute and enrich (thee)?
9. Therefore the orphan oppress not,
10. Therefore the beggar drive not away,
11. Therefore of the bounty of thy Lord be thy discourse.

SÛRAH 94

Al-Inshirâh "Solace", takes its name from a word in verse 1, and also from its subject, which is relief from anxiety. It was probably revealed upon the same occasion as Sûrah 93; and, at a time when the Prophet was derided and shunned after having been respected and courted, must have struck the disbelievers as ridiculous. It refers to the inward assurance which the Prophet had received by revelation, and speaks of future events as accomplished, as is usual in the Koran, the revelation coming from a plane where time is not. Verse 4, speaking of his fame as exalted, must have seemed particularly absurd at that time of humiliation and persecution. But today, from every mosque in the world, the Prophet's name is cried as that of the messenger of God, five times a day, and every Muslim prays for blessings on him when his name is mentioned.

An early Meccan Sûrah

THE SOLACE

Revealed at Mecca

In the name of Allah, the Beneficent, the Merciful
1. Have We not caused thy bosom to dilate,
2. And eased thee of the burden
3. Which weighted down thy back;
4. And exalted thy fame?
5. But lo! with hardship goeth ease,
6. Lo! with hardship goeth ease;
7. So when thou art relieved, still toil
8. And strive to please thy lord.

SÛRAH 95

At-Tîn, "The Fig", takes its name from a word in verse 1. The sense is mystical, referring to man in relation to the revealed Law of God and His judgement.

A very early Meccan Sûrah

THE FIG

Revealed at Mecca

In the name of Allah, the Beneficent, the Merciful
1. By the fig and the olive,
2. By Mount Sinai,
3. And by this land made safe
4. Surely We created man of the best stature.

5. Then we reduced him to the lowest of the low,

6. Save those who believe and do good works, and theirs is a reward unfailing

7. So who henceforth will give the lie to thee about the judgement?

8. Is not Allah the most conclusive of all judges?

SÛRAH 96

Al-'Alaq takes its name from a word in verse 2. Verses 1-5 are the words which the Prophet received in the vision at Hirâ, therefore the first of the Koran to be revealed.

A very early Meccan Sûrah

THE CLOT

Revealed at Mecca

In the name of Allah, the Beneficent, the Merciful

1. Read: In the name of thy Lord who createth,

2. Createth man from a clot,

3. Read: And thy Lord is the Most Bounteous,

4. Who teacheth by the pen

5. Teacheth man that which he knew not.

6. Nay, but verily man is rebellious

7. That he thinketh himself independent!

8. Lo! unto thy Lord is the return.

9. Hast thou seen him who dissuadeth

10. A slave when he prayeth?

11. Hast thou seen if he (relieth) on the guidance (of Allah)

12. Or enjoineth piety?

13. Hast thou seen if he denieth (Allah's guidance) and is forward?

14. Is he then unaware that Allah seeth?

15. Nay, but if he cease not. We will seize him by the forelock-

16. The lying, sinful forelock-

17. Then let him call upon his henchmen

18. We will call the guards of hell.

19. Nay! Obey not thou him. But prostrate thyself, and draw near (unto Allah).

SÛRAH 97

Al-Qadr takes its name from a word in verse 1. It refers to the night (one of the last nights of Ramadân) on which the Prophet received his call and the first verses of the Koran were revealed in the vision of Mt. Hirâ. It is said to be the night on which God's decrees for the year are brought down to the earthly plane.

A very early Meccan Sûrah

POWER

Revealed at Mecca

In the name of Allah, the Beneficent, the Merciful

1. Lo! We revealed it on the Night of Power.

2. Ah, what will convey unto thee what the Night of Power is!

3. The Night of Power is better than a thousand months.

4. The angels and the Spirit descend therein, by the permission of their Lord, with all decrees.

5. (That night is) Peace until the rising of the dawn.

SÛRAH 98

Al-Beyyinah takes its name from a word in the first verse. There is no certainty as to the period of revelation. Many regard it as a late Meccan Sûrah. I follow the attribution in the Mushaf which I have followed throughout.

The probable date of revelation is the year 1 A.H.

THE CLEAR PROOF

Revealed at Al-Madînah

In the name of Allah, the Beneficent, the Merciful

1. Those who disbelieve among the People of the Scripture and the idolaters could not have left off (erring) till the clear proof came unto them,

2. A messenger from Allah, reading purified pages

3. Containing correct scriptures.

4. Nor were the People of the Scripture divided until after the clear proof came unto them.

5. And they are ordered naught else than to serve Allah, keeping religion pure for Him, as men by nature upright, and to establish worship and to pay the poor-due. That is true religion.

6. Lo! those who disbelieve, among the people of the Scripture and the idolaters, will abide in fire of hell. They are the worst of created beings.

7. (And) Lo! those who believe and do good works are the best of created beings.

8. Their reward is with their Lord: Gardens of Eden underneath which rivers flow, wherein they dwell for ever. Allah hath pleasure in them and they have pleasure in Him. This is (in store) for him who feareth his Lord.

SÛRAH 99

Az-Zilzâl takes its name from a word in verse 1. A very early Meccan Sûrah

THE EARTHQUAKE

Revealed at Mecca

In the name of Allah, the Beneficent, the Merciful
1. When Earth is shaken with her (final) earthquake
2. And Earth yieldeth up her burdens,
3. And man saith: What aileth her?
4. That day she will relate her chronicles,
5. Because thy Lord inspireth her.
6. That day mankind will issue forth in scattered groups to be shown their deeds.
7. And whoso doeth good an atom's weight will see it then,
8. And whoso doeth ill an atom's weight will see it then.

SÛRAH 100

Al-A'âdiyât takes its name from a word in the first verse. A very early Meccan Sûrah

THE COURSERS

Revealed at Mecca

In the name of Allah, the Beneficent, the Merciful
1. By the snorting coursers.
2. Striking sparks of fire
3. And scouring to the raid at dawn.
4. Then, therewith, with their trail of dust,
5. Cleaving, as one, the centre (of the foe),
6. Lo! man is an ingrate unto his Lord
7. And Lo! he is a witness unto that;
8. And lo! in the love of wealth he is violent.
9. Knoweth he not that, when the contents of the graves are poured forth.
10. And the secrets of the breasts are made known,
11. On that day will their Lord be perfectly informed concerning them.

SÛRAH 101

Al-Qâri'ah takes its name from a word in verse 1, recurring in the next two verses.

A very early Meccan Sûrah

THE CALAMITY

Revealed at Mecca

In the name of Allah, the Beneficent, the Merciful
1. The Calamity!
2. What is the Calamity?
3. Ah, what will convey unto thee what the Calamity is!
4. A day wherein mankind will be as thickly-scattered moths,
5. And the mountains will become as carded wool.
6. Then, as for him whose scales are heavy (with good works),
7. He will live a pleasant life.
8. But as for him whose scales are light,
9. The Bereft and Hungry One will be his mother.
10. Ah, what will convey unto thee what she is!
11. Raging fire.

SÛRAH 102

Al-Takâthur takes its name from a word in the first verse. A very early Meccan Sûrah

RIVALRY IN WORLDLY INCREASE

Revealed at Mecca

In the name of Allah, the Beneficent, the Merciful
1. Rivalry in worldly increase distracteth you
2. Until ye come to the graves.
3. Nay, but ye will come to know!
4. Nay, but ye will come to know!
5. Nay would that ye knew (now) with a sure knowledge!
6. For ye will behold hell-fire.
7. Aye, ye will behold it with sure vision.
8. Then, on that day, ye will be asked concerning pleasure.

SÛRAH 103

Al-'Asr takes its name from a word in verse 1.
A very early Meccan Sûrah.

THE DECLINING DAY

Revealed at Mecca

In the name of Allah, the Beneficent, the Merciful
1. By the declining day,
2. Lo! man is in a state-of loss,
3. Save those who believe and do good works, and exhort one another to truth and exhort one another to endurance.

SÛRAH 104

Al-Humazah takes its name from a word in verse 1. The idolaters waylaid all newcomers to Mecca and warned them against the Prophet, in order to prevent them listening to his preaching.

An early Meccan Sûrah

THE TRADUCER

Revealed at Mecca

In the name of Allah, the Beneficent, the Merciful
1. Woe unto every slandering traducer,
2. Who hath gathered wealth (of this world) and arranged it.
3. He thinketh that his wealth will render him immortal.
4. Nay, but verily he will be flung to the Consuming One.
5. Ah, what will convey unto thee what the Consuming One is!
6. (It is) the fire of Allah, kindled,
7. Which leapeth up over the hearts (of men).
8. Lo! it is closed in on them.
9. In outstretched columns.

SÛRAH 105

Al-Fîl, "The Elephant", takes its name from a word in the first verse. The allusion is to the campaign of Abraha, the Abyssinian ruler of Al-Yaman, against Mecca, with the purpose of destroying the Ka'bah in the year of the Prophet's birth. He had with him an elephant which much impressed the Arabs. Tradition says that the elephant refused to advance on the last stage of the march, and that swarms of flying creatures pelted the Abyssinians with stones. Another tradtion says that they retired in disorder owing to an outbreak of smallpox in the camp. At the time when this Sûrah was revealed, many men in Mecca must have known what happened. Dr. Krenkow, a sound Arabic scholar, is of opinion that the flying creatures may well have been swarms of insects carrying infection. In any case the Ka'bah was saved from destruction after its defenders had despaired.

A very early Meccan Sûrah

THE ELEPHANT

Revealed at Mecca

In the name of Allah, the Beneficent, the Merciful
1. Hast thou not seen how thy Lord dealt with the owners of the Elephant?
2. Did He not bring their stratagem to naught.
3. And send against them swarms of flying creatures,
4. Which pelted them with stones of baked clay.
5. And made them like green crops devoured (by cattle)?

SÛRAH 106

Ash-Shitâ is so called from a word occurring in verse 2. It is also often called Qureysh. A very early Meccan Sûrah

"WINTER" OR "QUREYSH"

Revealed at Mecca

In the name of Allah, the Beneficent, the Merciful
1. For the taming of Qureysh
2. For their taming (We cause) the caravans to set forth in winter and summer,
3. So let them worship the Lord of this House.
4. Who hath fed them against hunger And hath made them safe from fear.

SÛRAH 107

Al Mâ'ûn takes its name from a word in the last verse. An early Meccan Revelation.

SMALL KINDNESSES

Revealed at Mecca

In the name of Allah, the Beneficent, the Merciful
1. Hast thou observed him who believeth religion?
2. That is he who repelleth the orphan,
3. And urgeth not the feeding of the needy
4. Ah, woe unto worshippers
5. Who are heedless of their prayer;

6. Who would be seen (at worship)
7. Yet refuse small kindnesses!

SÛRAH 108

Al-kauthartakes its name from aword in the first verse. The disbelivers used to turn the prophet with the fect that he had no son, and therefore none to uphold his religin after him.

ABUNDANCE

Revled at Mecca

In the name of Allah, the Beneficent, the Merciful
1. Lo! We have given thee Abundance;
2. So pray unto thy Lord, and sacrifice.
3. Lo! It is thy insulter (and not thou) who is without posterity.

SÛRAH 109

Al-Kâfirûn takes its name from a word in verse 1. It was revealed at a time when the idolaters had asked the Prophet to compromise in matters of religion.

THE DISBELIEVERS

Revealed at Mecca

In the name of Allah, the Beneficent, the Merciful
1. Say: O disbelievers!
2. I worship not that which ye worship;
3. Nor worship ye that which I worship.
4. And I shall not worship that which ye worship.
5. Nor will ye worship that which I worship.
6. Unto you your religion, and unto me my religion.

SÛRAH 110

An-Nasr takes its name from a word in the first verse. It is one of the very last revelation, having come to the Prophet only a few weeks before his death. Though ascribed always to A1-Madînah, tradtion say that it was actually revealed at Mecca during the day the Prophet spent there when he made his farewell pilgrimage. It is described in Ibn Hishâm and elsewhere as the first announcement that the Prophet received of this approaching death.

The date of revelation is the tenth year of the Hijrah.

SUCCOUR

Revealed at Mecca

In the name of Allah, the Beneficent, the Merciful
1. When Allah's succour and the triumph cometh
2. And thou seest mankind entering the religion of Allah in troops,
3. Them hymn the praises of thy Lord, and seek forgiveness of him. Lo! He is ever ready to show mercy.

SÛRAH 111

Al-Masad takes its name from a word (to the Arabs a very homely word) in the last verse. It is the passage in the whole Koran where an opponent of the Prophet is denounced by name. Abû Lahab (The Father of Flame), Whose real name was Abdul 'Uzzâ, was an uncle of the Prophet and was the only member of his own clan who bitterly opposed the Prophet. He made it his business to torment the Prophet, and his wife took a pleasure in carrying thorn bushes and strewing them in the sand where she knew that the Prophet was sure to walk barefooted.

An early Meccan revelation

PALM FIBRE

Revealed at Mecca

In the name of Allah, the Beneficent, the Merciful
1. The power of Abû Lahab will perish, and he will perish.
2. His wealth and gains will not exempt him.
3. He will be plunged in flaming fire,
4. And his wife, the wood-carrier,
5. Will have upon her neck a halter of palm fibre

SÛRAH 112

At-Tauhîd, "The Unity", Takes its name from its subject. It has been called the essence of the Koran, of which it is really the last sûrah. Some authorities ascribe this Sûrah to the Madînah period, and think that it was revealed in answer to a question of some Jewish doctors concerning the nature of God.

It is generally held to be an early Meccan Sûrah

THE UNITY

Revealed at Mecca

Revealed at Mecca
In the name of Allah, the Beneficent, the Merciful
1. Say : He is Allah, the one!
2. Allah, the eternally Besought of all!
3. He begetteth not nor was begotten.
4. And there is none comparable unto Him.

SÛRAH 113

Al-Falaq, "The Daybreak", takes its name from a word in the first verse. This and the following sûrah are prayers for protection, this one being for protection from fears proceeding from the unknown. The two sûrahs are known as Al-Mu'awwadhateyn, the two cries for refuge and protection.
An early Meccan Sûrah

THE DAYBREAK

Revealed at Mecca

In the name of Allah, the Beneficent, the Merciful
1. Say: I seek refuge in the Lord of Daybreak
2. From the evil of that which he created;
3. From the evil of the darkness when it is intense
4. And from the evil of malignant witchcraft,
5. And from the evil of the envier when he envieth

SÛRAH 114

An-Nâs, the second of the two cries for refuge and protection, takes its name from a recurring word which marks the rhythm in the Arabic. In this case protection is sought especially from the evil in a man's own heart and in the hearts of other men.
An early Meccan revelation

MANKIND

Revealed at Mecca

In the name of Allah, the Beneficent, the Merciful
1. Say : I seek refuge in the Lord of mankind,
2. The King of mankind,
3. The God of mankind,
4. From the evil of the sneaking whisperer,
5. Who whispereth in the hearts of mankind,
6. Of the Jinn and of mankind.

INDEX

Aaron, 2:248; 4:163; 6:84; 7:122, 142, 150-151; 10:75, 87, 89; 19:28, 53; 20:30-35; 20:42, 70, 92-94; 21:48; 23:45, 48; 25:35-36; 26:13; 26:48; 28:34-35; 37:114-122

'Abasa, S.80

Abbreviated letters, see *Muqatt'at*

Ablution, see Purification, 4:43, 5:6

Abraham, 2:133, 136, 140, 260; 3:33, 84; 4:54; 6:74-84; 12:6, 38; 19:41; 21:51; 29:27; 33:7; 37:83

  and the Ka'bah, 2:125-127; 3:96-97; 14:37; 22:26

  and the messengers, 11:69-76; 15:51-60; 29:31-32; 51:24-34

  angels visit him to announce son, 11:69-73; 15:51-56; 51:24-30

  an excellent example to follow, 60:4-6

  approached his Lord with a sound heart, 37:84

  argues with a skeptic, 2:258

  argues with father against idolatry, 4:74, 19:41-50

  argues with his people against idols, 21:51-71; 26:70-82, 29:16-18, 24-25; 37:83-98

  Book of, 53:37-54; 87:18-19

  chosen by Allah, 2:130; 16:121; 19:58

  confounds Nimrod, 2:258

  Friend of Allah, 4:125

  fulfilled Allah's command, 2:124

  Hanif, the true in faith, 2:135; 3:67, 95; 4:125; 6:79; 6:161; 16:120, 123

  His example in dealing with unbelievers, 60:4-6

  in the ranks of the Righteous, 2:130; 16:122; 26:83; 29:27

  a model, 16:120-123

  not Jew nor Christian, 3:67

  not pagan 3:95

  of the company of the Elect and the Good, 38:47

  people of, 3:33; 9:70; 14:37; 22:43; 60:4-6

  Power and Vision, 38:45-46

  prayer of, 2:126-129; 14:35-41; 19:48; 26:83-89; 37:100; 60:4-5

  preaches to his people, 6:80-83

  religion of, 2:130-133; 2:135; 3:65-68, 95; 6:161; 22:78; 42:13

  remonstrates with Azar, 6:74; 9:114; 19:42-48; 21:52; 26:70-82; 37:85-90; 43:26-27

  rejects worship of heavenly bodies, 4:75-79

  sacrificing his son, 37:101-107

  saved from the fire, 21:68-71; 29:24; 37:97-98

  Station of, 2:125; 3:97

  tried by Allah, 2:124; 37:106

  versus the idols, 6:74; 14:35; 21:52-67; 26:70-77; 29:16-18; 29:25; 37:91-96

  was sent revelation, 4:163; 57:26

  watches the heavens, 6:75-78; 37:88-89

Abrogation, 2:106

Abortion, 6:151; 17:31; 60:12

Abu Lahab, (father of flame), 111:1-3

'Ad, people, 7:65-72, 74; 9:70; 11:50-60, 89; 14:9; 22:42; 25:38; 26:123-139; 29:38; 38:12; 40:31;

INDEX

438

INDEX

440

INDEX

60, 164; 8:24; 10:4, 23, 45, 56;
11:3, 4; 15:25; 19:40; 21:35;
23:79, 115; 24:64; 28:70, 88;
29:8, 57; 30:11; 31:15; 32:11;
36:22, 32, 83; 39:44; 43:85;
45:15; 67:24; 96:8

towards Him you are turned,
7:125; 26:50; 26:227; 29:21;
43:14

trust in, 3:159-160, 173; 4:81;
5:11, 23; 7:89; 8:2, 61; 9:51, 129;
10:71, 84-85; 11:56, 88, 123;
12:67; 13:30; 14:11-12; 16:42, 99;
17:65; 25:58; 26:217; 27:79;
29:59; 33:3, 48; 39:38; 42:10, 36;
58:10; 60:4; 64:13; 65:3; 67:29

turn all your attention to
Him, 94:8

watchtower, 89:14

what is with Him will
endure, 16:96; 28:60; 42:36;
55:27

will change evil into good,
25:70

will gather you together, 3:9;
45:26

will not change the condition
of a people until they change,
13:11

will not suffer the reward to
be lost, 3:195; 9:120; 12:56, 90;
18:30; 21:94; 52:21

will prevail, 12:21; 58:21

with Him is the outcome of
all affairs, 31:22

worship Him (alone), 1:5;
3:64; 6:56, 102; 7:59, 65, 85, 206;
11:2, 26, 50, 61, 84, 123; 12:40;
13:36; 17:23; 19:65; 21:25; 22:77;
23:23, 32; 24:55; 25:60; 26:61;
39:66; 41:37; 46:21; 53:62; 71:3;
98:5; 106:3

Allah's artistry, 27:88;
Allah's attributes, 7:180;

17:110; 20:8; 59:24

All-Embracing (cares for al)
[Al Wasi7, 2:115, 247, 261, 268;
3:73; 4:130; 5:54; 24:32; 53:32

answers petitions [Al Mujib],
11:61; 37:75

Aware (Well-acquainted) [Al
Khabir], 2:234, 271; 3:153, 180;
4:35, 94, 128, 135; 5:8; 6:18, 73,
103; 9:16; 11:1, 111; 17:17, 30,
96; 22:63; 24:30, 53; 25:58-59;
27:88; 31:16, 29, 34; 33:2, 34;
34:1; 35:14, 31; 42:27; 48:11;
49:13; 57:10; 58:3, 11, 13; 59:18;
63:11; 64:8; 66:3; 67:14; 100:11

Beneficent [Al Barr], 52:28

Best of judges [Al Khayr al
Fasilin], 6:57

Best of those who show
mercy
[Arham ar Rahimin], 7:151;
12:64, 92; 21:83
[Khayr al Rahimin], 23:109,
118

Bestower of Forms and
Colours [Al Musawwir], 59:24

Best to decide
[Ahkam al Hakimin], 11:45;
95:8
[Khayr al Hakimin], 7:87;
10:109; 11:45; 12:80

Blots out sins [Al 'Afu], 4:43,
99, 149; 22:60; 58:2

Calls to account [Al Hasib],
4:6, 86; 6:62; 17:14; 21:47; 33:39

Cherisher and Sustainer[Al
Rabb], 1:2; 6:45, 162-163; 7:54,
58, 61, 67; 10:10, 32; 13:16,
18:42; 21:92; 23:52; 26:16, 23-28,
77; 29:59; 37:126, 182; 39:6;
44:8; 45:36; 81:29; 96:1; 98:8;
114:1; etc.

Creator [Al Khaliq; Al
Khallaq], 6:102; 13:16; 15:28, 86;

441

INDEX

INDEX

INDEX

INDEX

INDEX

not to be sold for a miserable price, 3:199; 5:44; 9:9

not to be treated as a jest or falsehood, 2:231; 4:140; 6:150; 7:37; 17:59; 18:56, 106; 23:105; 37:14; 45:9, 35; 46:26; 62:5; 54:10; 78:28; 88:13

shown in the furthest regions and in souls, 41:53; 51:21

the Greatest, 53:18

see also Signs in creation

Allah's Throne, 2:255; 7:54; 10:3; 11:7; 13:2; 20:5; 25:59; 39:75; 40:7; 57:4; 69:17. see also Allah's

attributes: - Lord of the Throne of Glory Supreme.

Allah's words, inexhaustible, 18:109; 31:27

Alms [Sadaqah], 2:271, 276; 9:58, 60, 79, 103-104; 51:19; 58:12-13; 75:31; 92:5

see also Charity

Al Yasa, see Elisha

An'am, al, S. 6

Anbiya,' al, S. 21

Anfal, al, S. 8

Angels, 2:161, 210, 248; 3:18, 39, 42, 45, 80, 87; 4:166; 6:8-9, 11, 111, 158; 11:12; 13:23; 15:7-8; 16:32-33; 17:40; 17:92; 95; 19:17; 21:103; 22:75; 23:24; 25:7, 21-22; 37:1-3; 41:14; 43:60; 53:26-27; 66:4; 79:1-5

and Adam, 2:30, 34; 7:11; 15:28-30; 17:61; 18:50; 38:71-73

appointed over the Fire, 39:71; 43:77; 66:6-7; 67:8; 74:30-31; 96:18

ascent of, 70:4

belief in, 2:177, 285; 4:136

creation of, 35:1; 37:150; 43:19

descent of, 16:2; 19:64-65;

25:25; 41:30-32; 97:4

fighting, 3:124-125; 8:9, 12; 9:26

given female names by Pagans, 53:27

guardian, 6:61; 13:11; 50:17-18; 82:10

implore forgiveness for all beings, 40:7-9; 42:5

on the Day of judgment, 34:40-41; 39:75; 50:21; 69:17; 78:38; 89:22

recording, 50:17-18; 82:11-12

send blessings, 33:43

send blessing on the Prophet, 33:56

serve and worship Allah, 2:30; 4:172; 13:13; 16:49-50; 21:19-20; 37:164-166; 39:75; 40:7; 42:5

take the souls of the dying, 4:97; 6:61, 93; 7:37; 8:50; 16:28, 32; 32:11; 47:27; 79:1-2

see also Gabriel, Michael; Malik; Israfil

Animals, 16:8, 49-50, 80; 22:18, 34, 36; 23:27; 24:45; 31:10; 42:29; 48:25; 81:5

in communities, 6:38

scattered through the earth, 2:164; 45:4

superstitions about, 4:119; 5:103; 6:138-139, 143-144;

see also names of animals, e.g. Cattle

Ankabot, al, S. 29

Ansar, al

Disciples of Jesus, 3:52; 61:14

of Madinah, 9:117-118, 120; 59:9

Ants, 27:18-19

Apes, transgressors become as, 2:65; 7:166

447

INDEX

INDEX

honour belongs to them, 63:8

loved by Allah, 19:96

make peace between your brothers, 49:9-10

men and women, 9:71-71; 33:35

on them is no fear, nor shall they grieve, 2:38, 62, 112, 262, 274, 277; 3:170; 5:69; 6:48; 7:35; 10:62; 39:61; 46:13

overflowing in their love for Allah, 2:165

protectors of one another, 8:72; 9:71; 42:39

rewarded, 2:62, 277; 17:9; 18:2-3; 23:10-11; 32:17; 33:35, 44, 47; 34:4, 37; 41:8; 45:30; 48:29; 57:7, 19; 84:25; 95:6

rewarded with Gardens, 2:25; 9:72; 13:22-24; 14:23; 19:60-63; 20:75-76; 22:23; 32:19; 42:22; 3:68-73; 47:12; 48:5; 57:12; 58:22; 61:12; 64:9; 65:11; 66:8; 70:35; 76:22; 85:11; 98:8

why say you that which you do not?, 60:23

see also Faith; Muslims; Ummah.

Balqis, 27:23-44

Bequest, 2:180-182; 2:240; 5:106

see also Inheritance

Birds, 2:260; 3:49; 5:31, 110; 6:38; 12:36, 41; 21:79; 22:31; 24:41; 34:10; 38:19; 67:19; 105:3-4

and Solomon, 27:16-17, 20-22;

held aloft by Allah, 16:79; 67:19

Blasphemy, to attribute begotton son to Allah, 19:88-92

Blood money, 2:178-179; 4:92; 17:33

Book, People of the, see People of the Book

Book, the, see Qur'an; Scripture

Booty, 3:152-153; 8:1, 41, 69; 48:15

Brass, 34:12

Bribery, 2:188

Brotherhood, 21:92; 23:52; 33:5-6

Burdens,

Allah does not burden a soul more than it can bear, 2:286; 6:152; 7:42; 65:7

borne on the Day of judgment, 16:25; 20:100; 29:12-13

no one can bear the burdens of another, 6:164; 17:15; 23:62; 35:18; 39:7; 53:38

removed by Muhammad, 7:157

removed from Muhammad, 94:1-6

Buruj, al, S. 85

Cain and Abel,

Calf, golden, see Children of Israel and the calf.

Call to prayer,

mocked, 5:58

on Friday, 62:9

Caller will call out from a place quite near, the, 50:41; 54:6

Camels, 5:103; 6:144; 7:40, 73, 77; 11:64-65; 12:65; 17:59; 22:27, 36-37; 26:155-157; 54:27-29; 59:6; 77:33; 81:4; 88:17; 91:13

Captives, 2:85; 8:67, 70; 33:26; 76:8

Cattle, 3:14; 4:119; 6:136, 138-139, 142-144; 7:179; 12:43, 46; 16:5-7, 10, 66; 20:54; 23:21-22; 25:44, 49; 26:133; 32:27; 36:71-73; 39:6; 40:79-80; 42:11; 43:12-14; 47:12; 79:33;

INDEX

INDEX

INDEX

every soul shall taste, 3:185; 21:35; 29:57

only happens once, 37:58-60; 44:56

Debt, remission of, 2:280; 9:60

Debts, 2:282-283; 4:11-12

Deities of Pagans, 4:117; 11:101, 109; 14:30; 18:15; 25:3; 27:24; 34:22; 36:23; 36:74-75; 37:86; 38:5-6; 40:73-74; 41:47-48; 46:22, 28; 71:23; Despair, 3:139; 146

Desert of Arabs, 9:90-99; 101-106; 48:11-12, 16; 49:14

Desertion in fight, 4:89-91

Determination, 81:28-29

Dhariyat, al, S. 51

Dhikr, see Remembrance of Allah.

D*hu* al Kifl, 21:85-86; 38:48

D*hu* al Qarnayn, 18:83-98;

D*hu* al Nun, 21:87-88; 68:48-50 also see Jonah

Difficulty, there is relief with every, 94:5-8

Discipline, 3:152; 61:4

Discord, incited by evil, 41:36

Disease in the hearts of hypocrites and unbelievers, 2:10; 5:52; 8:49; 9:125; 22:53; 24:50; 33:12; 32:60; 47:20, 29; 74:31

Disputations, 29:46

Distribution of charity, 2:177

Distribution of property taken from the enemy

anfal, if after fighting, 8:41

fay if without fighting, 59:7-8

Ditch, Battle of the, see Confederates

Divination, 5:90

Divorce, 2:227-233, 236-237; 2:241; 33:4, 37, 49; 58:2-4; 65:1-7; 66:5

Dog, parable of, 7:176

Doom, see Day of judgment

Dower, 2:229, 236-237; 4:4, 19-21; 5:5; 33:50; 60:10-11

Dreams,

of Egyptian prisoners, 12:36, 41

of Joseph, 12:4

of Muhammad about Ka'bah, 48:27

of Muhammad at Badr, 8:43

of the King of Egypt, 12:43-49

Duha, al, S. 93

Dukhan, al, S. 44

Earnings, 2:134, 141, 286; 4:32, 111-112; 6:129; 31:34; 42:23; 45:14-15, 22

Earth,

all that is on it will perish, 5:26

as a resting place, 40:64

becomes green, 22:63

blessings and nourishment, 41:10

creation in four days, 41:9-10

given life after its death, 2:164; 7:57; 16:65; 22:5; 25:49; 29:63; 30:19, 24, 50; 35:9; 36:33-36; 41:39; 43:11; 45:5; 50:11; 57:17

is Allahs, 7:128

life and death on, 77:25-26

made manageable for you, 67:15

mischief (corruption) in, 2:251; 7:56, 74; 8:73; 11:116; 12:73; 13:25; 26:152, 183; 27:48; 30:41; 47:22

noble things of, 26:7; 31:10; 50:7

on the Day of judgment, 14:48; 18:47; 20:105-107; 39:67, 69; 50:44; 52:9-10; 56:4-6; 69:14;

INDEX

INDEX

INDEX

INDEX

Healing, 9:14; 10:57; 16:69; 17:82; 26:80

Hearts,

a gift of Allah, 16:78; 23:78; 46:26; 67:23

and the remembrance of Allah, 8:2; 13:28; 22:35; 39:23; 39:45

disease in, 2:10; 5:52; 8:49; 9:125; 22:53; 24:50; 33:12; 33:60; 47:20; 47:29; 74:31

hardened, like rocks, 2:74; 5:13; 22:53; 39:22; 57:16

intention of, 33:5

open to the truth, 22:54; 39:22

sound, for approaching Allah, 26:89; 37:84

tested for piety, 49:3

transformed, 24:37

turned in devotion to Allah, 50:33

Heaven, lower, adorned with lights, bedecked with stars, 37:6-10; 41:12; 50:6; 67:5

Heavens,

almost rent asunder by Allahs Glory, 42:5

as a canopy, 2:22; 21:32; 40:64; 52:5; 79:28

constructed with power and skill, 51:47; 91:5

creation in two days, 41:12

(hypothetical) ladder to, 6:35; 52:38

like smoke (primeval matter), 41:11

no flaws in them, 50:6; 67:3-4

on the Day of judgment, 14:48; 21:104; 25:25; 39:67; 52:9; 55:37; 69:16; 70:8; 73:18; 75:8-9; 77:8-9; 78:19; 81:1-2, 11; 82:1-2; 84:1-2

raised by Allah, 13:2; 55:7; 79:27-28

returning, 86:11

seven in number, 2:29; 17:44; 23:17, 86; 41:12; 65:12; 67:3; 71:15; 78:12

starry, 85:1; 86:1

with numerous Paths, 51:7

Heavens and earth, creation of, see Creation.

Heifer, sacrifice of, 2:67-71

Heights, the, 7:46-49

Hell, 2:206; 3:12, 103, 131, 151, 191-192, 197; 4:56, 121; 7:18, 38; 39:35; 9:81; 14:16, 28-30; 15:43-44; 16:29; 17:97; 18:29; 21:98-100; 22:19-22; 23:103-108; 25:65-66; 29:54-55; 32:20; 36:63-64; 38:55-64; 39:16, 60; 40:71-76; 43:74-77; 44:43-50; 45:10; 50:24-26; 52:13-16; 54:48; 55:43-44; 56:41-56, 94; 57:15; 58:8; 59:3; 69:30-37; 70:15-18; 72:23; 73:12-13; 74:26-31, 42-48; 76:4; 77:29-33; 82:14-16; 83:16-17; 88:4-7; 90:20; 102:6-7

a place of ambush, 78:21-30

blazing in fury, 25:11-12; 67:7-8; 77:31-33; 81:12; 92:14-16; 101:11; 111:3

Hell, *(contd.)*

breaks to pieces, 104:4-9

filled with jinn and men, 7:18, 179; 11:119; 32:13; 38:85

fuel is men and stones, 2:24; 66:6

inhabitant there is viewed by former companion in Paradise, 37:51-59

insatiable 50:30

neither dying nor living there, 14:17; 20:74; 35:36; 43:77; 74:28; 84:11; 87:13

INDEX

penalty of Eternity, 10:52; 32:14; 41:28

placed in full view, 79:36-39; 89:23

Helpers, see Ansar

Hereafter, 2:94, 200-201, 220; 3:22, 85, 145, 148; 4:77, 134; 6:135; 9:69; 10:64; 12:57, 101; 13:34; 16:107, 122; 17:72; 20:127; 22:11, 15; 24:14, 19, 23; 27:66; 29:27; 38:46; 39:9, 26; 40:43; 41:16, 31; 59:3; 60:13; 68:33; 75:21

belief in, 2:4; 6:92, 113, 150; 7:45; 11:19; 16:23; 17:19; 27:3; 31:4; 34:21; 39:45; 41:8

better than worldly life, 2:86; 2:102; 2:201; 3:77; 3:152; 4:74; 6:32; 6:169; 9:38; 13:26; 14:27; 16:30; 17:21; 18:46; 20:131; 28:80; 29:64; 33:29; 40:39; 42:20; 43:35; 57:20; 87:17; 93:4

see also Day of judgment; Gardens of Paradise; Hell; Resurrection of the dead.

Hijab, 33:53,

Hijr, see Rocky Tract, Companions of the

Hijrah, see Muhajirs.

Himyarites,

Homicide, 2:72; 4:92-93; 5:30, 32; 6:151; 25:68

compensation for, 2:178; 4:92; 17:33

Homosexuality, 7:81; 11:78-79; 15:67; 26:165-166; 27:54-55; 29:28-29

Honour, depends on righteousness, 49:13

Hoopoe, 27:20-28

Horses, 3:14; 8:60; 9:92; 16:8; 38:31-33; 59:6; 100:1-5

Hospitality of Abraham, 11:69; 51:25-28

Hour, the, see Day of judgment, appointed time of

House of Allah, see Ka'bah.

Houses, manners about entering, 24:27-29

Hud, S. 11; 7:65-72; 11:50-60; 26-123,140; 46:21-25

Hudaybiyah, introduction to surah 48; introduction to surah 60;

Hujurat, al, S. 49

Humazah, al, S. 104

Humility, 4:42-43; 7:161; 57:16

Hunayn, battle of, 9:25-26

Hunting, 5:4, 94-96

forbidden during Pilgrimage, 5:1-2

Hur (Companions in Paradise), 33:33; 37:48-49; 38:52; 44:54; 52:20; 55:56- 58, 70-76; 56:22-23, 35-38; 78:33

Hypocrites, 2:8-20; 4:61-64, 88-91, 138-145; 8:49; 9:64-68, 73-80; 24:47-50, 53; 29:10-11; 33:1, 12-20, 25-26, 48, 60-62, 73; 47:16, 25-30; 48:6; 57:13-15; 58:8, 14-19; 59:11-17; 63:1-8; 66:9

Iblis, 26:95

refused to prostrate, 2:34; 7:11-18; 15:31-40; 17:61-65; 18:50; 20:116; 38:74-85

see also Satan

Ibrahim, S. 14

'Iddah, 2:231-232; 33:49; 65:1-2, 4, 6

Idols and idolatry, 6:74; 7:138-139; 14:35; 21:52-67; 22:30; 74:5

Idris, 19:56-57; 21:85-86

Ignorance (Days of), 5:50; 44:33; 48:26

Ihram, 5:1, 95-96;

459

INDEX

INDEX

belief in, 4:159

covenant with Allah, 33:7

cursed the Children of Israel, 5:78

Disciples of, 3:52-54; 5:111-113; 57:27; 61:14

given the revelation, 2:87, 136, 253; 3:48, 84; 4:163; 5:46; 19:30; 57:27

gives glad tidings of Ahmad, 61:6

in the ranks of the Righteous, 6:85

is not Allah, 5:17, 72; 9:30-31

like Adam, 3:59

Messenger to Israel, 3:49-51; 5:46, 72; 43:59; 61:6, 14;

miracles of, 5:110, 113-115

no more than a Messenger, 4:171; 5:75; 43:59

raised to Allah, 3:55; 4:158

religion of, 42:13

serves Allah, 4:172; 19:30; 43:64

spoke in infancy, 3:46; 5:110; 19:29-33

testifies before Allah, 5:116-118

was not killed, 4:157; 5:110

Wisdom of, 43:63

Jewish scriptures, see Torah.

Jews, 2:111, 113, 120, 135; 4:160; 5:18; 288; 16:118; 22:17

among them some believe, 2:62; 4:162;-5:69

became apes and swine, 2:65; 5:60; 7:166

cursed, 2:87; 4:46-47; 5:78; 9:30

enmity of, 5:64, 82

greedy of life, 2:96; 62:6-8

judged according to the Tawrah, 5:44

slew prophets, 2:87, 91; 3:21,

181; 4:155; 5:70

took usury, 4:161

unbelief and blasphemy of, 5:41, 64; 59:2, 11

work iniquity, 5:41-42, 78-81; 59:2-4, 11-17

write the Book with their own hands, 2:79

see also Children of Israel; People of the Book.

Jihad, 25:52; 29:15, 69; 60:1; 61:11; 66:9

see also Fighting in the cause of Allah; Striving; Warfare

Jinn, al, S. 72

Jinn, 6:100; 6:112, 128; 7:30, 177; 11:119; 17:88; 18:50; 32:13; 34:41; 37:158; 38:85; 41:25; 46:18; 55:33, 39, 56, 74; 114:6

creation of, 15:27; 38:76; 81:36; 55:15

employed by Solomon, 21:82; 27:17, 39; 34:12-14; 38:37-38

message preached to, 6:130; 46:29-32; 72:1-5

Jizyah, 9:29

Job, 4:163; 6:84; 21:83-84; 38:41-44

was sent revelation, 3:163

John (the Baptist), see Yahya

Jonah, 6:86; 21:87-88; 37:139-148; 68:48-50

people of, 10:98; 37:147-148

was sent revelation, 3:163

Joseph, 6:84; 12:4-101; 40:34

prayer of, 12:33, 101

Judgement Day see Day of judgement

Judi, mount, 11:44

Jumu'ah, al, S. 62

Justice, 4:58, 127, 135; 5:8; 6:151-152; 7:29, 181; 10:4, 47; 11:85; 16:76, 90; 39:75; 40:20;

461

INDEX

INDEX

of Muhammad, 53:37-38;
33:50-52

prohibited degrees in,
4:22-24; 24:31; 33:37;

with women of the People of
the Book, 5:5

see also Wives.

Martyrdom, 2:154; 3:140,
168-171, 195; 9:111; 22:58;
47:4-6;

Marut, 2:102

Mary, 4:156, 171; 5:17, 116;
21:91

annunciation of Jesus,
3:42-51; 19:16-21

sign for all peoples, 21:91;
23:50

woman of truth, 5:75

birth of, 3:35-37

chosen and purified by
Allah, 3:42

devout worship of, 3:43;
66:12

gives birth to Jesus, 19:22-26

guarded her chastity, 21:91;
66:12

"sister of Aaron" 19:27-29

Masad, al, S. III

Masjid, al al Harim, 2:144,
149-150, 191, 196, 217; 5:2;
86:34; 9:7, 19,28; 17:1; 22:29;
48:25, 27

Masjid, al, al Aqsa', 17:1, 7

Masjid, al, al Aqsa', 17:1, 7

Ma'un, al, S. 107

Mawlas, 33:5

Measurement and Weigh, give
full, 17:35; 83:1-3

Meat, see Food, lawful and
forbidden.

Mecca, see Makkah

Medina, see Madinah (see also
Yathrib)

Men, protectors and

maintainers of women, 4:34

Mercy, 3:159; 6:12, 54,
154-155; 7:52, 154, 203-204;
10:21, 57; 11:28, 63; 12:111;
16:64, 89; 17:8, 54, 82; 21:107;
23:109, 118; 24:56: 27:77; 28:43;
30:33, 36; 31:3; 42:48; 45:20;
49:9; 57:13; 90:17

see also Allahs mercy

Messenger, the, see
Muhammad.

Messengers, 2:87, 213,
252-253; 3:144; 4:163-165; 5:19;
6:42; 7:53; 9;70; 10:103; 11:120;
12:109-110; 13:38; 14:47; 15:10;
16:43-44; 17:77, 95; 21:7-9, 25;
22:75; 23:51; 25:20; 28:59; 30:47;
36:52; 41:43; 46:35; 57:25-27;
58:21; 65:8, 11; 72:27-28

angels, 35:1; 42:51

see also Messengers to
Abraham

assisted by Allah,
37:171-173; 40:51; 59:6

belief in, 2:177, 285; 3:179;
4:171; 5:12; 57:19, 21

bringers of glad tidings and
warners, 4:165, 5:19; 6:48, 130;
17:15; 18:56; 26:115: 34:44

did not ask rewards from
people, 10:72; 11:29, 51; 12:104;
25:57; 26:109, 127, 145, 164;
26:180; 34:47; 36:21

mocked, 6:10; 13:32; 15:11;
18:100; 21:41; 25:41-42; 36:30

peace be upon them, 27:59;
37:181

preach the Clear Message,
16:35; 29:18; 36:17; 38:46

rejected by their people,
3:184; 4:150; 5:70; 6:34; 7:101;
10:13, 74; 14:9-13; 16:113;
22:42-44; 23:44, 69; 26:105-191;
30:9; 34:34-35, 45; 35:4, 25;

INDEX

INDEX

INDEX

INDEX

Musk, 83:26

Muslims, 2:128, 132, 136; 3:52, 64, 80, 84, 102; 4:131; 5:111; 6:109, 163; 7:126; 8:26; 10:72, 84, 90; 11:14; 12:101; 16:89, 102; 22:78; 28:53; 33:35; 41:33; 43:69; 46:15; 66:5; 68:35; 72:14

    see also Believers; Righteous; Allah's servants; Islam; Ummah.

Naba', al, S. 78

Nahl, al, S. 16

Najm, al, S. 53

Names of Allah, most beautiful, see Allah's attributes.

Naml, al, S. 27

Nas, al, S. 114

Nasr, al, S. 110

Nazi'at, al, S. 79

Neighbors, 4:36

New moon, 2:189

Night and day, alterations of, 2:164; 3:27; 3:190; 7:54; 10:6; 10:67; 13:3; 16:12; 17:12; 22:61; 23:80; 24:44; 25:47; 25:62; 27:86; 28:71-73; 31:29; 35:13; 36:37; 36:40; 39:5; 40:61; 41:37; 45:5; 56:6; 73:20; 74:33-34; 78:10-11; 79:29; 81:17-18; 84:16-17; 89:1-5; 91:4-5; 92:1-2; 93:1-2; 97:5

    Night of Power, 44:3-6; 97:1-5

Nisa, al, S. 4

Nuh S. 71

Nur, al, S. 24

Noah, 3:33; 6:84; 7:59-64; 10:71-73; 11:25-48; 17:3, 17; 19:50; 21:76-77; 23:13-30; 26:106-121; 29:14; 33:7; 37:75-83; 54:9-15; 71:1-28

    people of, 9:70; 11:89; 14:9; 22:42; 23:37; 26:105; 38:12; 40:5, 31; 50:12; 51:46; 53:52; 54:9; 71:1-28

    prayer of, 54:10

    religion of, 42:13

    son of, 11:42-46

    was sent revelation, 4:163; 57:26

    wife of, 66:10

Oaths,

    in the Qur'an,

    of fealty, 48:10, 18; 60:12

    of unbelief, 6:109; 16:38; 24:53; 27:49; 35:42; 58:16, 18; 63:2; 68:10

    rules regarding, 2:224-226; 5:89; 9:12-13; 16:19-92, 94; 24:22; 66:2

    when giving testimony, 5:106-108; 24:6-9

Obediance to Allah and His messenger, 2:285; 3:32, 132; 4:59, 64, 66, 80-81; 5:92; 8:1, 20, 46; 24:54; 47:33; 58:13; 64:11-12, 16

Obligations to be fulfilled, 5:1,

Old age, 16:70; 17:23; 22:3; 28:23; 30:54; 36:68; 40:67

Olive, 6:99, 141; 23:20; 24:35; 80:29; 95:1

Orchards, 27:60; 36:34

Orphans, 2:177, 215, 220; 4:2-6, 8, 36, 127; 8:41; 76:18; 89:17; 90:15; 93:6, 9; 107:2

    property of, 4:2, 6, 10; 6:151; 17:34; 18:92; 59:7

Pagans and polytheists, 4:117; 6:121; 9:1-17, 28, 33; 16:35, 100; 22:17; 48:6; 61:9; App X, P. 1538; 98:1

    attribute to Allah what they hate for themselves, 16:57, 62; 17:40; 37:149-157; 43:16-20; 52:39; 53:19-23

    companions of Fire, 9:113; 98:6

INDEX

INDEX

INDEX

INDEX

473

INDEX

INDEX

INDEX

33:48; 96:19

do not take for friends or helpers, 3:28; 4:139; 4:144; 5:57; 9:23; 60:1-2; 60:9; 60:13

doubt Revelation, 6:7-8, 25; 16:101; 25:4-8; 30:58; 34:31; 37:12-17, 35-36, 170; 38:5-8; 40:70; 43:31; 45:11; 48:25; 50:2; 52:30-44; 67:9; 68:15; 74:24-25; 84:20-22

faces turned upside down, 33:6

forbidden Paradise, 7:50; 70:38-39

forbid the votary to pray, 96:9-10

fuel for the Fire (Companions of the Fire), 3:10-12, 151; 5:10, 86; 21:98; 22:19; 40:6; 57:19; 64:40; 67:10-11; 72:15

Unbelievers, *(cont'd.)*

granted respite, 22:44; 68:45

hearts are sealed, 2:7; 7:101; 10:74; 16:108; 30:59; 40:35; 45:23; 47:24; 63:3; 83:14

humiliated, 58:5-6, 20

in delusion, 67:20-21

kind and just dealing with, 60:8

laughing at believers, 83:29-36

led to Hell in crowds, 29:71-72; 41:19

lost their own souls, 6:12, 20; 11:21; 39:15; 42:45

mutual recriminations at judgment, 34:31-33; 37:24-32; 38:59-64; 40:47; 41:29

persecuting the Believers, 85:4-8, 10

plotting and planning, 8:30; 13:42; 14:46; 52:42; 71:22; 74:18-20; 86:15-17; 105:2

protectors of one another, 8:73; 45:19

rage of, 48:29

ransom not accepted, 3:91; 5:36; 13:18

slander and calumnies, 68:11; 104:1

summoned to bow, but do not, 68:42-43; 77:48

takes as his god his own desire, 45:23

their deeds are like a mirage, 24:39

their deeds rendered astray, 47:1; 47:8-9

their hearing and seeing is covered, 2:7; 17:45-46; 18:57; 36:9; 41:5; 45:23

their own deeds seem pleasing, 6:122; 8:48; 9:37; 27:4; 35:8

turn away from them, 51:54; 54:6

unforgiven, 47:34

will never triumph, 8:59; 23:117

wish for Islam, 15:2

worst of creatures, 98:6

yokes on their necks, 34:33; 36:8; 40:71

Understanding, see Hearts.

Unseen, the

belief in, 2:3; 52:41

keys of, 6:59

Usury, 2:275-279; 3:130; 4:161

'Uzayr, 9:30

'Uzza, 53:19

Vice, to be avoided, 2:169, 268; 3:135; 4:15, 19, 22, 25; 6:151; 7:28, 33, 80; 12:24; 16:90; 17:32; 24:19, 21; 29:28, 45; 33:30; 42:37; 53:32; 65:1

see also Sin.

478

INDEX

INDEX

List of Qur'an Translations

The Qur'an by Abdullah Yusufali:

English Translation (Pocket size)	Paperback	$ 5.95
English Translation	Paperback	$ 9.95
Arabic - Translation - Commentary	Hardcover	$30.00
Arabic - Translation - Commentary	Paperback	$25.00
Arabic - Translation - Transliteration	Hardcover	$25.00
	Paperback	$20.00

The Qur'an by M.H. Shakir

English Translation	Paperback	$9.95
Arabic - Translation	Paperback	$12.00
Arabic - Translation		
(Featuring 41 translations of the	Hardcover	$24.00
First Chapter)	Paperback	$19.00
Wedding Edition	Hardcover	$24.00

The Glorious Qur'an by Muhammad Pickthall

English Translation	Paperback	$ 9.95
Arabic - Translation	Paperback	$12.00
Arabic - Translation - Transliteration	Hardcover	$25.00
	Paperback	$20.00

The Holy Qur'an by S.V. Mir Ahmed Ali

English Translation	Paperback	$ 9.95
Arabic - Translation - Commentary	Hardcover	$59.95
	Paperback	$39.95

The Glorious Qur'an by S. V. Ahamed

English Translation (Pocket size)	Paperback	$5.95
English Translation	Paperback	$9.95
Arabic - Translation	Paperback	$12.00
A simplified translation for young people		

El Coran by Julio Cortes

Spanish Translation	Paperback	$12.00
Arabic & Spanish	Hardcover	$24.00

The Qur'an by 'Ali Quli Qara'i

A Phrase by Phrase Translation	Hardcover	$19.95
The Concordance of the Qur'an	Hardcover	$29.00

Tahrike Tarsile Qur'an, Inc.
80-08 51st Avenue • Elmhurst, New York 11373
www.koranusa.org • e: read@koranusa.org

Notes

Notes

Notes

Notes

Notes

Notes

Notes

Notes

Notes

Notes

Notes

Notes

Notes

Notes